Second Edition

Young Offenders and Juvenile Justice

A Century After the Fact

Sandra J. Bell
St. Mary's University

THOMSON

NELSON

Australia   Canada   Mexico   Singapore   Spain   United Kingdom   United States

Young Offenders and Juvenile Justice
Second Edition
by Sandra J. Bell

Editorial Director and Publisher:
Evelyn Veitch

Executive Editor:
Joanna Cotton

Marketing Manager:
Karen Howell

Senior Developmental Editor:
Edward Ikeda

Production Editor:
Julie van Veen

Production Coordinator:
Hedy Sellers

Copy Editor/Proofreader:
Joan Rawlin

Creative Director:
Angela Cluer

Interior Design:
Sylvia Vander Schee

Cover Design:
Angela Cluer

Cover Image:
(c) David Wise/Photonica

Compositor:
W.G. Graphics

Printer:
Transcontinental

National Library of Canada Cataloguing in Publication Data

Bell, Sandra Jean, 1943–
Young offenders and juvenile justice: a century after the fact

2nd ed.
Includes bibliographical references and index.
ISBN 0-17-616993-8

1. Juvenile delinquency—Canada.
2. Juvenile justice, Administration of—Canada. I. Title.

HV9108.B44 2002   364.36'0971
C2002-900218-4

Table of Contents

CHAPTER 3:   The "Facts" of Youth Crime   68

CHAPTER 4:   The Social Face of Youth Crime   105

CHAPTER 5:   Explaining Crime and Delinquency: In the Beginning ...   135

CHAPTER 6:   New Directions in Theorizing about Youth Crime and Delinquency   164

CHAPTER 7: The Influence of Family, School, and Peers on Youth Crime and Delinquency   189

CHAPTER 8: First Contact: Police and Diversionary Measures   212

CHAPTER 9:   Going to Court   239

CHAPTER 10:   Youth Corrections: Going to Jail   280

CHAPTER 11:   Perpetuating Social Injustice   313

CHAPTER 12:   A Century after the Fact: Where Do We Go from Here?   332

Preface

My concern for young offenders began in 1980. I was employed in a residential facility for juvenile delinquents and at the time the justice system for them was framed by the Juvenile Delinquents Act. The young people whom I worked with there had all been transferred from training schools, a euphemism for children's prisons under that act. I wanted to work at the facility because I liked young people and believed that I could effect a positive change in their lives. Unfortunately, for the most part, I was wrong. I found myself hopelessly enmeshed in a justice system that could not meet even the basic needs of these young people. Worse, I discovered it was a system that inflicted even more damage on their already shattered lives.

I was unable to prevent the suicide of a gentle 15-year-old poet who could not bear the continual rejection of his parents. Nor could I prevent the pregnancies of 15-year-old girls, so desperate for loving families that they believed they could create them by becoming child mothers. I could not prevent the sexual exploitation of these imprisoned girls by an unscrupulous male employee. Management refused to act on or even hear my complaints because, in their words, this individual had a "calming" influence on the girls. And I was unable to convince a 15-year-old that the police officer who arrested her when she was 13, and subsequently had an ongoing sexual relationship with her, was not likely to leave his wife and children to marry her, as she believed. In spite of my efforts and good intentions, I could not shield these children from the devastating social and psychological effects of arbitrary and oftentimes cruel administrative policies and staff indifference. Nor could I prevent them from committing more crimes while on the run from the institution: cold, hungry, frightened, and exhausted. A few committed particularly violent offences on these escapes, not because they were somehow inherently violent, as some might suggest, but rather because they were desperate not to be caught and sent back to prison.

My knowledge of young offenders and juvenile justice continued while I researched the youth court after the Young Offenders Act was implemented in 1984. Here, I interviewed parents and came to understand better why their children behaved as they did. Some parents were caring and doing their best with meagre resources, though insufficient to provide a decent lifestyle for themselves or their children. Others were struggling to cope with family tragedies—a spouse lost through desertion, divorce, or death; a missing or dead child; a demeaning and debilitating life of poverty, drugs, alcohol, or abuse. Most of the parents I talked to were tired and worn beyond their years. Far too many, it seemed, quite simply did not like or want their children.

This book is dedicated to these children—to Paul, Michelle, Geoff, Tammy, Fred, Jane, and Kenny—and to all the children in Canadian society whom we have failed to protect, guide, provide for, and teach: to all the children who have been failed by our social services, our justice system, and who have been maligned as young criminals in public discourse. Royalties from the sales of this book will be shared with these young people through Phoenix House, a safe haven for homeless youth, and with the Community Justice Society, an organization working toward restorative justice as a means of getting and keeping young people out of the justice system.

ABOUT THE TEXT

Nearly a century has passed since the Canadian government created for juveniles a justice system separate from the adult criminal justice system. Yet, youth crime and juvenile justice is today a major public issue, and many seem to think that the juvenile justice system is not working to control youth crime. *Young Offenders and Juvenile Justice: A Century After the Fact* is about the issue of youth crime and justice, and, as such, it is organized around the concerns expressed in public forums designed to address youth crime issues, which assisted the Minister of Justice's attempts to reform the justice system. Is youth crime on the increase? Did young offenders receive merely "a slap on the wrist" for their offences under the Young Offenders Act? Are youth more violent today than in the past? Will youth justice be different under the Youth Criminal Justice Act?

Beyond these immediate concerns is a more fundamental question, one not addressed in public forums. How far have we come in 100 years of juvenile justice? What did we know about youth crime and justice in the past, and how does that compare to what we know today? More important, have we changed what we think at all about youth crime and our responses to it? To address these broader questions, the book takes a historical comparative approach and locates contemporary youth justice issues in a historical context. Where appropriate, chapters begin with a discussion of either contemporary and/or historical issues, and proceed to a discussion of contemporary knowledge, practice, policy, and issues. Where it is relevant, the chapters offer comparisons of the new Youth Criminal Justice Act with the Young Offenders Act both in legislation and practice.

Young Offenders and Juvenile Justice differs from other texts in its approach to youth crime and justice in that it is not just a collection of "facts" and "theories" about crime and delinquency, nor is it a book *about* delinquents or young offenders. Rather, it is about how we think about youth and their behaviour, and about how these views are reflected in public discourse, scholarly theorizing, public policy, and institutional responses to "troublesome" youth behaviour. As such, the book is also not one that decontextualizes, depersonalizes, or objectifies young people or their behaviour. The voices of youth, past and present, together with the voices of people who work in the justice system, are brought into the discussion of the issues in the form of boxed inserts that appear throughout the text. This material is intended to give students an opportunity to reflect on the realities of other lives and views.

This book also differs from other texts on the subject in that it moves away from a presentation of youth as "perpetrators" of crime and emphasizes in various ways that they are also victims and survivors. As Schissel (1997) succinctly points out, young offenders are "victims first and offenders second ... survivors who are punished by law for offences viewed out of context" (108). I believe that discussions of youth crime and justice devoid of this context will never result in appropriate or effective responses.

Of course, since this is a textbook, I have presented an accumulation of facts, theories, and knowledge about youth crime and justice but I have not been exhaustive. With the exception of the chapters on theory, I have focused on Canadian literature and research, particularly in the chapters on juvenile justice. Other sources have been used when they are central to an understanding of an issue or when Canadian literature is lacking. I do not intend that this book be used as a source of "objective fact" but rather as a tool for college and undergraduate university students in developing their own understanding of public issues about youth crime and justice. This is particularly important as we begin a new era of youth justice under the Youth Criminal Justice Act and likely one of intensified public debate. In addition, there is sufficient knowledge and information in the book to provide students with a solid foundation to pursue professional careers or more advanced academic studies in the field.

In this edition, the challenge was how to present and discuss the justice system during this time of transition. Until at least April 2003, the YOA will govern the structure and functioning of the system, and it will continue to be reflected in official statistics for the next three years. In keeping with the overall premise of this book, that we need to know where we have come from in order to understand where we are today and where we are going tomorrow, I discuss both the YOA and the YCJA throughout each chapter. Relevant sections of the Youth Criminal Justice Act are presented in detail and compared to the YOA in legislation and practice and implications for change and new issues are discussed.

This book divides easily into two parts. The first half focuses on youth crime and how we explain it, while the second half addresses the justice system. Chapter 1 sets the stage for the remainder of the book by raising contemporary questions about youth crime and justice by examining those questions in historical context and by attempting to provide answers. Chapter 2 continues this historical framework with a discussion of the creation of the juvenile justice system and Canada's ongoing reform process, from the Juvenile Delinquents Act, to the Young Offenders Act, to the Youth Criminal Justice Act. Comparative discussions of the content of these acts and the public issues associated with them are presented. A central theme in this chapter, linking it to the first chapter, comes from a discussion of public opposition to each act and the similarities in the debates between each historical era. Chapter 3 revisits the central questions raised in Chapter 1. Here, we examine crime statistics and their sources and demonstrate that statistics can be misleading without a thorough understanding of their origin. This chapter exposes students to a variety of statistics so that comparisons of varying statistical interpretations are possible. Chapter 4 discusses youth crime statistics in a social context by focusing on race, class, gender, and victimization, and the issues associated with these concepts in making sense of statistics. Chapters 5 and 6 examine attempts at scholarly explanations of youth crime. Chapter 5 presents "the beginnings" of scholarly efforts at explaining youth crime, while Chapter 6 discusses "new directions" in thinking—those based on critical and feminist directions, as well as on recent efforts at integrating classic versions of control, conflict, and learning theory.

There is a wealth of research and critique associated with most theories of youth crime and delinquency, and it is beyond the scope of this book to review it all. Instead, Chapter 7 focuses on the factors most consistently identified theoretically as the keys to explaining and understanding youth crime—family, school, and peers. This chapter reviews the most recent empirical evidence pertaining to these factors and summarizes "what we know" about the relationships between youth crime and family, friends, and school.

The focus of the book then shifts to the justice system. Since the next three chapters present thorough descriptions of the structure of the justice system and of how youth were processed through the system under the YOA, students may want to review parts of Chapter 2 before moving on. The role of police and alternative measures programs are discussed in Chapter 8, the courts and sentencing issues in Chapter 9, and youth correctional programs and institutions in Chapter 10. Attempts are made throughout to present different regions as examples and to discuss variations across the country.

Chapter 11 addresses the issue of minority youth in the justice system. The focus is on girls and Aboriginal youth, and examples of alternative programming are presented. The final chapter returns to the fundamental question about youth crime and juvenile justice by examining what has changed over the last century. The discussion here focuses on various reform proposals ranging from those that offer "more of the same" to those that reflect fundamental shifts in how we respond to youth crime.

NEW IN THE SECOND EDITION

The major impetus for this edition is the new Youth Criminal Justice Act. While Chapters 1, 5, 6, 7, 11 and 12 are largely unaffected by the introduction of the YCJA, Chapters 2, 8, and 9 have undergone major revisions. The content of Chapters 3 and 4 will change substantially but not until at least 2005 when 2003 statistics become available. Nonetheless, every chapter in the second edition of *Young Offenders and Juvenile Justice: A Century After the Fact* has been revised to include the latest statistics, the latest Canadian research or publication, relevant sections of the Youth Criminal Justice Act, and, where appropriate, comparisons to the YOA in legislation and practice.

Chapters **3 and 4,** formerly Chapters 2 and 3, contain an updated "violent crime debate" as well as the most recent *Juristat* reports, youth court, police, and victimization statistics. Chapter 4 also provides a more detailed discussion and profile of violent youth crime and offenders including the debate about increasing levels of girls' violent behaviour.

Chapters **5 through 7,** formerly Chapters 4 through 6, have been expanded to include discussions of Gottfredson and Hirschi's General Theory of Crime, routine activity, and rational choice theory, and recent work on social capital theory and lifecourse developmental theory.

Chapter 8 introduces students to the YCJA concept of "extrajudicial measures" and presents a discussion of the variety of ways in which diversion has been practiced in Canada from informal police practices under the JDA to alternative measures under the YOA and the new structure and practices required by the YCJA. This chapter now offers a detailed discussion of YCJA provisions and principles, a comparison with the YOA, and a discussion of new issues including the creation of a "bifurcated" youth justice system.

Chapter 9 provides specific details on YCJA sentencing principles; custodial requirements and limitations, and the extensive range of sentencing options including the entirely new "intensive support and supervision"; "intensive rehabilitative custody and supervision"; and "custody and conditional supervision" options. The new offence categories "presumptive offence" and "serious offence" and their effect on eliminating the issues associated with transfer hearings are discussed in detail. The implications for youth justice of automatic liability to adult sentences are introduced and YOA sentencing statistics are updated.

Chapter 10 offers considerable discussion of how the YCJA will change the youth correctional system as well as legislative details on the new custodial sentencing requirements and options. New custodial issues are introduced including the implications of eliminating judicial powers in determining levels of custody. YOA custodial statistics are updated and elaborated for girls and aboriginal youth.

Chapter 11 includes recent statistics, research, and publications on girls and aboriginal youth.

Chapter 12 includes recent innovative and regressive proposals for change, for example, restorative justice initiatives and Alliance MPs' dissatisfaction with certain aspects of the YCJA such as no changes to age jurisdiction.

IN-TEXT LEARNING AIDS

Chapter Objectives and Introductions

Chapter objectives and an introduction are presented at the beginning of each chapter to give students an overview of major topics and act as an aid for reviewing the central points of each chapter.

Key Terms and Glossary

Key terms are presented at the beginning of each chapter to alert students to important concepts and to also provide a review. These terms are highlighted in bold print in the chapter and defined when this does not disrupt students' reading. All key terms are defined in the glossary section at the back of the book (new to the second edition).

Chapter Summary

Each chapter ends with a concise summary of key points, "facts," people, and theoretical perspectives. The summary is designed as a review for students, not as a study replacement to reading the chapter.

TEXT SUPPLEMENTS

Instructor's Manual/Test Bank

The Instructor's Manual portion provides chapter outlines, chapter summaries, chapter objectives, student learning objectives, key terms and people, issues for discussion, and additional ideas (suggestions for guest speakers, student projects, etc.). A revised Test Bank is available with over 2,000 review, multiple choice, short answer, and essay questions. Questions are designed to test conceptual understanding, concept application, or factual knowledge, and a text page reference is provided for each answer.

The Instructor's Manual/Test Bank was written by the author of the text.

www.bellyoungoffenders2e.nelson.com

This text features a companion Web site designed for both students and instructors. Features of the Web site include chapter links and quizzes, degree and career information, study resources, and much more.

Infotrac College Edition

InfoTrac® College Edition is automatically bundled FREE with every new copy of this text! InfoTrac® College Edition is a world-class, online university library that offers the full text of articles from almost 4000 scholarly and popular publications—updated daily and going back as much as 22 years. Both adopters and their students receive unlimited access for four months. Visit the text's Web site.

ACKNOWLEDGMENTS

A few special people made it possible for me to write this book. Above all, I wish to thank my parents, Jeanne and John Best, and grandmothers, Florence Roy and Louise Best, whose guidance, support, teaching, and example saved me from the juvenile justice system. The book is also due, in large part, to my gentle and generous partner in life, Rick Edwards, who kept me going throughout this project. Others have supported and assisted me along the way, through various stages. I am beholden and grateful to Marianne Parsons, Angela Dinaut, and Tena Boutilier, and to my research assistants, Cindy Bayers, Nancy Slipp, and Wendy Stephens.

I am also indebted to the reviewers who took the time to offer constructive comments on manuscript drafts. These include K.M. Campbell, University of Ottawa; Irwin Cohen, Simon Fraser University; Ruth M. Mann, University of Windsor; Kim Luton, University of Western Ontario; Bill O'Grady, University of Guelph; Michael G. Young, Camosun College; Jana Grekul, University of Alberta; Rebecca Volk, Algonquin College; and Tracey Moore, John Abbott College. The book is greatly improved because of their efforts.

Finally, I wish to thank the publisher, Evelyn Veitch, for supporting this project, Charlotte Forbes who, as acquisitions editor at Nelson, convinced me to take on this project, and Joanna Cotton, the executive editor who provided the inspiration for the second edition. My gratitude also extends to Joan Rawlin for her skilled final touches and to Edward Ikeda, senior developmental editor and Julie van Veen, production editor, for their patience and gentle prodding to keep the project moving on schedule.

Sandra J. Bell
Saint Mary's University
Halifax

CHAPTER 1

The Rise and Fall of Delinquency

CHAPTER OBJECTIVES

1. To situate contemporary public issues about youth crime in a historical context.

2. To demonstrate that concerns about youth crime are created as much by particular sociohistorical circumstances as by actual levels of youth crime.

3. To provide a sociological perspective on youth crime and public issues.

4. To recognize that youth misbehaviour is a concept that has been understood in a variety of ways at different times in Canada's history.

5. To examine the nature and level of youth involvement in crime throughout Canada's history.

6. To understand what is new about contemporary youth crime and public issues.

KEY TERMS

Public issues
Juvenile justice system
Penitentiary
Primary data
Secondary data
Discourse

Rehabilitate
Juvenile delinquent
Reformatories
Official crime
Structural
Demographic

Denied adulthood
Marginalized
Moral panic
Decontextualize

INTRODUCTION

This chapter examines youth crime issues from a historical perspective. Through an examination of historical documents and sociohistorical analyses, public concerns about youth crime in the 18th and 19th centuries are compared with contemporary **public issues** about youth crime. This approach provides a framework and background for a presentation of a sociological perspective on the subject and a broader understanding of public issues regarding youth crime.

The chapter begins with a discussion of the issues as we understand them today and then proceeds to compare these views to perceptions of youth crime, crime statistics, and public issues from the past. Three distinct periods in Canadian history are discussed: the pre-Confederation period, in which children and youth were treated the same as adults; the Victorian period, in which the behaviour and well-being of children and youth became a subject of concern; and the post-Victorian period, in which youthful offenders were separated from adults in an attempt to prevent them from developing a criminal lifestyle that could last a lifetime.

By putting the current issue of youth crime in a historical context, we will see that youth crime has always been a part of Canadian society, but not always a public issue. The last 150 years of Canada's history has witnessed the rise and fall of youth crime as a public issue, as well as the rise and fall of delinquency itself.

THE PUBLIC ISSUE

Over the last decade, youth crime has been the subject of considerable public concern and discussion. Across Canada, newspaper headlines warned of a serious crime problem if appropriate steps were not taken to curb youth crime. Headlines in the *Calgary Herald* warned of imminent danger: "Youth Violence Soaring" (Oct. 15, 1992, B15); "No End Seen to Spiral in Teenage Crime" (May 14, 1992, A1); "Toll Keeps Mounting as Violent Youth Spawn an Epidemic of Violence" (June 27, 1992, G4). While on the other side of the country, *The Chronicle-Herald* in Halifax reported, "Youth Crime Puts the Squeeze on Business" (July 1993, A4) and "The YOA a Slap on the Wrist for Violent Offenders" (May 1992). Beyond the headlines, newspaper articles painted horrific accounts of the criminal deeds of young Canadians. In one summer month in 1995, we were informed that five teens in Prince Rupert, British Columbia, were charged with second-degree murder for the fatal beating of a fisherman (Fisherman Murdered, 1995); a 7-year-old boy in La Ronge, Saskatchewan, was responsible (along with a 14-year-old) for the murder of another 7-year-old child (Riley, 1995); a 15-year-old in Winnipeg was charged with first-degree murder in the fatal drive-by shooting of a 13-year-old Aboriginal youth (Oosterom, 1995); and four

Halifax teenagers were charged with aggravated assault for trying to kill a man who was a total stranger to them (MacKinlay, 1995).

By the end of the decade, newspaper and magazine headlines and stories were fueling public concerns about violent events involving girls. Headlines in *The Globe and Mail* such as "Teen's Torture Again Reveals Girls' Brutality" (January 20, 1998, A1) and "Police Arrest Members of Girl Gang" (January 22, 1998, A12) reinforced images of out of control teenage girls created by journalists' coverage of the death of Reena Virk in Victoria, British Columbia, in 1997. A 16-year-old boy and 15-year-old girl were convicted in adult court of second degree murder in Reena's death and six teenage girls, aged 14 to 16 were also convicted of aggravated assault in youth court for their part in Reena's final ordeal (Purvis, 1997; Chisholm, 1997; Joyce, 2000). In the same year, two 15-year-old girls were charged with first-degree murder for stabbing Helen Montgomery to death in her North Battleford, Saskatchewan, home. The girls had been living in her home under an open-custody arrangement at the time of her murder (Cross, 1998).

Most recently, school violence has been added to the list of horrors presented about youth behaviour. The *National Post* informed readers that "Teen Felt Good After Killing Girl …" (May 30, 2001, A8) and *The Chronicle-Herald* that "High Schools [are] Simmering with Angry, Verbally Abusive Teens" (November 18, 2000, A6), "Teen Charged in Taber School Shooting … Listens Calmly … in Court" (August 29, 2000, C10), and "Teen in Beating Case Not Rehabilitated or Reformed" (December 14, 2000, A5). All are stories about beatings and killings in Canadian schools by seemingly unconcerned youth.

Not surprisingly, newspaper headlines, stories, and the personal experiences of a few have prompted many Canadians to voice their concerns about "today's youth" and about the effectiveness of our youth justice system in curbing youth crime. Politicians responded to these concerns by presenting youth crime and the Young Offenders Act (YOA) as a major election issue in the 1993 federal election campaign (see Table 1.1). Legislators, for their part, revised the YOA three times before finally proposing legislation to replace it. In 1995, while deliberating reforms for the third time, then-Justice Minister Allan Rock requested that the House of Commons Standing Committee on Justice and Legal Affairs undertake a comprehensive review of the **juvenile justice system** and that a Federal-Provincial-Territorial Task Force review the YOA and its application. The recommendations contained in these reports provided a foundation for further modifications to the justice system. In the spring of 1998, then-Justice Minister Anne McLellan announced plans to introduce new legislation, (McIlroy, 1998a, 1998b). By the fall of 2001, the Youth Criminal Justice Act, Bill (C-3), was poised to replace the YOA. Modifications to the juvenile justice system will be discussed in greater detail in the next chapter.

TABLE 1.1

Federal Party Platforms on Young Offenders and Juvenile Justice, 1993

Liberal	Recommends that the Young Offenders Act be amended to increase sentences for violent crimes.
Conservative	Recommends increasing the severity of punishment under the Young Offenders Act.
NDP	Advocates a review of the Young Offenders Act.
Reform	Advocates an overhaul of the Young Offenders Act.
National	Expresses general concern about handguns and repeat violent offenders.
Bloc Québécois	No set policy in this area, but expresses concerns about law-and-order rhetoric.

Source: Adapted from Voter's Guide (1993).

Two Opposing Sides

In 1995, as part of the review of the juvenile justice system, the House of Commons Standing Committee on Justice and Legal Affairs undertook public and special interest group consultations. Public forums were held in various communities across the country to discuss youth crime and propose solutions or make recommendations to the standing committee. At the heart of the public issue were questions about whether the YOA effectively controlled youth crime: the public was clearly divided into two camps on the youth crime issue as demonstrated, for example, at the Halifax public forum.

The youth advocates in this forum, often including social workers, lawyers, and others who work directly with young offenders, saw children and youth as victims in need of protection and believed that neither youth nor the YOA was a problem. The important issues, as they saw it, were those related to the difficulties that youth encounter in an increasingly complex society. From this perspective, current economic, social, and political realities are a source of tremendous hardship for some young people and their families. Often, economic or social problems exacerbate other problems within families and young people are forced to leave home as a matter of survival (see Box 1.1). One lawyer who works with youth poignantly reflected, "I look at these kids and their horrible family lives, and I think, 'There but for the grace of God go I.'"

Youth advocates were primarily concerned with the problems experienced by young people rather than youth crime. It was their view that youth crime had been

BOX 1.1

Street Kids' Perspectives

Ocean, 18, female:

I'm a ward. Social services took me out. They took me out of the home because I was sexually abused ... It was my stepfather that abused me. It went on from the age of seven until I was fourteen ... My Dad left when I was three. It was really hard because we had no money at all. Nothing. He took everything. I was in grade three when the abuse started. My mother knew about it a year later. She did something in a way but she didn't go to anybody. She said, "If he ever does anything again, come tell me." That night he came into my room and it started all over again ... I was in grade seven and I told Mum again and she still didn't do anything. It was at this time that I was put into my first foster home. For me if they had put me in with a family that wanted me I think I would have been okay. Jane was okay but she and everyone turned against my mother for kicking me out of the house and staying with him ... Me and my Mum never got along. We fought and fought. I guess it was from all the abuse and all the tension. I guess I took it out on my Mum and my brother. I used to abuse my brother. I used to beat him ... I'm real sorry for that. The day my Dad went to jail my Dad's second-youngest brother came up to me in a car and stopped and said, "Thanks a lot. You just put your Dad in jail for five years." ... From there I went to live with my aunt in B.C. Things were no better there, and I left there and came home to Nova Scotia ... Things were real bad here. I even tried to kill myself at one point and was put into the N.S. Hospital for five months ... Things were no better when I got out. Nobody wanted me, so they put me into Phoenix house. I have been there ever since.

Clarissa, 17, female:

When did we move there ... I think I was eleven ... but once I was twelve I decided I wanted out ... so I ran. When I got off the bus, the police were waiting for me. So I was, well, quickly returned home and I was put into a foster home ... It was only a temporary agreement, voluntary, for three months. My parents had to sign a thing so after three months were up I was supposed to be returned to them ... I did go home for Christmas and I got a big bawling out from my stepmother about how I wasn't there and they weren't going to get their tax deductions at the end of the year … It didn't make me feel very good, like, well jeez, is that all you want me for, the money … My Dad is a pervert, put it that way … oh yeah, I lived with that for years … I was five and a half when it started, that's as far back as I can remember … My stepmother knows but she denies that she knows, she denies that it is true … I lived in many different group homes. I got kicked out because I wasn't following the rules … I was fourteen when I started doing it [prostitution] but now it is just when I need the money … I gotta chill out because I'm doing the dope again … The system sucks … They don't do anything for us … they take us and stick us in a group home and that's all they do … they stick you there … I don't have a place I would call home. I have been basically without a roof over my head and you bunk where you can find a spot … I have had to stay out on the streets and all I do is get so stoned out of my tree I don't know whether I am comin' or goin' and the night passes like that.

Source: *Homeless Youth* (1994: 12–21).

exaggerated and misrepresented in most public accounts, particularly by the media. At the Halifax public forum, youth advocates presented statistics from the Department of Justice showing that crime in Nova Scotia had dropped in all categories since 1986, and that recent increases in violent crime had "flattened out." Other statistics indicated that youth were being treated far more harshly under the YOA than they ever were under the former legislation, the Juvenile Delinquents Act (Leschied and Jaffe, 1991). Further, with the exception of the most serious offences of murder and manslaughter, youth were treated at least as harshly as adults who had committed the same offences (Doob, Marinos, and Varma, 1995; Bell and Smith, 1994). Among other things, youth advocates prefer policies that will address poverty and high youth unemployment rather than focus on punitive justice reforms.

The other perspective presented at the Halifax public forum was the one most often seen in the media. The law-and-order group viewed children and youth accused of crimes as an enemy from whom adults needed protection (Sherr, 1996). Proponents of this view saw youth as "out of control" and favoured a law-and-order approach to youth crime. Included in this group were what one police officer described as the "old buffalo police officers," store security personnel, small-business owners, and homeowners associations. From their perspectives, both youth and the YOA were problems. Youth were a problem because they were said to (1) lack respect for anyone or anything, as was often reflected in foul language and "no fear of using it"; (2) lack a sense of responsibility for their criminal behaviour; and (3) be increasingly involved in violent criminal behaviour. The YOA was viewed as a problem because it was believed that (1) youth could not be identified; (2) youth were not punished for their crimes; (3) youth had more rights than their victims; and (4) youth were too protected by the YOA.

Law-and-order proponents at the Halifax forum cited a recent Statistics Canada release reporting an 8 percent increase in youth involvement in violent crime. They were further armed with information about incidences of particularly violent youth crime, readily supplied from news media. These stories usually portray the young offender in such cases as remorseless and lacking feeling—the "superpredator" (Sherr, 1996). The law-and-order view advocates a get-tough approach to young offenders.

"THE GOOD OLD DAYS"

Perhaps the most basic assumption underlying many public views about youth crime, particularly the law-and-order perspective, is the notion that today's youth are worse than they were in "the good old days." Interestingly, every generation of adults seems to remember a time when things were "better" and not what they are "today." Yet, available crime statistics do not indicate any such period in Canadian history. Canadian crime statistics, as far back as 1885 (see Table 1.2), indicate that young people have always been involved in criminal activity, some of it serious violent crime.

Moreover, young people have always been responsible for a considerably smaller amount of criminal activity than adults, and most of their offences have involved petty property crime. According to Carrigan (1991:216), this pattern of criminal activity was established in early pioneer days and has continued to the present. In 1909–10, for example, documents in the annual reports for the City of Halifax indicate that youth under 18 were responsible for 18 percent of all criminal charges (City Marshal, 1909–10). The Nova Scotia Department of Justice reports that in 1993–94 youth accounted for the same proportion of all criminal activity—18 percent (Bell, 1995). For Canada as a whole, youth under 18 accounted for 19 percent of all criminal code charges and 16 percent of all violent crime in 1998 (Statistics Canada, 1999:18–19).

Some youth crimes are particularly horrendous, such as the 1993 abduction and brutal murder of 2-year-old James Bulger by two 10-year-old boys in Liverpool, England. Some view this crime as "evidence" that children are far more criminal now than ever before. However, most people have no way of knowing what crimes occurred decades ago. Few of us would recall that an 11-year-old girl in England murdered two children in her care in 1968; fewer still would know that in 1861 two 8-year-old boys murdered a 2-year-old in a case very similar to the James Bulger murder. Similarly, Carrigan (1991:204) tells of a 10-year-old boy who, on a hunting party in March 1802, took a loaded gun to a tent and shot a man dead. The lawyer representing one of the

TABLE 1.2

Juvenile Convictions for Indictable Offences, 1885–1899

Type of Offence	Under Age 16		16–20	
	Male	Female	Male	Female
Offences against the person	371	16	1,593	62
Offences against property with violence	805	4	1,456	3
Offences against property without violence	7,750	398	7,328	704
Malicious offences against property	161	10	106	5
Forgery and offences against the currency	24	1	106	5
Other offences not included in the above classes	125	40	336	169
Totals	9,236	469	10,963	948

Source: Adapted from *Statistical Yearbook of Canada, 1899*.

young Liverpool defendants argued to the judge hearing their case that "there is no evidence of an increase during this century of crimes of murder by young children" (Reduced Sentences, 1996).

Unfortunately, historical data on youth crime and public responses are not readily available since youth crime statistics were not always kept in the manner that they are today. In the early years of European settlement, crime information was recorded in the reports of colonial administrators. Some statistics are available for Upper and Lower Canada (Ontario and Quebec) after Confederation, and slightly more detailed information is available in general reports from city administrators. Prison records provide a source of information on youth crime, but the ages of prisoners were not always recorded. There are no consistent prison records until 1835, the year in which Kingston **Penitentiary**, the first Canadian prison, opened. Beyond these **primary data**, there are a few academic analyses of youth crime that provide **secondary data** (such as Carrigan, 1991). These analyses are scant since contemporary Canadian scholars and researchers seem to have been far more interested in the justice system than in the actual behaviour of children and youth in Canada's history. Most Canadian criminologists now studying in this area have relied more on the work of historians than criminologists (Smandych, 1995:13).

Lawless and Disobedient Youth: The 17th and 18th Centuries

Information on youth involvement in crime in Canada during the 17th and 18th centuries is sketchy. Although we cannot ever know the actual incidence of lawbreaking among youth during this period, what information is available indicates that concerns were expressed about youth as a problem in the North American colonies as early as the late 17th century. In his analysis of youth in New France, Moogk (1982) documents the concerns expressed by colonial administrators regarding the children of the colonies:

> The great liberty of long standing which the parents and Governors have given to the youth, permitting them to dally in the woods under the pretext of hunting or trading ... has reached such an excess that from the time children are able to carry a gun, fathers are not able to restrain them and dare not anger them. (Governor Brisay de Denonville, 1685, cited in Moogk, 1982:17)

Other reports described boys in New France as "lawless" and "disobedient," and girls as "vain" and "lazy." Similarly, in 1707, an intendant of the colony described the children of New France as "hard and ferocious" (Moogk, 1982:18).

Carrigan (1991: 203, 205) examined the historical records of crime and punishment from the earliest European records and reports that the majority of documented cases were of a petty nature. They involved vandalism, petty theft, brawling, swearing, immorality, violations of local ordinances, and the abandonment of indentured service contracts. There were young people involved in serious crimes and murders, but their ages are often not recorded. One recorded example is the case of a 10-year-old indentured servant who set fire to his master's house in Annapolis, Nova Scotia, on April 19, 1737; the house and contents were totally destroyed.

Throughout recorded history, children in European society have had a different legal status than adults. Mostly, this meant they had no rights and were at the mercy of their parents and the state. Infanticide, child slavery, and child labour were common. The idea that children had rights as individuals independent of their parents, or that they had a right to protection from adults, did not gain popularity until the 19th century (Bala and Clarke, 1981:1–6). With regard to crime, from about the 11th century, English common law recognized that a child's capacity to understand the wrongfulness of crime was limited. Hence, children under 7 were considered to lack the "capacity to commit a crime" (*doli incapax*) (Bala and Clarke, 1981:163). Evidence of capacity was required to convict children 7 to 13 of a crime. Nonetheless, 7-year-old children were charged with crimes, tried in court with adults, and faced with the same punishments upon conviction (163).

Colonial administrators brought these legal codes and traditions to the New World. The first European settler executed in the territories of Canada was a 16-year-old girl who had been found guilty of theft in 1640. Her execution was ordered by Champlain (Carrigan, 1991), and she was hanged by a male offender who escaped execution by agreeing to act as her hangman (Adelberg and Currie, 1988). Smandych (1995) cautions that we should not conclude that children were always or usually treated exactly like adults in the colonial justice system; rather, they "were usually shown an even greater degree of mercy than adults" (15). Thus we find that in 1672, a 13-year-old girl who had helped her parents murder her husband escaped execution because of her age; instead, she was required to attend the execution of her parents (Carrigan, 1991:203).

The Colonial Public Issue

The issue for colonial administrators in the territories of Canada was the freedom and independence that young people had relative to their counterparts in the Old World. In Europe, children were subservient to adults and dependent on parents. As Moogk (1982) notes,

> The official culture of France glorified submission to authority ... The family, the church, and the state were organized as hierarchies in which authority descended from the top. An orderly society was one in which people accepted their hereditary social rank and obeyed their superiors. (42)

However, the largely rural nature of the population in New France meant that parents were dependent on their children's labour for economic success. Hence, rural and working-class children in the New World had considerable independence from their parents. In the view of colonial administrators, parental authority was significantly undermined by this arrangement and this lack of authority was evident in young people's behaviour. According to administrators' reports:

> Rural children stole produce from their parents in order to buy trifles ... [and] among "the common people" ... "boys of ten or twelve years of age ... run about with a pipe in their mouth" ... Young *Canadiens* drank brandy, refused to doff their hats in the presence of ladies while indoors, and rode about on their own horses ... The fact that in New France young peasants rode horses and country girls dressed in the finery of gentlewomen did not accord with the outsider sense of propriety. (Moogk, 1982:41–42)

The freedom and independence displayed by young people in New France likely posed a significant threat to the authority of the administrators themselves since 42 percent of the population was composed of children under 15 (Moogk, 1982:42–43).

"Causes" and Solutions: An Era of Control and Punishment

From historical documents of the colonial period two factors emerge as perceived "causes" of youth crime—parents and the fur trade. Overindulgent parents were often cited by administrators as a reason for youth problems:

> The residents of this country have never had a proper education because of the over-indulgence (la foiblesse) resulting from a foolish tenderness shown to them by their mothers and fathers during their infancy. In this they imitate the Amerindians. It prevents them from disciplining the children and forming their character. (Intendant Jacques Raudot, 1707, cited in Moogk, 1982:18)

Some officials complained about the children of "gentlemen," accusing them of "debauchery" and "abusing the daughters and wives of the natives" (Denonville, 1685, cited in Carrigan, 1991:204). Another identified problem was the fur trade, one of the most lucrative businesses of the times. Since the seigneurial system of inheritance in New France dictated that only eldest sons inherited family farms, other children had to look elsewhere for a livelihood. The fur trade promised freedom, adventure, and a lucrative career. Merchants and military officers also saw business opportunities for their sons in the fur trade and apprenticed them to experienced voyageurs. According to Carrigan (1991), the fur trade was "rife with fraud, immorality, theft, assault, and murder," and teenagers "probably contributed their fair share to the lawlessness" (204). Apparently, many carried these habits back to their homes after they left the fur-trading business, for they were accused of having contracted "an habitual libertinism" (cited in Carrigan, 1991:204).

Beyond this, a very real source of problems came from the active promotion of immigration to the New World. Impoverished Europeans had been lured to the New World with promises of a prosperous life, but once there, many found only unemployment, sickness, destitution, or death. Countless numbers of children found themselves in desperate circumstances because of the hardships faced by their parents in the New World. Some parents died as a result of these hardships, while others simply abandoned their children once they reached the New World.

> Between 1752 and 1760 the Orphan House in Halifax admitted a total of 275 children. Of that number 114 were orphans while the remainder were either neglected or abandoned ... One ship that arrived in Halifax in 1752 landed eight orphans whose parents had died during the voyage. More deaths shortly afterwards increased the number of parentless children to fourteen. (Carrigan, 1991:206)

In the 18th century a variety of disciplinary measures were proposed as solutions to youth crime. Some are remarkably similar to modern proposals. While such solutions as more schools, more priests, and confinement to settled parts of the colony were, as informal forms of legal governance (Hogeveen, 2001:45-47), uniquely suited to the political, social, and economic structures of this period, other proposals, such as fines and punishment for parents of offenders, military justice, and an increase in garrison troops [read police] should sound very familiar to a modern reader (Moogk, 1982:18).

A Question of Immorality: The 19th Century

Urban problems associated with immigration and poverty continued and worsened throughout the 19th century. Carrigan (1991) reports that one relief agency in York cared for 535 orphans over a two-year period in the early 1800s. Some fathers were deserting their families "in despair of bettering their situation," and York was "overwhelmed with Widows or Orphans" (Archdeacon John Strachan, 1831, cited in Carrigan, 206). The Irish famine exacerbated the orphan problem in Canada by increasing the number of people emigrating to the New World. The effect of these increased numbers was to worsen the quality of life on the ships and to make passengers more susceptible to typhus fever.

> In 1847 an estimated 20,000 immigrants died from sickness. Some 5,000 died at Grose Isle, the quarantine station in Quebec, the rest in places like Quebec City, Montreal, Kingston, and Toronto. One estimate suggested that 500–600 orphans were left in Montreal from this epidemic. (Carrigan, 1991:206)

By the mid 1800s, British and Canadian authorities had developed policies to send Britain's orphaned, poor, and destitute children to Canada as indentured servants. Between 1873 and 1903, over 95,000 children came to Canada under the sponsorship of child immigration agencies (Carrigan, 1991:208). While the migration scheme was seen as a means of providing a better life for the children of Britain's poor and destitute families, many of these children found only a life of misery and harsh working conditions in Canada. In the words of one young female immigrant, "'doption, sir, is when folks gets a girl to work without wages" (cited in Sutherland, 1976:10). Some children abandoned their contracts (even though to do so was a punishable offence), which left them dependent on their own resources for survival.

Life for the poor was very difficult in Victorian Canada. Fingard (1989) contrasts the lifestyle of the "respectable middle-class" with that of the people who lived in the poorer sections of Halifax and vividly documents the difficulties faced by urban young people in 19th-century Canada. Many did not have work, and those who were lucky enough to secure employment were often at the mercy of unscrupulous employers. Girls were particularly vulnerable. Those working as domestics and servants for shopkeepers were often forced to "service" male customers in order to keep their jobs. They were not free to leave these places of employment because to do so would require them to forfeit a letter of reference without which they would be unable to secure other employment (Fingard, 1989:101–2).

This situation was only too common in most North American cities. Stansell's (1986) analysis of sex and class relations in New York City documents the grim lives of girls who sought self-reliance.

> Juvenile prostitution stemmed not just from class encounters but from the everyday relations of men and girls in working-class neighborhoods. Rape trials ... show that sex with girl children was woven into the fabric of life in the tenements and the streets ... Poor girls learned early about their vulnerability to sexual harm from grown men, but they also learned some ways to turn men's interest to their own purposes. Casual prostitution was one ...
>
> Laboring girls ran across male invitations in the course of their daily rounds—street selling, scavenging, running errands for mothers or mistresses, in walking home from work, in their workplaces and neighborhoods ... Opportunities proliferated as New York's expanding industry and commerce provided a range of customers extending well beyond the traditional clientele of wealthy rakes and sailors. Country storekeepers in town on business, gentlemen travellers, lonely clerks and working men were among those who propositioned girls on the street. (182–83)

Most of our information on youth crime from the Victorian period comes from city police records and prison reports. Juvenile institutions were not built until after 1857, so when young offenders were imprisoned they were sent to adult jails. This included the penitentiary in Kingston, which opened in 1835. In 1846, 16 children were imprisoned at Kingston Penitentiary (Bowker, 1986). Carrigan (1991) reports that in 1849–50, 36 of the prisoners released from Kingston Penitentiary were between the ages of 10 and 17. One of these prisoners had been convicted of murder at age 15, and another of manslaughter at age 10. The 1848–49 report from a government inquiry on the Kingston prison, the Brown commission report, tells of children 8, 11, and 12 being housed with adult criminals. Six percent of the convicted population in other jails scattered throughout Upper and Lower Canada were under 16. Compared to today's institutionalized populations, a much higher percentage of imprisoned youth were girls. In 1859, 29 percent of youth detained in the jails of Upper and Lower Canada were girls under 16 (Carrigan, 1991:209–15). This may be because arrest rates for female offenders were higher in the 19th century than they are today (Boritch, 1997:46–47).

Many incarcerated youth had been convicted of relatively minor offences and many were as young as 7. Throughout the 19th century, it was not uncommon to find children not yet in their teens in city jails as well. In 1881, for example, the annual prison report for the City of Halifax indicates that 7.9 percent of the prison population that year was between 8 and 14 (Prison Report, 1881:113). Many youth were imprisoned because they were "habitual" offenders. Houston (1982:134) tells of a 10-year-old break-and-enter artist in Toronto who was outdone in his crimes by three 7-year-olds who, when convicted of felony in 1890, already had three previous convictions for break and enter.

After Confederation in 1867, the proportion of youth in jails declined somewhat, especially in regard to girls and young women.

> In 1869 approximately 6.6 per cent of all people put in Ontario jails were juveniles. The percentage dropped to 4.2 in 1879 and to 3.9 in 1889. The percentage fluctuated over the years but there was never any significant increase ... In 1869 girls accounted for 21.8 percent of juvenile incarcerations, dropping to 11.3 per cent in 1879 and to 9.2 per cent in 1889. (Carrigan, 1991:210)

Rates for boys continued to fluctuate. In Ontario, Houston (1982) notes,

> Males under sixteen years old fluctuated as a proportion of total male committals to provincial gaols within a relatively short span from Confederation to 1890. At its highest (7.8 per cent) in the late 1860's, the figure dropped in the 1870's, rising briefly in 1882 to its decade high of 6.7 per cent, falling again to its lowest percentage for the total period (3.8 per cent) in 1886. (133)

Houston cautions that fluctuations in the use of institutions should not be seen as indicative of changes in criminal behaviour. Committals to prisons tended to reflect "governmental and judicial faith" in the institutions rather than any actual change in youth behaviour. "There is little to suggest that the behaviour of youngsters altered. Larceny dominated the list of offences committed; only the addition in 1880 of "incorrigibility" as a grounds for committal significantly altered the picture" (Houston, 1982:133). In addition, some of the decline and fluctuation in youth incarceration was likely due to changing attitudes about young offenders, the development of separate institutions for children, and the ability of boards of directors of these institutions to affect court commitments to their facilities (Rains and Teram, 1992:27–31).

Passed in 1857, An Act for Establishing Prisons for Young Offenders provided for separate institutions for youth (Hagan and Leon, 1977). Two facilities were opened shortly thereafter, one in an unused military barracks in Penetanguishene on Georgian Bay in Upper Canada and one at Isle aux Noix on the Richelieu River in Lower Canada. When the institution at Penetanguishene opened, it housed 40 boys; by 1872, there were 193 inmates. The institutionalized population at Penetanguishene reached a record high of 263 boys in 1882 (Jones, 1988:279). Many of these boys were very young; according to Carrigan (199:212), 55 percent of the boys admitted to Penetanguishene in 1889 were under 14.

The Victorian Public Issue

By the mid-1800s, the urban middle class in North America began to express concerns about the morality of those who were poor and destitute. Various urban relief agencies sprang up in cities across the continent to address such problems as illiteracy, prostitution, alcohol abuse, juvenile delinquency, and "family squalor" (Fingard, 1989:119). The **discourse** surrounding those agencies and their activities served to define problems, their "causes," and seemingly appropriate solutions. In Halifax, one agency instrumental in bringing social issues to public attention was the Halifax City Mission. Established in 1852, the mission identified three problems—prostitution, the liquor trade, and infanticide—and lobbied the city and provincial governments to take action (Fingard, 1989:122). The criminal activity of young people was also of some concern to the agency. In 1862, an annual report for the City of Halifax reports that "juvenile offenders of both sexes are constantly brought before the Police Court, charged with thefts and other similar offences ... The numbers of these youthful criminals are far greater than would be imagined" (Mayor's Report, 1862:14). The 1898–99 report of the Chief of Police for the City of Halifax indicates that 10.8 percent of the convicted offenders whose ages were known were under 16, while 18.9 percent were between 16 and 20 (Annual Report, 1898–1899:76). In other words, almost 30 percent of the convicted offenders in Halifax a century ago were under 21.

Throughout the latter half of the 1800s, the issue of youth crime seemed to be a moral one. Because of poverty and destitution brought on by a lack of employment and severe working conditions, countless numbers of children and young people were spending a good portion of their lives on city streets, which they worked by begging, stealing, and selling whatever they could to make a living. In Toronto, these children were referred to as "waifs," "strays," and "street arabs" in public discussions (Houston, 1982). The public issue was not poverty and destitution, however. Rather, it was the morality of an impoverished working class. The parents of these children were perceived as immoral and unable or unwilling to control their children. Attitudes toward the poor were very unsympathetic. One of the brothers at St. Patrick's Home for Boys in Halifax made the following observation:

> I find that boys sent to us for theft have absolutely no realization of its gravity. I had two lads committed here not long ago for stealing clothing. I questioned them, and they replied with perfect directness, that they stole the clothes because they needed them. ("Suspended Sentences," 1908)

Much of the morality discourse about youth problems revolved around discussions about "children on the streets." The 1890 Annual Report of the Chief Constable of Toronto states that "vagrant bands parading the streets at night have given the police a good deal of trouble, composed as they are, of rowdy youths" (48). The report goes on to indicate that the police had received numerous complaints "from all parts of the City respecting the conduct of boys in the streets" (49). Concern is expressed that the police are fighting a losing battle because "boys are ubiquitous" and the constables are "not omnipresent." The report of the following year continues to express police frustration with youth crime. "Juveniles are responsible for depredations of all kinds, and, as a class, are more difficult to deal with than the professional thief ..." (21, cited in Doob, Marinos, and Varma, 1995:1).

City administrators in other parts of the country reported similar concerns. The people of Halifax debated the merits of a curfew to solve the problem of youth on the streets at night. It would seem that boys were the curse of authorities everywhere at the turn of the century. As the Halifax *Morning Chronicle* reported on May 11, 1909:

> The problem of the nation is the problem of the City, and the problem of the City is the "Boy Problem" ... The problem of the boy is largely one of providing him with a proper environment during his "off hours" ... The boy, if neglected during the character forming period of his life, has in him the power of making the future as black as night. (Y.M.C.A., 1909)

Young women on the streets were also a concern, not for their safety, as we might assume, but for perceived danger to their morality. This view is evident in an article that appeared in the Halifax *Evening Mail* on January 11, 1908. The author of "Danger of the Street: Where Lieth Responsibility?" had this to say about the perils of the street for young women:

> Perhaps there is merely a rendezvous of young friends, but in no case can these boys and girls be improving their minds, characters or their manners. The whole effect upon them is insidious and degrading. The young girl must hear conversation unfit for her ears, she must attain worldly knowledge that she never should attain, she must grow careless, 'flip', and used to the 'license of touch'. **She will lose the essential qualities of womanliness that command every man's respect. In some cases, the girl will go down and out, and the end will be ruin, sorrow and misery.** [boldface in original]

"Causes" and Solutions: An Era of Social Reform

According to Rothman (1980), a reform movement swept North America in the latter half of the 19th century. The essential tenets of this movement were a focus on the individual, a widespread belief in the goodness of humanitarian sentiment, and, above all, a belief in the ability of the state and professionals to reform individuals. The emergence of the progressive reform movement marked the birth of rehabilitative philosophy. Reformers maintained that it made no sense to return "evil with evil" by imprisoning and punishing criminal offenders. They argued that it was far more effective in the long run to return "evil with good" by trying to **rehabilitate** individuals who had committed crimes.

This reform philosophy applied most readily to children and young people. For the "child savers" it was easy to believe that, if young enough, a child could be "saved" from a life of crime through interventions designed to correct the factors believed to influence children in the development of criminal ways (Platt, 1969a). Consistent with this idea, the practice of confining children in prison with adults also fell into public disfavour. Prisons were seen by many as "schools of crime" where children would associate with, and learn the habits of, "hardened" adult criminals.

One of the recommendations of the 1848–49 Brown commission report on Kingston Penitentiary was that a separate justice system be created for juveniles. The opening of juvenile institutions at Penetanguishene and Isle aux Noix was the first of a series of reforms that culminated in the establishment of a separate law governing the misdeeds of children and youth. Implemented in 1908, the Juvenile Delinquents Act (JDA) made **juvenile delinquent** a legal status (Hagan and Leon, 1977:591). This is not to imply that there was unanimous agreement as to the problem of youth crime or the most appropriate solution. Few seemed to object to separating children from adults, but there was disagreement over how this should be done. Some reformers believed that lengthy sentences in **reformatories** were necessary to rehabilitate young people, while others were opposed to institutionalizing young people, whether in youth or adult prison (Leon, 1977).

W.L. Scott, one of the people instrumental in drafting the first juvenile legislation, posed the question, "What wise parent would place a naughty child with other naughty children in order to make him better?" (cited in Leon, 1977:591). J.J. Kelso, another important player in the Canadian reform movement, elaborated upon this sentiment:

> Gradually we are coming to see that youthful offenders against criminal law cannot be reclaimed by force but must be won over to a better life by kindness, sympathy and friendly helpfulness; that we should substitute education for punishment and secure the hearty co-operation of the boy or girl in his or her own reclamation by awakening in them the dormant ambition to excel and to show themselves capable of responding to good influence ... To save the lad through humane agencies, to awaken in him true repentance, promise of restitution and determination to retrieve the past, is far nobler work, and decidedly more in the public interest than to send him to a felon's cell, with revenge in his heart, and continuance in crime his only ambition. (1907a:106)

Others worried that anything less than a term in an institution would serve to "cheapen" the offence in the mind of the offender. An apparent rash of thefts in the City of Halifax in 1908 was attributed to a growing tendency toward "lenient" sentencing.

> The boys know perfectly well that their youth is sure to plead eloquently and with probable success for 'release on suspended sentence'. There was a time when a boy suffered death for stealing a shilling ... The pendulum has now swung to the extreme point in the opposite direction ... the present tendency is directly responsible for an increase in the very serious crime of dishonesty. (E.H. Blois, Superintendent of the Protestant Industrial School, cited in "Suspended Sentences," 1908)

A century earlier, it had been argued in public debates that improper parenting was the cause of youth problems. By the end of the 19th century, improper parenting was once again emerging in the public discourse as the primary "cause" of youth crime. This time around, the claims took on a new dimension. Now, youth problems were attributed not to a lack of parental discipline or a loss of authority, but to neglectful or immoral parents. Poor working-class parents were viewed as inadequate or as bad role models for their children (See Box 1.2). The public issue in the latter decades of the 19th century was the moral state of youth and children, in particular those from working-class backgrounds. As West (1991) notes,

> Juvenile crime and misbehaviour were seen as not only evils linked to working-class and immigrant parents' drunkenness, sexual immorality, laboural sloth, and resultant poverty, but also as a challenge to a moral crusade for the construction of a New Jerusalem on this 'virgin' continent. (6)

By the end of the 19th century, the juvenile delinquent had been born, and "growing up on the street became the subject of public condemnation and regulation ... a life style—a street culture—had become the most common definition of juvenile delinquency" (Houston, 1982:131).

BOX 1.2

Early 20th-Century Analysis of Case Files from an Orphanage

Analysis of Case Files from an Orphanage

CASE A:

Samuel, age 7, entered the institution January 12, 1917.

The Problem

1. Delinquency
   (a) Petty pilfering.
   (b) Sexual precocity.
   (c) Uses obscene language.
   (d) Tells lies.

2. School
Expelled after a few months in kindergarten class, because of attack on little girls.

3. Home
    (a) Disobedient and impertinent.
    (b) Unmanageable.
    (c) Attempted sex act on mother.

4. Society
    (a) Lured little girls in hallways and lavatories.
    (b) In a number of boarding homes, foster-mothers complained that he was troublesome and constantly annoying little girls.
    (c) Friendly and good-tempered.
    (d) Rifled pockets, purses, drawers, any place where he knew money was kept, or suspected that it was hidden.
    (e) Offered his stolen gains to little girls for the privilege of taking liberties with them.
    (f) Juvenile Court Record (at age of seven):

Sexual precocity. Stealing and lying. Minor without proper care ...

The Analysis

1. Mental
    (a) Examination—Psychiatrist's Report:
         Intelligence: Apparently normal.
         Character: Poor basis and poor organization.
         Health: Normal.
         Impression: Definite sexual pervert.
    (b) Personality Traits:
         Sweet, winning manners. Ready smiles. In appearance, an overgrown, innocent, and lovely baby.
         Hearty eater. Excessively fond of ice-cream, soda-water, and candy.
         Plays with dolls and picture-books. No desire for any boy's toys.
         Sleeps like a baby, and sucks his thumb ...

3. Social
    (a) Heredity:
         Father: unknown. Boy believed to be illegitimate.
         Mother: slovenly, brazen, and of questionable character. Has no known relatives or friends. Claims that she was married to boy's father and divorced him. Has no proof to substantiate her claims. Does not know the man's whereabouts.
         Was living with a man as his common-law wife, and her neighbors said she frequently entertained men visitors.

Had no women callers.

Blond. Extremely attractive in appearance.

Siblings: Unknown.

  (b) Developmental:

Healthy, normal, eight-pound baby.

Had been cared for till three years of age by a very young colored girl, paid by the mother, and was not known to have had any illnesses, major or minor.

After that age, he was left to himself in the streets, and would be found by the neighbors asleep in their hallways and upon their doorsteps. Mother seemed engrossed in her own affairs, and was either unable or unwilling to give any care to the child.

When her attention was called to the neglect of the child, she was said to have told the well-intentioned neighbors to "mind their own business."

At the age of four, he was taken by the mother to the Psychiatric Clinic and examined upon her complaint that, when sleeping with her, he had attempted to assault her.

The mother also said that she had noticed he had marked sexual tendencies since babyhood, and was always trying to entice little girls into her home, for the purpose of attacking them.

She further complained that he stole money, used vile language, and was very unreliable and troublesome.

At the age of five, the neighbors reported him as a menace to their children and an incorrigible.

He was then taken from his home and sent to a boarding home ...

Samuel's Story

... In spite of the fact that he was only seven years old, he spoke with the knowledge of a man of the world. His mother had been a prostitute, and had entertained men in his presence ever since he could remember anything. She had never done any cooking, but had fed him on delicatessen stuff and beer since babyhood. He had been made to join his mother and her "friends" at their cardgames, and told how he had seen his mother and the men at times steal money from one another, "in a cute way." "Nobody was ever caught," he said, "and I asked the smartest one, Mr. Hinky, to learn me how, and he learned me."

There were even worse things that the poor little lad learned. Sometimes some men would give him money for candy and send him out of the room for a while; but others did not even heed the presence of the child. The mother seemed entirely indifferent to his presence or absence; and the boy in describing the immorality of which his mother had accused him, said, as if he were narrating some very usual incident, "Honest, I didn't mean to do any wrong. I seen the men do it and I wanted to do it too."

He also described, in full revolting detail, the acts of sex-perversion his mother's visitors had taught him; and added that they all laughed when he did it and said he was "a smart kid."

It was easy to understand how the spirit of imitation had prompted the child to wrongdoing, of the serious consequence of which he was utterly unconscious; and how, in his many foster homes, he had easily succumbed to the temptations excited by the propinquity of little girls (329–34).

CASE C:

Mary, age 15, entered the institution July 20, 1916.

The Problem

1. Delinquency
    (a) Attempted suicide by drinking carbolic acid.
    (b) Morbid; melancholic; obsessed by thoughts of suicide and death.
    (c) Exceedingly difficult case—first in child-caring institution, and then in girls' home, working girls' club, and in different private homes—by reason of extreme untidiness, disobedience, and impertinence.
    (d) Very quarrelsome and unwilling to do any work.
    (e) Indolent; defiant and anti-social.
    (f) Undesirable associations.

2. The School
    (a) Very poor scholarship. Had not gone beyond the Fourth Grade.
    (b) Antagonized teachers by attitude of indifference and general carelessness.
    (c) Frequent truancy.

3. Home
    (a) Unmanageable and very troublesome in institutions, and defiant and quarrelsome in own and private homes.
    (b) Obstinate, sullen, and bitter.
    (c) Discontented and very miserable, brooding over possibilities of revenge, and encouraging sentiments of hatred, resentment, and rebellion, to one and all alike.

4. Society
    (a) Intolerant of reproof; bitterly incensed against any criticism.

(b) Disobedient and disrespectful to elders, and very quarrelsome with girls of the same age.

(c) Freely expressing hate and scorn for her superiors.

(d) Disliked; ostracized by young people of both sexes ...

The Analysis

[1.] (a) Examination—Psychiatrist's Report:

Intelligence: Normal. I.C. 1.00.

Character: Poor organization, with poor hereditary basis.

Health: Poor. Congenital syphilis. Should be under anti-syphilitic treatment.

Impression: Peculiar circumstances affecting the case render institutional adjustment impossible. Superior private home should prove beneficial. Wholesome, sympathetic environment, and essential for improvement.

(b) Personality Traits:

Untidy in habits. Careless about person.

Deep wrinkles marked by an habitual frown strongly outlined on the young face.

Sullen, unfriendly attitude to strangers, very retiring, and very anxious to avoid the least attempt at social intercourse.

Pessimistic, bitter, biting words ready to flow from her lips at the smallest provocation.

Hasty, furtive glance, as if both ashamed and afraid.

Hands never still: either fingers interlacing, or pulling at the knuckles, or the nails being bitten.

Sad, unyouthful drooping of the head.

3. Social

(a) Heredity:

Father: born in Germany, passed his boyhood in England, and emigrated to America in his early manhood. Though he claims to be a college graduate, and, when he so desires, gives every evidence of really possessing an excellent education, he is uncouth and unpolished. The first impression usually formed of him is that of an illiterate, ignorant, and besotted wretch ...

A gambler and a common drunkard, he attributed his inability to keep a job for any length of time to the fact that his employers were unable to appreciate his talents and devotion to them ...

He found his near-sightedness a very convenient explanation for many of his delinquencies, even offering his defective vision in exculpation of the brutal beating he had administered to his wife. He claimed that he had been "somewhat affected by a drink," and was unable to see his wife clearly at the time, and gave her the beating thinking it was an enemy of his. His gross sensualism and corrupt morals stamped him a moral degenerate. He was afflicted with syphilis in an infectious state ...

The four children had been sent to institutions, when their mother's insanity deprived them of her care. In April, 1911, the man suddenly appeared in the institution where his daughter and two younger sons were living, and demanded that the children be returned to him ...

During the next few years, the man repeated his career of vagabondage, gambling, drunkedness, and brutality, while the Charities assisted in the maintenance of his family.

In February, 1915, his daughter, then a girl of fourteen, attempted to commit suicide by poison. In the hospital, she gave as the reason for her act seduction by her father.

The man was arrested and in March, 1915, was sentenced to three years in the penitentiary, on the charge of incest.

Mother: American parentage, fine family connections, had the advantages of a high-school education and excellent environment in childhood and girlhood. Two of her brothers are successful and honored merchants, and two sisters have married well and are quite happy. The offspring of these families are normal.

The woman met the man at some public function, fell madly in love with him, and, against the wishes, and in spite of the violent opposition, of her parents, married him. They at once disowned her, and never, during the rest of her troubled life, did they manifest any further interest in her.

In addition to her four living children, she had a number of miscarriages and abortions. Steeped in direst poverty, ill-treated and constantly deserted by her husband, the poor woman, whatever her reasons may have been for clinging to the creature she married, at no time manifested any independence of thought or action, but submissively accepted her ruined life without complaint. When her neighbors, outraged at the treatment accorded her, had the man brought to court, she always intervened in his favor and had him pardoned.

She was infected with syphilis by her husband, first became paralyzed, then insane, and was sent to the State Hospital for the Insane, where she remained till her death, in 1916.

(b) Developmental:

No trustworthy record of her early childhood was obtainable. She herself has no definite recollections of her mother or remembers any home life. Paralysis at first incapacitated the mother from caring for her, and at the age of five, she was put into an institution by the Charities ...

She hailed with sincere delight the opportunity to return to the home her father told her he was reestablishing. Neither she, nor the boys who were then in the institution with her, had any recollection of the mother, who at the time was in the Insane Asylum, and readily believed the father, who told them that the woman he brought to them was their mother.

The home life to which she was now introduced was exceedingly unhappy and wretched. With poverty were combined drunkedness, bad company, and gambling at all hours; while her portion in the home was the care of two sickly babies and the haphazard household. The "mother" was constantly out, or busy entertaining "friends," and the girl looked after the family and the housework.

There were frequent quarrels, and during the woman's loss of temper, at a time when the girl was twelve years old, the facts of the mother's insanity were cruelly presented to the child, who never recovered from the effect of the awful revelations which then followed.

As she grew older, her father displayed a certain fondness for her, to the jealous rage of the woman he called his "wife." Her attendance at school had been very poor, and then ceased entirely. The wretched existence at the miserable "home" terminated with the pitiful attempt at suicide made by the girl.

She stated that she thought death the best way out of her dilemma, as her father had threatened her with "terrible things" if she exposed him ...

Mary's Story:

... "It's no use," she ended bitterly, "wherever I'll be, wherever I'll go, they'll soon know all about it. Why didn't they let me die at the hospital? I can't live, and they won't let me die. What do they want me to do?" ...

She was sent to a trade school and carefully watched for any preference that might manifest itself in an individual line of work. Ultimately she evinced great enthusiasm for the milliner's art, and while she was learning to become "a hat artist," as she quaintly expressed it, efforts were made to give her the benefits of well-regulated and wholesome home life. The sympathies and interest of her boarding-home mother had been enlisted, by informing the woman only of such facts as were necessary to awaken her pity, with the happy result that she was very gentle and patient with the girl's faults.

After six months apprenticeship, she became the "hat artist" she yearned to be, and shortly earned a salary sufficient to support herself.

"It's not such a bad thing to be alive," she confided, as with the joy of achievement shining in her eyes, she told of the "creations" which had brought her a substantial raise; "that is," she hastily caught herself, "if they let you live" (352–65).

Source: Drucker and Hexter (1923).

The Era of the Juvenile Delinquent: The 20th Century

The turn of the century saw continued increases in population and a rapid growth of cities that was accompanied by a variety of social issues including increases in youth crime. As cities grew and commercial activities expanded, there were more opportunities for criminal activities and for different types of crime. The expansion of the railway brought breaches of the Railway Act, the introduction of the automobile brought car theft, and the growth of the banking industry brought increases in bank robberies—all offences engaged in by teenagers as well as adults (Carrigan, 1991:218–19).

Statistics for all of Canada show dramatic increases in youth crime rates throughout the 20th century. Convictions of children under 16 increased by over 124 percent between 1911 and 1921, and by over 67 percent between 1921 and 1931 (Carrigan 1991:219). During the 1920s drug use and drug dealing surfaced as a social issue and led to a number of arrests and convictions of young people in Canadian cities.

> Authorities in Vancouver claimed that drugs were in common use among boys and girls fifteen to eighteen years of age, and children were brought before the courts on drug charges in a number of cities ... Newspapers carried stories claiming that young boys were selling in the streets. Dope dealers, it was claimed, were offering free drugs to young people to get them addicted. (Carrigan, 1991:221)

One city particularly troubled by high rates of delinquency and an apparent rise in serious offences during this period was Winnipeg. According to Kaminski's (1994) analysis of delinquency rates in Manitoba, from 1926 to 1935 rates of youth crime in Winnipeg surpassed any other Canadian city, including Toronto. "In the 1920's and early 1930's, the years just before and just after the stock market crash of October 1929 and into the decade of the Great Depression, youth crime trends were regarded with alarm" (Kaminski, 1994:1). Public concern in Manitoba about youth crime was such that in 1934 the province's attorney general asked the Welfare Supervision Board to conduct a study of juvenile delinquency (Kaminski, 1993:1). The commissioning of this study and the final reports of the board are notable for the fact that by the time the study began, youth crime rates were on the decline. Nonetheless, the board continued to speak of "the crime problem," arguing that immigrants and their children were responsible (Kaminski, 1994).

While crime rates in Manitoba during the 1930s declined to levels lower than they had been in the early 1920s, statistics from other provinces show a continued escalation in juvenile convictions through to 1945. The statistics for the country as a whole (see Table 1.3) show a similar growth, with minor fluctuations from year to year (Statistics Canada, 1947). From 1963 to 1983, youth crime continued to increase, with some fluctuations. Table 1.4 shows a decline in the theft category from 1971 to 1976 and declines in all categories except theft, offensive weapons, and municipal bylaws from 1980 to 1983. Overall, the figures suggest there was more youth crime in 1983 than 20 years earlier and that youth crime levels were higher in both these periods than they were in 1945.

Increases in the numbers of youth involved in criminal activity do not necessarily mean that young people were or are behaving in a more criminal manner. As the total number of people in a population increases, the amount of crime will also increase simply because there are more people to engage in criminal activity. Another way of looking at youth crime is to compare standardized rates, which account for differences in overall population size and composition. These statistics also show increases in youth crime throughout the 20th century. In 1911, the conviction rate for youth 10–15 years of age was 172 per 100,000 population. In 1921, the rate was 300 per 100,000 and by 1931 it had climbed to 423 per 100,000. From 1940 to 1954, it dropped to slightly under 300 per 100,000, but rose to a high of 459 per 100,000 in 1966 (Carrigan, 1991). In 1989, the rate of youth crime was 2568 per 100,000 (Winterdyk, 1996:15). Of course, as we will see in Chapter 2, the 1989 rate is not directly comparable to earlier rates because it is indicative of criminal activity while the earlier rates refer only to convicted young people.

Another comparative technique is to examine what proportion of all crime is accounted for by young people. In 1972, juveniles accounted for 19.5 percent of all persons charged with Criminal Code offences; by 1980, they accounted for 32.2 percent (Carrigan, 1991:238). Winterdyk (1996:15) reports that in 1989 young people under 18 years of age were responsible for 22 percent of all Criminal Code charges and by 1999, 19 percent (Statistics Canada, 1999:19). Thus, while there may be higher numbers of youth involved in crime, youth today may account for the same proportion of crime as youth in earlier periods; as we reported at the start of the chapter, in Nova Scotia youth under 18 accounted for 18 percent of all Criminal Code charges in both 1909–10 and 1993–94.

A SOCIOLOGICAL PERSPECTIVE ON YOUTH CRIME

It is tempting to conclude from the foregoing discussion of youth crime in Canadian history that nothing has changed for at least 200 years. However, what we are able to

TABLE 1.3

Convictions of Juveniles for Major Offences, by Province, Years Ended September 30, 1922–1945

Year	P.E.I.	N.S.	N.B.	Que.	Ont.	Man.	Sask.	Alta.	B.C.	Canada
1922	5	167	45	655	1,852	627	196	240	278	4,065
1923	10	253	60	864	1,633	581	249	246	268	4,165
1924	31	251	59	782	1,977	750	362	192	251	4,655
1925	18	263	77	971	2,064	915	280	215	277	5,080
1926	6	187	55	870	2,081	1,002	246	326	317	5,090
1927	21	174	169	888	2,033	989	253	267	362	5,156
1928	11	225	145	880	1,800	970	273	340	419	5,063
1929	7	158	130	882	1,962	976	318	349	374	5,106
1930	10	203	131	1,033	2,155	869	381	443	428	5,653
1931	14	155	166	1,260	1,758	885	297	430	346	5,311
1932	4	184	186	1,293	1,772	820	229	306	302	5,096
1933	9	209	262	1,426	1,686	786	149	261	356	5,144
1934	9	300	155	1,444	1,814	635	185	409	401	5,353
1935	33	240	247	1,633	2,059	428	239	318	317	5,514
1936	20	321	204	1,324	2,021	275	228	315	262	4,970
1937	46	344	276	1,392	2,016	196	311	344	299	5,224
1938	21	283	224	1,357	2,162	222	225	298	263	5,055
1939	45	228	244	1,245	2,164	293	201	321	277	5,018
1940	41	195	251	1,461	2,229	286	208	364	262	5,298
1941	58	244	344	1,637	2,588	315	263	378	377	6,204
1942	60	220	279	1,617	3,071	503	397	472	301	6,920
1943	53	373	337	1,455	2,804	363	359	349	401	6,494
1944	82	362	363	1,212	2,901	345	356	431	477	6,529
1945	55	390	221	1,239	2,394	277	282	384	516	5,758

Source: From *Canada Yearbook 1947*, Cat. No. 11-402, p. 253.

TABLE 1.4

Juvenile Crime: Selected Offences, 1963–1983

Offences	1963	1971	1976	1980	1983
Assaults	652	1,390	1,926	7,792	6,439
Robbery	345	790	1,339	2,641	1,354
Breaking and entering	8,052	14,989	23,212	42,175	34,524
Theft—motor vehicle	3,736	5,178	7,680	10,064	5,651
Theft over $50	1,849	4,663	2,263*	6,120*	6,329*
Offensive weapons	202	340	700	1,601	2,104
Provincial statutes	3,974	8,860	12,062	21,666	20,116
Municipal by-laws	1,571	1,345	1,023	2,420	2,959

*Theft over $200.

Source: Adapted from Statistics Canada, Cat. Nos. 85–201, 85–202, 85–205.

glean from historical information is limited and not always comparable from one period to another. We will see in our discussion of crime statistics in the next chapter that modern information also has its limitations. In short, statistics do not speak for themselves; their meaning is a matter of interpretation, and interpretations differ dramatically.

A sociological perspective on youth crime is different from other perspectives because the sociologist goes beyond the question of whether crime levels are increasing or decreasing. The sociologist will ask questions about the meaning of crime, about how we as a society respond to it, and about how meanings and responses affect both criminal behaviour and crime statistics. With this in mind, we can now attempt to answer questions implied earlier in the chapter by the opposing views represented in public forums: Is youth crime more serious now? Is youth crime a new problem? Why is youth crime a public issue? What are the "facts" of youth crime?

Is Youth Crime More Serious Now?

According to Carrigan (1991), a non-critical social historian, youth crime in the 1990s was out of control:

> The post-World War Two era witnessed some dramatic changes in juvenile delinquency. Offences increased significantly and the trend was toward more major crimes

and more violence. Manifestations of the new direction were found in all parts of the country as young people turned to alcohol and drugs, and captured media attention by the commission of major and sometimes brutal crimes. The violent turn taken by many delinquents in the form of assaults, weapons offences, and destruction of property had continued; indeed, this trend seems to have worsened by the early 1990's. The most publicized examples are the gangs of teenagers who now terrorize many communities across the country ... The nature of these gangs, in contrast to those of an earlier day, offers a vivid illustration of the changed direction that modern delinquency has taken. In 1965 the Department of Justice Committee on Juvenile Delinquency reported that "gang delinquency is generally not a problem in the large urban areas of Canada." Obviously things have changed. (242)

A more sociological reading and interpretation of youth crime statistics would point to a number of factors that could account for increases that have little or nothing to do with changes in actual delinquent or criminal behaviour among youth. As we will see in the next chapter, the 20th century was the period in Canadian history when the juvenile court was created, and it was also a period of rapid population growth. Hence, we should expect increases in criminal activity over time for at least two reasons. The Canadian population increased and a new organization was created specifically to work with children who were involved in criminal and delinquent activity. Schissel's (1997) examination of Criminal Code charges for youth from 1973 to 1995 clearly indicates that the Young Offenders Act created increased crime rates because more youth were arrested and brought to court than under the Juvenile Delinquents Act (80–81).

Furthermore, as we will see in Chapter 8, changes in policing, juvenile legislation, and administrative practices affect **official crime** rates, as do public pressures to "crack down on crime." Therefore, even though official crime statistics show increases in youth crime over the last century, we cannot assume that youth behaviour is any worse now than in past decades. Contrary to Carrigan's view, Tanner (1996), a sociologist, argues that youth crime and even gang activity are no more or less serious today than they were in the past. He reminds us that, in the 1940s, the Toronto *Globe and Mail* was given to such proclamations as "Another outbreak of street gang fighting has reawakened citizens to the extent of the problems these young people present" (1996:1). This particular story concerned Halloween riots in 1945, which had ended with some 7000 people besieging a police station in Toronto's west end because 13 young men had been arrested for setting fires and vandalism (1996:3; Campbell, 1998). Similarly, Bernard (1992:24) points out that street gang violence drives the action in Shakespeare's *Romeo and Juliet*, a play that takes place in 15th-century Italy.

"Outbreaks" of crime and gang activity are also a matter of interpretation. Zatz's (1987) research on gangs in Phoenix, Arizona, cautions us that gang activity is often overreported and exaggerated by both the news media and the police. According to her study, notwithstanding news and police reports of increasing gang activities in Phoenix, police files and records showed no difference between gang members and nongang delinquency in terms of level or type of offences. Both the police and the media have a vested interest in crime—it ensures their jobs. For journalists, crime is "news"; for the police, "crime waves" usually mean increased funding for policing activities.

Is Youth Crime a New Problem?

Youth crime has always existed in Canada. What has changed over the last century is how Canadians have perceived, defined, and responded to the misdeeds and criminal acts of children and youth. In 1887 the public view of youth crime was of delinquents engaged in juvenile delinquency. One hundred years later, the view was of young offenders engaged in youth crime (Smandych, 1995:14, 20). And now as we begin the 21st century, the legislative terminology is poised to frame the public issue as one of "youth criminals" (Hogeveen and Smandych, 2001:166). The next chapter discusses changes in Canadian laws and public perceptions regarding children and crime. In brief, we no longer think of young people as children in need of care and guidance. Over the last 20 years, Canadians have come to believe that young people need to be held "responsible" for their criminal behaviour. This way of thinking is not new; it brings us closer to treating child and youth offenders in the same manner as adult offenders, and thus to the response of authorities in the colonial era to children and youth involved in criminal behaviour.

Comparing crime statistics from different periods and drawing anything other than tentative conclusions is extremely difficult. Throughout this chapter, the terms "youth crime" and "delinquency" have been variously used depending on which term was used in the original reports. However, the terms are not necessarily measuring the same behaviours. Legally speaking, the behaviour "delinquency" and the "delinquent" young person ceased to exist with the passage of the Young Offenders Act; they were replaced with the terms "youth crime" and "young offenders." "Youth crime" statistics tend to measure Criminal Code offences while "delinquency" statistics also include noncriminal "offences" such as incorrigibility. Chapters 2 and 3 discuss the differences between these terms in more detail.

Why Is Youth Crime a Public Issue?

The question of why or even when youth crime becomes a public issue is easier to answer than questions about crime levels. Public issues (in particular, youth crime issues) are influenced more by **structural**, social, **demographic**, and political factors than by actual criminal behaviour. As discussed earlier in the chapter, children made up a significant portion of the population of Upper and Lower Canada. Before industrialization, life expectancy was considerably lower than it is today. As a result, more than half the population was usually under 25 years of age, and there were twice as many school-age children as middle-aged people (Gottlieb, 1993). By the 19th century, these population proportions began to change and today they are roughly equal. Smandych (1995:15) argues that these demographic shifts partially explain why the "deviant" behaviour of children began to be viewed differently by adults. These shifts stimulated structural changes (such as legislation restricting child labour and enforced compulsory schooling), which in turn had consequences for the social status of children and youth, as well as their physical development.

Young people are physically different today. They mature physically and sexually at a much earlier age than in the past. Girls in England reached menarche at 15.7 years in 1832 and by age 13 in 1973 (see Table 1.5). With regard to the onset of puberty in boys, Mitterauer reports that "we know the ages at which the great composers had to leave boy's choirs. In the case of Haydn it was 18, Schubert 16, Bruckner 15, but in the 20th century it is often as early as 14 or 13" (1992:5). These biological changes are not independent of sociological factors. Changes in physical and sexual maturity are directly related to social and class position, for it is mostly a sedentary lifestyle that leads to early maturity. When children worked long hours at physical labour and were undernourished, as were poor and working-class children, their maturity was delayed (Mitterauer, 1992).

As children were moved out of factories as a result of child labour laws in the 19th century, they became a sedentary population and, at the same time, a surplus population. Children were no longer useful as labourers and producers. As a result, their social status and position within their communities and families changed from one of economic asset to one of economic liability (Smandych, 2001:18) and consequently to one of dependence on adults for their survival. West (1991:12) describes the status of youth in the 20th century as that of **denied adulthood**. Children and youth in the 20th century have become subordinate to adult authority and are not permitted such adult rights as holding decision-making positions, working for a wage, obtaining credit, getting married, or engaging in adult pleasures. Youth and children are marginal to adult society and exist on the periphery, their status is a **marginalized** one. Yet, at the same time, they now mature physically and sexually at an earlier age. The end result is that "our young are seen as unappreciative of our past, unsocialized, menacingly strong and healthy, and seductively sexy—the quintessential strangers in our midst" (West, 1991:10).

Some take the position that the media play a major role in the production of public issues, particularly with regard to youth crime. According to Hartnagel and Baron (1995), "the media are primarily responsible for constructing youth crime into a social issue" (56). Since youth are threatening to adult society (the quintessential strangers) and are perceived as continually "troubled" or "troubling" (Tanner, 1996:17), sensationalistic media coverage of youth crime easily arouses public fear and moral indignation. Stanley Cohen (1972) refers to this phenomenon as **moral panic**. The media

TABLE 1.5

Average Age of Menarche, Selected European Countries

Country	Year/Average Age	Year/Average Age
Germany	1808 16.8	1981 12.5
France	1830 15.3	1979 13.0
England	1832 15.7	1973 13.0
Denmark	1850 17.3	1968 13.2
Sweden	1844 16.2	1976 13.1
Finland	1883 16.6	1971 13.2
Netherlands	1873 16.1	1976 13.4
Norway	1839 17.0	1973 13.2

Source: Mitterauer (1992:3).

generate a panic about youth crime through continual and sensationalized crime reporting. It then reinforces this panic through selective reporting of public outrage toward "out of control" youth (outrage that often implicated the YOA as a "cause").

Schissel (1997) argues that media crime reporting does more than sensationalize. In his view, it presents "hateful, stereotypical views of youth misconduct" (49) and identifies the poor and marginalized as dangerous people from whom law-abiding citizens need police protection. In these media accounts, race and class are "code words for gang criminality," and class and gender are code words for factors that "cause" youth crime. "Bad" youth, for example, are said to come from homes with working mothers or mother-headed households. In this regard, Schissel argues, media crime reporting borders on hate literature (51). He states,

> Hatred and fear are political emotions that people in positions of political and economic power use to garner public opinion. Fear and hatred are staples of popular culture and populist politics … [T]hey exist as an unquestioned part of our ideology and discourse. Hatred is fundamental to news accounts [about crime], and fear is what sells them (31) … [T]he groups who dominate the media—white, male, professional, capitalist classes—hold hateful, stereotypical views of youth misconduct. Further, when they present these views, they obliterate other, more favourable images of youth. (1997:31, 49–50)

Criminologists have identified a variety of ways in which printed news media promote panic, hatred, and fear about youth. As we saw in examples of headlines at the beginning of this chapter, headlines frame the discussion to follow in a "predetermined ideological context" (Schissel, 1997:41)—teens are violent and out of control. The stories that follow take the form of morality plays that prey on peoples' fear of crime and an immoral world by presenting atypical, unusual youth crimes as typical and representative of youth behaviour (Schissel, 1997:33). Most importantly, the media **decontextualizes** criminal events and the lives of those accused of the crimes. Crimes are always, by the nature of newspapers, discussed out of the context within which they occur. Context is provided by the journalist, usually in a manner that generates a number of emotions: fear, moral outrage, despair, panic, and hatred. These emotions are easily displaced to the vulnerable in society, the marginalized youth, by the details provided about the crime event—such as "teen shows no remourse." In this way, media discourse is extremely powerful in promoting the "law and order " agenda and reinforcing a sense that nothing can be done about youth crime but to implement punitive repressive measures. (Schissel, 1997:37; Kappeler, Blumberg and Potter, 1996)

Myths and Facts about Youth Crime

Bernard (1992:12) argues that, with regard to the history of youth crime, there are three myths: a myth of progress, a myth of the good old days, and a myth that nothing changes.

The "myth of progress" is the notion that things are somehow better now than in the past. Not many people believe this myth. Nonetheless, as we will see in Chapter 3, for some types of crime (such as murder today compared to murder 20 years ago) the progress myth is actually true.

The "myth of the good old days" is the most commonly held myth. It is characteristic of the law-and-order group. More people seem to believe that youth crime is worse today than ever before and that youth no longer respect authority. Since youth crime has varied over time, Bernard argues that this myth is "true some of the time and false some of the time." The problem is that people "believe it without any particular concern about whether it is true. People always like to believe in the 'good old days,' whether delinquency was actually better or worse back then" (1992:13).

The "myth that nothing changes" is more widely believed than the "myth of progress," but it is false. It is a belief typically shared by some youth advocates. While it is true that youth crime has always existed, we have seen that how it is perceived does change over time, as do the kinds of activities in which young people are involved. On the other hand, some things have remained the same. Over the last century in Canada, the sheer volume of official crime has increased, but the overall pattern of youth crime has not. Most youth crime has consisted of minor property crime, with a small proportion involving serious personal injury or death to others. Young males have always been responsible for the largest share of criminal activity. Nonetheless, the specific aspects of some youth crime may have changed, such as school shootings. Furthermore, as West (1991) observes, a century ago Canadian streets were filled with "errant youths: but, now, in addition to the traditional mainstay of petty property crime, instead of selling newspapers and pencils, they offer 'speed,' 'crack,'" ecstasy, and they still offer their bodies "if not their very souls and lives" (9).

SUMMARY

The argument presented in this chapter is that the problem of youth crime is not new. What is new is the fact that youth crime has once again become a public issue and the issue now has a different definition. We seem to have come full circle from a century ago when delinquency was first defined and coded in law. Now, instead of "delinquency," the problem is defined as "youth crime."

A common view of youth crime, the one most often reflected in the media, is the law-and-order perspective. This view sees youth crime as out of control and far more serious than it was in the past. An opposing perspective, that of youth advocates, argues that youth crime is probably no better or worse than in other periods in history. From this perspective, the most important issues are social problems affecting youth, not youth crime.

In the colonial era, from the earliest time of European settlement in North America to the early 1800s, anyone over the age of 7 who committed a crime could be treated the same as an adult. Some convicted children were imprisoned with adults, while others were executed. English common law allowed leniency for children 7–14, and many were indeed treated more leniently than adults. Colonial administrators worried that children and youth had too much freedom and lacked respect for authority.

The mid-1800s to the turn of the century, the Victorian period, witnessed increasing numbers of poor, abandoned, orphaned, and neglected children in North American cities. This period also witnessed perceptions of a rise in criminal activity by children and young people. Concerns were expressed about children's well-being as well as their behaviour. Reformers wanted to "save" the children of the poor from corrupting and criminalizing influences.

The post-Victorian era, the modern period, was characterized by a rise in official criminal and delinquent behaviour by children and young people. Much of this increase can be attributed to demographic changes, changes in the administration of juvenile justice, and changes in police practices.

Despite the limitations of historical records pertaining to youth crime, it appears that we have always had youth crime, that young men are responsible for most of this crime, and that most youth crime is of a petty nature, with only a small proportion involving serious violent crime.

Public concerns about youth crime today are similar in many ways to those expressed in the past. People worry today as they did in the colonial era that children have no respect for authority, that they have too much freedom, and that we need more policing of youth. Similarly, in the Victorian era, people worried about bad parenting and lack of appropriate guidance for youth. As for type of crime, young people and children have long been involved in the same types of crime. A small proportion of young people have always been involved in violent crime, some particularly horrific, young girls have always been sexually exploited in the prostitution trade by men, and children and youth have always stolen what they needed to ensure their material survival. What is different today is the specifics of the violence and the availability of different goods to sell (e.g., crack, speed, and ecstacy).

CHAPTER 2

Creating a Juvenile Justice System: Then and Now

CHAPTER OBJECTIVES

1. To trace the history of the Canadian juvenile justice system from its origins in the 19th century to the present.

2. To situate opposition to the Young Offenders Act and the Youth Criminal Justice Act in a historical context.

3. To discuss details and interpretations of the principles underlying the JDA, the YOA and the YCJA.

4. To discuss the juvenile justice law reform process from the JDA to the YCJA.

5. To identify concerns about the Youth Criminal Justice Act.

KEY TERMS

Child savers
Welfare
Parens patriae
Indictable
Probation
Status offences

Responsibility
Limited accountability
Justice
Modified justice
Crime control
Restorative justice

Reparation
Reintegration
Bifurcated
Cycle of juvenile justice

INTRODUCTION

Although today we tend to associate the justice system with notions of crime prevention and crime control, the creators of the system had other objectives in mind. According to some scholars, the juvenile justice system was created as a response to problems generated by an emerging system of capitalism that served to undermine traditional family supports. Two resulting problems were growing numbers of poor children on the streets and higher levels of street crime committed by young people. This street crime generated fear and a sense among middle-class Victorians that the children of the poor and working class (the "dangerous class") needed to be controlled (Alvi, 1986; West, 1984; Platt, 1969b).

According to other scholars, the juvenile justice system was the creation of Victorian reformers, or **child savers** (Platt, 1969a), who were motivated primarily by humanitarian concerns and a desire to save children from harmful family influences.

The Canadian juvenile justice system was created in 1908 through the passage of the Juvenile Delinquents Act. Prior to the Act's implementation, other legislation was introduced that affected the position and status of children in Canadian society (see Box 2.1). This chapter discusses the development, philosophy, and structure of the juvenile justice system under the JDA; how the system was modified by the introduction of the YOA and YCJA; and the reform process for each modification to the system. Interestingly, while there have been significant legal, philosophical, and structural changes to the system over the last century, much of the public opposition surrounding it has remained the same.

THE SOCIAL AND LEGAL UNDERPINNINGS OF THE JUVENILE JUSTICE SYSTEM

The 19th century was a period of industrialization, urbanization, and rapid population growth, much of it from immigration. It was also a period of social reform and increasing concerns among urban middle-class Canadians about the welfare of children and the family. As Sutherland (1976) notes in his analysis of Canadian children in the late-19th and early-20th centuries, this was a period when English Canada "intensified a century-long effort to impose higher standards of order on itself" (95). Governments at all levels were enacting laws designed to curb immorality and encourage moral behaviour. Drinking and spitting in public were prohibited, as was child labour in factories. Campaigns were waged against alcohol and cigarettes, regular school attendance was required, and vaccinations and child welfare programs were encouraged (Sutherland, 1976:95).

BOX 2.1

Some Precursors to the Juvenile Delinquents Act

1799—An Act to Provide for the Education and Support of Orphaned Children

1813—An Act to Provide for the Maintenance of Persons Disabled and the Widows and Children of Such Persons as May be Killed in His Majesty's Services

1827—An Act Respecting the Appointment of Guardians

1837—An Act to Make the Remedy in Cases of Seduction More Effectual, and to Render the Fathers of Illegitimate Children Liable for their Support

1847—An Act for Compensating Families of Persons Killed by Accident, and for other Purposes therein Mentioned

1851—An Act to Amend the Law Relating to Apprentices and Minors

1857—(Ontario) An Act for Establishing Prisons for Young Offenders

1857—An Act for the More Speedy Trial and Punishment of Young Offenders

1862—An Act to Incorporate the Boy's Industrial School of the Gore of Toronto

1869—An Act Respecting Juvenile Offenders within the Province of Quebec

1870—An Act to Empower the Police Court in the City of Halifax to Sentence Juvenile Offenders to be Detained in the Halifax Industrial School

1874—(Ontario) An Act Respecting Industrial Schools

1877—(Ontario) An Act Respecting the Reformatory Prisons

1880—An Act Respecting the Reformatory for Juvenile Offenders in Prince Edward Island

1884—An Act Respecting a Reformatory for Certain Juvenile Offenders in the County of Halifax in the Province of Nova Scotia

1886—An Act Respecting Public and Reformatory Prisons

1888—(Ontario) An Act for the Protection and Reformation of Neglected Children

1890—(Ontario) An Act Respecting the Custody of Juvenile Offenders; An Act Respecting the Commitment of Persons of Tender Years

1891—An Act Respecting Certain Female Offenders in the Province of Nova
  Scotia

1893—An Act Relating to the Custody of Juvenile Offenders in the Province
  of New Brunswick

1894—An Act Respecting Arrest, Trial and Imprisonment of Youthful
  Offenders

1903—An Act Respecting the Good Shepherd Reformatory in the City of
  Saint John, New Brunswick

Source: Leon (1977: 75–79, 82–83, 88).

Neglected and Delinquent Children

The Victorian child savers were primarily concerned with the welfare of children and families. Thus their activities and reforms did not focus solely on crime. Of particular concern to reformers were neglected, dependent, and delinquent children (Sutherland, 1976:97–98). Notions of delinquency came from English common law and applied to children between the ages of 7 and 14 who broke any municipal, provincial, or federal law. This encompassed a broad range of children. Among those considered delinquent were "waifs, arabs, strays, newsboys, hawkers, beggars, habitual truants, and other children of the streets, and children whose parents instructed them in intemperance, vice, and crime" (Sutherland, 1976:97). If it was determined that an accused child aged 7–14 was capable of discerning right from wrong and good from evil, then that child could be convicted and suffer the same penalty as an adult, including execution. Youth over 14 were subject to the same law as adults, while children under 7 were considered unable to distinguish right from wrong. Dependents were children who were considered to be without families, either because they were deemed illegitimate or because they had been abandoned to orphanages (Sutherland, 1976:98). Neglected children were those deemed to be not properly cared for by their parents (see Box 2.2).

Public concern about neglected children was part of a larger anticruelty movement that began with the creation of Humane Societies mandated to address animal cruelty. While Canadian historians generally credit Toronto and Ontario with developing the first child-protection laws, Fingard (1989:171) maintains that Nova Scotia was the first province to establish a Humane Society. In 1876, the Nova Scotia Society for the Prevention of Cruelty was founded. Initially mandated to address animal protection, by 1880 its activities had been extended through legislation to include neglected women and children (see Box 2.3). Montreal followed Halifax's lead in 1882 (Fingard, 1989:171–72). The Toronto Humane Society was established five years later. In 1893, Ontario passed its first child-protection legislation, an Act for the Prevention of

BOX 2.2

Legal Definitions of Neglect

Ontario's Act for the Prevention of Cruelty to, and Better Protection of Children, passed in 1893, provided for this period the most wide-ranging and widely used descriptions of what, in law, was a neglected child. The Act empowered various officers to apprehend without warrant and bring before a judge as "neglected" any child "apparently under the age of 14" who fitted into one of five general groups. A neglected child, the Act stated, was any child

(1) who was found "begging or receiving alms or thieving … or sleeping at nights in the open air";

(2) who was found "wandering about at late hours and not having any home or settled place of abode, or proper guardianship";

(3) who was found "associating or dwelling with a thief, drunkard or vagrant," or who "by reason of the neglect or drunkenness or vices of the parents was 'growing up without salutary parental control and education' or in circumstances which were exposing him 'to an idle or dissolute life'";

(4) who was found "in any house of ill fame, or in company of a reputed prostitute"; and, finally,

(5) who was found "destitute, being an orphan or having a surviving parent" who was "undergoing imprisonment for a crime."

Source: Sutherland (1976:97).

Cruelty to, and Better Protection of Children, also known as the Children's Charter (Sutherland, 1976:97). Although legislation addressing neglect and cruelty did not begin in Ontario, most of the impetus for the juvenile justice system came from social reformers in Ontario, largely due to the superior financial resources available to Ontario reformers (Fingard, 1989; Sutherland, 1976).

Reformers may have identified different types of "problem" children, but they made no distinctions when responding to these children. For the child savers, only the end result mattered, and the desired result was for children to be "saved" from a life of crime. For Victorian reformers, the only difference between a neglected child and a

BOX 2.3

Society for the Prevention of Cruelty Cases, 1 March 1884–March 1885

Children (sometimes involving more than one child)

Sent out begging by worthless parents	20
Neglected by drunken father	42
Neglected by drunken mother	6
Neglected by baby-farmers (8); ill-treated by aunt (6); father (10); adoptive parents (5); strangers (6); stepmother (1); mother (3)	39
Abandoned by father (4); mother (3); mother & father (3)	10
Persons with vicious dogs that injured children	3
Excessive punishment by school teacher	1
Rescued from improper houses or company—girls under 16	5
Clothes provided (7); food, etc., when sick (6)	13
Cautioned at request of parents 3 boys & 4 girls	7
Homeless—sent to homes or institutions	14
Reward to boy for rescuing drowning child	1

Women

Neglected by drunken husbands	28
Ill-treated by husbands	24
Husbands eloped with women	2
Husbands improperly conducting themselves with wife's sister	2
Neglected by sons legally liable for their support	3
Absconding husbands traced & made to support	3
Assaults by various persons	4
Death supposed by violence at hands of husband	2
Assisted to get stove & other articles	3
Rescued from bad life	3
Insane, advised & assisted relatives	3
—to families	7
Homeless—suitably provided for	8

Men

Seamen ill-used by captain	9
Sick, homeless or oppressed	5
Destitute & in search of work	7

Source: Nova Scotia SPC, *9th Annual Report*, 1885, 18. Reprinted in Fingard (1989:176).

delinquent child was the difference between a "potential" criminal and an "actual" one (Houston, 1972:263). Leon (1977) elaborates:

> Because of [reformers'] focus on control, or the lack thereof, in the family context, distinctions between behaviour attributed to parental absence or neglect, and behaviour characterized as criminal or delinquent, were not seen to be relevant. The rationale for the control of juvenile misbehaviour, and hence for the prevention of future criminal behaviour, mixed the perceived need for the protection of others from children with the perceived need for the protection of children from themselves and others. The question was not whether a child would be held accountable for his or her behaviour— criminal or otherwise—but rather how best to treat the child in order to effect adequate socialization before the child became a "convicted criminal." If the family was not capable, then the state would intervene to reform the child. (76)

Canadian Child Savers

While many women were involved in the activities of the child-saving movement, two men are credited by historians with creating the juvenile justice system—J.J. Kelso and W.L. Scott. Kelso (1907a, 1907b) was a Toronto newspaper reporter who, through his concern about the plight of poor children in the city, became a driving force behind the establishment of the Toronto Humane Society and the Children's Fresh Air Fund. Following passage of the Ontario Children's Charter in 1893, Kelso was appointed Provincial Superintendent of Neglected and Dependent Children (Sutherland, 1976:112). In this capacity, he began campaigns aimed at getting children, including delinquents, out of institutions and into foster homes.

Kelso's reform activities were complemented by the children's court movement. In 1892, the federal Criminal Code was amended to allow separate nonpublic trials and custody for those under 16 (Sutherland, 1976:115; Leon, 1977). For its part, the Ontario Children's Charter provided for separate magistrates to hear cases involving youth under 16. It also provided, for youth under 21, separate trials and commitment to places other than prisons (Leon, 1977:83).

Meanwhile children's courts were being established in American cities. In 1906, W.L. Scott, a lawyer and president of the Ottawa Children's Aid Society, went to Philadelphia to examine that city's system of separate children's courts, judges, and probation officers. Before the end of the year, he had persuaded Ottawa to appoint two probation officers for the supervision of child offenders. Scott went on to draft the juvenile delinquents bill, which was accepted in the House of Commons and became law on July 8, 1908 (Sutherland, 1976:119, 121). This legislation created a justice system for children and youth separate from the adult system.

THE CANADIAN JUVENILE JUSTICE SYSTEM

JDA: Philosophy and Definitions

Section 31 of the Juvenile Delinquents Act states,

> This Act shall be liberally construed to the end that its purpose may be carried out to wit: That the care and custody and discipline of a juvenile delinquent shall approximate as nearly as may be that which should be given by its parent, and that as far as practicable every juvenile delinquent shall be treated, not as a criminal, but as a misdirected and misguided child, and one needing aid, encouragement, help and assistance.

The JDA created a juvenile justice system based on **welfare** principles (see Table 2.1 on page 53). The main philosophy underlying the legislation, the justice system it created, and the decision making of justice personnel who implemented the act, came from the doctrine of ***parens patriae***, meaning "parent of the country" (Reitsma-Street, 1989–90:512). The doctrine originated in medieval England where it began as the king's right to control the property of orphaned heirs for the purpose of protection. By the 18th century, *parens patriae* had been expanded to include a "best interest" principle as a means of actively promoting the well-being of a child or young person. By the 19th century, the doctrine had extended beyond the monarch to the state and to children without property who were orphaned or neglected by parents or guardians. The numerous acts of legislation passed in the 19th century to protect young people in need (see, for example, Box 2.1) were supported and reinforced by the principle of *parens patriae*. Thus, a doctrine that began as "the King's prerogative" had by the 19th century become "legitimized in common and statutory law in various English-speaking countries" (Reitsma-Street, 1989–90:512–13).

Whereas in the United States delinquency was considered a state of being or a condition, in Canada a youth had to break a law to be adjudicated delinquent by the court. The JDA defined delinquency as the violation by persons under 16 (varying by province) of any federal, provincial, or municipal law for which a fine or imprisonment was the penalty, or the commission of any other act that would make the young person liable to be committed to an industrial school or reformatory. In 1924, the act was revised to include a much broader range of behaviour. Following the addition of this omnibus clause, a delinquent was defined in s. 2(1) of the act as "any child who violates any provision of the Criminal Code or of any Dominion or provincial statute, or of any bylaw or ordinance of any municipality, or who is guilty of sexual immorality or any similar form of vice, or who is liable by reason of any other act to be committed to an industrial school or juvenile reformatory under the provisions of any Dominion or provincial statute" (cited in West, 1991:33).

JDA: The System

The JDA gave the courts extensive powers. Cases were to be handled summarily. If an offence was **indictable**, it was up to the court to decide if the youth would be tried in an adult court. More like hearings than trials, juvenile cases were conducted privately and notices of delinquency hearings were sent to parents or guardians. Separate detention and jail facilities were mandated for delinquents. In addition, the JDA provided for a wide range of sentences or dispositions. Within the broad requirement to act in "the child's own good and the best interests of the community," the court could adjourn the hearing, impose a fine for as much as $10, place the child in a foster home or in the care of a Children's Aid Society, impose a probationary sentence, or send the child to an industrial school or reformatory. **Probation** was a central element of the juvenile court with the probation officer playing a key role (see Box 2.4). The court could place a child in the custody of a probation officer as a form of sentence. The JDA required probation officers to conduct investigations for the court, to assist and direct the court, and to represent the interests of the child in the court (Leon, 1977:100; Sutherland, 1976:122).

BOX 2.4

W.L. Scott on the Role of the Probation Officer

By far the most important element in the system is probation. It is the keystone of the arch. Without it the Juvenile Court would be almost powerless for good. With it, and nothing else, a vast amount can be done. You cannot deal with children as a class. You must deal with them as individuals. You must win the confidence, the respect, even the love of each individual child, would you make of it what you desire it to be. It is the personal touch that counts, and that touch is supplied by the Probation Officer.

The duties of the Probation Officer are threefold: before trial, at trial, and after trial.

As soon as the child is arrested, or informed against, a Probation Officer is at once notified. Her first duty is to see the child as a friend, to get its confidence, and to hear its story. She then visits its home, school, or place of employment and any other place where information about its habits and its history may be obtained ...

In the Court the Probation Officer appears to represent the child, as friend, though not as excuser. She represents to the Judge the course which the result of her inquiries has led the Juvenile Court Committee to consider would be for the best interest of the child. In most cases the issue will be the release of the child on probation in charge of the officer. The Judge takes advantage of the occasion to make as strong an impression as possible on the mind of the child, and the Probation Officer seizes on this precious psychological moment, immediately after the trial, to deepen and supplement the impression already made by a serious talk and words of advice.

After the trial comes her most important range of duty. She must see the child frequently, at first it should be every day, and by her personal influence endeavour to form it into what it should be. She comes into touch with the home, and occasionally reforms the whole family as well as the child. She visits the school, or place of employment, and enlists the teacher, or the employer, in the work of helping the child. While the keynote of all this is kindness, yet there is behind her the firm hand of the law. The child and its parents both know that on her report he may be sent to the reform school, and the knowledge adds greatly to her influence, and to the respect in which she is held. If all care fails, she brings the child before the Judge, for commitment to an institution. If the home is so bad that reform there is hopeless, she recommends that the child be placed in a foster home.

The question of the sex of the Probation Officer is an open one. The feminine gender is here used because experience has shown hitherto that women, intended by nature for motherhood, are better fitted for the work than men. Moreover, it is important that Probation Officers should be chosen from the best class—should represent the highest order of men and women—and the better class of women than of men can frequently be got for the money available ...

Source: Scott (1908:895–96).

Once adjudicated as delinquent, children remained wards of the court until the court released them or until they reached the age of 21 (Sutherland, 1976:122). Under the JDA, the provinces were allowed to set the maximum age under which a youth could be adjudicated as delinquent. By the late 1970s, the maximum age of delinquency was 16 in Saskatchewan, Ontario, New Brunswick, Nova Scotia, and Prince Edward Island; 17 in British Columbia and Newfoundland; and 18 in Manitoba and

Quebec. Alberta had a separate age for boys and girls—18 for girls, 16 for boys—until 1978, when the age for both sexes was set at 16.

Because the juvenile justice system required probation officers, separate courts, separate judges, and separate detention facilities, its implementation was costly. In order to allow provinces to put in place these necessities, the JDA did not require immediate implementation; as a result, its implementation across the country was sporadic.

In February 1909, the first juvenile court under the JDA was set up in Winnipeg in the dining room of a house on Simco Street. The judge of this court was the Honourable T. Mayne Daly (Sutherland, 1976:125). Within five years, courts had been set up in Halifax, Charlottetown, Montreal, Ottawa, Toronto, Vancouver, and Victoria. Within a decade, Alberta and Saskatchewan also had juvenile courts (Sutherland, 1976:125). The JDA was not implemented in Prince Edward Island until 1974, in the Yukon until 1978, and in the Northwest Territories until 1979. Newfoundland never did implement the JDA, but rather established juvenile courts through provincial legislation (Wilson, 1982:17). While men were the major actors in creating the justice system, once the JDA was passed, women played a major role in the system, both as probation officers and as judges. Helen Gregory-MacGill was a youth court judge in British Columbia, and Emily Murphy was one of the first judges in Alberta (Leon, 1977:82).

Opposition to the JDA

The JDA was not passed without opposition. Those who opposed the bill did so either on the grounds that it was not punitive enough or out of concern about potential abuses to childrens' and parents' rights. Two police officials (Inspectors William Stark and David Archibald) and two police court magistrates (George Dennison and R.E. Kingsford) were the most outspoken in the opposition to a juvenile justice system and the proposed legislation (Leon, 1977). Kingsford was concerned that since the new juvenile court would replace existing children's courts—which were run by police magistrates—the employees connected with those courts would also be replaced. "It would be a great pity," he stated, "if the notion got abroad that the police were so harsh in their dealings with juveniles that it was necessary to take from them that portion of work." Archibald, on the other hand, was more concerned about the motives of the reformers:

> [The reformers] work upon the sympathies of philanthropic men and women for the purpose of introducing a jelly-fish and abortive system of law enforcement, whereby the judge or magistrate is expected to come down to the level of the incorrigible street arab and assume an attitude absolutely repulsive to British Subjects. The idea seems to be that by profuse use of slang phraseology he should place himself in a position to kiss and coddle a class of perverts and delinquents who require the most rigid disciplinary and corrective methods to ensure the possibility of their reformation. I would go fur-

ther to affirm from extensive and practical experience that this kissing and coddling, if indiscriminately applied, even to the best class of children, would have a disastrous effect, both physically, mentally, morally and spiritually. (cited in Leon, 1977:96)

Typical of the reformers Archibald opposed was J.J. Kelso, whose views are expressed in Box 2.5.

There was some minor opposition to the proposed legislation from Children's Aid Societies in Toronto, in particular the Saint Vincent de Paul Society. According to Leon (1977), this opposition was based on concern over the ability of probation officers to "properly" supervise delinquent children. The bill was supported by members of the Senate, with the exception of Senator Wilson, who echoed the concerns of the Children's Aid Societies:

BOX 2.5

Parens Patriae as Expressed by J.J. Kelso

[T]here are so many problems of a social and domestic character involved in the child's delinquency that to expect the ordinary magistrate and police authorities in a large city to deal with it is simply to invite failure. Anyone can decide in five minutes whether or not a youth is guilty of theft or some other offence, and liberate or banish him to a reformatory, but either decision may be equally unjust, and the problem still remain[s] unsolved. The court should be parental in the truest sense and should be so constituted in all its branches as to make the child intuitively realize that love and not hostility is the atmosphere into which he has entered. When one has had the experience of years in dealing with wayward youth, has studied the moral conditions, visited the wretched homes, comprehended the utter absence of real affection, the heart hunger, the longing for appreciation and sympathy, then [one] begin[s] to recognize that what is needed is not severity, not flogging, not jail or reformatory, but a true friend and an opportunity under clean auspices to develop worthy character. It is an intense realization of the erring boy's need, gained in many a sad interview with the children themselves, that entails the writing of these lines.

Source: Kelso (1907b:164–65).

We are all desirous of making every child as it grows up a useful member of society, but we may differ as to the means of accomplishing that. Here we pass an act to permit a child being taken away from its parents and put in other charge, and who is as solicitous for the welfare of the child as the parent? We put young children in the hands of an officer and that officer has absolute power and control over them. He may do anything under the Act and he is protected. I say that it is an unreasonable proposition to make, and I am fearful that instead of lessening the criminal juvenile class it will increase them. (cited in Leon, 1977:98)

Among members of Parliament, only Mr. Lancaster, a lawyer from Ontario, opposed the bill. Lancaster, who was clearly 60 years ahead of his time, worried that children's rights would not be protected by the new law or the new justice system. In particular, he feared that children would not be represented by lawyers, that their fate would rest entirely in the hands of probation officers, and, most important, that they would be denied the right to a trial (see Box 2.6).

BOX 2.6

The Right of Trial by Jury

The following exchange between Lancaster and Leighton McCartney (also an Ontario lawyer) took place in the House of Commons.

Mr. M.: If the child is allowed the inherent right of trial by jury, which he undoubtedly has under the British Constitution, it is put in the hands of the child to do away with the entire benefit of the Act. We are passing extraordinary legislation for the protection of the child, and to amend that as my Hon. friend suggests would be to do away with the benefits of the Act.

Mr. L: You are providing that the parents shall be notified. On being notified, if the case is a serious one, the parent will employ counsel, and the child will have the advice of both the parents and the counsel, and the decision can be safely left to them. But you are leaving the decision entirely in the hands of someone [probation officer] who has no direct interest in the child's welfare.

Mr. M: It is the converse of the case which the Hon. gentleman puts. We are passing an enactment for the benefit of the juvenile delinquent.

Mr. L.: How do you know it is?

Source: Cited in Leon (1977:99).

Victorian reformers shrugged off the opposition. Most were not the least concerned about children's rights because they were convinced that what they were doing was protecting children. Since this was their motive, they believed that decisions and actions of those working in the justice system would similarly always be in the "best interest" of children. The system itself was focused on meeting children's needs, on "helping" rather than punishing and the objective was to treat and rehabilitate. The belief that this welfare-based justice system would act to ensure the best interest and welfare of the child was not significantly challenged until 1967 when an American Supreme Court Justice concluded, in connection with the Gault case, that *parens patriae*—the basis of the justice system—accords very different rights to children and adults: more specifically, adults have autonomous legal rights; children do not.

> The right of the State, as *Parens Patriae* to deny the child procedural rights available to his elders was elaborated by the assertion that a child, unlike an adult, has a right "not to liberty but to custody … If his parents default in effectively performing their custodial functions—that is, if the child is "delinquent"—the State may intervene. In doing so, it does not deprive the child of any rights, because he has none. It merely provides the "custody" to which the child is entitled. (Justice Fortas, cited in Wilson, 1982:5)

MODIFYING THE JUVENILE JUSTICE SYSTEM

Serious challenges to the Juvenile Delinquents Act began to surface in the 1960s, a period in which the United States witnessed the civil-rights movement and Canadians created their first Bill of Rights. It was in this environment that more and more people began to question *parens patriae* as a foundation for juvenile justice as well as the ability of the JDA to ensure due process for young people.

Serious criticism was directed at the JDA with regard to **status offences**. These were behaviours, such as sexual behaviour, truancy, or incorrigibility, acts not criminal if engaged in by an adult. Critics argued that lumping together all child and youth offences, be they status offences or criminal offences, undermined the seriousness of some criminal offences and thereby inhibited any deterrent effect of punishment on criminal behaviour. Others maintained that treatment provisions were not consistent across the country and gave social workers far too much discretionary power. Since social workers were not part of the justice system, they were not accountable to the courts for their decisions. Anticipating current debate, other critics charged that the JDA failed to provide adequate public protection from the criminal behaviour of children and youth (Hylton, 1994:232–33). According to Hylton (1994), a major factor contributing to the demise of the JDA was changing public and political attitudes about youth crime. In addition, as we will see in Chapter 10, critics were also sceptical about the efficacy of treatment.

Reform attempts began in 1965 with the release of a federal report from the Committee on Juvenile Delinquency in Canada. A number of legislative proposals followed this report and the YOA (see Box 2.7) was the end product of nearly two decades of fine-tuning. Most of the opposition during this period came from provincial governments who, concerned about what changes would cost them, looked for federal funds to support implementation. Important points of contention in these debates included the maximum age at which youth would be brought into the juvenile system from the adult system, and the cost of alternative measures programs.

The first drafted legislation, the Children and Young Persons Act of 1967, was rejected because of provincial objections to changes in jurisdiction and federal cost sharing. The first Young Offenders Act, introduced in 1970 and supported by the Canadian Bar Association, met with considerable opposition from welfare professionals and other interest groups because it was seen as too legalistic and too punitive—a "Criminal Code for children." In 1975, legislation entitled the Young Persons in Conflict with the Law also met with provincial concerns over costs and jurisdiction. By 1977, a new Young Offenders Act had been drafted. It contained aspects of the earlier Young Persons in Conflict with the Law bill—that is, accountability, responsibility, and legal rights—but it added as a central guiding principle the protection of society (Corrado and Markwart, 1992:148–50; Hylton, 1994:232).

As described in Corrado and Markwart (1992), there was extensive discussion of these draft legislative proposals and the eventual YOA submission. Presentations on the proposed YOA were made to a parliamentary subcommittee by more than 40 interest groups. There was a general acceptance of the bill's philosophy and legal rights orientation; debate centred on more narrow issues, such as the meaning of legal rights for young people (Corrado and Markwart, 1992:151). Finally, in April 1984, the Young Offenders Act came into effect, replacing the Juvenile Delinquents Act.

The actual passage of the YOA was fairly straightforward. The act was generally seen as a progressive piece of legislation, as reflected in the comments of Judge Omar Archambault (1986), who played a significant role in drafting the legislation:

> [The YOA] is based on a new set of fundamental assumptions reflecting [cultural] evolutions and inspired, as well, by extensive research and a more sophisticated knowledge of human behaviour generally, and the moral and psychological development of children in particular. (45)

Principles of Juvenile Justice

The Young Offenders Act created a juvenile justice system very different from that which had prevailed under the JDA. Whereas the JDA referred to delinquents as "misdirected and misguided" children in need of "aid, encouragement, help and assistance," the YOA referred to young persons as in a "state of dependency" who have "special

BOX 2.7

General Principles of the YOA

3 (1)   It is hereby recognized and declared that:

(a)   crime prevention is essential to the long-term protection of society and requires addressing the underlying causes of crime by young persons and developing multi-disciplinary approaches to identifying and effectively responding to children and young persons at risk of committing offending behaviour in the future (December 1, 1995);

(a.1)   while young persons should not in all instances be held accountable in the same manner or suffer the same consequences for their behaviour as adults, young persons who commit offences should nonetheless bear responsibility for their contraventions;

(b)   society must, although it has the responsibility to take reasonable measures to prevent criminal conduct by young persons, be afforded the necessary protection from illegal behaviour;

(c)   young persons who commit offences require supervision, discipline and control, but, because of their state of dependency and level of development and maturity, they also have special needs and require guidance and assistance;

(c.1)   the protection of society which is a primary objective of the criminal law applicable to youth, is best served by rehabilitation, wherever possible, of young persons who commit offences, and rehabilitation is best achieved by addressing the need and circumstances of a young person that are relevant to the young person's offending behaviour (December 1, 1995);

(d)   where it is not inconsistent with the protection of society, taking no measures or taking measures other than judicial proceedings under this Act should be considered for dealing with young persons who have committed offences;

(e)   young persons have rights and freedoms in their own right, including those stated in the Canadian Charter of Rights and Freedoms or in the Canadian Bill of Rights, and in particular the right to be heard in the course of, and to participate in, the

(f)   processes that lead to decisions that affect them, and young persons should have special guarantees of their rights and freedoms;

(f)   in the application of this Act, the rights and freedoms of young persons include a right to the least possible interference with freedom that is consistent with the protection of society, having regard to the needs of young persons and the interests of their families;

(g)   young persons have the right, in every instance where they have rights or freedoms that may be affected by this Act, to be informed as to what those rights and freedoms are; parents have responsibility for the care and supervision of their children, and, for that reason, young persons should be removed from parental supervision either partly or entirely only when measures that provide for continuing parental supervision are inappropriate.

needs and require guidance and assistance" as well as "supervision, discipline and control" (see Box 2.7). More specifically, the YOA introduced new principles to the juvenile justice system that gave emphasis to youth responsibility, protection of society, special needs, alternative measures, and legal rights and freedoms.

Accountability

For the first time since its creation, a principle of juvenile justice was established (s. 3(l)(a.1)) that young people who commit criminal offences would have to assume **responsibility** for their behaviour. However, the YOA also recognized, in the same section, that young people have **limited accountability**. This was and is an important principle, for without it there would be no need for a separate system for youthful offenders. If we were to hold youth as accountable for their offences as adults, we could simply process all young people through the adult system. This subsection of the YOA also underscored the significance of provisions relating to the transfer of youth to the adult system. In the absence of these special provisions, a youth's accountability for his or her offence following transfer would be the same as that of an adult. Thus we find in other sections of the YOA provisions for shorter maximum sentences for youth. Initially, the maximum sentence for young offenders was three years; this was changed to five years in 1991. By December 1, 1995, the maximum sentence for teens was ten years for first-degree murder and seven years for second-degree murder. This issue of limited accountability continued as a major source of contention for opponents

Different Models of Juvenile Justice

	Welfare	Justice	Crime Control	Restorative
Focus	The individual offender's needs	Individual rights	Protection of society	Harm caused by crime Repair harm done to victims Reduce future harm by crime prevention
Philosophy	Best interests of the child and family *Parens Patriae*	Minimal interference with freedoms Right to due process	Law and order in society are paramount State responsibility for maintaining order	Peacemaking Reparation of past harms Reconciliation between victims, offenders, and communities
System Features	Informality Indeterminant sentencing Focus on unacceptable behaviour	Focus on criminal offences Determinant sentences	Crime/status offences Punishment Determinant sentences	Full and equal participation of victims, offenders, and communities in the justice process Mediation, conferencing, circles
Key Professionals	Child care and social workers	Lawyers	Lawyers Criminal justice professionals	Community agencies, volunteers, non-profit organizations, criminal justice professionals play a minor role
View of Crime/ Delinquency	Determined by social, psychological, and environmental factors	Free will Individual responsibility	Responsibility Accountability Determinant	A violation of people and relationships
Purpose of Intervention	Treatment	Appropriate sanction	Protection of society Retribution Deterrence	For parties to a crime to work out satisfactory solutions
Purpose of System	Individual rehabilitation	Ensure justice is done Maintain individual rights	Maintenance of social order	Redress for victims Recompense for offenders Community reintegration of victims and offenders

Sources: Adapted from Reid and Reitsma-Street (1984); Reid-MacNevin (1991:28); Corrado (1992:4).

of the YOA (as we see below) and transfer rules were significantly altered by the YCJA.

Protection of Society

The protection of society, a principle expressed in s. 3(1)(b) of the YOA, was revisited in the 1995 amendment, subsection (c)(c.1), which underscored its importance as a guiding principle for juvenile justice by stating that it is a *primary objective of the criminal law*. This principle has an even more prominent position in the YCJA.

Special Needs

Section 3(1)(c)(c.1) outlined more specifically the rationale for a youth justice system. Because of their immaturity and dependency relative to adults, young people are said to have "special needs." According to Reid and Reitsma-Street (1984) and Reid-MacNevin (1991), the welfare principles expressed in the JDA lived on in this section of the YOA. Other scholars and Canadian judges interpreted this section to mean that any intervention with regard to special needs should be commensurate with the youth's offence (Bala and Kirvan, 1991; Bala, 1992). This latter interpretation was supported by the 1995 amendment, subsection (c.1), which requires that the needs of young persons be addressed in a manner that is relevant to their "offending behaviour." This too, as we will see below, is made a cornerstone of youth justice by the YCJA.

Alternative Measures

Section 3(1)(d) expresses the principle of diversion: that where the protection of society is not compromised, measures other than formal court processing, with its potentially negative effects, should be considered. In most provinces only first offenders and young persons guilty of relatively minor offences are processed through alternative measures. Once again, the "protection of society" principle is expected to balance the use of alternative measures. As we will see below, this is still an important principle under the YCJA, so important that "societal protection," as a principle, expanded to the point where it may have a significant impact on the very structure of the juvenile justice system. Diversion principles and practices are further entrenched and expanded with the YCJA.

Rights of Young Persons

It is in s. 3(1)(e) and (g) that one finds the major difference between the YOA and the JDA. In addition to rights and freedoms guaranteed through the Canadian Charter of Rights and Freedoms and the Canadian Bill of Rights, the YOA established that young people would have special guarantees, including the right to legal representation and the right to be informed as to their rights and freedoms under the act. Some of these pertained to statements made to "persons in authority." These rules most clearly applied to questioning by police officers and other officials such as teachers or school principals. Section 56 of the YOA outlined a complex set of procedures governing the questioning of young people. Interestingly, parents were not usually considered "persons in authority," so that things said to them by their children, in confidence, would be admissible regardless of cautions regarding legal rights (Bala, 1992:41). Other parts of the YOA made it clear that youth had fewer justice rights than adults with respect to preliminary hearings, jury trials, and issues of privacy and search. Many of these have been changed with the YCJA.

Minimal Interference with Freedom

Section 3(1)(f) applied to every aspect of youth justice and affected every young offender, except in cases where there were concerns having to do with the protection of society. This principle of "least possible interference" encouraged the use of alternative measures, but it also encouraged police officers to divert youth from the system altogether. This principle also influenced bail proceedings and sentencing: it encouraged the court to apply sentences more lenient than custody, and discouraged the court from effecting transfers to the adult system. This principle has been maintained by the YCJA but is no longer stated as a principle in its own right.

Parental Responsibility

Section 3(1)(h) marked another major difference between the YOA and the JDA systems. Under the JDA, parents or guardians whom the court considered to be providing inappropriate parental care could be held responsible for their children's offences; they could be made to pay fines or provide financial support for their children. In contrast, the YOA did not consider parental responsibility. Rather, it addressed parental involvement with youth and the justice proceedings. Parents or guardians were required to be notified of their child's arrest (s.8) or of youth court proceedings (s.9), and they could be ordered to attend court (s.10). Other sections of the YOA allowed parents to make statements to the court regarding dispositions and transfers.

At the same time, s. 3(I)(h) indicated that parents were to be judged along with their children. If they were not considered "responsible" parents, the court could remove children from the parents' guardianship. In this regard, Bala (1992) cautions that

> It is important ... not to "romanticize" the role of parents in the lives of their children ... Some young offenders have been victims of physical, emotional or sexual abuse at the hands of their parents, and some youths have ceased to have meaningful relationships with their parents before they are involved in the youth court system. The fact that a youth is charged with a criminal offence often strains the relationship with parents, and those involved with dealing with young offenders need to be realistic about the role that parents are likely to play in their children's lives. (32)

From another perspective, LaPrairie (1988) argued that the parental responsibility principle expressed in the YOA had a negative impact on Aboriginal youth, precisely because of the impoverished state of many First Nations communities, particularly those in remote regions of the country. In one case, an Aboriginal youth was sentenced to two years' custody for a second break-and-enter offence because of his family's impoverished circumstances (Bala 1992:28–29). Some of these issues were addressed by the YCJA and in some ways, to be discussed below, parents now have more responsibility for their children's offences.

Because of the predominance of justice principles over welfare principles in the YOA, some argued that it was based on a **justice** model (see Table 2.1 on page 53), others described the system as one of **modified justice** because it maintained some of the welfare principles that underpinned the JDA (Corrado, 1992). Most of the revisions to the YOA moved it in the direction of a **crime control model**.

Modifications to the YOA

Most resistance to the YOA came after its enactment. Much of this controversy originated from the different ways in which its principles were interpreted. A good deal of opposition also came from conservative interest groups who advocated a crime control approach to juvenile justice (see Table 2.1). Their efforts were bolstered and reinforced by provincial governments who remained concerned about the cost of correctional programs (Corrado and Markwart, 1992:160–62) and the actual introduction of "get tough" policies and programs by Ontario and Manitoba (Hogeveen and Smandych, 2001:148). In addition, media coverage of youth crime helped both to create and to fuel a sustained opposition to the YOA. By engaging in sensationalism and overreporting of the most violent cases of youth crime, the media created, maintained, and reinforced public perceptions that violent youth crime was on the rise and that the YOA was too lenient to be of any consequence in preventing or controlling it (Corrado and Markwart, 1992:161; Sprott, 1996).

The debate over the YOA was reminiscent of the debates provoked by the creation of the juvenile justice system 100 years ago. Not unlike police then, police groups in the YOA debates expressed concerns about children under 12 committing criminal offences, about restrictions on record keeping, and about restrictions on obtaining confessions (Sapers and Leonard, 1996:86). A survey of professional groups in the juvenile justice system conducted by the Ministry of the Solicitor General in 1982 found that attitudes toward the YOA varied by role in the system. Police and Crown prosecutors were the most negative, while defence counsel and probation officers were the most positive. Judges, who were somewhere in the middle, expressed concerns about setting the maximum age at 18, as well as about the destruction of records, reviews of custodial dispositions, and the three-year maximum on sentences for offences that adults would receive a life sentence (Moyer and Carrington, 1985). Among politicians, Reform MPs (now Alliance) were the most vocal proponents of crime control principles. They continually raised concerns, both in the House and the media, that

- horrible crimes committed by youth were going unpunished;
- the YOA was incapable of controlling youth violence;
- youth rights were protected at the expense of their victims;
- the YOA was far too problematic to ever be "fixed"; and
- youths' legal rights were a major obstacle to the protection of society (Hogeveen and Smandych, 2001).

After the YOA was implemented, there were three sets of major revisions all of which moved the justice system closer to a **crime control** model (see Table 2.1 on page 53) (Corrado and Markwart, 1992; Hylton, 1994; Sapers and Leonard, 1996). The first set of YOA amendments were made in 1986 (Bill C106) and addressed technical and procedural changes (Sapers and Leonard, 1996: 95). Nonetheless, opposition to the YOA continued (Bala,1989) particularly with regard to serious youth crime. More specifically, judges could choose only between the extremes of a three-year sentence in youth court or a life sentence in adult court. Following a number of consultative meetings, a second set of amendments were made (Bill C-12) and passed by Parliament in December 1991. These changes included raising maximum sentences for first- and second-degree murder to five years less a day and changing parole eligibility for youth transferred to adult court to five and ten years in adult custody (Hylton, 1994:237; Sapers and Leonard, 1996:90–91).

In spite of the 1986 and 1991 revisions, some interest groups were still not satisfied with the YOA. Following the 1991 amendments, public concerns continued to be expressed regarding the so-called leniency of the YOA and its perceived inability to control youth crime. In addition, those analyzing the youth courts were beginning to notice a trend toward an increased use of custody. Arguments were made that this trend was dangerous in that, in the long run, it thwarted the goals of societal protection. In June 1994, the federal government responded to these concerns with a two-part strategy of reform for the juvenile justice system. Part 1 of the strategy involved more amendments to the YOA (Bill C-37). Part 2 mandated a parliamentary subcommittee with the assistance of a Federal-Provincial-Territorial Task Force to assess public opinion with respect to the act, and to provide a public consultative process and make recommendations for reform. Bill, C-37, was approved by Senate in June 1995 and came into force on December 1, 1995. Once again, the YOA had been amended in the direction of crime control, but the extensive use of custody was also addressed. The major change to the YOA this time included

- sentences of ten years for youth convicted of first-degree murder and seven years for second-degree murder;
- automatic transfer to adult court for 16- and 17-year-olds charged with serious "personal injury" offences unless able to satisfy a judge that the two objectives— public protection and rehabilitation—could be achieved better through the youth court;

- an emphasis that rehabilitation for youth charged with minor offences is best achieved in the commmunity.

Still, law-and-order groups were not satisfied. Sapers and Leonard (1996) observed that "the level of public involvement in the current debate will likely spur politicians to get more tough rather than to look at issues already identified as important ... [C]rime control policy will [likely] continue to reflect muddled, reactionary tinkering" (97). Unfortunately, their prediction came true.

1997–98 Recommendations and Proposals for Reform

Bill C-37 had been the first phase of the federal government's plan for reform. For the second phase, the House of Commons Standing Committee on Justice and Legal Affairs was given a mandate to undertake a comprehensive review of the youth justice system, youth crime, and the operation of the YOA. They were to accomplish this review by surveying a broad cross-section of the Canadian public, as well as those who worked in the system. On the basis of their meetings with individuals and groups, their visits to youth facilities, the information presented at local and national forums, and the recommendations of the Federal-Provincial-Territorial Task Force, the standing committee made 14 recommendations. These recommendations included changing the declaration of principle to a statement of purpose, with the primary purpose being the protection of society; supporting crime prevention and rehabilitation as "reinforcing strategies" for this crime control principle; increasing federal funding for community-based crime-prevention initiatives and public education on youth crime and justice issues; more use of alternative measures, mandatory parental/guardian attendance in court; and lowering the minimum age to 10 (Cohen, 1997:73–76). These recommendations reflected an emphasis on protection of society that ran counter to the emphasis on rehabilitation and prevention in Quebec's Youth Protection Act. It was an emphasis that led to the Bloc Québécois's dissenting position on the standing committee's recommendations and their continued rejection of government reform proposals including the YCJA (Cohen, 1997:115–17; Hogeveen and Smandych, 2001).

Interestingly, the Federal-Provincial-Territorial Task Force's recommendations, which were based on a review of research and literature rather than public consultation, were as oriented to crime control as those of the standing committee—with two notable exceptions. The task force recommended no change to the minimum age and presented a very different view of the conflicting principles issue. Rather than proposing a statement of purpose (protection of society), the task force recommended a review of the YOA's principles for the purpose of distinguishing between "fundamental principles" and "other principles." It also recommended that "other principles" should include

1. the circumstances of Aboriginal youth;
2. the involvement of families in the justice process;

3. the interests of victims;
4. the need for coordination between youth justice and other youth services; and
5. sentencing principles (Report, 1996:629).

These recommendations (see Box 2.8), with the exception of item 4, were adopted in the YCJA.

As with the recommendations of the standing committee, the task force's recommendations did not meet with unanimous approval. A meeting of federal and provincial attorneys general (Alberta, Manitoba, Ontario, P.E.I.) in December 1997 led to recommendations to lower the minimum age, impose mandatory jail terms for weapons offences, make it easier to transfer youth to adult court, and allow media publication of young offenders' names (B.C. Anticipates Tougher Young Offenders Act, 1997:A15). In May 1998, then-Justice Minister Anne McLellan responded to these recommendations with a Youth Criminal Justice Act proposal to replace the YOA .

Responses to this proposed legislation were predictable. The Reform Party (now Alliance) justice critic endorsed the punitive crime control aspects of the proposal. Progressive Conservative and New Democrat critics charged that the Minister was merely "tinkering" with the system. And provincial governments worried that the changes would increase their costs (McIlroy, 1998b). Newspaper articles and editorials ran the gamut, from "YOA Changes 'Right Approach'" (Borden, 1998) to "More Dressing Than Meat" (1998).

The YCJA was eventually introduced in the House of Commons on March 11, 1999, as Bill C-68. It was debated in the House and reintroduced October 14, 1999, as Bill C-3. Following this debate, it was referred to the Standing Committee on Justice and Human Rights and hearings were conducted through to the spring of 2000. As a result of the federal election of 2000, the act had to be reintroduced to the House of Commons in May 2001, now as Bill C-7, and went to the House of Senate in June 2001. It was reintroduced to the House of Commons for final reading in fall 2001 and will come into effect in April 2003. It took 7 years, 3 drafts, and more than 160 amendments to accomplish.

Throughout this process, Reform MPs (Alliance) and conservative interest groups such as victims' rights groups continued to argue that the YCJA had not gone far enough and the Bloc Québécois continued its opposition that the YCJA constituted a step backward for youth justice in Quebec and constituted a substantial problem for any real attempts to rehabilitate and reintegrate youth. Their position was that youth problems could be resolved with the existing YOA (Hogeveen and Smandych, 2001:163–165). In the end, Quebec won the right to "opt out" of the YCJA and continue operating juvenile justice through their Protection Act.

The Youth Criminal Justice Act

The general principles of the Youth Criminal Justice Act are found in its Declaration of Principle, Section 3(1).

the youth criminal justice system is intended to

(i)   prevent crime by addressing the circumstances underlying a young person's offending behaviour,

(ii) rehabilitate young persons who commit offences and reintegrate them into society, and

(iii) ensure that a young person is subject to meaningful consequences for his or her offence in order to promote the long-term protection of the public;

(b) the criminal justice system for young persons must be separate from that of adults and emphasize the following:

(i)   rehabilitation and reintegration,

(ii) fair and proportionate accountability that is consistent with the greater dependency of young persons and their reduced level of maturity,

(iii) timely intervention that reinforces the link between the offending behaviour and its consequences, and

(iv) the promptness and speed with which persons responsible for enforcing this Act must act, given young persons' perception of time;

(c) within the limits of fair and proportionate accountability, the measures taken against young persons who commit offences should

(i)   reinforce respect for societal values,

(ii) encourage the repair of harm done to victims and the community,

(iii) be meaningful for the individual young person given his or her needs and level of development and, where appropriate, involve the parents, the extended family, the community and social or other agencies in the young person's rehabilitation and reintegration, and

(iv) respect gender, ethnic, cultural and linguistic differences and respond to the needs of aboriginal young persons and of young persons with special requirements; and

    (d) special considerations apply in respect of proceedings against young persons and, in particular,

        (i) young persons have rights and freedoms in their own right, such as a right to be heard in the course of and to participate in the processes, other than the decision to prosecute, that lead to decisions that affect them, and young persons have special guarantees of their rights and freedoms,

        (ii) victims should be treated with courtesy, compassion and respect for their dignity and privacy and should suffer the minimum degree of inconvenience as a result of their involvement with the youth criminal justice system,

        (iii) victims should be provided with information about the proceedings and given an opportunity to participate and be heard, and

        (iv) parents should be informed of measures or proceedings involving their children and encouraged to support them in addressing their offending behaviour.

    (2) This Act shall be liberally construed so as to ensure that young persons are dealt with in accordance with the principles set out in subsection (1).

Principles of Justice under the YCJA

As we see in Box 2.8, the Youth Criminal Justice Act has maintained the principles introduced by the YOA, but the way in which it has done so creates a very different justice system both in terms of its structure and its focus. First, the crime control thrust introduced to the system by YOA amendments are maintained, but there are a number of important differences in how this has been accomplished. Unlike the JDA and YOA, the YCJA is explicit about the purpose and objectives of the juvenile justice system. The YCJA specifies clearly that the purpose of a *youth* (no longer defined as *juvenile*) justice system is protection of the public through crime prevention, rehabilitation, and meaningful consequences (s. 3(1)(a)(i-iii)). So, while maintaining the JDA principle of rehabilitation, this is to be undertaken for the sole purpose of protection of the public in the context of "meaningful consequences" rather than as an end in itself. Further, it is no longer sufficient to establish, as the YOA did, that youth will be held responsible, now the system will emphasize "fair and proportional accountability" (s. 3(1)(b)(ii)). We will also see in Chapter 9 that there have been other changes, such as the introduction of sentencing principles, that will have a crime control impact on the system and on youth charged with "serious" and violent offences.

Interestingly, at the same time that the YCJA moves juvenile justice more in the direction of crime control, s. 3(1)(c)(ii) and (iii) open the door for **restorative justice** principles (see Table 2.1 on page 53) to be realized through encouraging **reparation** and the involvement of parents, victims, families and communities in the justice process (also discussed in Chapter 12). Section 3(1)(b)(i) also introduces **reintegration** as a goal of the justice system. Further, in keeping with the Federal-Provincial-Territorial Task Force recommendations, the YCJA justice system is progressive in that s. 3(1)(c)(iv) recognizes that the legislation and system has differential impacts on youth depending on their status in society, thereby at least paving the way for a more equitable justice system in practice.

Justice principles are preserved through s. 3(1)(b) and (d). While s. 3(1)(d)(i) preserves the rights and freedoms of youth, including special rights because of their social status and age (s. 3(1)(c)(iv) to be discussed further in Chapter 8 and 9), justice principles are enhanced through s. 3(b)(iii)(iv) and (v). These subsections emphasize the need for timely intervention and prompt and speedy processing of cases, all of which are recognized as of particular importance for young offenders. Sections 3(1)(d)(ii) and (iii) further extend justice principles by addressing the role and rights of victims in the justice process, a first in the juvenile justice system.

Finally, the YCJA has revived the JDA principle of rehabilitation as an objective, one that was lost in the YOA system with its justice and crime control orientation. While rehabilitation and reintegration is established as a goal, s. 3(1)(c)(iii) specifies that these processes should involve the parents and extended family and that parents should be encouraged to support their children in these efforts. This is a more positive, welfare-orientated statement than that contained in the YOA (3(1)(f)) which merely established the powers of the justice system, relative to parents, with regard to removing children from parental custody. The YCJA also maintains the welfare system orientation toward the "special needs" of young people through s. 3(1)(d)(i) and (b)(ii) by maintaining the YOA focus on the "greater dependency of young persons and their reduced level of maturity." As before, this principle serves as the justification for a separate system of justice for youth. It is significant though that this is stated as a given in s. 3(b) and is therefore no longer a matter of interpretation. This principle, as we will see in later chapters, also now serves as a fundamental guideline for every other aspect of the act's implementation, from police contact, court proceedings, sentencing, and correctional provisions.

One of the most significant changes to the system comes through the omission of alternative measures as a stated principle. Nonetheless, diversionary aspects of the youth justice system remain, but they have been redefined as "extrajudicial measures" and now occupy a separate section in the new act. Part 1 of the YCJA begins with the principles and objectives of diversion (referred to as extrajudicial measures), and proceeds to lay out appropriate responses, conditions, restrictions and the role of police, parents, and victims in the diversionary process. Hence, the familiar practices of YOA alternative measures are far more formalized in the YCJA. Depending on how these practices are implemented by individual provinces and jurisdictions, the end result may be a mini youth justice system in its own right. The specifics of these new sections (s. 4 through s. 12) will be discussed in greater detail in Chapter 8.

Minimal interference is no longer a stated principle of youth justice under the YCJA. Rather, this principle is implied through changes to other sections of the act. So, for example, police are advised in s. 6(1) to consider that no action beyond a warning or referral to a community program might be sufficient action toward a young offender to satisfy the principles laid out in s. 3 of the YCJA.

A New/Old Justice System

The youth justice system under the YCJA is substantially and structurally different from that under the YOA and the JDA. It has retained the welfare focus on rehabilitation and individual needs, the justice focus on individual rights, due process, and individual responsibility as well as the crime control focus on protection of society and accountability. While these principles have been retained, they have also been revised in ways that give a new focus and structure to the system. So, for example, instead of "special needs," the YCJA speaks of rehabilitation, reintegration, and the need to involve families and communities in this process. Gone as fundamental overriding principles are alternative measures, least possible interference, parental responsibility and the right to be informed of rights and freedoms. These principles have been revised and restated elsewhere as principles applying to specific sections of the act such as the new "extrajudicial measures." The new concepts and principles are reintegration; meaningful consequences; timely intervention; parental, family, and community involvement; victim rights; reparation; and a recognition of special needs groups. As we will see in later chapters, many aspects of the YCJA are regressive revisions of old principles and practices while many are indicative of a restorative justice model and as such offer a potential for progressive changes.

And so we have it. As Sapers and Leonard (1996) predicted, politicians got tougher, public concern over the juvenile justice system continues, and involved parties—lawyers, judges, police officers, and social workers—take positions adopted by their predecessors a century ago. Have we come full circle? First we were punitive and made few distinctions between youth and adult offenders. Then we were concerned about the welfare of children and separated youth offenders from adult offenders. Now we are moving in the direction of putting more youth into the adult justice system while at the same time trying to keep minor offenders out of the system. As will become more apparent in later chapters, we have created a **bifurcated** youth justice system— one set of rules for minor offenders and another for those charged with more serious offences. Are we returning to the point at which we started? Maybe so. In the Western world, juvenile justice is an ever-revolving cycle. Bernard (1992) describes this **cycle of juvenile justice** in his analysis of two centuries of criminal justice in the United States:

> This cycle arises from the fact that, at any given time, many people are convinced that the problem of high juvenile crime rates is recent and did not exist in the "good old days." These people conclude that the problem lies in the policies for handling juvenile offenders, whether those are harsh punishments or lenient treatments. The result is a cycle of reform in which harsh punishments are blamed for high juvenile crime rates and are replaced by lenient treatments, and then lenient treatments are blamed for high juvenile crime rates and are replaced by harsh punishments. (22)

SUMMARY

A century ago, middle-class Victorians in Canadian cities were concerned about the welfare of neglected and delinquent children and believed that housing them in penal institutions and adult prisons was too punitive. As a result of their reform efforts, a juvenile justice system was created with the passage of the Juvenile Delinquents Act in 1908. Some critics argued that the system was not punitive enough, others that children would be deprived of their legal rights. Now, nearly a century later, the juvenile justice system has been significantly modified to incorporate due process rights and legal responsibility for criminal behaviour. Still, law-and-order groups worried that the system was not punitive enough. Politicians responded with punitive recommendations and the Youth Criminal Justice Act. The cycle of juvenile justice reform continues.

Prior to the creation of the juvenile justice system in Canada, English common law dictated that anyone over 14 was subject to the same law as adults. Those under 7 were considered unable to distinguish right from wrong. Children between the ages of 7 and 14 could suffer the same consequence as adults if it was determined that they had the ability to distinguish right from wrong.

J.J. Kelso and W.L. Scott are credited with creating the juvenile justice system, which began with the passage of the Juvenile Delinquents Act in 1908. The justice system under the JDA was based on the doctrine *parens patriae*, which required the court and justice system to act in "the best interest of the child." Under this welfare-based system of justice, delinquents were viewed as "misdirected and misguided" children in need of "aid, encouragement, help and assistance."

Serious challenges to the JDA began to surface in the 1960s, largely as a result of the human-rights movement in North America and rising public concerns about youth crime and public protection. After a 20-year debate, the Young Offenders Act was enacted in 1984. The system it created was described as a modified justice system because it maintained some welfare principles, incorporated justice principles, and used crime control principles to modify both. This combination of conflicting principles fueled a 15-year debate over the purpose and effectiveness of the juvenile justice system.

The principles of juvenile justice under the YOA were accountability, protection of society, special needs of youth, alternative measures, due process rights of young persons, minimal interference with freedom, and parental responsibility.

The YOA was amended three times after it was implemented. All revisions moved the justice system further from welfare principles and closer to a crime control model. The Youth Criminal Justice Act continues this trend toward crime control principles by allowing more youth to be placed into the adult justice system while at the same time keeping more youth out of the juvenile justice system by means of extrajudicial measures. In so doing, the new justice system is a bifurcated one.

Under the YCJA the new aspects of youth justice are reintegration; meaningful consequences; timely intervention; parental, family, and community involvement in rehabilitation and reintegration processes; victim rights; reparation; and a recognition of special needs groups.

APPENDIX

The United Nations Convention on the Rights of the Child

In 1992, over 100 countries, including Canada, ratified the Convention on the Rights of the Child. The United States and Somalia have refused to ratify because of Article 37(a). Children are defined as those under the age of 18. Among other things, U.N. Document A/44/736 (1989) addresses the special needs of children, the concept of "best interests," children's rights, and juvenile justice systems.

Recalling that, in the Universal Declaration of Human Rights, the United Nations has proclaimed that childhood is entitled to special care and assistance, *convinced* that the family, as the fundamental group of society and the natural environment for the growth and well-being of all its members and particularly children, should be afforded the necessary protection and assistance so that it can fully assume its responsibilities within the community,

Recognizing that the child, for the full and harmonious development of his or her personality, should grow up in a family environment, in an atmosphere of happiness, love and understanding, ...

Bearing in mind that, as indicated in the Declaration of Rights of the Child, "the child, by reason of his physical and mental immaturity, needs special safeguards and care, including appropriate legal protection ..."

Article 3

1. In all actions concerning children, whether undertaken by public or private social welfare institutions, courts of law, administrative authorities or legislative bodies, the best interests of the child shall be a primary consideration.

Article 12

1. States Parties shall assure to the child who is capable of forming his or her own views the right to express those views freely in all matters affecting the child, the views of the child being given due weight in accordance with the age and maturity of the child.

2. For this purpose, the child shall in particular be provided the opportunity to be heard in any judicial and administrative proceedings affecting the child, either directly, or through a representative or an appropriate body, in a manner consistent with the procedural rules of national law.

Article 37

States parties shall ensure that:

(a) No child shall be subjected to torture or other cruel, inhuman or degrading treatment or punishment. Neither capital punishment nor life imprisonment without possibility of release shall be imposed for offences committed by persons below 18 years of age;

(b) No child shall be deprived of his or her liberty unlawfully or arbitrarily. The arrest, detention or imprisonment of a child shall be in conformity with the law and shall be used only as a measure of last resort and for the shortest appropriate period of time;

(c) Every child deprived of liberty shall be treated with humanity and respect for the inherent dignity of the human person, and in a manner which takes into account the needs of persons of his or her age. In particular, every child deprived of liberty shall be separated from adults unless it is considered in the child's best interest not to do so and shall have the right to maintain contact with his or her family through correspondence and visits, save in exceptional circumstances;

(d) Every child deprived of his or her liberty shall have the right to prompt access to legal and other appropriate assistance, as well as the right to challenge the legality of the deprivation of his or her liberty before a court or other competent, independent and impartial authority, and to a prompt decision on any such action.

Article 40

1. States Parties recognize the right of every child alleged as, accused of, or recognized as having infringed the penal law to be treated in a manner consistent with the promotion of the child's sense of dignity and worth, which reinforces the

child's respect for the human rights and fundamental freedoms of others and which takes into account the child's age and the desirability of promoting the child's reintegration and the child's assuming a constructive role in society ...

3. States Parties shall seek to promote the establishment of laws, procedures, authorities and institutions specifically applicable to children alleged, accused of, or recognized as having infringed the penal law, and, in particular:

   (a) the establishment of a minimum age below which children shall be presumed not to have the capacity to infringe the penal law;

   (b) whenever appropriate and desirable, measures for dealing with such children without resorting to judicial proceedings, providing that human rights and legal safeguards are fully respected.

4. A variety of dispositions, such as care, guidance and supervision orders; counselling; probation; foster care; education and vocational training programmes and other alternatives to institutional care shall be available to ensure that children are dealt with in a manner appropriate to their well-being and proportionate both to their circumstances and the offence.

CHAPTER 3

The "Facts" of Youth Crime

CHAPTER OBJECTIVES

1. To discuss the meaning of crime statistics through an examination of the strengths and limitations of various sources: media, official, self-report, and victimization surveys.

2. To emphasize that official crime statistics underestimate the prevalence of crime in general and the crimes of white middle-class youth.

3. To profile youth crime patterns and trends and provide a focus on selected offences and associated issues.

4. To discuss the violent-crime debate and contradictions in statistics and interpretations.

5. To discuss issues of validity and reliability in relation to official, self-report, and victimization data.

6. To revisit questions raised in Chapter 1 about youth crime by considering what is measured by the various sources, by comparing statistics from periods under the JDA and the YOA, and by comparing rates of adult and youth crime.

KEY TERMS

Concept
Social control agencies
Field research
Aggregated
Crime index
Administrative charges

Self-report survey
Victimization survey
Clearance rates
Administrative offences
Empirical
Zero-tolerance policies

Reliability
Validity
Unfounded
Telescoping
Self-fulfilling prophecy

INTRODUCTION

This chapter is about the interrelated activities of defining and measuring youth crime. Before youth crime can be understood or explained, it must be measured or counted. Prior to counting, the meaning of the term "youth crime" must be formalized. In other words, youth crime cannot be accurately counted or measured without an exact definition of the term. For example, we used to talk about (or measure) a person's height in feet and inches. This implicitly sets the definition of the **concept** "height" in terms of inches. Of course, many now count in terms of centimetres rather than inches. In this case, "height" would be defined as the number of centimetres a person would measure from head to toes. All concepts must be defined before they can be measured with any accuracy or reliability. Youth crime, as a concept, has been defined and measured in different ways over the last 150 years. This knowledge has important implications for our efforts to make sense of youth crime statistics.

As mentioned in the last chapter, under the Juvenile Delinquents Act youth misbehaviour was defined, measured, and recorded as delinquency. Hence, statistics predating the Young Offenders Act include behaviours other than criminal acts as defined by the Criminal Code of Canada. As we saw in Chapter 2, delinquents were often children or youth who were deemed to be unmanageable by their parents and a Family Court judge. Since 1984 and the implementation of the Young Offenders Act, statistics have included only behaviours that are charged under the Criminal Code or various special provisions of the YOA such as failure to comply with a court order, which would mean that a youth might have not complied with the conditions attached to her or his probation. As well, delinquency law applied to a different age group than the YOA and this varied by province and over time. For example, the Juvenile Delinquents Act applied to those aged 7–17 in Quebec and 7–15 in Ontario and Nova Scotia.

Even the concept "young offender" has not been defined in a consistent manner. When the YOA was implemented in 1984—some sections did not become effective until 1985—it did not apply to 16- and 17-year-olds. This changed in 1986. So, for the first two years, 1984 and 1985, youth crime statistics for Ontario and Nova Scotia included only youth aged 12 to 15. Thus, statistics gathered prior to 1985 are not directly comparable to those gathered in later years.

Beyond the question of definition, we also need to know something about crime measurement. This chapter begins with a discussion of the sources of statistics on youth crime and what they are measuring. It moves on to develop a profile of youth crime by discussing types of youth crime and what we know about crime from different sources. The chapter ends with a discussion of measurement issues and a revisiting of key questions about youth crime that were raised in Chapter 1.

MEASURING YOUTH CRIME

Measuring youth crime, or delinquency, is not an easy task because what gets counted depends on the source of the information. The most common source of information on youth crime for many people is the media. The other major source, less accessible to the average person, is statistics provided by **social control agencies**. These agencies include police, courts, and various correctional institutions. Only some of this information is available to the public through Statistics Canada. Other information on youth crime comes from researchers who, over the years, have developed various techniques for measuring youth and adult crime through population surveys and **field research**. The two most common types of surveys are victimization surveys, which ask people if they have been victimized, and self-report surveys, which ask about a person's involvement in criminal and delinquent activities. Most field research has been done with "street kids" and institutionalized populations. Each source is useful, but each has shortcomings as a measure of youth crime. Unless we understand the strengths and weaknesses of each of these sources, youth crime can easily be misunderstood or misrepresented in some very significant ways. Further, and most important, what we think we know about youth crime will depend on which source has been used.

Sources of information on crime and delinquency vary considerably as measures of actual criminal activity. Table 3.1 illustrates that surveys and field research are more representative of actual criminal activity than is the information we get from control agencies such as police, courts, and prisons. Among agencies, a steadily diminishing amount of criminal activity is measured depending on whether the source is police records, court records, or correctional records. For example, not all crimes known to police result in charges as charges may be dropped or reduced before going to court and not all convictions result in probation or prison sentences. Further, agency statistics tell us as much (or more) about the activities of the agencies themselves than about youth crime. In fact, the statistics that we get from these agencies have not been designed to measure youth crime. Rather, they have been designed by agencies to be used for their own purposes. Courts, for example, need to know how long it takes to process a case for scheduling purposes. Survey and field information on youth crime provides a more valid measure of what we would consider to be the actual amount and character of youth crime, primarily because these measuring tools and techniques have been designed by researchers solely for the purpose of measuring criminal activity.

SOURCES AND WHAT THEY TELL US ABOUT YOUTH CRIME

The Media

Most people obtain information about youth crime exclusively from newspapers and television news reports. Sometimes journalists write books about youth crime. An example is Kevin Marron's *Apprenticed in Crime*, in which he tells his readers that the rate of violent offenses ... has been increasing steadily in recent years, and such crimes now account for about 18 percent of the charges before youth courts. Between 1987 and 1989, violent offenses by youths rose by about 10 percent, while property crimes decreased by 8 percent. Ontario, which accounts for 40 percent of all convictions under the Young Offenders Act in Canada also has the highest rate of violent offenses, which appear to be endemic in large urban centres. (1993:49)

While this information is correct, when it is presented without a historical context or discussion of the limitations and shortcomings of the sources, it becomes misleading and contributes to public fears of a youth crime wave.

Bortner (1988) argues that all too often what appear to be crime waves may be more accurately described as "media waves." To make her point, she discusses Mark Fishman's analysis of how New York City's three daily newspapers and local television stations reported a surge of violent crime against elderly people. A public outcry for greater protection followed the news coverage. Politicians responded with get-tough measures and additional resources to increase policing activities. Fishman compared the media reports to police arrest statistics and found that youth violence had not increased. In fact, there had been a 19-percent decrease in violent criminal activity in the areas of the city that had been reported in the news as being particularly violent (Fishman, 1978:531–43).

Closer to home, we find that Canadians seem increasingly concerned about crime and violent crime in particular. This concern becomes centred on youth when a few high-profile cases involving teenage killers fuel public fears about youth crime. Surveys indicate that 4 in 10 Canadians rate juvenile delinquency as a "very serious problem" (Bibby, 1995:101). Diane Ablonczy, as justice critic for the Reform Party, stated that

TABLE 3.1

Relationship between Criminal Activity and Criminal Statistics

Criminal Activity	Source of Information
Actual crime	None
Voluntary admission of crime	Self-report survey
Detected crime	Victimization survey
Known about and Cleared Crime	
Reported, recorded, arrested	Police statistics
Convicted crime	Court records
Offenders serving terms of probation, prison, parole	Corrections agencies

more young people were accused of homicide in 1994 than in 1993 and that violent crime by youths has increased at a faster pace than adult violent crime. Many Canadians and politicians, notably former Reform Party Leader Preston Manning, have been calling for the public to rule on reinstating the death penalty. An opinion poll conducted in June 1995 reports that 69 percent of those surveyed strongly or moderately support capital punishment. Yet, figures recently released by Statistics Canada (July 1998) show that the crime rate for young offenders charged with Criminal Code offences dropped for the sixth year in a row, and that the violent crime rate for youths has been on the decline since 1995 (Kong, 1998:20).

Criminologists tend to have a very different view of youth crime than politicians and the general public. Their interpretations of the statistics would suggest that Canadians are experiencing a media wave rather than a crime wave. According to Neil Boyd, a criminologist at Simon Fraser University, "all of the evidence is contrary to the majority of public perception, that crime is something that we are losing control of. In fact, the best evidence is something to the contrary" (quoted in Cox, 1995). Elliott Leyton, a professor of anthropology at Memorial University of Newfoundland, argues that Canadians are in a "violence panic ... and are unaware that the threat of real crime 'in Canada is low by world standards'" (quoted in Bailey, 1995). Schissel (1997) concludes from an analysis of street youth and police statistics that

> the logic and rhetoric of politics and news is so flawed and poorly struck that malicious intentions cannot be dismissed ... the reality of youth crime shows that there is no substance to the contention that youths are progressively becoming more criminal and more dangerous. (99)

Police Statistics

Crimes "known to police" refer to crimes for which the police have been provided information through complainants or from their own observations. Crimes "cleared by the police" refer to crimes for which police are satisfied they have a suspect and are prepared to process the case. Cases are processed either through laying charges or some other action such as deciding to take a youth home to her or his parents, or referring the youth to a community agency or program. Whether police clear a charge varies considerably by type of offence.

Table 3.2, which provides 1992 youth crime statistics for Ontario, clearly indicates the amount of discretion that police have in deciding whether or not to charge a youth. The more serious the offence, the more likely it is that police will lay a charge and take a youth to court. As Table 3.2 shows, the proportion of youth charged increases with the severity of assault. Charge rates, which are 63.1 percent for first-level assault, increase to 98.6 percent for third-level assault. Similarly, the charge rate for theft over $1,000 is almost 74 percent, but only 52.5 percent for theft under $1,000.

TABLE 3.2

Crime Statistics: Ontario (Selected Offences), 1992

Offence Type	Youth Charged	Youth Not Charged	Percentage of Apprehended Youth Who Are Charged
Assault I	4,243	2,480	63.1%
Assault II	1,597	320	83.3%
Assault III	145	2	98.6%
Robbery	1,223	112	91.6%
Theft over $1,000	605	216	73.7%
Theft $1,000 & under	12,857	11,626	52.5%
Drugs: Cocaine	217	7	96.9%
Drugs: Cannabis	590	56	91.3%

Source: Statistics Canada, Canadian Crime Statistics, 1992. Adapted from Doob, Marinos, and Varma (1995:7).

Individual police departments produce the majority of statistics on criminal activity in Canada. Record keeping is limited to 132 Criminal Code offence categories and several drug and traffic offences (Creechan, 1995:99). Police data in Canada were standardized by the Uniform Crime Reporting (UCR) system in the early 1960s. These standardized reports are sent to the Canadian Centre for Justice Statistics in Ottawa where they are **aggregated** and made available to the public. Police statistics are often reported as general indexes—the violent **crime index**, property crime index, and "other" crime index (Creechan, 1995:100). UCR statistics include all police departments across the country. Since 1988, a revised UCR survey has collected, from a sample of police departments, detailed information concerning individual incidents.

What Police Statistics Tell Us about Youth Crime

UCR statistics comparing offences from 1986 to 2000 indicate that the number of youth charged with Criminal Code offences has both increased and decreased on a year-to-year basis over this time period (see Table 3.3 and Figure 3.1). The total number of youth charges rose steadily from 107,698 in 1987 to a high of 142,316 in 1991 and dropped to a low of 99,322 in 1999, then increased to 100,861 in 2000.

TABLE 3.3

Youth Charged in Criminal Code Incidents, Canada, 1986–2000[1]

	1986	1987	1988	1989	1990	1991	1992	1993	1994r	1995	1996	1997	1998	1999	2000
Population (aged 12–17)	2,272,400	2,260,900	2,249,500	2,245,700	2,260,100	2,284,800	2,315,800	2,341,200	2,360,400	2,348,600	2,417,500	2,445,400	2,449,696	2,449,097	2,451,701
Violent crime															
number	9,275	10,165	11,437	13,780	15,690	18,919	20,028	21,477	21,629	22,375	22,521	22,252	22,195	21,102	22,635
rate	408	450	508	614	694	828	865	917	916	938	932	910	906	862	923
% change in rate from previous year	...	10.2	13.1	20.7	13.1	19.3	4.4	6.1	-0.1	2.4	-0.9	-2.3	-0.3	-4.9	7.2
Property crime															
number	78,862	74,769	74,316	76,317	83,741	91,656	83,603	74,981	68,907	68,138	66,702	59,532	54,104	48,009	46,248
rate	3,470	3,307	3,304	3,398	3,705	4,012	3,610	3,203	2,919	2,857	2,759	2,434	2,209	1,960	1,886
% change in rate from previous year	...	-4.7	-0.1	2.9	9.0	8.3	-10.0	-11.3	-8.8	-2.1	-3.3	-11.8	-7.6	-11.2	-3.8
Other Criminal Code															
number	20,869	22,764	24,136	25,865	27,118	31,741	31,651	30,429	29,089	30,119	30,187	29,952	31,153	30,211	31,978
rate	918	1,007	1,073	1,152	1,200	1,389	1,367	1,300	1,232	1,263	1,249	1,225	1,272	1,234	1,304
% change in rate from previous year	...	9.6	6.6	7.3	4.2	15.8	-1.6	-4.9	-5.2	2.5	-1.0	-1.9	2.3	-3.0	5.7
Total Criminal Code															
number	109,006	107,698	109,889	115,962	126,549	142,316	135,282	126,887	119,625	120,632	119,410	111,736	107,452	99,322	100,861
rate	4,797	4,764	4,885	5,164	5,599	6,229	5,842	5,420	5,068	5,059	4,939	4,569	4,386	4,055	4,114
% change in rate from previous year	...	-0.7	2.6	5.7	8.4	11.2	-6.2	-7.2	-6.5	-0.2	-2.3	-7.5	-3.5	-7.5	1.4

[1] Rates are calculated on the basis of 100,000 youths. Population estimates from Statistics Canada Census and Demographic Statistics, Demography Division.

Populations as of July 1st: revised intercensal estimates from 1985 to 1990, final intercensal estimates for 1991 to 1995, final postcensal estimates for 1996 and 1997, updated postcensal estimates from 1998 to 1999, and preliminary postcensal estimates for 2000.

r Revised

... Figures not appropriate

Sources: Adapted from *Juristat*, Cat. No. 85–002, 15(12); Cat. No. 85–002, 21(8).

FIGURE 3.1

Young Offender Index Crime

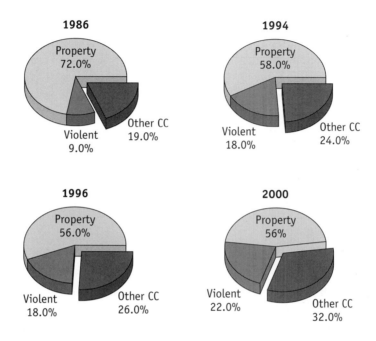

1986
Property 72.0%
Violent 9.0%
Other CC 19.0%

1994
Property 58.0%
Violent 18.0%
Other CC 24.0%

1996
Property 56.0%
Violent 18.0%
Other CC 26.0%

2000
Property 56%
Violent 22.0%
Other CC 32.0%

Sources: Statistics Canada (1990b; 1995; 1997, 2001).

However, the number of youths charged with violent offences consistently increased until 1995 before showing declines and then began to increase again in 2000. On the other hand, charges for property incidents began to decrease after 1991 and continue to do so. Of the 110,861 youth charged with Criminal Code offences in 2000, 22 percent were charged with violent crimes, 46 percent with property crimes, and 32 percent with other Criminal Code offences (Kong, 1998:20; Logan, 2001:12,20).

While these figures certainly support public concerns, particularly regarding violent crime, viewing the statistics in a more detailed or comparative context presents a less dramatic view of youth crime. First, about half of the young people charged with violent crimes are charged in connection with minor assault incidents which involves behaviour like pushing and shoving, incidents not resulting in physical injury (Statistics Canada, 1995:29). Second, the most serious offence, homicide, is consistently low with a rate that has fluctuated from 2 to 3 per 100,000 youth. Furthermore, as we will see later in the chapter, adults are responsible for considerably more crime including crimes of violence than are young people. Compared to youth violence at 22 percent, violent crimes accounted for 31 percent of all adult Criminal Code offences in 2000 (Logan, 2001:12). Finally, an examination of the ratio of youth to adult charges compared to total incidents from 1973 to 1995 shows a dramatic increase in youth charges for violent offences after the YOA was implemented, which suggests that youth are processed through the justice system for violent offences in greater numbers than adults (Schissel, 1997:80–81). Hence, official adult rates for violent crime are also likely underestimated compared to youth rates, and the gap is greater than official statistics suggest.

Nonetheless, despite decreasing rates of reported youth crime since 1986, the violent crime rate is now considerably higher than it was a decade ago (695 vs. 923 per 100,000), and this is fuel for public concern. In 1986, as we see in Figure 3.1, 9 percent of all police charges against young people were for violent crimes; by 1996, this proportion had doubled to 18 percent and by 2000 had increased again to 22 percent (Logan, 2001:12).

Court Statistics

Court statistics are kept by individual courts and yield smaller numbers than police statistics. Not all people who are known to police end up arrested, and not all arrested people end up in court. The value of court records is that they can provide information about offenders and their offences. Court files can provide detailed information, for example, on whether other people were involved in the offence or who the victims might be. If a report on a young offender has been prepared, information is also available on the young person's family, school records, prior criminal activity, and various other information of a social nature that is not ever available from police records. In addition, court records provide information about sentences. Youth court records are not accessible to the public in every province, but basic data are sent to Ottawa and compiled for public distribution by the Canadian Centre for Justice Statistics. These public statistics are similar to police statistics in that the information is aggregated. An advantage of police and court statistics is that they are usually available for the entire country. Part of the negotiations for acceptance of the YOA by provincial governments involved a commitment on the part of the federal government to provide record keeping for young offender courts. To this end, the federal government set up a special branch of the Centre for Justice Statistics to compile youth court data. This information is published on a yearly basis (Annual Youth Court Statistics) for the entire country and for individual provinces.

What Court Statistics Tell Us about Youth Crime

Figure 3.2 shows court statistics comparing 1986–87 with 1996–97 and 1999–2000. We see the same patterns that are evident in police statistics. In 1986, 67 percent of all cases heard in youth court were property offences, 13 percent were violent offences, and 19 percent were all other offences. By 2000, property offence cases going to court had decreased to 40 percent and, with the exception of drug cases and other federal offences, all other types of offences showed continual increases over this period. Court cases involving violent offences increased to 22 percent while other criminal code charges rose to 18 percent. The most dramatic increases occurred for YOA offences. These increased from 3 percent of court cases in 1986–87 to 13 percent in 2000.

Despite the same general pattern that exists between court statistics and index crimes, a word of caution is in order regarding comparisons of anything other than broad patterns. First of all, with index crime categories, "other" offences include only

FIGURE 3.2

Youth Court Cases by Offence Category, Canada: 1986–87, 1996–97, 1999–2000

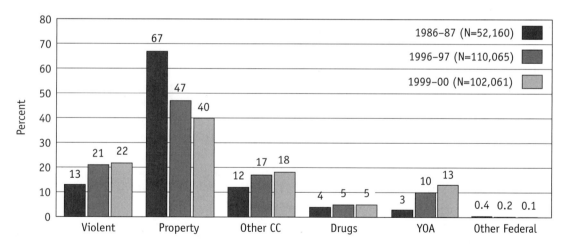

Note: Data exclude Ontario and the Northwest Territories in 1986–87.

Sources: Adapted from de Souza (1995); Statistics Canada (1998:xiii); 2001:4, 14.

Criminal Code charges, whereas in court statistics the "other" category also includes **administrative charges** under the Young Offenders Act. A major weakness with youth court statistics—particularly problematic when we try to compare across years—is that, in 1986, Ontario and the Northwest Territories were not included in the statistics. Ontario is not included in youth court statistics until after 1992, and, even then, only partially. Nonetheless, this exclusion is not likely to affect proportions or rates by category of offence but only the figures for numbers of cases appearing before the courts. Finally, youth court statistics measure only cases going to court and are therefore not a valid measure of youth criminal activity. As such, they are more useful as a measure or indicator of youth justice than youth crime.

Self-Report Surveys

An interesting way of measuring crime and delinquency is to use a **self-report survey**. Under this approach, people are simply asked about their involvement in criminal or delinquent behaviour. Typically, surveys are administered to school population samples. Some recent Canadian research has surveyed people in natural settings. Such field research is often conducted on the streets. McCarthy, for example, surveyed young people who hung around the Eaton Centre on Toronto's Yonge Street (McCarthy & Hagan, 1992). In some ways, as we will see in Chapter 5, nothing changed the face of criminological theory more than the discovery of self-reported measures of delinquent behaviour.

According to Creechan (1995:97), the use of self-report studies originated with a sociologist named Austin Porterfield who experimented with them at Texas Christian University in the 1940s (Porterfield, 1946). The first self-report study of delinquent behaviour to have a significant impact on criminologists' thinking about delinquency was that done by Nye and Short (1957:328) (see Box 3.3 on page 96). Prior to this research, the only statistics available on the criminal and delinquent behaviour of young people came from official sources (i.e., courts, police, or institutions). When the self-report questionnaire was introduced, it became immediately apparent that the actual amount of criminal and delinquent behaviour by young people was much higher than had ever been reported through official statistics. In addition, self-report studies revealed a profile of people involved in crime and delinquency that was very different from that gleaned from official records. Official records tend to underrepresent the offences of middle-class youth, presenting instead a profile of delinquents and young offenders as poor, working class, and members of visible minorities.

In the mid-1990s, Statistics Canada and Human Resources Development Canada began a joint project to collect longitudinal data on children and youth. Beginning in 1994–1995, the project began collecting information on a sample of 22,000 children up to age eleven. These children will be interviewed every two years until they reach age twenty-five. To date, four surveys have been collected. Limited information is now available on child and youth delinquency since there are a few questions included in the survey about child and youth engagement in stealing, vandalism, and aggressive behaviours directed toward others. Parents and teachers are asked to report on children's behaviours and youth self-report their own delinquency once they reach age ten (Dauvergne and Johnson, 2001:2; Sprott, Doob and Jenkins, 2001:2–3).

What Self-Report Surveys Tell Us about Youth Crime

Typically, results from self-report studies indicate that delinquent and criminal behaviour is far more widespread than one would ever think from looking at official statistics. According to Bortner (1988:144), self-report measures of delinquency report estimates that range from four to ten times the amount reported by official statistics. In one American study she cites, 88 percent of the 13- to 16-year-old youth surveyed admitted to participating in at least one delinquent act during the three years prior to the study; less than 3 percent of these offences had been detected by police, while only 22 percent of the juveniles had ever had contact with police and less than 2 percent had ever gone to court (Bortner, 1988:145).

One of the first Canadian self-report studies was done by Mark Le Blanc. Seven surveys were carried out by Le Blanc and his colleagues in Montreal schools between 1967 and 1976. A relatively stable proportion of adolescents (approximately 90 percent in each of the seven surveys) admitted to having committed a delinquent act (Le Blanc, 1983:33–35). Things have not changed much since then; a comparative study of self-reported delinquency in Montreal in 1974 and in 1985 showed no change in the level or nature of self-reported delinquency (Le Blanc and Tremblay, 1988).

Most recently, Steven Baron surveyed 200 male street youth, all under the age of 24, about their illegal behaviour over a 12-month period. Most of the boys and young men that he surveyed had not had a fixed address or had lived in a shelter during the last year. Among those who were homeless, most had spent almost five months living exclusively on the street during the survey period, and 19 percent had been without shelter for at least six months. Baron's survey yielded the following results:

> These 200 youth reported committing some 334,636 crimes during the twelve months prior to the interview—an average of 1,673 per respondent. Although this figure seems astronomical, analysis by type indicates that drug offenses are responsible for 72 percent of the reported crime. Thus, most of the crime takes place between willing participants on the street ... [T]he bulk of the non-related offenses ... appears to be directed against others leading similar 'risky lifestyles'. The group fights, the robberies and the assaults are all a result of interactions in the risky areas frequented by the respondents. (Baron, 1995:145)

Baron's self-report survey of criminal activity among male street youth provides a very different picture of criminal activity from that provided by official statistics or the earlier Montreal studies. While the most frequent offence reported by the youth in Baron's sample was drug-related (72 percent), violent offences accounted for only 5 percent of all the reported offences. Aggravated assault and common assault most often stemmed from disputes, horseplay, or drunkenness, or from a situation that "called for revenge," such as somebody getting "ripped off" in a drug deal (Baron, 1995:143–44).

Property crime accounted for only 20 percent of the offences reported by the male youth in Baron's sample. Usually, a small number of male offenders are responsible for the majority of property offences. This result is consistent with findings in other studies. Twenty-four of the 200 youth Baron surveyed "insisted that they had been involved in a combined total of over 500 property offences" (1995:141). McCarthy and Hagan (1992), who used self-report measures in their survey of 475 homeless youth in Toronto during 1987 and 1988, argue that the crimes of homeless youth are directly related to the adversity of living on the streets: "Consistently, hunger causes theft of food, problems of hunger and shelter lead to serious theft, and problems of shelter and unemployment produce prostitution" (623).

Victimization Surveys

A more recently developed method of acquiring information about criminal behaviour is the **victimization survey**. This approach involves asking people if they have ever been victimized by the criminal behaviour of others. Although victimization data do not provide a direct measure of the nature or prevalence of youth crime, they do provide considerable information that is useful in combination with other sources.

The U.S. government collects victimization data on an annual basis from a sample of the population. The first national survey in the United States was conducted in 1966. Since that time, victimization surveys have become the principle method of gaining information about the volume of specific types of crime and delinquency. (See Box 3.4 on page 98 for examples of questions used in victimization surveys.) The U.S. government also conducts victimization surveys of high-school students to determine how crime affects the daily lives of teenagers (Creechan, 1995:98).

The first Canadian victimization survey was conducted by the Ministry of the Solicitor General and Statistics Canada in the early 1980s. Known as the Canadian Urban Victimization Survey (CUVS), it gathered data from some 61,000 Canadians aged 16 and over. The respondents, who consisted of residents of seven cities (Greater Vancouver, Edmonton, Winnipeg, Toronto, Montreal, Halifax/Dartmouth, and St. John's) were interviewed about their experiences with certain crimes during the 1981 calendar year (Johnson and Lazarus, 1989:311). Since then, information collected by Statistics Canada about crime victimization has been incorporated into the federal government's General Social Survey (GSS). In this survey, which began in 1988 and is undertaken every five years, a sample of more than 10,000 Canadians over the age of 15 are asked questions about assault, robbery, sexual assault, personal theft, break and enters to their house, theft of household property or cars, and vandalism. In 1999, questions on spousal violence were added to the GSS (Besserer and Trainor, 2001:2). In addition, in 1993, Statistics Canada conducted a survey (Violence Against Women Survey (VAWS)) of women regarding their experiences of sexual and physical assault, and some victimization data is available for children and youth from the national longitudinal survey of children and youth.

What Victimization Surveys Tell Us about Youth Crime

Victimization surveys focus on crimes against individuals and households and thus do not measure other common offences such as shoplifting. Nonetheless, victimization surveys do tell us something about crime trends. Comparisons between the 1988 and 1993 GSS clearly show a flat trend with respect to the victimization rate; 24 percent of respondents in both surveys said they had been victimized (Gartner and Doob, 1994). While public fears of increased crime may thus be unwarranted, these surveys also make it clear that not all crime in Canada is reported to the police. From the 1993 GSS we know that 68 percent of assaults and 32 percent of household break and enters either were not reported to the police or were reported but did not lead to the charging of a suspect with the offence (Gartner and Doob, 1994).

What is particularly useful about victimization surveys, then, is that they allow us to know something about police **clearance rates** for specific offences and about which offences will be underestimated in police statistics. Comparisons of victimization survey results with police clearance rates show considerable variation by type of offence. With respect to vandalism, 54 percent of the cases do not get reported to the police and, among those reported, only 15 percent are cleared. For household break and enters, 17 percent of the cases reported to the police are cleared. Reporting and clearance rates for crimes against persons are very different from property crimes in that reporting rates for crimes against persons tend to be lower while clearance rates for property crimes are higher. In sexual-assault cases, about 10 percent are reported to police and a suspect is named in about two-thirds of these cases. Most homicides are reported and police are able to name a suspect in 84 percent of the cases (Doob, Marinos, and Varma, 1995:5).

With regard to measuring the offences that young people commit, victimization surveys are not able to give us information about an offender's age if there has not been any contact between the victim and the offender. Even if the victim saw the offender in a particular case, age is not always easily discernible. Hindelang and McDermott (1981) report that sex is the easiest characteristic for victims to recall, race is somewhat difficult, and age is the most difficult. Nonetheless, they did find that victims' accuracy rates for estimating the age of an offender was not less than 89 percent for any age, group. On the other hand, Doob, Marinos, and Varma (1995) point out that if an offender is a stranger and around the age of 18, victims are not likely to be able to judge whether the offender is an adult or a youth. In addition, victimization surveys cannot measure victimless crimes such as drug offences. Nor can they measure crimes against people who are not aware that they have been victimized. For example, jewellery may be stolen and not missed by the owner until months or even years after the theft; at that point, the owner may simply assume that the item is lost. Offences committed against businesses or corporations are also not counted in victimization surveys.

Some critics have raised concerns about victimization surveys because of the possibility that victim reports may be influenced by popular stereotypes of criminals. Media crime images are such that minorities and young people may be more likely reported as offenders. Hindelang and McDermott's (1981) findings from victimization surveys in the United States indicate that actual crimes committed by juveniles contradict media portrayals of juvenile crime. Their comparisons between juvenile offenders (under 18 years), youthful offenders (18 to 20 years), and adult offenders (over 21 years) show that juvenile crime is "demonstrably less serious than youthful offender and adult crime in three major areas." There is less weapon use by juveniles; juveniles are less successful than adults in committing theft-motivated offences; and there are lower rates of victim injury for juvenile offences (72). These facts are contradicted by many media images of juvenile crime.

PROFILING YOUTH CRIME

Property Crime

As we have seen, according to police statistics, property crime is the most common of all youth offences but its frequency has been on the decline over the last ten years relative to other types of offences. Most youth property crime is of a petty nature, the majority of which involves shoplifting (Creechan, 1995:102–3). Index crime figures for property offences in 2000 indicate that most property crime charges were for theft (44 percent) followed by break and enter (27 percent). Both have been declining such that the rate of youth charged for these offences is one-half in 2000 what it was in 1990. Motor vehicle theft rates, on the other hand have shown more fluctuation with a rate, on average, of one half to one-third that of break and enter (Logan, 2001:20). The peak age of property crime charges for youth is 16 (Kong, 1998:11).

Baron's (1995) study of male street youth also found that most property crime is of a petty nature. He reports that stolen items tended to be things easily concealed and distributed, such as clothes, game cartridges, and cassette players. Cash, jewellery, guns,

TVs, VCRs, and stereos were the kinds of items most often taken during a break and enter. Baron further notes that respondents usually received only 10 to 15 percent value for their stolen property. Not surprisingly, the primary motivation for property crime among Baron's respondents was purely utilitarian: they needed the money. Sometimes their thefts were directly related to their homelessness in that they would often break into houses or buildings in order to sleep or steal food. Cars were sometimes stolen so that goods from burglaries could be moved, but most of the motor vehicle thefts involved joy riding (Baron, 1995:142).

Violent Offences

In 2000, 77 percent of all violent crime charges were for assault, 15 percent were for robbery, 8 percent were for sexual assault, and 0.2 percent were for homicide (Logan, 2001:20). As with property crime, the majority of violent crimes that young people commit are minor (in particular, minor assault). This is particularly true for girls. In 1998, more than two-thirds (67.3 percent) of violent crime charges for girls were for common assault, the corresponding proportion for boys was 46 percent. However, girls are charged at younger ages than boys. Violent offence charges peak for male youth at age 16 and 17, but at 14 and 15 for girls. The next most frequent violent offence charges for both male and female youth are assault causing bodily harm (20 percent and 16 percent respectively) and robbery (19 percent and 9 percent). These proportions have changed little over the past ten years. What has changed, and dramatically, is robbery. The rate of youth charged with robbery has doubled over the last ten years, from 7 to 15 per 10,000 (Savoie, 1999:5,6,9). While offence patterns have remained consistent since the YOA was implemented (Corrado and Markwart, 1994; Carrington, 1995), violent crime rates have increased largely due to increases in common assault and robbery (Savoie, 1999:6). As we will see in the next chapter, while girls' patterns are similar to boys, their crime rates are significantly lower. Later in the chapter, we will discuss the extent to which increases in violent offence charges can be accounted for by changes in police charging practices.

Contrary to media impressions, the elderly, the very young, and strangers are not the primary targets of youth violence. As Figure 3.3 shows, in 1998, only 2 percent of the victims of youth violence are age 55 or older, 11 percent are younger and the majority (52 percent), are their own age. Two thirds (60 percent) of the victims were acquaintances of the youth, and boys' offences more often involve strangers (22 percent) than girls' offences (12 percent). Youth are also no more likely than adults to use weapons. Fourteen percent of youth violent charges involved a weapon compared to 13 percent of adult charges. Nonetheless, boys and girls used knives with the same frequency, which was more than adult males (48 percent vs. 38 percent) and about the same as women (45 percent). Boys (15 percent), similar to men (18 percent), used firearms

FIGURE 3.3

Age and Sex of Victims of Violent Crimes Committed by Youth, 1998

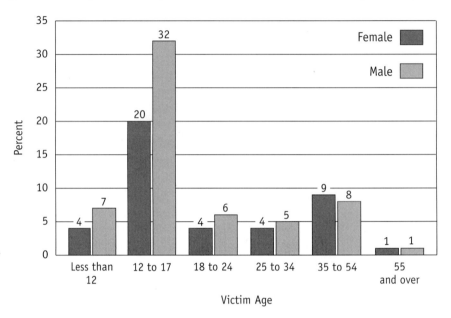

Note: Percentage may not add to 100% due to rounding.

Source: Statistics Canada, Cat. No. 85-00219(13).

more than girls and women (3 percent). Location of the offence is one area where youth violence differs from that of adults.

Where most adult violence occurs in the home (60 percent), youth violence most often occurs in public places (35 percent), 24 percent occurs at school and 24 percent at home. Of all youth violence charges in 1998, only 10 percent occurred on school property, but charge rates are lower for school related violence than other types suggesting that this is an underestimate (Savoie, 1999:9–12). School self-report surveys indicate that there is more minor assault on school property than is suggested by police statistics. A 1995 survey of Calgary middle and high schools reports that 31 percent of boys and 41 percent of girls reported having slapped, punched, or kicked someone in the last year and 24 percent of the girls and 33 percent of the boys reported having threatened to hurt someone (Smith et al, 1995). Another Canadian survey, focusing on more serious acts of violence found that half the boys surveyed (52 percent) and one-fifth of the girls (21 percent) reported that "they had beaten up another kid once or twice" (Artz:1998:27).

Sexual Assault

Sexual assault, an area of youth violence about which we know relatively little, appeared to be on the increase after the YOA was implemented. From 1986 to 1988, sexual-assault charges increased from .94 percent of all police youth charges to 1.10 percent. Corrado and Markwart (1994:352) report a 103 percent increase in the rate of sexual-assault charges against youth from 1986 to 1992. However, it declined for six years in a row until 2000 when the rate increased by 18 percent from 58 to 69 per 10,000, accounting for 1.7 percent of all police youth charges and 7 percent of all sexual assault charges (Logan, 2001:12,14, 20). On the other hand, children and youth are most likely to be victims of sexual assault. Two-thirds of the victims of sexual assault (62%) in 1997 were under the age of 18 and 82% are girls and women. Sixty-nine percent of the victims under age 12 are girls and one third (31 percent) are boys. Victimization survey results suggest that child and youth sexual victimizations are less likely to be reported to police indicating that police based statistics for youth victimizations are underestimates (Statistics Canada, 1999:11). The next chapter discusses youth victimization in more detail.

Until recently, sexual assault by young people tended to be ignored or dismissed as minor or experimental in nature (Brayton, 1996). Increases in rates of sexual assault may thus be explained by changing attitudes. To the extent that the public is more sensitized to some behaviours as constituting sexual offences, people are likely reporting more behaviours as sexual offences and police are likely responding and charging these offences more often. As with overall violent crime increases, a large portion of sexual assault is accounted for by minor offences (e.g., touching) (Carrington, 1995:67).

While some sexual assault may be characterized as "experimental" or "minor," even these offences can have serious consequences for both victims and offenders. A sexual assault interpreted as "experimentation" may involve an older child taking advantage of a younger child. In these situations, the older child has often been placed in a position of trust. More specifically, babysitters (most often male) have sexually assaulted children (most often female) in their charge, and older children sometimes sexually assault younger siblings (see Box 3.1). Some youth sexual assault does involve rape, and the accused may be very young. In one recent case, an 11-year-old boy was accused of raping a 13-year-old girl; according to court testimony, four boys (aged 10, 11, and 13) "ripped off her jeans" and held her down "so that the eleven year old could rape her" (Wattie, 1996).

Murder

While public fears have been fuelled by media reports of particularly violent murders, as mentioned earlier, there are not major gaps between murders known to and reported by police and cases that go to court. Of all crime statistics, those on homicide are the most reliable and they indicate that homicide rates, where young offenders are

BOX 3.1

Typology of Adolescent Sex Offenders

Naive Experimenter

- Offender: young boys, 11–14 years of age
- Victim: younger child, 2–6, usually female
- Usually involves one or a few acts that are sexually explorative (fondling)
- Offences not usually progressive
- No use of force or threat

Undersocialized Child Exploiter

- Offender: older boys aged 12–17
- Victim: younger child, aged 10–12, usually female, but not always
- Involves intercourse, masturbation, oral sex, exposure to pornography
- A high risk of reoffending
- Uses manipulation, rewards, and enticement

Pseudo-Socialized Child Exploiter

- Offender: is similar to the undersocialized but has good social skills and acts self-confident—is himself a victim of ongoing abuse

- Gets sexual pleasure through exploitation of others

Sexual Aggressive

- Offender: male 13–18
- Victim: generally female
- Offences violent, involve penetration with victim degradation—respond to resistance with aggression
- Desires power through domination and humiliation
- Offender often a victim of family violence and sexual assault

Sexual Compulsive

- Offender: male aged 14–18
- Victim: either sex, any age
- Behaviour results from psychological disorder, substance abuse, severe family dysfunction
- Offence is impulsive

Peer-Group Influenced

- Offender: male, young teen
- Victim: females of own age
- Offence often involves gang rape
- Motivated by peer pressure and desire for approval

Source: O'Brien and Bera (1986).

the accused, are no higher today than they were 25 years ago. In fact, youth homicide rates were considerably higher 25 years ago than they were for most of the YOA years (see Figure 3.4). Both Silverman (1990) and Silverman and Kennedy (1993) found no increase in the per capita rate of youth homicide in Canada between 1970 and 1990.

Homicide rates have remained fairly constant since 1986, when there were 38 homicide cases accounting for .03 percent of all young persons charged by police. By 1988, the number of youth homicide cases had increased to 48, or .04 percent of total young persons charged by police. Even the addition of 16- and 17-year-olds to the youth justice system in 1985 did not impact significantly on the numbers of youth charged (Statistics Canada, 1996). Throughout the 1990s, young offenders accounted for, on average, 9 percent of all persons accused of homicide and 14 percent of these were girls. Two-thirds of those accused of homicide are in the 16–34 age group which accounts for only 27 percent of the total population in Canada (Fedorowycz, 1999:8,12). In 2000, 41 young offenders were charged with murder or manslaughter, which amounted to .04 percent of all police youth charges for that year (Logan, 2001:20).

FIGURE 3.4

Youth Aged 12–17 Accused of a Homicide Offence

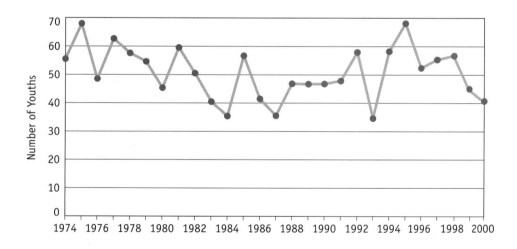

Sources: Canadian Criminal Statistics (1994); Doob, Marinos, and Varma (1995), Fedorowycz (1999); Logan (2001).

Meloff and Silverman's (1992) examination of homicide rates for Canadian youth between the years 1962 and 1983 is the most detailed and it provides us with the following information about youth homicide during this period:

1. Eighty percent of youth homicides in Canada involved one offender and one victim; only 3 percent involved more than three victims and offenders (21).
2. Thirty-five percent of youth homicide cases involved guns, 30 percent involved stabbing, and 22 percent involved beating. All other means of homicide (drowning, strangling, arson, etc.) accounted for 13 percent of the events (22).
3. Similar to homicide cases involving adults, homicides committed by youth most commonly involved parents, family, and acquaintances as the victims. Parents were victims in 14 percent of the cases, other family members in 19.5 percent of the cases, and acquaintances in 35 percent of the cases. Strangers accounted for 31.5 percent of the victims (23). The most recent homicide statistics from Statistics Canada indicate the same pattern of victim/offender relationship. In 1998, 30 percent of the victims of youth homicides were strangers, 21 percent were family members and the remainder were acquaintances (Fedorowycz, 1999:12).
4. Crime-based homicide is proportionately small, and when it does occur it usually involves strangers. Of all crime-based homicides committed by youth in Canada during this 20-year-period, 70 percent were theft-related, 21 percent involved sex, and 9 percent involved some other crime (24).
5. Youth homicide rates in the United States are 10 times higher than those in Canada (28).

Administrative Offences

Administrative offences, which occur after a person has been arrested, involve interference with the administration of justice. Some of these offences appear in police statistics, others in court data. The category includes failure to comply with a disposition, failure to appear (in court), escape from lawful custody, being unlawfully at large, failure to comply with a probation order, and less common offences such as breach of recognizance or contempt against the youth court. Administrative offences occur at different stages of the judicial process. For example, failure to appear in court and failure to comply with an undertaking occur before a disposition is imposed. Offences that take place after the court disposition include escape from lawful custody, being unlawfully at large, and failure to comply with a probation order. Some administrative offences, such as failure to appear, or escape from lawful custody, are Criminal Code offences. Other offences involve charges under the Young Offenders Act or Youth Criminal Justice Act. YOA and YCJA administrative charges, such as failure to comply, are connected with a disposition (usually probation or a community service order) that is ordered under the authority of the YOA or YCJA.

According to Statistics Canada figures, between 1987 and 1992 the number of cases involving offences against the administration of justice almost doubled, rising from 9,440 to 17,007 (these figures exclude Ontario, British Columbia, and the Northwest Territories). In 1991–92, one-quarter of the youth court caseload (26 percent) were offences against the administration of youth justice (Gagnon and Doherty, 1993:3). In 1994–95, when all provinces and territories were included in court statistics, there were 10,704 YOA charges, 10,633 of which involved failure to comply with a disposition; in addition, there were 10,041 Criminal Code charges for failure to appear. These two charges together accounted for most of the administrative charges against young offenders (Statistics Canada, 1996:9–12).

More recent figures are not directly comparable to pre-1992 statistics, but they do demonstrate that administrative offences continue to make up a considerable and steadily increasing portion of youth court cases. In 1999–2000, two offences accounted for almost one-quarter of all cases going before the court. Eleven percent of the cases were charged with failure to appear in court and 13 percent were charged with failure to comply with a court disposition. Combined YOA and Criminal Code administrative offence charges accounted for approximately 30 percent of all cases appearing before youth court in 1999–2000. This is particularly significant since these offences are more likely than any other offence category to result in a custody sentence (48 percent and 39 percent of cases respectively) (Sudworth and deSouza, 2001:5,8,14). It is also significant because some portion of the increase in the overall youth crime rate may be due to these increases in administrative charges (Schissel, 1997:82), a point we will return to later in the chapter. The characteristics of youth charged with these offences, in particular girls and Aboriginal youth, are discussed in the next chapter.

MEASUREMENT ISSUES

The Violent Crime Debate

While the public is concerned about violent crime, and its concerns are fueled by the reporting of specific cases in the news media, the academic community is divided on the question of whether or not violent crime is on the rise. The main concern for academics stems from an awareness that levels of reported or official crime are a "political as well as an **empirical** issue" (Doob, Marinos, and Varma, 1995:16). As discussed earlier, determining how much crime we have in our society depends on what statistics we look at, on how police are behaving in relation to public pressures to clamp down on criminal activity, and on people's willingness to define or report activities as criminal. Concerns about violent crime have given rise to an interesting debate among Canadian criminologists.

BOX 3.2

Kids Who Kill

Jason Gamache ... [was a] strapping six foot one inch handsome 15-year-old youth ... Before October 24, 1992, there was nothing to suggest that this boy would lure an unsuspecting younger child into darkened woods, rape and ... murder her ... What the neighbours did not know was that the youth was already on probation for two previous minor sex offences ... [A] B.C. supreme court jury in Victoria convicted him of Dawn's murder. He is now serving a life sentence.

The 13-year-old boy left his house and walked down a short makeshift road, across the highway and through the woods to the comfortable cedar home where the Jarvis family lived. He rang the door bell and waited. When John Jarvis, 43, opened the door, the boy shouldered the pump-action shotgun and blew off the businessman's face from six feet away ... Reta Jarvis, 41, was also shot and seriously injured on the same night by the boy that had shot her husband ... [W]arning signs had been flashing. The youth allegedly came from a home marked by poverty and domestic violence. It was common knowledge that the youth also had a drinking problem, as well as an addiction to chewing tobacco ... "It just happened, I was angry," he told the RCMP. The question of what sort of anger could make a 13-year-old commit that sort of atrocity still haunts all those touched by the crime. The boy, who turned 14 in February, pleaded guilty to second-degree murder and attempted murder, and received the maximum sentence allowed under the Young Offenders Act at that time—five years less a day.

The inside of Robert's quarters could be that of any teenager—an album of family photos even lies open on the desk ... "When I got these pictures a few weeks ago," Robert says thoughtfully, "I could see the proof that they really did love me." But that simple realization, which so many sons and daughters take for granted, was far beyond Robert's grasp on Mother's Day of 1992. That is when he took a 12-gauge pump-action shotgun and killed his 17-year-old brother, 42-year-old mother and 49-year-old father at the home they shared. Robert had just turned 14 ... [He] is now 16, faces three counts of first-degree murder and a possible life sentence ... "He saw himself as helpless, worthless and completely dependent on his parents ... yet he saw his parents as preventing him from living" ... Robert has his own ideas about what would constitute an appropriate punishment. "I don't think it's possible," he says, "but if a judge wanted to give me the death penalty, I would accept that. I can't die three times, but I will never have a normal life."

Source: Excerpted from Kahila (1994).

According to a 1992 report prepared for Statistics Canada (Frank, 1992), the per capita rate of youth violence doubled after 1986. In 1986, the rate of crimes against the person was 41.5 per 10,000 youth. By 1992, the rate had more than doubled to 90 per 10,000 youth—an increase of 117 percent. Frank suggests that the overall increase in violent charges was largely owing to minor assaults. He adds, however, that some of this rate change may have been created by changes in public attitudes toward violence—changes that led to increases in the reporting of violent crime and/or changes in law-enforcement practices and the willingness of the Crown to prosecute cases.

By way of contrast, Corrado and Markwart (1994) argue that there has been a real increase in violent crime committed by Canadian youth. They present data for the same years as Frank, but calculate rate changes for specific offence categories. Their calculations show increased rates in all categories of violent offences. From 1986 to 1992, the rate of Assault Level I (minor assault) increased by 142 percent, assault causing harm by 90 percent, robbery involving firearms by 267 percent, and robberies involving other weapons by 121 percent. Contrary to Frank, Corrado and Markwart argue that these rate increases cannot be accounted for by changes in policing. UCR statistics indicate that, between 1986 and 1992, there was no change in the rate of police charging to not charging for assault causing harm or robbery. Although there was an increase (from 50 to 61 percent) in the proportion of youth charged (vs. not charged) with common assault, Corrado and Markwart argue that this change in charging practice "can only account for approximately 20 percent of the increase in that period" (1994:351).

While it can be argued that a fear of further victimization would result in greater reporting of these incidents, Corrado and Markwart take the position that there are no survey data to support the hypothesis of a greater social sensitivity toward violence. Further, since half the victims of minor and aggravated youth assaults are other youth (Frank, 1992), they suggest it is equally plausible "that the fear of retaliation, or peer group ostracization, might inhibit youth victims from reporting" (1994:353). And while Frank (1992) suggests that **zero-tolerance policies** toward youth violence in many Canadian school districts can also lead to more crimes being reported to police, Corrado and Markwart argue that it is equally plausible that increased reporting is a reflection of increasing levels of crime in schools. They point out that the Toronto-based Safer Schools Task Force reported an almost 40 percent increase in crimes on school grounds between 1987 and 1990. Similarly, a survey of 4,392 high-school students in Vancouver (McCreary Centre Society, 1993, as cited in Corrado and Markwart, 1994:354) found that 40 percent of males had been involved in a fight in the previous year, while in the previous month 23 percent had carried a weapon, most notably knives and razors (Corrado and Markwart, 1994).

Carrington's Challenge

Carrington (1995) disputes Corrado and Markwart's interpretation of UCR statistics and challenges their conclusion about the reality of violent crime increases. More specifically, he takes exception to the following two statements by Corrado and Markwart (1994):

> The per capita rate of young persons charged with Criminal Code offences increased by a relatively modest 25 percent between 1986 and 1992. (350)

> There has been a real and substantial increase in youth violence in Canada in recent years. (354)

With regard to the first statement, Carrington maintains that it is not useful to use police charges as a method of comparing changes in crime rates over time. He agrees with Frank that police charging practices are susceptible to changing public attitudes and zero-tolerance policies. For this reason, Carrington argues that rate comparisons should be based on crimes reported to police rather than on crimes charged by police. Making just such a comparison, he finds that between 1986 and 1992 violent crime increased by 19 percent, not the 25 percent reported by Corrado and Markwart. Since reported crime increases are lower than charge increases, police charging practices did change between 1986 and 1992.

Perhaps the most compelling evidence against Corrado and Markwart's position comes from a comparison of crime rates in 1992 to years prior to 1986. Compared to earlier years, 1986 was a year with one of the lowest rates of violent offence charges for young offenders while the rate for 1992 was one of the highest. Carrington points out that comparisons based on these two years are meaningless. "Using 1986 as a base-line year for comparison of youth crime rates is like using the employment rate in the depths of a recession as a baseline for assessing annual employment rate: in comparison, any other year will seem high" (Carrington, 1995:62).

In Carrington's view, a more appropriate approach is to compare the average level of reported crime for different periods. This type of comparison reveals increases in most violent offence categories and a decrease in robbery with firearms. Nonetheless, none of Carrington's comparisons show the kinds of increases reported by Corrado and Markwart. On the basis of these new figures, Carrington concludes,

> [much] of the increase in police reported violent youth crime is actually in offenses against the person that are generally nonviolent; but there has been a substantial increase in the police reported rate of assaults causing harm. This indeed represents a substantial increase in police reported violent crime. (1995:70)

Carrington links this increase to a much wider trend toward increased police reporting of violent crime. The most recent Canadian victimization survey results support the notion that crime hasn't increased but police reporting has. According to Gartner and Doob (1994),

> essentially the same proportion of the population (24 percent) experienced at least one incidence of criminal victimization in 1993 as compared to 1988. Any change in public attitudes, especially with regard to violent offenses is likely to result in increases in crime rates known to police, specifically because such a small proportion of these offenses, in particular assaults and sexual assaults, are reported to police. In 1993 only 32 percent of assaults and 10 percent of sexual assaults of all levels were reported to police. (13)

Meanwhile, Gabor (1999) entered the debate and questioned Carrington's use of crime statistics aggregated for the whole country. He maintains that increases in violent charges for youth in specific Canadian cities are not likely attributable to increases in police charging. Gabor provides no evidence to support his claim, only the illogical suggestion that because motor vehicle thefts are consistently reported and have shown a doubling in charge rates from 1986 to 1996, this must also be true of violent youth crime in major Canadian cities (387). As we will see later in the chapter, Carrington (1999) also examines provincial level data and provides strong evidence of major increases in police charging after the YOA was implemented.

Validity and Reliability

As suggested by the violent crime debate, another major issue for academics concerned with the measurement of criminal activity, be it youth or adult, is the **reliability** and **validity** of the measuring instrument. Reliability refers to whether or not we can repeat the results that we get; validity refers to whether we are measuring what we think we are measuring. We have come to accept that a ruler is a reliable and valid measure of length or height. Things are not as simple when it comes to measuring crime. Both reliability and validity can be compromised in official statistics. We have already seen how easy it is to find inconsistencies in police-based statistics that depend on what is compared and how the comparisons are made. In addition, the validity of police statistics is always an issue because crimes known to police and clearance rates are susceptible to public and political pressures, as well as changes in policy, police administration, training, and recruitment practices. Similarly, court statistics are susceptible to public, institutional, and political pressures, as well as police, Crown prosecutor, and judicial behaviour. In later chapters, we will also examine how race, class, and gender affect who is charged and who is taken to court.

Lying about Crime

Self-report survey results are generally accepted as reliable in that researchers can get relatively comparable results from their surveys. Nonetheless, some are sceptical about self-report questionnaires because of an assumption that people will not be truthful in filling them out. This is particularly a concern with regard to young people because it is thought that they, more so than adults, may feel a sense of bravado about misdeeds and will want to elaborate and exaggerate their involvement. Adults, on the other hand, are thought to be more likely than young people to underreport their criminal activities because they fear the consequences of being caught.

A very interesting study was undertaken to address just this issue. Hindelang, Hirschi, and Weis (1981) conducted a large survey in Seattle, Washington, throughout the years 1978 and 1979 for the purpose of testing the reliability and validity of self-report questionnaires. Their research involved surveying a sample that included high-school students and young people not in school who had police records and/or court records. Responses to the self-report questions were then cross-checked with police records, court records, school records and parents to determine the truthfulness of responses. Relevant to our question, they found that, in general, young people do not lie about their misdeeds.

What Are We Measuring?

It is validity that is considered particularly problematic with respect to self-report questionnaires. The issue concerns the types of questions that have been included in the survey, what they measure, and the usefulness of responses for making assessments about crime levels. Box 3.3 presents questions from Nye and Short's (1957) self-report questionnaire. These questions, which include *have you ever skipped school? ... disobeyed your parents? ... defied openly the authority of your parents?*, are very different from the ones used by Tribble (1972) in one of the first Canadian self-reported delinquency studies. All of Tribble's questions (e.g., *Have you ever seriously hurt an animal? ... beat up another person? ... damaged someone's property? ... forged a cheque?*) refer to behaviours that are controlled by the Criminal Code. Only some of Nye and Short's questions (such as *Have you ever hit children that haven't done anything to you? ... hurt or inflicted injuries on someone just for kicks?*) cite behaviours that could refer to Criminal Code items. Many of their questions concern delinquencies, not crimes. The result, of course, was that their questionnaire yielded much higher rates of delinquent and criminal behaviour than Tribble's.

This is not to say that one questionnaire is right and the other is wrong. Rather, it is important to be knowledgeable about what is being measured when we interpret the results of self-report surveys. Since Nye and Short's questionnaire yields higher rates than Tribble's, it would be wrong to interpret their results to mean that the young people in Nye and Short's survey were more criminal or delinquent in their behaviour than those in Tribble's survey. As we will see in Chapter 5, what is known about delinquent behaviour, and how it is explained and understood, depends a great deal on the kinds of questions that have been asked in self-report studies and on how the results of these studies have been interpreted.

Other validity problems stem from attempts to compare self-report or victimization surveys with police statistics or court statistics. It is often assumed that self-report questionnaires measure the true incidence or prevalence of crime and that police statistics do not. Strictly speaking, results from the two are not comparable because of the nature of police activity and the role of police in the criminal justice system. As we saw earlier, police have discretionary power with respect to the kinds of behaviours they will charge and also in their interpretation of the Criminal Code. A police officer must determine if someone's behaviour is a criminal offence in law. Some offences known to the police are determined by them to be **unfounded**. Police may categorize an offence as "unfounded" after investigating a complaint and determining that either no crime took place or there wasn't enough evidence of a crime for a charge to be laid. Alternatively, police may use their discretionary power and determine that an offence is not serious enough to proceed with a charge (in lieu of a charge, the officer may give the person a warning). Yet, persons who have been involved in "unfounded" situations might report in a self-report questionnaire that they had committed a crime—or, in a victimization survey, that they had been victimized. In either case, it is a judgment call as to which source is valid as a "true" measure of whether a crime took place.

Recalling Crime

A related methodological problem stems from people's ability to recall with any accuracy the things they have done or experienced. For example, a teen may have broken into someone's house, but not recall when he did so. Nonetheless, the incident might stand out in his mind as a significant event. Assuming, then, that the incident occurred 15 months ago, the teen may report that it happened in the last 12 months. In this hypothetical example, the reporting of the incident, even if it had resulted in police charges and court appearances, would not appear in official statistics for the year in which it was reported to have occurred. Similarly, comparisons of self-report results

Self-Report Questionnaire

Have you ever:

1. Skipped school?
2. Been in a fist fight with another person?
3. Disobeyed your parents?
4. Driven a car without a driver's licence?
5. Left home?
6. Defied openly the authority of your parents?
7. Driven a car dangerously or beyond the speed limit?
8. Taken small objects (less than $2.00) that did not belong to you?
9. Taken objects of an average value (between $2.00 and $50.00) that did not belong to you?
10. Taken objects of greater value ($50.00 or more) that did not belong to you?
11. Taken things, ignoring that they didn't belong to you?
12. Taken part in teenage gang fights?
13. Taken a car for a spin without the permission of the owner?
14 Entered into sexual relations with someone of the same sex?
15. Hit children that haven't done anything to you?
16. Been expelled from school or put on trial?
17. Bought or drunk beer, wine, or some other alcoholic drinks?
18. Hurt or inflicted injuries on someone just for kicks?
19. Intentionally damaged or destroyed public or private property that does not belong to you?
20. Used or sold drugs (narcotics, goofballs, etc.)?
21. Entered into sexual relations with someone of the opposite sex?

Source: Nye and Short (1957:328).

with court statistics are problematic because of the way in which people are processed through the courts. What a person has done, what she or he is charged with, and whether charges are dropped or modified through various plea negotiations can vary considerably. More important, as we will see in Chapters 8 and 9, these decisions vary by race, class, and gender. Hence, the resulting police and court statistics may not accurately reflect the actual offence that occurred.

In victimization surveys, people are even more likely to confuse or forget the time of occurrence because these events are usually always significant and sometimes frightening or traumatic. In addition, Bortner (1988:149) suggests that victimization surveys would give a less reliable picture of unreported crime than self-report surveys because victims are more likely to remember events that they reported to the police. Victimization surveys also suffer from the problem of **telescoping**—victims report an event correctly, but place it in the wrong time period. Finally, it is impossible to estimate the number of offenders involved in a particular offence because the unit of measurement in a victimization survey is the event, not the offender. Hence, unlike self-report surveys, victimization surveys do not allow us to determine if a small number of offenders account for a large portion of offences.

REVISITING QUESTIONS ABOUT YOUTH CRIME

Which Source of Information Is the "Best"?

As we have seen, all three major sources of information on young offenders—official statistics, self-report surveys, and victimization surveys—yield useful information if used appropriately. More to the point, all three sources provide answers to questions about how much and what type of crime young people commit. However, the answers they provide are different, and some seem contradictory. Thus we are left with the question, Which source is the most accurate for the purpose of measuring youth crime? There are two very different answers to this question.

Hindelang, Hirschi, and Weis (1981) take issue with the question itself. Alleged discrepancies between official statistics, self-report surveys, and victimization surveys are an illusion, they argue. Because each source is measuring something very different, no one source is more accurate than the other. Official statistics, whether from police sources or court records, generally measure more serious criminal behaviour. Self-report surveys tend to measure minor delinquent behaviours such as mischief or vandalism.

While there may be some truth in this argument, Bortner (1988) cautions against the belief that official statistics are representative of all youth involved in serious crime. Her argument suggests that there may be something of a **self-fulfilling prophecy** operating with regard to official statistics. To the extent that official statistics include

---

BOX 3.4

Sample Questions in Victimization Studies

Household Questions

Now I'd like to ask some questions about crime. They refer only to the last 6 months [for example, between January 1, 1987, and June 30, 1987].

- During the last 6 months, did anyone break into or somehow illegally get into your (apt./home), garage, or another building on your property?

- (Other than the incident(s) just mentioned) Did you find a door jimmied, a lock forced, or any other signs of an attempted break-in?

- Was anything at all stolen that is kept outside your home or happened to be left out, such as a bicycle, a garden hose, or lawn furniture (other than any incidents already mentioned)?

- Did anyone take something belonging to you, or to any member of this household, from a place where you or they were temporarily staying, such as a friend's or relative's home, a hotel or motel, or a vacation home?

- What was the total number of motor vehicles (cars, trucks, etc.) owned by you or any other member of this household during the last 6 months?

- Did anyone steal or try to steal, or use (it/any of them) without permission?

- Did anyone steal or try to steal parts attached to (it/any of them), such as a battery, hubcaps, tape-deck, etc.?

Individual Questions

The following questions refer only to things that happened to you during the last 6 months [for example, between January 1, 1987, and June 30, 1987].

- Did you have your (pocket picked/purse snatched)?

- Did anyone take something (else) directly from you by using force, such as by a stickup, mugging, or threat?

- Did anyone try to rob you by using force or threatening to harm you (other than any incidents already mentioned)?

- Did anyone beat you up, attack you, or hit you with something, such as a rock or bottle (other than any incidents already mentioned)?

- Were you knifed, shot at, or attacked with some other weapon by anyone at all (other than any incidents already mentioned)?

- Did anyone threaten to beat you up or threaten you with a knife, gun, or some other weapon, not including telephone threats (other than any incidents already mentioned)?

- Did anyone try to attack you in some way (other than any incidents already mentioned)?

- During the last 6 months, did anyone steal things that belonged to you from inside any car or truck, such as packages or clothing?

- Was anything stolen from you while you were away from home, for instance, at work, in a theatre or restaurant, or while travelling?

- (Other than any incidents you've already mentioned) was anything (else) stolen from you during the last 6 months?

- Did you find any evidence that someone attempted to steal something that belonged to you (other than any incidents already mentioned)?

- Did you call the police during the last 6 months to report something that happened to you which you thought was a crime? (Do not count any calls made to the police concerning the incidents you have just told me about.)

- Did anything happen to *you* during the last 6 months which you thought was a crime, but did not report to the police (other than any incidents already mentioned)?

Source: Hindelang and McDermott (1981).

minority and poor youth more than other youth, and to the extent that courts and police believe that these are the people most likely to be involved in serious criminal activities, police responses to minority and poor youth will be relatively severe. Similarly, a belief that middle-class, nonminority youth are less likely to be involved in serious criminal activity, or more likely to be involved in minor kinds of offences, decreases the likelihood that the official police response will be severe. The end result is that we may continue to respond severely to disadvantaged youth while ignoring the offences of more privileged youth (Bortner, 1988:150–52). These responses are then reflected in official statistics, which in turn reinforce stereotypical beliefs about who is involved in crime.

We can never say for certain that crime is increasing or decreasing because none of the three major sources of information provides a direct measure of criminal activity. Nonetheless, there does seem to be some evidence that crime levels, overall, may be levelling off (Doob, Marinos, and Varma, 1995:16). And, in spite of various measurement problems, all three sources of information confirm that most criminal activity involving young people is property crime, and that only a small proportion of youth criminal activity involves violent crime, the largest portion of which is minor assault.

Crime under the YOA versus Crime under the JDA

Many people were concerned and are convinced that the YOA was responsible for increasing youth crime. According to a nationwide survey in the mid 1990s, 95 percent of Canadians maintained that the Young Offenders Act needed to be toughened (Bibby, 1995:105) and a survey of a sample of Torontonians indicated that a majority believed that the youth court under the YOA was too lenient (Sprott, 1996). As we have seen, a majority of academics disagree.

Schissel (1995:122) takes the position that official rates of youth crime are more related to the changing political nature of crime control than to increases or changes in the criminal activity of youth over the last 20 years. His research examines the relationship between rates of Criminal Code offences for young offenders and the formal and informal processing of these cases in the years 1970 to 1990. Formal processing refers to cases handled through the courts, in which the accused enters a plea and has her or his case adjudicated by the judge. Informal processing refers to cases handled outside of courts, in which youth are not charged but are instead released to the custody of their parents or a social agency.

Schissel's work shows a dramatic increase in Criminal Code offences in 1984, the year in which the Young Offenders Act came into effect. Another increase followed in 1985, when 16- and 17-year-old youth were brought into the system. While these increases could be interpreted to mean that young people were more criminal, Schissel suggests otherwise. He points out that as the Young Offenders Act was being implemented, and as older youth were being brought into the system, the number of cases processed informally began to drop and there was a dramatic increase in the formal processing of young offenders. Hence, after the introduction of the YOA, there was more formal processing of teenagers through the courts than was evident under the Juvenile Delinquents Act (Schissel, 1995:123–25). Schissel argues that police were far more disposed to laying a charge under the YOA than they were under the JDA. Hence, any statistics based on police charges will reflect this change in police behaviour.

Carrington (1999) also addresses this issue by examining youth crime rates from 1977 to 1996 through a comparison of police reported crime to police charges for each province. His results confirm Schissel's findings. Carrington concludes that police charging practices did change such that with the introduction of the YOA police increased their charges for young offenders compared to their practices under the JDA. However, this change "was especially pronounced" in Saskatchewan and Ontario, but also occurred in Nova Scotia, Prince Edward Island, and the Northwest Territories. New Brunswick and Manitoba maintained a fairly high apprehension and charge rate with both the JDA and YOA whereas British Columbia and Newfoundland and Labrador began to decrease formal charging after a brief period of increases when the YOA was first implemented. Quebec's charge rate declined into the 1990s, hence their use of discretion increased and Alberta and the Yukon had consistently high charge ratios throughout the YOA period that are not clearly attributable to the YOA (24–25). With an increased emphasis on diversion for non-violent offences, we should expect youth charge rates to decline dramatically with the implementation of the YCJA.

Increases in youth charge rates under the YOA aside, comparisons with rates of delinquency under the JDA show the same pattern of offences that we now see under the YOA. Statistics Canada figures for juvenile courts in 1980 (excluding British Columbia) indicate that there were 97,264 charges of delinquency. The most frequent juvenile offences in 1980 were break and enter (accounting for 26 percent of all charges laid) and theft (21 percent). Violent crimes accounted for 4.2 percent of total charges, and charges under the Narcotic Control Act were 2.3 percent of the total (Statistics Canada, 1981:2). Figures for 1982, which included British Columbia, indicate a total of 121,379 charges. The most common offences were break and enter (35 percent) and theft (29 percent). Overall, property offences accounted for 83 percent of total charges, and violent offences for 4.8 percent of the total (Statistics Canada, 1984:3).

Youth Crime Waves

Another way of assessing the volume, severity, or magnitude of youth crime is to compare youth rates over time to crime rates for adults. While youth crime rates have shown an increase from 1962 to 1990, so too have adult crime rates; hence, youth crime rates are simply mirroring overall crime rates. Starting in 1962, property crime rates increased for about 20 years, began to level off in the early 1980s, and increased slightly in the early 1990s. Violent crime rates and other Criminal Code charges show a steady increase over the 28-year period. Minor assaults have consistently accounted for the majority of violent crimes, increasing from 71 percent in 1962 to 77 percent in

1990 (Statistics Canada, 1992:4–5). This crime pattern mirrors that of young offenders. Moreover, since victimization rates have not changed since at least 1988 (Gartner and Doob, 1994), it can be argued that young people were not more involved in crime in the 1990s than they were in the 1980s or the 1970s.

Parallels notwithstanding, there are some important differences between adult crime and youth crime. Comparisons of all persons charged by police with Criminal Code offences for the years 1986 to 1988 show a greater increase in adult crime (7 percent) than youth crime (1 percent). In addition, three-year averages for the 1986–88 period indicate that adults are more likely than teens to be involved in more serious offences (Statistics Canada, 1990b:3).

Table 3.4 indicates clearly that adults are responsible for far more criminal activity than youth. For 2000, the only areas in which young people even began to approximate adult activity are motor vehicle theft and arson. Youth account for 41 percent of all police charges for motor vehicle theft and 48 percent for arson. The next highest figures for youth are break and enter (37 percent), mischief (33 percent), robbery (34 percent) and theft under $5,000 or petty theft (27 percent).

The proportionate figures for violent offences are even more striking. With the exception of robbery, every offence category is disproportionately represented by adults. Only 8 percent of homicide charges, 9 percent of attempted murder charges, and 15 percent of assault charges involved young offenders. In view of the larger crime picture, then, youth crime does not seem as alarming as is suggested by media reports. Young people are responsible for 16 percent of all violent crime, 27 percent of all property crime, and 21 percent of all other Criminal Code offences. While some would argue that this type of comparison is misleading because the youth age group is considerably smaller than other age groups, as we will see in the next chapter, even comparisons of more specific age groups show that adults far outnumber young people in criminal activity.

SUMMARY

The major sources of information about youth crime are the media, official statistics, self-report surveys, and victimization surveys. Making sense of this information requires a knowledge of the source and what is being measured, as well as an understanding of the limitations of various crime measures. Making sense of public issues and conflicting discourses about the prevalence and severity of youth crime requires a consideration of all sources in a historical comparative context and a recognition of the political nature of information gathering.

Most people get their information about crime from the media. While statistics presented in the media may be correct, they can also be misleading in the absence of (1) an understanding of the limitations of data sources and (2) a historical or social context.

TABLE 3.4

Persons Charged[1] by Age Status, Selected Incidents, 2000

	Age Group	
	Adult	**Youth (12–17)**
	%	%
Homicide[2]	92	8
Attempted murder	91	9
Assaults	85	15
Sexual assaults	82	18
Other sexual offences	83	17
Abduction	96	4
Robbery	66	34
Violent crime—Total	**84**	**16**
Breaking and entering	63	37
Motor vehicle theft	59	41
Fraud	92	8
Theft over $5,000	87	13
Theft $5,000 and under	73	27
Property crime—Total	**73**	**27**
Mischief	67	33
Arson	52	48
Prostitution	98	2
Offensive weapons	78	22
Criminal Code—Total	**79**	**21**
Impaired driving[3]	99	1
Cocaine offences	95	5
Cannabis offences	83	17
Other drug offences	85	15

1. Represents all persons charged in Canada, Uniform Crime Reporting Survey, Canadian Centre for Justice Statistics.

2. Homicide Survey, CCJS.

3. Includes impaired operation of a vehicle causing death, causing bodily harm, alcohol rate over 80 mg., failure/refusal to provide a breath/blood sample. Age of persons charged with impaired driving comes from the incident based survey (UCR2).

Source: Adapted from Statistics Canada (2001), *Juristat,* Cat. No. 85–002-XPE 21(8), p. 19.

Official statistics come from police and courts. These statistics are more a measure of the activities of the agencies themselves than they are of actual criminal or delinquent behaviour. As such, they are particularly susceptible to changing public attitudes and shifts in police surveillance, policy, charging, and sentencing practices. The exercise of discretion decreases with the severity of the offence. Police statistics indicate that youth crime is predominantly property related and that a minority of this crime involves violence. Official statistics for homicide, which are the most reliable, indicate that youth homicide rates were higher 25 years ago than they are today. Overall, youth crime declined for eight years in a row beginning in 1992 and showed a slight increase of 1.4 percent in 2000.

Despite this general decline, official rates for some violent crimes are showing an increase. While there is agreement among criminologists that the majority of violent offences are minor, there is no agreement as to the reason for the increases. Some argue that youth behaviour has changed and cite evidence that serious violent crime is on the increase. Others question the validity of this evidence and point out that there has been a change in police reporting and processing practices. Victimization survey data also suggest changes in police reporting rather than in actual criminal behaviour of youth.

Self-report and victimization surveys give us a better indication than official statistics of the actual volume of crime. Self-report studies demonstrate that the volume of crime is considerably higher than that indicated in police statistics. Estimates range from four to ten times the amount reported in official statistics. A comparative study in Montreal shows no change in the level or nature of self-reported delinquency from 1974 to 1985.

Although Canadian victimization surveys do not give us specific information about youth crime, these general surveys are useful in telling us something about general crime patterns and can be used with other sources to arrive at a more complete picture. Since overall rates of victimization are no higher today than they were in the 1980s, and since police statistics show that youth crime rates parallel adult rates, it would appear that youth are not responsible for more criminal activity today than in the past.

Claims that the YOA is "soft on youth criminals" and led to a youth "crime wave" seem unfounded. Comparisons of youth charges under the JDA and YOA show that patterns of youth crime did not change with the YOA, and that more youth offences were charged and processed through the courts under the YOA than was the case under the JDA.

Claims that youth crime is "out of control" also seem unfounded. Comparisons of official crime rates for young offenders and adults over the last 30 to 35 years show that youth crime rates have not increased as rapidly as adult rates, that adult crime far surpasses youth crime, and that adults are far more likely that youth to be involved in violent offences and drug offences.

CHAPTER 4

The Social Face of Youth Crime

CHAPTER OBJECTIVES

1. To discuss who young offenders are with respect to race/ethnicity, gender, and age.

2. To emphasize the racialization and sociopolitical nature of public images of youth crime.

3. To discuss age-specific crime rates and their significance in understanding trends in youth crime rates.

4. To clarify gender differences by examining different sources of information.

5. To discuss the other side of youth crime: youth victimization and the links between youth crime, victimization, and the status of youth and children in Canadian society.

KEY TERMS

Ethnographic method	Socioeconomic status	Birth cohorts
Longitudinal studies	First Nations	Remedial
Race	Gender	
Ethnicity	Status offences	

INTRODUCTION

In the preceding chapter, we examined official, self-report, and victimization survey statistics on young offenders. The next step in understanding youth crime is to develop a social portrait of young people who have found themselves in conflict with the law. As we saw in Chapter 1, a number of public issues and questions about youth crime stem from assumptions about the social characteristics of youth who break the law. A central aspect of the public discourse on youth crime is that it identifies certain youth as more threatening than others. Age is a concern in the debates in that some interest groups insist that youth criminals are younger now than ever before and that youth under 12 are committing crimes with impunity. Some of the discourse is gendered in that young women are said to be more criminal and more violent than in the past.

Perhaps the most destructive and vitriolic discourse is that which racializes youth crime. It seems that nothing fuels the fires of moral panic more than the image (a patently false one) of nonwhite youth gangs preying on the innocent. Depending on the region of the country, Aboriginal or black youth, or the children of Asian, West Indian, or South American immigrants, are consistently portrayed in the media as more criminal, more dangerous, more "out of control"—and hence more threatening—than Caucasian youth. Toward the end of the 19th century, middle-class Victorian Canadians living in cities felt threatened by "street arabs," their term for the children of the poor. Today, at the beginning of the 21st century, visible-minority youth have been defined in public discourse as a threat. In 1994, there were news stories about violence erupting at Toronto high-school basketball games. While this "hooliganism" was defined as a "black problem," violence is actually more frequent in hockey games and yet is not defined in terms of a "white problem" (Tanner, 1996:119–20).

For criminologists, the social face of youth crime has always been gendered and classed; the young offenders to be studied were impoverished and working-class males living in the urban core areas of large cities. As we saw in the last chapter, research findings from self-report surveys challenged this image. Only in the last 20 years have researchers begun to acknowledge the importance of class, race, and gender—as well as their interconnectedness—in the social construction of youth crime images. By the 1970s, it was apparent to some criminologists that the social face of youth crime was a sociopolitical construction that varied depending on the source of information, be it the media or police and court records. Furthermore, it is now also recognized that youth crime itself is a sociopolitical construction that is reinforced by media portrayals of crime.

Along with the self-report survey, two other methodological developments have altered the face of youth crime for criminologists. The **ethnographic method** of data collection, exemplified by Baron's (1995) research on "street kids" (discussed in the last chapter), is a type of field research in which the details of people's lives are documented through direct participation, observation, or comprehensive interviews. **Longitudinal studies** (data collected for the same group at different periods of time) have lead to a greater emphasis on age and its relation to crime over the life of an individual. Tremblay et al's (1991) research on intervention programs for disruptive schoolboys in Montreal, to be discussed in Chapter 12, is an example of longitudinal research. Here, the effect on the boys of the intervention program was tested for a number of years after the intervention program had been completed.

Only in the last decade have criminologists begun to address the other side of youth crime—youth and children as victims of crime. The growing body of ethnographic information concerning the lives of young offenders has directed attention to the fact that young people are not involved in perpetrating crimes only. In many instances, they are more likely than adults to be the victims of crime. The links between youth victimization and youth criminality are coming under increasing scrutiny as criminologists seek to understand the criminal behaviour of young people. More important, an

---

BOX 4.1

Joey: "The Crime"

It was the night of the grade nine graduation, and Joey and nine friends made plans for a memorable evening. [Joey's friend] Dale was the bait. He perched on the fence circling Citadel Hill, hoping to lure one of the men cruising for sexual partners ... A prospect in a 1991 Dodge truck drove up and the man pulled over ... Dale hopped in, while the other boys piled up beside the driver's window. The man tried to pull away, but Joey and the other boys [opened the door and] pulled him out of the truck ... Joey hit him with the truck door when the man tried to get up ... Dale slid behind the wheel and drove off and the other boys scattered ...

Later, in the small hours of the morning, Dale returned to where the other boys were. Dale had nicked a tree with the truck and had abandoned it on Spring Garden Rd. At 4:00 am, Joey and some of his friends returned to the truck to find that the keys were still in the ignition ... While in the truck they found the man's jacket and in the pocket was his wallet. In it there was approximately 8,000 dollars ... Joey and his friends took the money and spent it.

Source: MacDonald (1994a:6).

understanding of the social face of youth crime is essential to the development of effective responses to youth crime. In this chapter, we will examine the social face of youth crime in terms of race/ethnicity, age, gender, and youth victimization.

RACE/ETHNICITY

"Race" and "ethnicity" are commonly used terms, but their definitions are neither common nor objective. Generally, the term **race** refers to a group of people who share observable physical traits (most commonly, skin colour). **Ethnicity** refers more to identity—a means by which people distinguish themselves, as a group, from others. Language, cultural traditions, and place of ancestral origin are commonly used as distinguishing characteristics among members of an ethnic group (Li, 1990:4–5). As categories, both race and ethnicity are social constructions in that "physical and cultural traits are the basis for defining [racial or ethnic groups] only in so far as they are socially recognized as important" (5). Unfortunately, racial and ethnic distinctions are most often produced and maintained by power differentials between a dominant "racial" or "ethnic" group and a subordinate one (5). As a result, it is often difficult to distinguish empirically between race or ethnicity and class, as measured by **socioeconomic status**. LaPrairie (1994), for example, found in her study of Aboriginal peoples in the city core areas of Regina, Edmonton, Toronto, and Montreal that class may be more important than race in understanding the overrepresentation of Aboriginal youth in the justice system.

While race is clearly a factor of some consequence in the criminal justice system, there is little Canadian information on criminal activity by race or ethnicity, particularly with regard to official statistics. Some provinces and police departments record information on race, but this information is not widely available. Police departments do categorize racial and ethnic information in their occurrence reports (Doob, 1991). These categories range from multiple listings (e.g., white, Hispanic, Negro, Oriental, Arabic, Native Indian, East Indian) to simple "white/other" distinctions. In the latter case, "other" is used to distinguish "Canadians" from people with different cultural backgrounds (Ericson and Haggerty, 1997:283–84). Some police departments have created multicultural units and specialized intelligence units for the purpose of identifying and gathering information on perceived racial and ethnic crime problems. In this regard, "Asian organized crime," "Aboriginal organized crime," and "Asian gangs" have been identified as priorities for criminal intelligence activities (288–89). Recently, Aboriginal "gangs" have become a focus of law-enforcement activities in Winnipeg. Ericson and Haggerty (1997:290) tell of one minority family that was targeted for plainclothes-officer intelligence gathering simply because it was the only minority family in a particular community.

Federal statistics do not provide public information on race and crime largely because human rights organizations have objected to the collection of justice statistics by race. While this prevents exploitation of the data by white supremacists and other racist groups, it also means that much potentially useful information is not available for research. Much of our information on race as a factor in justice systems comes from media reports, police accounts, and court-based research in which race can be ascertained, albeit imperfectly, on a direct observational basis. Other information comes from government inquiries and special reports. This research will be examined in Chapters 8 and 9 when we discuss the processing of youth through the justice system.

Immigrant Gangs

In the context of discussions of gang-related behaviour, the Canadian media have identified four groups of youth as problematic: Asian, Vietnamese, Latin, and Black. Fasiolo and Leckie (1993) examined how gangs are presented in the media by analyzing gang stories that appeared in Canadian daily newspapers between the months of July and October 1992. Most of the gang stories, 77 percent of which came from Vancouver, Montreal, Calgary, Ottawa, and Toronto, had not focused on a specific event, such as a gang-related crime. The gang most frequently cited was the Asian gang. The following example of Asian gang mythology appeared in *The Calgary Sun*:

> For only when *they* [Asian gangs] live in fear that *our* investigators will almost certainly uncover their nefarious deeds, *our* courts will certainly find *them* guilty and *our* prisons await *them*, will *they* stay away from *our* shores. *We* must let the purveyors of these obscenities know that *their* filth is not welcome in *our* city or in *our* province. [italics in original] (Fasiolo and Leckie, 1993:25, cited in Tanner, 1996:6)

As Tanner (1996:6) points out, the most horrifyingly racist aspect of Asian gang mythology is that Caucasian youth gang activities are not ever linked to their race. The terms used in the media are broad, generic identifiers such as "Asian" that serve to brand all visible-minority individuals who are perceived to fit the category.

Gordon (1993, 1995), who researched gang members in British Columbian jails, reports that 68 percent of gang members serving prison sentences in British Columbia are Canadian-born (1995:315). Vancouver's street gangs do draw members from particular ethnic groups (Latin-American, Chinese, Iranian, or Vietnamese), but most gangs are multicultural. Asians are no more likely to be involved in street gangs than any other ethnocultural group or community. Gordon (1995) reports that while the Lotus Jung gang (also known as Jung Ching) "consisted of approximately 40 young males of Chinese and Vietnamese descent, there were two branch gangs (White Lotus and the Sparrows), which had a predominately European and mixed ethnic membership ..." (315).

Joe and Robinson (1980) studied youth gangs in Vancouver's Chinatown over a four-year period, from 1975 to 1979. What is interesting about this study is that of the four gangs that had been in existence in 1975, none was still active by 1979. The gangs had either ceased to exist or were no longer engaging in criminal activity (in some cases, members had graduated to adult gangs). Twenty years later, Gordon (1993, 1995) and Young (1993) report the same finding: youth gangs are not long-lived. In spite of these findings, notions of immigrant gangs persist. As Schissel (1993) states,

> in public policy research the conviction predominates that certain ethnic groups are especially prone to violent and anti-social behaviour. Carrigan (1991) and Fowler (1993) report, for example, that not only are youth gangs becoming increasingly common in Canada's major cities, but that they are drawn from Latin America or specific countries like China or Viet Nam. The underlying message in much of the social analysis is that with immigration comes violence prone youth. (14)

Defining the children of immigrants as particularly troublesome is not a new phenomenon. You may recall from Chapter 1 that in the 1920s and 1930s Winnipeg's youth crime problems were blamed on immigration.

Black Youth

While little is known about the offences of black youth, public discourse began to identify a "black crime problem" in such major cities as Toronto and Montreal in the early 1980s. Solomon (1992), who studied black male students (all recent immigrants from the West Indies) in a Toronto high school, argues that the subcultural practices of black students are in direct conflict with the all-white school authority structure. The "argot-patois" spoken among these students, their reggae music, their dreadlocks and tams are all seen as threats to authority. The hip-hop subculture, with its street-style fashion and (particularly) its "gangsta rap," is also perceived as threatening (Tanner, 1996:89).

Current fears about young black men can be understood as a moral panic brought on by public apprehension about the profound social changes we have been experiencing in recent decades. Tanner (1996) applies Cohen's (1972) views on moral panics to Canadian society in arguing that

> a growing inclination to link youth crime to race is symbolic of broader uncertainties about the impact of newcomers or cultural and racial outsiders on the fabric of Canadian society ... For many citizens, and the police as well, the sight of what appears to be large numbers of black youth hanging out together, publicly playing music ... and wearing strange clothes, is frightening and leads to exaggerated fears about "black crime." (11)

Aboriginal Youth

Only recently have researchers begun to investigate Aboriginal young offenders. The most common offences committed by Aboriginal youth are theft, break and enter, and wilful damage (Shkilnyk, 1985:30). Shkilnyk (1985) and York (1990) suggest that some criminal activity by Aboriginal youth stems from the boredom and despair of life on impoverished reserves. One youth counsellor in Winnipeg estimates that "30 percent of the reserve's teenagers are prepared to commit criminal offences to escape the reserve" (cited in York, 1990:142). York (1990) reports that 75 percent of the young people in the Winnipeg Youth Detention Centre are Aboriginal. Aboriginal youth crime often occurs in the context of substance abuse and the violence that often accompanies it. This violence is often self-inflicted, as the tragic events at Davis Inlet, Newfoundland, testify.

> About 42 of 340 kids regularly sniff gas in this remote Innu island off the coast of Labrador, where six teens high on fumes tried to kill themselves last month. Youths have blown holes in their stomachs with shotguns. Some sniff gas until they're hallucinatory or brain-damaged. (Gorham, 1993:A34)

York (1990:97) reports that the suicide rate for Aboriginal peoples under 25 is six times higher than that for non-Aboriginal youth in the same age group.

While little can be said about actual criminal activity, we do know that Aboriginal youth are overrepresented in court populations. Schissel (1993) found that 18 percent of young offenders processed through an Edmonton court were **First Nations** youth. Bell (1994a) examined a court in London, Ontario, and found that Aboriginal youth were the accused in 12 percent of the court cases. Schissel (1993:11) suggests that much of this overrepresentation may be owing to a high concentration of policing in Native reserve areas. Police are also concentrated in urban core areas, which in some cities (particularly in the west) furthers the risk of apprehension for Aboriginal youth. Ratner (1996) reports that in the early 1990s there were about 6,000 Native youth in Vancouver. Half were said to be "problematic," about 200 were "hard-core" street kids, and many were reserve runaways.

> Most of the reserve émigrés chose to flee the reserve and entertain dreamy expectations of the future—expectations that are quickly dashed, given that they lack work skills transferable to the urban area. Girls turn to prostitution and shoplifting; boys to car theft, stealing, and running drugs. Immersion in alcohol, sex, and drugs (often from the age of 12) ensures school failure, joblessness, and chronic welfare dependency. The predictable sequence for native youths caught in this spiral begins with entry into the child welfare system, advances to more serious delinquencies as the youths "rise" through the criminal justice system, and ends with a slow weaning off the latter, accompanied by burnout and apathy. Thus, the study of native youth delinquency epitomizes, with special poignancy, the obstacles to cultural regeneration faced by off-reserve Aboriginals. (Ratner, 1996:188)

The National Indian Brotherhood, Assembly of First Nations, expressed concern for their youth in a recent discussion paper:

> A study entitled "Locking Up Indians in Saskatchewan" concluded that a treaty Indian boy turning 16 in 1976 had a 70% chance of at least one stay in prison by the age of 25. The corresponding figure for a non-Indian was 8%. Put into context, in Saskatchewan, prison for young treaty Indians had become the equivalent to the promise of a just society which high school and college represented to the rest of Canada. (Canada, 1991:2)

BOX 4.2

How Adults Treat Teens: Some Teenage Views

Students in a Grade 8/9 class were asked to write about how adults treat them. Some of their responses—unedited—follow.

Female, 14, Grade 9

They treat you bad just about everywhere you go. And depending on where you go they'll treat you worse because your black and young. They follow you around, accuse you of stealing, try to rip you off they also give you bad service.

Female, 13, Grade 8

I don't really have any experiences to talk about. But I think it unfair the way adults think that we're suspisious/dangorous. Just because some teenagers are not trustworthy dosen't mean we all are. It's like your going into MacDonolds with your parents and the guy at the door says "This way Man, Sir, points to the teenager, you go to the side door." Hello! There's something wroge here. Why should adultes be treated higher than teenagers. They commit just as many crimes as teenagers do!

Female, 13, Grade 8

When ever I walk into a store the people look at me as if I am going to steel things. I can't bring my friends into a store so if I can buy them a candy because they (the people who work at the store) tell my friends to "Get out!" it they don't have money. Sometimes it takes 10 minutes or more for them to actualy serve me. When an adult walks in they get served before me even if i am first in line. Often they don't notice me even after I have said "Excuse me," or if they do its to say "What are you doing? Get out of my store!" They see us as infereor.

Female, 13, Grade 8

I think there is an unfair advantage for students. Adults consider teenagers a threat to there bussiness or place of work this is my opinion. But I always think that certain adults degrate some teenagers even more because of there sex or race. For exemple there is one store on Bayers road that there is only aloud people with money to enter, it could be a terrible storm and your *teenage* friend had money but you did not you would be asked to leave. But on the other hand if the same situation happened to 2 adults it would have been Okay, also I don't completely understand the actions of adults would treat you with this disrespect because they have probably been in this position before. The only logical explanation I could think of was they were misbehaving when they were young so they assume that we would do the same.

Fisher and Janetti (1996:240–41) report that the proportionate representation of Aboriginal youth in British Columbian correctional institutions increased from 19 percent in 1983–84 to 25.5 percent in 1990–91. Over the same period, Aboriginal representation in community correctional programs increased from 15 percent to 18 percent. The Aboriginal Justice Inquiry of Manitoba reported that Aboriginal youth in Manitoba had higher arrest rates than non-Aboriginal youth, were more likely to be denied bail, and were more likely to be held in detention prior to trial (cited in Hamilton and Sinclair, 1991). A two-year study of a northern Canadian community reported similar results; the same study found that Aboriginal youth become involved in the justice system at an earlier age than non-Aboriginal youth (LaPrairie, 1983). Similar results were found in Ontario (Jolly, 1983). Correctional statistics for 1998–99 indicate that 23 percent of admissions to custodial institutions are Aboriginal youth, the highest proportion of Aboriginal admissions are still in Manitoba and Saskatchewan, and British Columbia is still about 25 percent (Statistics Canada, 2000: 25, 35).

Meloff and Silverman (1992) and Moyer (1992) examined Canadian youth charged and convicted of murder and manslaughter between 1961 and 1983. Meloff and Silverman found that Aboriginal youth are overrepresented as offenders in homicide cases. Thirty percent of young persons convicted of homicide during the 1961–83 period were Aboriginal youth. At the same time Aboriginal peoples are also overrepresented as victims of homicide (Fedorowycz, 2000:14). Meloff and Silverman report that most Canadian juvenile homicide is intraracial. Sixty-eight percent of all the homicides committed by youth involve Caucasians killing Caucasians. When Aboriginal youth kill, the victim is an Aboriginal person 87 percent of the time. Aboriginal youth more than non-Aboriginal youth have killed a member of their family (49 percent vs. 30 percent). Homicides by Aboriginal youth less often involve another crime (3 percent), and victims are more often friends and acquaintances than are the victims of non-Aboriginal offenders (in other words, non-Aboriginal youth have killed more people who are strangers to them).

AGE

Age is one of the most important factors to consider in attempting to explain youth crime patterns and changes in criminal activity over time. Three age-related issues in the public discourse surrounding youth crime are increased criminal activity by youth under 12 years of age, increases in overall youth crime (particularly after the Young Offenders Act was implemented), and increases in violent crime.

Youth under 12

In 1980, in all of Canada, 1155 young people under the age of 12 appeared in juvenile court (Statistics Canada, 1981). This figure amounted to 3.5 percent of the entire juvenile court population. Bala and Mahoney (1994) report that in the year before the YOA was implemented (1983), 7 to 11 year olds made up "just under" 2 percent of the charges under the JDA. In other words, children under 12 were not highly involved in criminal activity. This is likely one of the major reasons youth under 12 were excluded from the jurisdiction of the YOA and the YCJA, particularly since, even with these small proportions, not all would have been charged with an offence under the Criminal Code. To learn about the behaviour of youth under age 12 since the YOA was implemented, Clark and O'Reilly-Fleming (1994) examined police files from 27 Canadian cities. Between 1988 and 1992, 4,757 of the 406,662 criminal incidents reported by police involved youth under the age of 12. Youth under 12 accounted for only 1.2 percent of the total offences; young offenders aged 12 to 17 for 21 percent of the total offences, and adults for the rest (307–8). Among young offenders, those under 12 accounted for approximately 5 percent of police apprehensions (DuWors, 1992:3). Ninety percent of the "under 12s" were males, and the majority (70 percent) were 10 or 11. Only 13 percent of those involved in criminal incidents were 7 or under.

Most of these children's offences were of a petty nature. For example, 41 percent had been involved in mischief and 23 percent in theft under $1000. Only 2 percent had been involved in violent offences of a serious nature, such as sexual assault and Assault Level II. Three percent had been involved in arson. These violent crimes most often involved casual acquaintances (82 percent) or family and friends (6 percent). The great majority of under 12s (74 percent) did not use weapons; of those who did, 8 percent used knives, 7 percent a club or stick, and 1 percent a firearm.

Most under-12 offences (63 percent) were committed alone. According to Clark and O'Reilly-Fleming (1994), "... either organized or spontaneous peer involvement in crime, of a youth group or 'gang' nature, is negligible" (311). Most important, public fears that older youth or adults are encouraging under 12s to be involved in criminal activity appear to be unfounded. When accomplices were involved in under-12 cases, they tended to be children 12 to 13 years of age (70 percent); only 6 percent of these cases involved accomplices over age 16 (Clark and O'Reilly-Fleming, 1994:309–11).

Increases in Youth Crime

As mentioned in the last chapter, a considerable portion of the increase in youth crime rates and increases in violent crime rates can be explained simply by the addition of 16- and 17-year-olds to the youth justice system in 1985. Prior to the implementation of the YOA, the youth justice upper-age limits were under 16 in New Brunswick, Nova Scotia, Prince Edward Island, Ontario, Saskatchewan, Alberta, the Yukon, and Northwest Territories; under 17 in Newfoundland and British Columbia; and under 18 in Quebec and Manitoba.

There are two reasons why age changes in the juvenile justice legislation accounted for increased crime rates. First, criminal activity increases with age, and, secondly, as we saw in the last chapter, police charge older youth, particularly male youth, at a higher rate than younger youth. Carrington (1998) for example found that a large part of the increase in youth crime rates in Ontario and Saskatchewan were due to older youth coming into the system and police laying more charges. Age-specific crime rates (i.e., rates of crime by age group) consistently show that the peak ages for persons charged with violent crime are the late 20s and early 30s. In particular, persons aged 15 to 28 account for the highest portion of violent incidents in Canada (Statistics Canada, 1995:29), and persons aged 15–32 are the highest risk group for committing homicide. They accounted for three out of five of the accused in 1999 (Fedorowycz, 2000:12). According to Meloff and Silverman's (1992) homicide study, Canadian youth homicide rates from 1961–83 ranged from .29 per 100,000 for those 13 years of age to 2.71 per 100,000 for those 17 years of age (21). Juvenile delinquency figures for 1980 indicate that 14- to 17-year-olds were the age group with the highest number of criminal charges for youth offenders. In provinces where 16- and 17-year-old youth were in the juvenile justice system, this age group constituted the largest percentage of youth offenders; in Quebec, for example, 16- and 17-year-old youth made up 67 percent of juvenile offenders (Statistics Canada, 1981).

Table 4.1 presents crimes known to police by age as a percentage of the total population. What this table shows is that the 18–24 and 31–45 age groups are responsible for far more crime than 12- to 17-year-old youth, and that 25- to 30-year-olds and 12- to 17-year-olds are responsible for about the same proportion of crime. Viewed in the context of their percentage of the total population, 18- to 30-year-olds are the group responsible for the greatest share (almost 50 percent) of police-recorded crime. Hence crime rates will continue to fluctuate as the proportion of 18 to 30 year olds in the population changes.

Increases in Violent Crime

Statistics Canada (1992) reports that in 1991, 12- to 17-year-olds were charged with property crimes at a rate of 47 per 100,000, or "about four times the adult rate of 11 per 100,000 persons aged 18 or more" (3). This is a very misleading comparison precisely because crime rates peak in the late 20s and decline thereafter. More meaningful comparisons of age-specific rates between youth and adults would involve five-year age groups for adults as well as youth. As we have seen, this type of comparison indicates youth rates that are considerably lower than adult crime rates. Not only are youth not as involved in criminal activity (contrary to what is suggested in the media and some government reports), but increases in crime rates resulted in large measure from the legislative inclusion of 16- and 17-year-olds in the justice system and changes in police charging practices.

TABLE 4.1

Accused Status by Age, Canada, 1991

		(Age Group as a % of)	
Age	Total	Total Accused	Total Population
Under 12	1,611	0.8	16.8
12–17	33,781	18.4	8.2
18–24	54,207	29.9	9.9
25–30	33,140	18.1	10.6
31–45	45,527	24.7	24.6
46–64	13,106	7.2	18.4
65 and over	1,963	1.1	11.6
Total	183,115	100%	100%

Sources: CCJS, UCR Survey, Cat. No. 85–205, 1991; 1991 Census of Canada. Adapted from Nova Scotia Youth Secretariat (1993).

Meloff and Silverman's (1992) study of homicide found that youth under 15 more often killed relatives than did youth aged 15 to 17. Over the 22-year period studied, 50 percent of the victims of youth under 15 were family members whereas only 30 percent of the victims of 15- to 17-year-olds were family members. This means, of course, that 15- to 17-year-olds killed more friends and acquaintances than did younger youth (Meloff and Silverman, 1992:25). Compared to adults, young offenders accused of homicide in 1999 killed more strangers (34 percent vs. 15 percent), fewer acquaintances (34 percent vs. 50 percent) and equal proportions of family members (30 percent vs. 33 percent) (Fedorowycz, 2000:14).

People aged 18 to 30 are responsible for more property crime and considerably more violent crime than young offenders. As Table 4.1 indicates, however, it is also the case that 48 percent of all accused people are between 12 and 24 and that this group constitutes only 18 percent of Canada's total population. These figures tell us something about the validity of expectations that the creation of presumptive offences and adult sentencing for 14- to 17-year-old youth in the YCJA will solve crime problems. On this question, which we will return to in later chapters, the Nova Scotia Youth Secretariat (1993) argues that

> efforts aimed at addressing crime among the total youth population (age 15 to 24) should not necessarily focus on "toughening up" the YOA. Factors other than so-called lenient juvenile justice legislation seem to be responsible for the high degree of criminal activity among young people in society. It is necessary to question the extent to which the criminal justice system alone can deal with the greater factors responsible for crime, especially among young people. (22)

GENDER

One of the facts of crime and delinquency that is most consistent and least disputed is that male youth are far more involved in crime and serious criminal activity than female youth of any age (see Table 4.2). Reports on female young offenders, based on police charges for 1990–91 (Conway, 1992) and 1994 UCR statistics, indicate that 18 percent of all youth charged with Criminal Code Offences in Canada were female. In 2000, female youth were responsible for 23 percent of all Criminal Code charges against youth (Logan, 2000:8). Interestingly, girls charge rates have always been higher than women's, even before the YOA was implemented and particularly for violent offences (Conway, 1992; Hatch and Faith, 1991:77). In 2000, girls accounted for 25 percent of all youth violent crime while women accounted for 16 percent of adult violent crime (Logan, 2001:19).

The consistency of these statistics notwithstanding, certain aspects of the "fact" of **gender** differences are debatable. At issue is the magnitude of the difference between

TABLE 4.2

Youth Charged by Sex, Selected Incidents, 2000

	Sex	
	Males %	**Females** %
Homicide[1]	88	12
Attempted murder	89	11
Assaults	71	29
Sexual assaults	96	4
Other sexual offences	96	4
Abduction	25	75
Robbery	85	15
Violent crime—Total	**75**	**25**
Breaking and entering	91	9
Motor vehicle theft	85	15
Fraud	63	37
Theft over $5,000	85	15
Theft $5,000 and under	66	34
Property crime—Total	**77**	**23**
Mischief	88	12
Arson	86	14
Prostitution	14	86
Offensive weapons	93	7
Criminal Code—Total	**77**	**23**
Impaired driving[2]	87	13
Cocaine offences	79	21
Cannabis offences	87	13
Other drug offences	83	17

1. Homicide Survey, CCJS.

2. Includes impaired operation of a vehicle causing death, causing bodily harm, alcohol rate over 80 mg., failure/refusal to provide a breath/blood sample. Age of persons charged with impaired driving comes from the incident based survey (UCR2).

Source: Adapted from Statistics Canada (2001), *Juristat,* Cat. No. 85–002, 21(8), p. 19.

male and female youth, whether the types of offences they are involved in differ, and whether girls are becoming more like boys in their behaviour. Answers to these questions are not straightforward and will depend on what type of statistics are used—official, self-report, or victimization.

Official Statistics

Almost half of young female offences (48 percent) involve petty theft, and most of these charges (86 percent) involve shoplifting. The next most common offences for female youth are minor assault (9 percent), break and enter (7 percent), and bail violations (5 percent). Like that for female offenders, male youths' most frequent charge is theft under $1000 (22 percent). The second most frequent offence for male youth is more serious, break and enter (21 percent), followed by mischief and damage (7 percent), and motor vehicle theft (7 percent). Both male and female youth have shown an increase in minor assault charges, but the increase is greater for girls. Since 1986, the number of assault charges against female young offenders has increased by 120 percent, compared with a 78 percent increase for male youth. Nonetheless, their overall rate is one-third the male rate and compared to boys, more girl violence involves common assaults (67 percent vs. 46 percent) (Logan, 2001:8; Savoie, 1999:5; Conway, 1992:1-5). In addition, while overall charges for violent crime have increased at a higher rate for girls than boys over the last 10 years, the charge rate is still considerably lower for female youth (481 per 100,000 vs. 1342 per 100,000) (Logan, 2001:8). The other area accounting for girls' increases in police charge rates is administrative offences, more specifically bail violation. In the first five years after the YOA was implemented, this charge rate increased by 71 percent (Conway, 1992:1–5). Carrington and Moyer (1998) conclude that increases in charges for girls was primarily due to increased charges for minor assaults and administrative offences (38).

A typical scenario for these charges occurred recently in Halifax. Two patrolling police officers noticed a 15-year-old girl on the street who they knew "was supposed to be at home." The officers chased the girl and a struggle ensued when they caught up with her. She was subsequently charged with assaulting a police officer, resisting arrest, and breaching an undertaking (Teen charged, 2000).

One of the most striking differences between male and female young offenders in official crime statistics is the difference in charges by age. Figure 4.1 shows that violent offence charges are more likely to involve younger females, in the case of males these charges increase with age. It is important to remember that these statistics are based on persons charged and do not necessarily reflect actual behaviour. We have already discussed that police charging practices do fluctuate and we will see in Chapters 8 and 9, that police and other justice officials are sometimes more likely to charge and process young females than young males. Greenberg (1992:4), for example,

FIGURE 4.1

Age and Sex of Youth Charged as a Proportion of
All Accused Youth, 1998

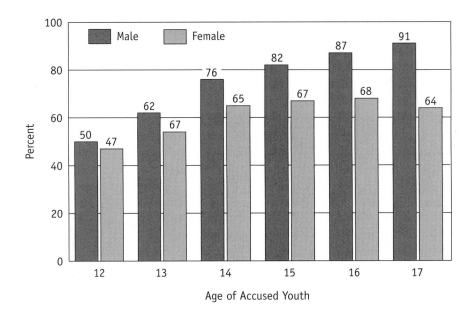

Source: Statistics Canada. Cat. No. 85-002, Vol. 19 No. 13, p. 12.

reports that, on a proportionate basis, female youth are charged more frequently than males with violent offences, particularly minor assault.

Age differences between boys and girls are also apparent with respect to administrative charges. Figure 4.2 shows that girls under 16 are more likely than older girls and boys the same age to be charged with offences against the administration of justice. Of female youth charged with administrative offences, 56 percent were under 16, almost twice the proportion for male offenders; only 36 percent of males charged with administrative offences were under 16 (Gagnon and Doherty, 1993:5).

Statistics from the youth courts show gender patterns similar to those reflected in police statistics. In 1999–2000, female youth accounted for 21 percent of all charges appearing before youth court (Sudworth and deSouza, 2001:6). Female offenders accounted for 22 percent of all violent charges appearing before youth court and 16.5 percent of all property offence charges. The dramatic difference between male and

FIGURE 4.2

Distribution of Young Offender Cases Involving Offences Against the Administration of Justice, by Age and Sex, 1991–1992

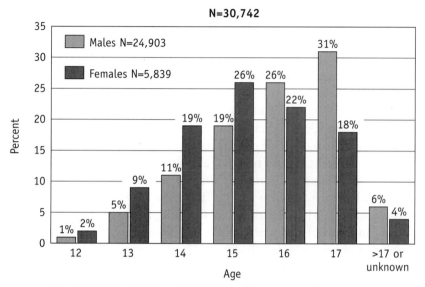

Note: YCS data for Ontario and British Columbia represent only 85 percent of their respective provincial caseloads.

Source: Gagnon and Doherty (1993:5); Statistics Canada: Canadian Centre for Justice Statistics.

female youth in this area is more apparent in the youth court statistics than in police statistics. In court, this is the only area in which female youth charges outnumber male youth charges. Female youth accounted for 25 percent of other criminal code charges, of these, 15 percent were escape custody, 19 percent unlawfully at large, 28 percent failure to appear, and they accounted for 26 percent of all YOA charges (Sudworth and deSouza, 2001:6). Girls rates for administrative charges rose from 6.1 percent in 1985–86 to 27.3 percent in 1995–96 and boys rose from 3.9 percent to 21.6 percent (Reitsma-Street, 1999:338-39). The significance of these increases is that, as discussed earlier, the chances of a custody sentence are higher for these than any other offences. Forty-eight percent of youth charged with a YOA offence in 2000 received a custody sentence as did 39 percent of those charged with a criminal code administrative offence (Sudworth and deSouza, 2001).

Self-Report Studies

Self-report studies corroborate official reports that there is more criminal behaviour among boys than girls, but suggest that the gap between them is much smaller than that indicated by official statistics. According to Le Blanc (1983), official statistics in the late 1970s were showing a ratio of one girl to every eight or ten boys. His self-report study in Montreal during the same period indicated a delinquency rate of one girl to three boys (1983:37). A more recent Canadian self-report study indicates little change in girls' behaviour—a 3:1 male–female ratio (Simourd and Andrews, 1996). Most recently, the longitudinal survey of Canadian children reports that for the years 1994–1997, 30 percent of girls aged 12–13 report involvement in property offences compared to 40 percent of boys the same age, and 29 percent an involvement in fighting with or attacking other people compared to 56 percent of the boys. For both types of behaviour, only 7 percent of the girls reported a high frequency of involvement. The percentages for boys are almost double; thirteen percent of the boys reported a high involvement in property offences and 16 percent a high involvement in fighting and physical aggression (Sprott, Doob and Jenkins, 2001:3)

Reitsma-Street's (1991a) discussion of Canadian self-report studies suggests that race and class, and possibly even gender, are not factors that differentiate involvement in delinquent behaviour (see Byles, 1969; Gomme, 1985; Le Blanc, 1983). Reitsma-Street argues that self-report studies in Canada and the United States "challenge the amount of real variation in delinquencies by background of the girls. They also question the numbers and rates of the official statistics" (1991a:253). Most self-report studies suggest that girls and boys are involved in the same kind of criminal and delinquent behaviour. According to Reitsma-Street (1991a:253–54), the rate of official charges for girls is infrequent, but most girls report at least one or more delinquencies in any one-year period; only a small proportion of girls report an involvement in more than 10 acts of crime or delinquency.

Chesney-Lind and Shelden (1992), in their thorough review of self-report studies in the United States, report that female delinquency is more prevalent than official statistics indicate. The majority of girls' delinquency, like that of boys', is trivial. Contrary to what is indicated by official statistics and reports, boys report running away from home and being involved in prostitution as much as girls do. Later in the chapter we will discuss how the consequences differ for boys and girls.

A major difference is that girls engage in delinquent behaviour far less frequently than boys (Conway, 1992:9; Chesney-Lind and Shelden, 1992:18). Hindelang (1979) has argued that frequency rather than type of delinquent behaviour accounts for the greater number of male offenders in official police statistics. By contrast, Chesney-Lind and Shelden (1992) argue that while frequency may help to explain why there are disproportionate numbers of males in violent offence categories, it does not account for the categories in which girls are overrepresented. More specifically, and with regard to

American youth, it does not account for the overrepresentation of girls charged with **status offences** (Chesney-Lind and Shelden, 1992:18). In the Canadian context, Hindelang's argument does not account for the high charges against girls for administrative offences. The questions of why girls are criminalized for some behaviours and not others will be addressed in later chapters.

Victimization Surveys

Results from victimization surveys confirm the aforementioned gender patterns, but only for face to face crimes and not in a manner that readily separates youth from adults. Johnson's (1986) report on the 1982 Canadian victimization survey found that

- only 5 percent of all victimizations involved one or more female assailants; the 1999 GSS reports that 18 percent of all assailants were female (Besserer and Trainor, 2000:21);
- the age distribution of offenders is similar for males and females;
- females are the victims of female assailants more often than male assailants (78 percent vs. 35 percent);
- female assailants are more likely to be acquaintances (50 percent) or relatives (15 percent) of their victims than men (25 percent and 5 percent respectively);
- males are more likely than females to use weapons (34 percent vs. 23 percent);
- females' victims are more likely to be injured (64 percent) than males' victims (48 percent) or victims of both sexes (59 percent);
- incidents involving males and females are more likely to be reported than incidents involving only a man or only women; and
- incidents perpetrated by a female are more likely to be described as a crime than a threat or an attempt (32 percent vs. 49 percent for male perpetrators).

It is sometimes suggested that female crime rates are low because men are too embarrassed to report having been victimized by a woman. Hatch and Faith argue (1991) that victimization survey results raise important questions about male hesitancy to report being victimized by women. The results also raise important questions about how similar acts may be interpreted differently depending on whether they are perpetrated by a male or a female (Hatch and Faith, 1991:71). Finally, victimization survey results suggest a considerable amount of police discretion in charging and support the argument that police and prosecutors are more inclined to charge and prosecute female offenders under 16 than they are older girls.

Delinquent Careers

Other important differences between male and female young offenders have been revealed from longitudinal research on **birth cohorts**. Chesney-Lind and Shelden

(1992) reviewed this type of research and confirmed a considerable gender gap over time. Male offence rates were found to be four times greater than female rates. The ratio of male to female rates was 9:1 for all index offences and 14:1 for violent offences. One possible explanation for this difference is that boys' delinquent behaviour is more long-lasting than girls'. Chesney-Lind and Shelden concluded from their review of American research, as well as research in England, Wales, and Scotland, that boys' delinquent careers are longer, boys are more likely to begin their careers at an earlier age, and boys are more likely to extend their delinquent careers into their adult lives. Girls' careers are not only shorter than boys', but they involve less-serious offences (Chesney-Lind and Shelden, 1992:19–20). Similarly, Biron's (1980:7) study of Montreal girls found an overall decrease in delinquent behaviour after two years, especially with regard to violent crimes. More recently, a self-report questionnaire administered to the student bodies of four secondary schools in Metropolitan Toronto found that girls were more likely than boys to abandon delinquent behaviour after police contact (Keane, Gillis, and Hagan, 1989).

Girls and Violence

An emerging public issue with regard to gender differences and criminal activity is the so-called growth of "girl gangs" and their propensity for violent behaviour. A *Globe and Mail* article in the mid 1990's entitled "Ruthless Violence Part of Girl Gang Reality" exemplifies this concern:

> Girls used to be made of sugar and spice and everything nice, but today experts on youth violence see some of them as a dangerous threat to society—ruthless, volatile and brutal ... [I]n its recently released Women in Canada report, Statistics Canada reported that, in 1993, females between the ages of 12 and 17 accounted for 24 percent of all young offenders charged with violent offences, compared with 21 percent charged with property crimes.

Research suggests that when viewed over time girls' behaviour has not changed in any dramatic fashion. Reitsma-Street (1999;1993b) compares court charges for female youth before the Young Offenders Act with those after the YOA, from 1980 to 1995–96. Table 4.3, presents these statistics and indicates a number of interesting things about girls' court charges. First, the most violent offences, and the ones least susceptible to low or changing charge rates—namely, murder, attempted murder, manslaughter, robbery, and arson—are very low and show little change from 1980 to 1996. While charges "against the person" have seen a steady increase, from 9.9 percent in 1980 to 20.3 percent in 1995–96, the majority of offences in this category are minor in nature. Moreover, Reitsma-Street reports that of all the court cases against female offenders in 1995–96, 3.16 percent involved aggravated assault or assault with a weapon. This means that 84.4 percent of all of the court charges in the crimes-against-the-person category are minor. This strongly suggests that a major portion of female violent crime is minor and any increases may be accounted for by the implementation of zero-tolerance policies in the 1990s. In spite of media claims that girls are becoming more violent, in 1998, 67 percent of girls' violent offence charges were for minor assault (Savoie, 1999:5).

With regard to the most violent offence, murder, Meloff and Silverman (1992) report that 63 percent of youth homicides involve males killing males. Female youth accounted for 11 percent of the youth homicides between 1961 and 1983. Compared to male youth, girls are more likely to kill family members (48 percent vs. 32 percent) than friends or strangers (27). In the 1961–83 period, 85 percent of the 65 people killed by female young offenders were relatives (28). According to Reitsma-Street (1993b), "street crime and stranger crime by female youth is definitely not a major source of public danger" (444). In 1989, of the 563 people charged with homicide, 458 were men, 57 were women, 43 were male youth, and only 5 were female youth (Frank, 1991:6–7). In 2000, there were 542 homicides; less than 10 percent involved young offenders. Overall, 36 male youth and 5 girls were charged, the same number of girls as in 1989. This seems a far cry from "ruthless, volatile and brutal." A subject we will return to in later chapters.

Boritch's (1997) review of the literature and statistics on juvenile crime trends for the last 30 years concludes that female crime has increased. Nonetheless, while involvement in criminal activity (especially minor crimes) has escalated, there have also been changes in both victim-reporting behaviour and "law enforcement attitudes toward, and policies affecting, female offenders" (46). Boritch also reminds us that female crime rates were considerably higher in the early 19th century, declined from 1860 to the 1920s, and began to increase again in the 1930s (1997:46–47). Recent increases are thus relative to the time frame under consideration.

YOUTH AS VICTIMS OF CRIME

While much public attention is focused on young people as offenders, very little concern is directed toward youth and children as victims of violence or the relationship between victimization as a child and later criminality. As a consequence, our thinking about the relationship between youth and crime is distorted and social policies are directed more toward punitive measures than **remedial** solutions. Yet child victimization surveys in the United States report that children are far more likely to be victimized than adults, girls are more likely to be sexually assaulted than boys, and boys are more likely than girls to be killed or physically assaulted (Finkelhor and Dziuba-Leatherman, 1994).

Victimization studies in the United States also report that the risk of violent criminal victimization in 1991 was greater for a 12-year-old than for anyone 24 or older, and that juveniles between 12 and 17 are more likely to be the victim of violent crime

TABLE 4.3

Charges Laid against Girls in Canadian Youth Courts for Criminal Code and Federal Statute Violations Pre- and Post-YOA (numbers in percentages)

Type of Charge	Pre-YOA (Includes Ontario)		Post-YOA (Excludes Ontario)		Post-YOA (Includes Ontario)
	1980 (N=7,919)	1983 N=9,876)	1986–87 (N=10,791)	1989–90 (N=13,361)	1995–96 (N=21,898)
Murder or attempt	.1	.1	.1	.02	.03
Robbery	1.1	1.3	1.5	.7	1.7
Arson	.5	.2	.4	.4	.2
Against person	9.9	9.5	13.0	12.5	20.3
Theft over/auto	5.4	5.3	3.7	3.1	2.4
Trafficking/possession	3.3	2.3	2.8	1.8	2.6
Break and enter	14.6	10.6	10.3	6.7	5.0
Fraud	5.8	6.9	7.2	7.2	2.6
Theft under/stolen goods	43.1	47.9	39.8	33.4	31.2
Mischief	5.6	4.5	4.5	4.6	3.0
Nuisance/disorderly	3.0	3.3	3.6	2.2	.8
Immorality/vice/soliciting	1.2	.6	(Decriminalized)		.9
Other/unknown	.6	.6	.9	5.9	2.1
Against administration of justice	5.7	6.9	12.2	21.5	27.3
TOTAL	100.0	100.0	100.0	100.0	100.0

Sources: Adapted from Reitsma-Street (1993b:441; 1999:343).

than are persons past their mid-20s (Snyder and Sickmund, 1995:14). While we usually hear that senior citizens are most afraid of violence, these victimization surveys indicate that senior citizens have much lower victimization rates than persons aged 18 to 24. In fact, 18- to 24-year-olds have the highest rate of victimization within the adult population. Among youth, victimization rates are so high for teenage youth that "if not a single younger child were victimized, the level of teen victimization alone would make the rate for all children higher than the rate for all adults" (Finkelhor and Dziuba-Leatherman, 1993:3).

Canadian figures are very similar. The Canadian General Social Survey reports that the victimization rate for youth aged 15–19 was more than double the national average in 1993 (217 per 1,000 vs. 92 per 1,000) and in 1999 the rate for youth aged 15–24 at 405 per 1000 was higher than any other age group older than 24. Compared to people over the age of 65, the rate of violent crime victimization for 15–24 year olds is 21 times higher, and for theft victimization 9 times higher (Besserer and Trainor, 2000:7, 19, 21; Johnson, 1995:6; Gartner and Doob, 1994). Twenty percent of all victims of violent crime reported to the police in 1994 were youth aged 12–19 (20 percent is double this group's proportion of the population). Some of this higher rate of victimization is attributable to lifestyle as rates of victimization are higher for students and those who spend time away from home in the evenings (Besserer and Trainor, 2000:7). Lifestyle, however, does not help account for the most violent offences against young victims.

Among victims of homicide, from 1991 to 1994, the age group with the highest rate of victimization was infants under one year of age (see Figure 4.3). Between 1988 and 1998, an average of 12 infants under the age of one and 52 children under the age of 12 have been murdered each year. Four out of five of these children were murdered by their parents (Fedorowycz, 2000:11–12). Wendy Regoeczi's (2000) research on all youth homicide victims from 1985 to 1995 shows that, on average, 29 youth aged 12–17 were killed each year and one-third were killed by a family member (497). Half (51.7 percent) were killed by a friend or acquaintance (498). One quarter of these homicides occurred because of a quarrel or argument and the other quarter occcured during the course of a criminal offence not of their making (501). As for other violence, in 1997 one in every five assaults reported to Canadian police involved a child under 18, one in four of the assailants was a family member, and children and youth were more likely than adults to be the victims of sexual offences (Kong, 1998:19).

Age and Gender

While Canada has not conducted child victimization surveys, data on victimization are available from the general Canadian victimization survey and from the revised UCR survey. In a study based on data from 13 police departments, Johnson and Lazarus (1989) report on personal victimization rates in seven Canadian cities in 1981 and 1984. The risk of victimization, they point out, is "not random." While young people aged 16 to 24 have higher victimization rates than any other group, male rates are generally higher than female rates. However, the differences vary by city and type of offence, and, as women age, their chances of victimization increase. Women and girls experience higher rates of sexual assault and personal theft victimization, while men and boys experience higher rates of robbery and assault (Johnson and Lazarus, 1989:312).

The 1993 GSS found that the total personal victimization rate for women over 15 was about 11 percent higher than that for men (151 per 1,000 vs. 136 per 1,000) and even higher in urban areas (Gartner and Doob, 1994; Kong, 1994). By 1999, the GSS reported very little difference in rates for women and men (189 per1,000 vs. 183 per 1,000), but 4 times more sexual assaults were perpetrated against women (33 per 1,000 vs 8 per 1,000) and men reported higher rates of assault and robbery (92 per 1,000 vs. 70 per 1,000 and 12 per 1,000 vs. 7 per 1,000, respectively). While the majority of persons accused of violent crimes are adults, this is less often the case when victims are teens; slightly more than half (52 percent) of those accused of violent crimes against teens between the ages of 12 and 17 were teens themselves (Besserer and Trainor, 2000:7,9).

In 1994, the chances of victimization were about equal for boys and girls, regardless of age. Nonetheless, there were important differences. More boys were the victims of homicide, attempted murder, assault, and robbery, while more girls were the victims of sexual offences (including sexual assault). Children under 12 were kidnapped or abducted in equal proportions regardless of sex, but girls over 12 were victimized in this manner far more than boys of the same age (Johnson, 1995:5). Interestingly, the RCMP Missing Children's Registry reports that, in 1991, only 0.1 percent of all recorded cases of child abduction involved strangers. The "stranger" category includes anyone other than a parent who does not have legal custody. Hence, "stranger abductors" can and do include grandparents and other relatives or friends of a child (Ericson and Haggerty, 1997:276–77). More girls are abducted by friends and acquaintances, while more boys are abducted by parents (Johnson, 1995:8).

FIGURE 4.3

Average Rates of Homicide by Age Group of Victims, 1991–1994

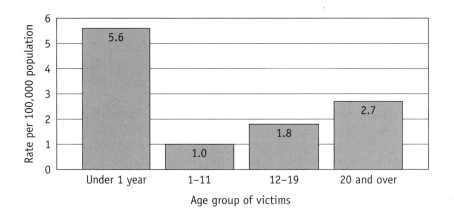

Source: Adapted from Statistics Canada, *Juristat*, Cat. No. 85-002, 15(15), p. 13.

Location

Public information campaigns designed to educate parents about "street proofing" children can create the impression that youth and children are more likely to be victimized by strangers. However, victimization studies of children, such as those done in the United States, indicate that juveniles are more likely than adults to be victimized by family members, friends, or acquaintances (88 percent vs. 58 percent) (Snyder and Sickmund, 1995:14). In a national family violence survey conducted in the United

---

BOX 4.3

Teenage Victims of Violent Crime: Facts to Consider

- Twenty percent of all violent crime victims were teenagers (between 12 and 19 years of age), two times their representation in the 1990 Canadian population.

- Both teenagers and children (under 12 years) constituted a larger proportion of victims of sexual assault than adults (20 and older). Of every ten reported sexual victims, four were teenagers and four were children.

- Twenty-three percent of those accused of crimes against younger teen victims were 12–15 themselves and a further 23 percent were 16–19.

- Between 1981 and 1990, 9 percent of homicide victims were teenagers, which is slightly lower than their 11 percent proportion in the population.

- One-third of younger teen victims (12–15) and one-quarter of older teen victims (16–19) were killed during the commission of another offence, in particular sexual assault.

- One-third of the homicides against older teenage victims and more than one-quarter of those against younger teenage victims occurred in public places.

Source: Adapted from Statistics Canada (1992b), *Juristat*, Cat. No. 85–002, 12(6).

States, adults reported almost twice as much severe violence against a child in their household as against their adult partners (Strauss and Gelles, 1990). Snyder and Sickmund (1995) report that offences against juvenile victims are less likely to be brought to the attention of police than adult victimizations (20 percent vs. 37 percent). This may be because juveniles are more likely to report offences to other officials (adults other than police) and/or because complaints from children and youth are less likely than adult complaints to be taken seriously.

More than half (56 percent) of juvenile victimizations happen in school or on school property, and three-quarters of these incidents involve personal thefts. With regard to violent crime, offences against juveniles are as likely to occur at home as they are at school (25 percent vs. 23 percent) (Snyder and Sickmund, 1995:16). More important, family members are often the perpetrators of violence against children, and girls are more likely than boys to be assaulted, sexually or otherwise, by a family member (Finkelhor and Dziuba-Leatherman, 1993). The 1994 revised UCR survey reports that in 37 percent of the child victim cases in Canada the accused was a parent or other relative; for youth aged 12–19, 17 percent of the violence cases involved family members. Johnson (1995:7–9) reports that girls are twice as likely as boys to be victimized by family members. Further, the risk of victimization is greater for children and youth in households where adults, most likely the mother, have been victimized. A 1998 review of research on exposure to domestic violence found between 45 and 70 percent of children exposed to family violence were victims of physical abuse (Margolin, 1998). Girls are particularly vulnerable to this type of victimization (Mitchell and Finkelhor, 2001:957). Since many of these statistics are based on police statistics, they include only incidents reported to police and thus underestimate the magnitude of child and youth victimization.

Many street youth describe their family lives as years of abuse that most commonly involved physical and sexual abuse by fathers (Webber, 1991; Homeless Youth, 1994; see also Chapter 7). My own analysis of young offender case files in a Southwestern Ontario Family Court for the years 1986–87 (Bell, 1993) revealed that a considerable number of young offenders in the court came from families where interpersonal relationships fall considerably short of an "ideal" family model. Fourteen percent of these families had a lengthy history of violence and abuse in the home, and another 14 percent were characterized by neglect and negative parent–child relationships. Six percent of the parents were very outspoken and insistent about wanting their child out of the family home. Fathers, stepfathers, and other male partners as well as older brothers were most often the source of violence and abuse.

Living on the streets also puts young people at great risk for violence (Baron, 1995). Whitbeck et al. (2001) report that living on the street increases a youth's risk of physical victimization by 5 times and that the risk of sexual victimization is 6 times greater for girls on the street than for boys (1200). Webber (1991) poignantly documents the plight of Canadian street youths. Among other things, she talks about a growing street trade for young boys:

> If new girls on the stroll are hot sellers, fresh "male meat," called "chicken," is an even hotter commodity among "chicken hawks," usually middle aged men who lust for boys, the younger the better. And since sexism translates on the street into self-employment, boys keep their earnings. Raised to control their own lives, most won't relinquish that power to pimps. Prepubescent boys, however, are vulnerable to being pimped, and some very young newcomers ... do fall into the hands of "sugar daddies." Usually these chicken hawk pimps—some gay, some bisexual—will rape the child to initiate him into his new role on the home front and his night work on the stroll. Like street girls, boys are beaten by bad tricks, plus they risk incurring the rage of "fag bashers." However, most are spared pimp violence. (123)

Youth are especially vulnerable to violence in their homes from parents and relatives but also on the streets from each other and from predators who exploit their vulnerability. Many youth run from neglect and physical or sexual abuse in their homes only to find themselves facing the same on the streets because they are ill prepared to protect themselves or are vulnerable because of a lack of education or employment opportunities that would allow them to fend for themselves economically. Hagan and McCarthy (1998) suggest that physical abuse at home is an important factor in youth running away and the number of nights they spend away puts them at further risk for involvement in theft, drugs, violence, and prostitution. Theirs and other Canadian studies estimate a range of 18 to 32 percent of runaways are or have been involved in prostitution, a majority of whom are girls (Fisher, 1989; Kufeldt and Nimmo, 1987; McCarthy, 1990; Hagan and McCarthy, 1998). Schissel and Fedec (1999) found that pregnancy is one significant consequence of prostitution for non-aboriginal girls in Saskatoon and Regina; in other words, they are more likely to be coerced into unsafe sex by johns and so are more vulnerable to AIDS. On the other hand, aboriginal youth are twice as likely to have been physically assaulted than non-aboriginal youth. And, both are more likely to have been sexually assaulted than youth not engaged in prostitution regardless of their race (49–50). Far too many youth meet a tragic end on the streets. Hagan and McCarthy report on their follow up on the Vancouver and Toronto youth in their study of street youth that

> More than one worker told us of a youth who was later found dead—in an abandoned building or alley-way—the victim of a sex crime, a drug overdose or a violent attack. Other youth survived the day-to-day living of street life only to die later from other problems—most often AIDS or other diseases—some of which originated on the street and others which were exacerbated by it. (2000:234)

Victimization and the Justice System

Until recently, the extent of violence inflicted on male young offenders by their families has gone largely unexplored, as has violence and abuse in the childhood lives of adult males. Research of female delinquents has documented a high incidence of physical and sexual abuse stemming from their family lives. One U.S. study of an institutionalized female population reports figures of 76 percent physical abuse with injury and 50 percent sexual assault among prisoners (Phelps, 1982). Sandberg (1989) reports that 66 percent of the residents of a juvenile facility population had a history of child abuse, and for 38 percent of the girls this involved sexual abuse (129). Chesney-Lind (1988) argues that precisely because of this abuse many female young offenders have good reason to have "bad relationships" with their parents (and sometimes with their male siblings and other male relatives) and to be "unmanageable" and "out of control." Closer to home, McCormack, Janus, and Burgess (1986) found family-related sexual abuse rates of 73 percent for girls and 38 percent for boys among youth in a Toronto shelter for "runaways." Schissel (1997) also found high rates of abuse and neglect among street youth and young offenders in Saskatoon and Regina, particularly among those displaying physically aggressive behaviour and problems with anger (94). Of 150 convicted women involved with a community helping agency in a Canadian city, one-third were victims of extensive physical and/or sexual abuse that dated back to their lives as children (Bell, 1994a). Artz (1997) reports from her analysis of Canadian girls with a history of violence that they are likely to have been subjected to or witnessed physical violence and sexual abuse. The National Longitudinal Survey of Children and Youth in Canada reports that children who have witnessed violence in their homes are more likely than other children to exhibit physical aggression, emotional disorders, and engage in property crime (Dauvergne and Johnson, 2001:11).

Children of convicted women are particularly vulnerable to abuse and sexual assault. Often, when women come into conflict with the law their children are placed in foster care or in the care of other relatives. In one particularly disturbing case, a teenage girl was placed in a foster home because of her mother's incarceration. The girl was subsequently murdered by her foster father; her younger sister remained in the same foster home, despite the mother's attempts to have her placed elsewhere. Another case involved a 14-year-old who bore her father's child. She was removed from her family home as a consequence, and her child was taken from her and placed in foster care. Sixteen years later, she was able to finally locate her child, only to discover that he had been physically and sexually abused while in foster care; he is currently serving time in a federal penitentiary for aggravated assault (Bell, 1994a).

A significant number of children and youth in the justice system were formerly under state care. Bell (1993) reports that 85 percent of the families in one youth court had prior involvement with a social service agency, while Thompson (1988) notes that

47 percent of the first 2539 individuals charged under the YOA in Alberta had previously been assigned child welfare status. Little is known about the welfare of children under state care or its relationship to criminal behaviour. Nonetheless, we know that institutional abuse exists because of recent court cases and investigations concerning abuse in residential schools and other specific youth institutions. Mount Cashel in Newfoundland, Kingsclear in New Brunswick, Shelburne in Nova Scotia, and Grandview in Ontario are but a few examples. Judi Harris, one of the survivors of the Grandview Training School in Ontario, "was in Grandview when she was 12 years old. She has memories of being locked up naked in solitary confinement; she also has memories of a guard who promised her a blanket for sex" (Edwards, 1992, cited in Reitsma-Street, 1993a:1).

As Harris and others continue to speak out about their abuse, we are left with a picture of institutional sexual and physical abuse of children that is far more common than previously assumed. We also know from these individuals that many of their problems with the justice system are attributable to their institutional and legal experiences (Schissel, 1997; Sandberg, 1989). As the investigations unfold, it is becoming increasingly clear that Canadian politicians and institutional bureaucrats bear some responsibility for the acts of violence committed against children and youth under state care. It is also clear from the records of child advocacy agencies that institutional abuse is not a thing of the past. According to the chief advocate of the Office of Child and Family Services Advocacy program in Ontario, one-third of the agency's annual requests for advocacy come from youth facilities (Dorey, 1997). The implications of child and youth victimization for juvenile justice and law reform will be discussed in Chapter 12.

SUMMARY

This chapter attempts to further deconstruct the public discourse on youth crime by addressing public issues that revolve around race, gender, and age. Once again, questions of the volume and seriousness of youth crime are addressed, but now in the context of social dimensions. The distorted view of youth as "perpetrators" of crime is balanced by an examination of statistics on youth as "victims" of crime.

Over the last 20 years, information on young offenders has been enhanced by the use of two new research tools. Ethnographic studies provide detailed information on the lives of youth and their families. Longitudinal studies of youth crime focus on age as an important factor in youth crime rates.

The public discourse on youth crime is highly racialized. Images of "out of control" visible minorities, "Asian" gangs, and "ruthless and violent" girl gangs fuel public fears of youth and their crimes. The crimes of Caucasian males are never presented as such in public discourse. The children of visible minorities are no more likely than

Canadian-born or Caucasian youth to be "gang" members. Aboriginal youth crime is part of a larger pattern of violence directly related to their oppressed status in Canadian society. This pattern of violence includes suicide, substance abuse, and physical and sexual victimization.

Young adults (primarily males 18 to 30 years of age) are responsible for far more violent crime than youth. Notwithstanding changes in policing practices, a not insignificant portion of the increase in violent crime, as well as in all categories of youth crime, can be explained by the introduction of 16- and 17-year-old youth into the juvenile justice system. Youth under 12 do not appear to be any more "criminal" than they were 20 years ago (less than 2 percent of all offences known to police). Nor are they being coerced into criminal activities by older youth or adults; only a small proportion of the under-12 cases in police files involved an accomplice over the age of 16.

Girls are far less involved in "official" crime than boys. Self-reported studies suggest that girls engage in the same behaviours as boys, but less frequently. Boys' criminal behaviour begins earlier than girls' and is more likely to extend into adulthood. There appears to be a gender gap with respect to charging practices. Proportionately more girls than boys are charged for minor crimes of violence (and at younger ages), and more girls are charged with administrative offences. As boys and girls age, violence charges increase for boys and decrease for girls.

The risk of violent victimization is greater for 12-year-olds than for anyone over 24, and 12- to 17-year-old youth are more likely to be victimized than anyone over 25. Twenty percent of all violent crime victims in Canada are youth aged 12–19, twice this group's proportion of the Canadian population. Of every ten reported victims of sexual assault, four are teenagers and four are children.

Men and boys are more likely than women and girls to be the perpetrators and the victims of violence. As women age, their chances of overall victimization increases relative to men. Women and girls experience higher rates of sexual assault and personal theft, while men and boys experience higher rates of robbery and assault. Girls are more likely than boys to have been assaulted, sexually or otherwise, by family members.

Almost half of those accused of crimes against teens are also teenagers. Adults are more violent with their children than with their adult partners. A majority of offences against children occur outside the home, but offences are as likely to occur at home as at school. In the home, adult males and older brothers are the most frequent perpetrators of violence against children and youth. For many young offenders, victimization at home leads to running away which in turn puts them at risk for criminal activity and further victimization on the streets by each other and from predators who exploit their vulnerability. Recent investigations into physical and sexual abuse in foster homes, correctional facilities, and other state institutions indicate that Canadian politicians and assorted institutional bureaucrats bear some responsibility for violence against children and youth under state care.

CHAPTER 5

Explaining Crime and Delinquency: In the Beginning ...

CHAPTER OBJECTIVES

1. To discuss scholarly and "taken for granted" understandings of events.

2. To learn the basics of empirical relationships, especially causal ones.

3. To understand theory and its relationship to research.

4. To outline the development of positivistic thinking about crime from the 19th century to the mid-20th century.

5. To understand the differences between biological, psychological, and sociological approaches to explaining youth crime and delinquency.

6. To introduce major perspectives and theories of youth crime and delinquency, along with general theoretical critiques of each.

KEY TERMS

Postmodernists	Classical school	Human ecology
Theory	Eugenics	Anomie
Research	Behaviourism	Strain theory
Facts	Conditioned	Delinquent subculture
Empirical	Cognitive	Consensus theory
Positivist	Development theory	Control theory
Concepts	Antisocial personality	Social bond

INTRODUCTION

Over the last 100 years, much has been written about the causes of crime and delin-quency. Perspectives range from the biological and physiological to the psychological and sociological. Some views are academic or scientific, while others are what Anderson (1996) refers to as "taken for granted understandings." Taken-for-granted understandings are beliefs that are accepted as true simply because they are either felt to be true or are commonly shared as true. They are based on "immediate experience" and are rarely examined (Anderson, 1996:11). Taken-for-granted understandings differ from scientific beliefs that are accepted as true because these beliefs have been subjected to empirical testing. **Postmodernists** would take the position that even scientific knowledge, including academic theory, has no more claim to "truth" than taken-for-granted understandings.

In this chapter, we will discuss the development of academic thinking and taken-for-granted understandings of crime and delinquency (thereby providing a framework for the examination of current theorizing in the next chapter). This chapter will trace the development of criminology theory, as it pertains to youth crime, from the 18th century to the 1960s. We begin, however, with a discussion of **theory**, expla-nation, **research,** and the important relationships between them.

THEORY AND RESEARCH

Theory and Explanation

Broadly speaking, theories and explanations are the means by which we attempt to understand our world. When we observe events or hear about them and ask questions such as why or how they happened, we are searching for explanations. When we pro-vide answers to these questions, we have essentially come to a theoretical under-standing of the event. So, for example, crimes are sometimes understood or explained as "copycat" events. In one recent incident a 12-year-old boy was struck and taped to a tree near a Halifax high school. The event was reported in *The Chronicle-Herald* as a "copycat assault" (see Box 5.1). To the extent that this copycat explanation is an idea, it can be said to be a theory. In other words, unless we experienced the event or talked to the boys, we wouldn't know if the copycat explanation was valid or not. Because the explanation makes intuitive sense to us, it seems plausible. It is an example of a "common sense" or "taken for granted" understanding.

One way of understanding theory is to look at it as a set of interrelated propositions. What offers the explanation is the relationship between the propositions. For example, if we look at the incident in Box 5.1, we see that there are at least five interrelated propositions from which can be drawn the conclusion that the Halifax incident was a copycat crime.

BOX 5.1

Copycat Assault

As we will see later in the chapter, acts or events are sometimes understood or explained as acts of imitation. The following excerpts from a newspaper article provide an example.

Copycat Assault Worries Parents

Duct tape and kids. It's a strange combination, but it's one that has police and parents fearful. Halifax Police confirmed ... they're investigating the assault of a 12-year-old boy outside a north end school. The boy apparently was struck and possibly taped to a tree ... [I]t was the second time in two weeks that a Nova Scotia junior high school student was attacked in that fashion ... Last week, a 15-year-old Cape Breton boy was jumped, taped up and strung upside down from a tree ... [The school] principal ... is concerned that media attention to the Cape Breton bullies might have led to the assault in Halifax. [A] police ... constable ... said, "We have a major concern that kids were copycatting the Sydney incident."

Source: Hoare (1995:A6).

The propositions might look something like this:

1. Some crimes occur because some people imitate or copy crimes that they see or read about in the news.
2. A Cape Breton boy is jumped, taped up, and strung upside down from a tree.
3. The incident is reported in the news.
4. A Halifax boy is struck and taped to a tree.
5. The first incident is "like" the second incident.
6. Therefore, the Halifax incident is a copycat crime.

It is the connections or interrelationships between these propositions that provide a sense that the explanation is correct or plausible. The explanation seems to make "sense" because the idea takes the form of a logical argument and a conclusion can be deduced from the propositions.

Research and the Scientific Method

A scientific or empirical mind would be sceptical about the copycat explanation of the Halifax incident, however. A more sceptical or critical mind would see that the propositions do not contain a logical argument, but are a rhetorical argument. They would also see that the argument in favor of a copycat theory is faulty. For example, if the copycat incident described in Box 5.1 is closely examined it becomes apparent that there are several unconfirmed assumptions. It is assumed that the boys referred to in proposition 4 learned about the first incident via the news, that "taped up" and "taped to" constitute the same action, and there is a question as to whether proposition 1 is true, or simply a taken-for-granted belief because it sounds plausible.

It is the widespread acceptance of the scientific method that makes us require empirically validated information, **facts**, as a basis for probable truth. The scientific method offers theory based on observation rather than theories based solely on ideas. Figure 5.1 presents a diagram of the scientific method showing the relationship between theory and research, which is also the relationship between the conceptual world and the physical/social world. In the lower half of the diagram is the physical/social world or the world of material objects and social relationships. This is the world in which we make our observations by, for example, reading an article in the newspaper about copycat crime. However, as we try to explain our observations, we have to move away from the physical/social world to the conceptual world, or the world of ideas. This is the upper half of the diagram, the realm of theory, and theory that is based on observations is "grounded theory." Once we have developed a theory

FIGURE 5.1

The Scientific Method

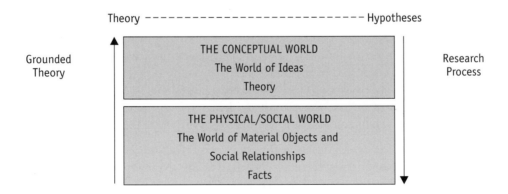

and begin to examine it by asking questions about the truth value of our propositions or assumptions, we are adopting an **empirical** approach to the problem. It is at this point that the research process becomes important.

Research may begin in the conceptual world with ideas or grounded theory or questions such as Did the boys in proposition 4 actually know about the first incident? If so, did they hear about it from the news? In order to answer these questions, we would have to move away from the realm of ideas to the physical/social world, the world of material objects and relationships. We would have to talk to the boys involved and find out if they had known about the first incident. Of course, the scientific method is not as simple as this example would suggest. It is more complicated simply because the sceptical mind would not be willing to accept that an observation of one incident would be sufficient to establish with certainty that new crimes occur because people imitate crimes reported in the news. We would need to examine many more incidents to satisfy the requirements of the scientific method.

Within the scientific method, research is the mechanism whereby we establish the truth value of our ideas, test our theories, and determine what will be accepted as factual. Strictly speaking, our facts are only as good as our research, and theories are never fact. Theory exists only as ideas and may be more or less supported by the information/evidence that is gathered by research. We have not always looked to the scientific method to provide explanations. As Anderson (1996) notes, Copernicus, Galileo, and others laid the foundations for the scientific method in the 17th century, but it was not until the 1800s that their ideas gained widespread acceptance. Initially, science was applied exclusively to the physical world; only as late as the 19th century was its application extended to the study of the social world.

Auguste Comte (1798–1857), the founding father of sociology, was among the first to argue that society could best be understood by applying the scientific method to its study. Practitioners of this new scientific method shared with mathematicians and physical scientists the belief that science would allow them to discover laws of society and behaviour. In other words, they assumed that human behaviour is determined by natural laws, and they believed that their task, as scientists, was to discover these laws. What differentiates such **positivist** thinkers from other scientific thinkers is the assumption that behaviour is determined by some factor or factors beyond the control of the individual. Positivist criminologists, past and present, seek to discover the causes of crime by applying the scientific method.

Causal Relationships

Establishing a law or a cause is one way of explaining an event. While we may suggest or imply cause through our daily conversations, establishing cause by means of the scientific method is a complicated process. Three conditions have to be met before causality can be established. First, it has to be established that there is a relationship between **concepts** both within and between the propositions that constitute a theory. Second, a time priority has to be established between these concepts. In other words, the cause has to come before the effect. If we take as an example the proposition that seeing a criminal act on television caused that act to be repeated, we would have to establish (1) that there was a relationship between seeing a crime on television and committing a crime, and (2) that the "seeing" preceded the "committing." Most often, statistical tests such as chi square or correlation are used to establish a relationship.

While we may be able to establish on the basis of a statistical test that there is a significant relationship between watching crime shows and committing crimes, it is not likely that we would ever be able to establish time priority. Returning to the example of the copycat assaults in Nova Scotia, the boys involved may have learned of the Cape Breton incident through television, but it is also possible that they had a history of tying people to trees, or had heard about others doing so (or had been tied to a tree themselves). Before we could say that seeing an incident on television or reading about it in a newspaper actually caused a similar incident to occur, we would have to establish that the people involved had not ever been exposed to such an incident before viewing it on television or reading about it.

A third criterion for determining causality concerns "spuriousness." In the copycat example, this would refer to whether we can be certain that there is no other "causal" factor related to both watching television and committing a crime. A possible third factor in that case might be boredom or having a lot of free time. People with a lot of free time often watch a lot of television. Moreover, when young people are bored, they are more likely to be involved in criminal or delinquent activities. Taking all of these considerations into account, it may very well be no more than coincidence that Halifax and Cape Breton boys tied someone to a tree. As for establishing the "cause" of crime, usually the best that we can do in the social sciences (and criminology in particular) is to establish relationships between our concepts. Seldom if ever are we able to establish causal relationships.

NINETEENTH-CENTURY THEORIZING ABOUT CRIME AND DELINQUENCY

Prior to the Enlightenment period in Western European history and the subsequent development of scientific methodologies, religion was the dominant force in society. Religious frameworks were used to understand and explain events and behaviours. When a person or his or her behaviour was viewed as bad or evil, the devil, or some type of devil possession would be blamed. Although such thinking declined in popularity with the rise of the scientific method, some people today claim that God or "voices in their head" made them commit their crimes. The scientific community is unable to confirm the existence of God and therefore whether God actually caused a

BOX 5.2

Sherlock Holmes and the Scientific Method

The scientific method didn't capture the public imagination, particularly with regard to the study of crime and criminals, until the late 1800s. One of the reasons Arthur Conan Doyle's detective stories so fascinated the Victorian reader was their application of science—and the scientific method—to solving crime. If you think about the methods used by Sherlock Holmes in his investigations, you can see Figure 5.1 in operation. First of all, Holmes makes an observation. From initial observation he develops a theory, which he puts to the test through further observation. If he is able to gather more evidence to confirm his theory, he is then convinced that he is on the right track to identifying the guilty party. The message of the Sherlock Holmes stories is that the scientific method is never wrong.

person to commit a crime. Nonetheless, psychiatry has legitimized the notion of insanity and used it to explain some bizarre or criminal behaviours. Today, rather than saying "the devil made them do it," people are more likely to blame some criminal acts on membership in things like satanic cults.

Classical Criminology

The earliest recorded scientific thinking about crime in Western thought comes out of the 18th century and is generally referred to as the **classical school** of criminology. A central tenet of the classical school is that people have free will—as opposed to being possessed by devils—and therefore must be held responsible for their misdeeds.

Cesare Beccaria (1819), an Italian philosopher, was one of the most influential writers of the classical school. Some of the ideas expressed in his famous essay "On Crimes and Punishments" (1764) sound remarkably similar to contemporary arguments. Among other things, Beccaria argued that offenders must be presumed innocent, that offences and punishments should be specified in a written code of criminal laws, that guilty people deserved to be punished because they had violated someone else's rights, that punishment should fit the crime, and that offenders must be held responsible for their behaviour. In a similar vein, the 18th-century English legal scholar, Jeremy Bentham, argued that repeat offenders should be punished more severely, that the punishment should fit the crime, and that people who commit similar offences should be punished in the same manner (Regoli and Hewitt, 1994:78–82).

Biological Positivism

While the ideas of the classical school had a significant impact on restructuring criminal justice systems, little attention was addressed to the offender or to the "causes" of criminal behaviour. By the end of the 19th century, positivism was gaining a strong hold and scholars were beginning to pay more attention to the criminal person. The first positivistic criminologists focused on biological and physiological factors in their search for the causes of criminal behaviour. This biological positivism had a profound effect on public thinking about crime at the turn of the century.

The Born Criminal

Perhaps the most influential among biological positivists was the Italian physician and criminologist, Cesare Lombroso, who has been called "the father of scientific criminology." It is clear in his chief work, *L'uomo delinquente* (1876), that Lombroso was influenced by evolutionary ideas such as those of Darwin that were popular at that time. As a prison doctor, Lombroso had cause to examine hundreds of prisoners. On the basis of these examinations, he argued that criminals and noncriminals were at different stages of evolutionary development. The physical features of convicted criminals constituted the "evidence" for Lombroso's theory that some people were quite simply born criminals. He states that

> at the site of that skull [of a notorious robber] I seem to see all of a sudden ... the problem of the nature of the criminal—an atavistic being who reproduces in his person ferocious instincts of primitive humanity and the inferior animals. These were explained anatomically by the enormous jaws, high cheekbones ... insensibility to pain, extremely acute sight, tattooing, excessive idleness, love of orgies, and the irresistible craving for evil for its own sake, the desire not only to extinguish life in the victim, but to mutilate the corpse, tear its flesh, and drink its blood. (cited in Regoli and Hewitt, 1994:97–98)

Types of People

A variant of Lombroso's idea of the born criminal came from studies of entire families. One such study was conducted by Richard Dugdale, an investigator for the Prison Association of New York. Dugdale's (1888) study of 709 members of the Jukes family found that a considerable number of the Jukes had criminal records, worked at prostitution, or were on welfare. Dugdale concluded that the Jukes family suffered from "degeneracy and innate depravity," and he went on to argue that pauperism, crime, and prostitution were all inherited traits.

Similarly, in the early part of the 1900s, Henry Goddard attempted to establish a connection between heredity, crime, and "feeblemindedness." Goddard's (1912) study of the Kallikak family identified two distinct types of people. One branch of the family was the progeny of a "feebleminded barmaid," while the other branch was descended from a "respectable girl of good family." According to Goddard, the former branch was full of paupers, criminals, alcoholics, and "mentally deficient" family members. By the end of the 19th century, lack of intelligence, or "feeblemindedness," was viewed as a major causal factor in criminal behaviour. It was believed that low intelligence made people incapable of understanding the potential immorality of their behaviour and less able to control their emotions (Shoemaker, 1990:49–50).

By the late 1800s, "tainted life blood" was believed to be responsible for passing on such vices as drinking and prostitution, as well as the condition of feeblemindedness (Weinberg, Rubington, and Hammersmith, 1981:17). People who engaged in these and other vices, as well as criminal behaviours, were generally classified into three broad categories: delinquent, dependant, and defective (Rubington and Weinberg, 1981). Delinquents were believed to be people who could change their ways if they received the right sort of guidance. Defectives were believed to have limited abilities, in some cases to be "feebleminded," and thus were not held responsible for what they did. Dependants were seen as people (not unlike children) whose well-being depended on the assistance of others. Understanding crime in these terms meant there was little need to explain delinquent behaviour because the concept was an explanation in itself. A person who committed a crime was a delinquent, dependant, or defective for the simple reason that he or she was a delinquent, dependant, or defective (as exemplified in Box 5.3). The categories were not reserved for juveniles—adults could be delinquents also. Hence, at the time, it was necessary to differentiate "juvenile" delinquents from other delinquents.

"Types of people" views grew in popularity at the turn of the century and were bolstered by **eugenics** studies like those of Dugdale and Goddard. People who were considered to be defective, inferior, or feebleminded were sterilized to prevent them from having children. By the 1930s, 31 U.S. states had passed laws permitting the sterilization of people who were determined to be feebleminded, mentally ill, or epileptic (Regoli and Hewitt, 1994:104). Involuntary sterilizations were carried out in Canada as late as the 1950s. Recent court cases have centred on the sterilization of young girls in Alberta who were considered to have low IQs.

The "Dangerous Class"

Another public concern at the turn of the century was a "class of people" that consisted largely of the poor, who were struggling to survive in the face of rapid industrialization and urbanization in European and North American cities. Henry Mayhew, an investigative reporter at the turn of the century, expressed concern in his writings about the growth of "this dangerous class":

There are thousands of neglected children loitering about the low neighbourhoods of the metropolis, and prowling about streets, begging and stealing for their daily bread ... They have been surrounded by the most baneful and degrading influences, and have been set a bad example by their parents and others whom they came in contact with, and are shunned by the honest and industrious classes of society. (cited in Sylvester, 1972:48)

Often, then, it was not children but their parents who were seen as defectives, delinquents, or dependants. Another of Mayhew's observations was that children, from their earliest years, "are often carried to the beer shop or gin palace on the breast of worthless, drunken mothers" (cited in Sylvester, 1972:51).

BOX 5.3

Girls of This Class

At a Charities and Correction Conference in Buffalo, New York, in June 1909, Mrs. Orphelia L. Amigh, Superintendent of the State Training School for Girls, spoke at a special session on the "Education of Backward, Truant, and Delinquent Children":

> When girls of this class [somewhat deficient but not feebleminded] come before a judge for commitment to an institution, it never occurs to him that they are irresponsible and need constant care to keep them from going wrong. The judge as well as her parents call such a girl wayward and incorrigible and sometimes vicious, but never defective. These are the girls who are used in the traffic in the white slave trade, who become the mothers of illegitimate children, and sometimes if possessed of a pretty face become the wives of men who later regret the confidence with which they enter them into matrimonial bonds. They are usually fond of excitement, dress and display and with the faculty and energy they possess they are turned in this direction. The power of reasoning out things for their own benefit seems to be an unknown quantity so far as good is concerned and they are easily turned aside from the right path and into the wrong one.

Source: Defective Children (1909:5).

TWENTIETH-CENTURY THEORIES OF DELINQUENCY

Biological Positivism

Although very influential in their time, "types of people" theories may seem quaint or far-fetched to a modern reader who is more inclined to consider social or psychological factors as causes of criminal behaviour. Nonetheless, the influence of biological positivism has continued to this day. Some of the most intuitively convincing research on hereditary effects has come from the study of twins and adopted children.

Twins and Adopted Children

Twin studies, which began in the 1930s, have consistently shown that identical twins tend to have higher delinquency rates than fraternal twins. Studies of adopted children have shown that children are more like their biological parents than their adoptive parents. Most of these early studies are problematic because they involved very small samples. In one of the most recent studies, Mednick, Gabrielli, and Hutchings (1987) looked at the court records of 15,000 adopted children in Denmark and compared their criminal records to those of their biological and adoptive parents. They found that crime rates for adopted boys were higher when their biological parents had a criminal record, and that crime rates were higher for adopted boys than for adopted girls. Most important, however, they found that the rate of criminality among adopted sons was less than 25 percent, which is lower than the rate implied by earlier studies (Mednick, Gabrielli, and Hutchings, 1987:86). Gottfredson and Hirschi (1990) re-examined these data, along with other adoption research, and concluded that "the magnitude of the 'genetic effect' as determined by adoption studies is near zero" (60).

Studies of twins and adopted children provide very poor evidence in support of heredity as a causal factor in crime and delinquency because they merely compare rates of offending in the different groups. None of these studies isolates or identifies a specific genetic factor that is responsible for the behaviour in question (Shoemaker, 1990:28–29).

Body Type

Modern variations on Lombroso's work were under way in the United States by the mid-1900s. Most notable is Sheldon's (1949) work, *Varieties of Delinquent Youth*. In the book, Sheldon argued that a young person's body type or "somatotype" affects his or her temperament and personality, which in turn can lead to delinquent behaviour. The basic body types or somatotypes are: endomorph, mesomorph, and ectomorph. Endomorphs tend to be soft and round, mesomorphs muscular and athletic, and ectomorphs thin and fragile. Not surprisingly, it was mesomorphic characteristics that were linked to delinquent behaviour. Sheldon found that both male and female offenders were more mesomorphic than nonoffenders. Glueck and Glueck (1950) provided considerable support for Sheldon's research. They compared male delinquents with nondelinquents and "found them to have narrower faces, wider chests, larger and broader waists, and bigger forearms and upper arms than nondelinquents." In later works (1956, 1959), they reported that mesomorphs were "more prone to delinquency" (Regoli and Hewitt, 1994:101).

Chromosomes

Some research has attempted to identify chromosomal abnormalities as causal agents. The average person has 46 chromosomes, two of which determine a person's sex. Males are typically XY and females are XX. Studies of sex chromosomes have found that some males (less than 1 percent) have an extra Y chromosome—the "super male." The extra Y chromosome has been used to explain violent criminal behaviour, the argument being that there is a higher proportion of males in prison populations with this chromosome than is found in the general population (Taylor, 1984). This evidence is not convincing for several reasons. First, the number of male prisoners with an extra Y chromosome is extremely small (1–3 percent). Second, the incidence of an extra X chromosome (Klinefelter syndrome) among male prisoners equals or exceeds that of the extra Y chromosome. Third, and most important, male prisoners with an extra Y chromosome are the least likely group within the prison population to have committed a violent offence (Akers, 1994:76).

IQ, LD, and ADHD

While we no longer talk about feeblemindedness, some researchers have focused on IQ (intelligence quotient). Research in this area has consistently shown a relationship between IQ and delinquency. The lower the IQ, the higher the probability of delinquency (Gordon, 1987). The findings from this research are difficult to interpret because of the class and race bias inherent in the IQ test itself. Most problematic is the question of how much of the IQ is determined by biological factors and how much by environmental factors.

More attention has been devoted to learning disabilities and delinquent behaviour. The actual cause of learning disabilities is not known, although it is widely assumed that a learning disability has a biological origin. Learning disabilities are seen to be related to delinquent behaviour in a number of ways. Some view the existence of a learning disability as leading to poor performance in school, association with similarly performing peers, and subsequent delinquency. Others argue that learning disabilities create physical and personal problems that make children susceptible to delinquency. Still others have suggested that children with learning disabilities are unable to understand the relationship between behaviour and punishment (Shoemaker, 1990:31–33).

The most recent disorder seen to be related to delinquent behaviour is attention-deficit hyperactivity disorder (ADHD). ADHD children are said to have difficulty concentrating, which affects their ability to learn and behave in an otherwise normal manner. While approximately 10 percent of American children are reported to suffer from ADHD, research has shown that the disorder is nine times more likely to be found in delinquent children (Moffitt, McGee, and Silva, 1987).

Explaining the "Biological" Facts

In evaluating the strength of biological theories, past and present, we need to consider what the facts were that people were trying to explain. While researchers like Lombroso were looking at a prison population, others were looking at boys who were delinquent. In most cases, researchers adopted a positivistic orientation to explanation, which meant they were trying to find the ways in which the people they were observing differed from noncriminals or nondelinquents. In every case, however, cause-and-effect relationships are confused, and those who espoused biological explanations failed to consider the possible spuriousness of the relationships they thought they had discovered. Recall that one of the most important criteria to be satisfied in establishing a causal relationship is time priority. The argument that feeblemindedness causes criminal behaviour—and there is little doubt that an IQ develops before a criminal act—is likely based on a spurious relationship. Poverty is something that may affect both one's IQ and criminal behaviour. Living a life of extreme poverty and deprivation cannot help but "cause" a person to have a measurably lower intelligence quotient than a person who has lived an enriched lifestyle, and poverty puts one at greater risk for criminal justice processing.

The major problem with early biological explanations of criminal behaviour is that they failed to account for environmental impacts on behaviour and, in so doing, overestimated the biological impact on behaviour. Consider the following observations about Down's syndrome children:

> Children [born] with Down's Syndrome have a specific genetic inheritance ... yet, even though the genotype remains the same for any such child, the behaviourial outcomes associated with this genotype differ ... Thirty years ago, Down's Syndrome children were expected to have life spans of no more than about 12 years. They were also expected to have ... low IQ scores. They were typically classified into a group of people who ... required custodial ... care. Today, however, Down's Syndrome children often live well beyond adolescence. Additionally, they lead more self-reliant lives. Their IQ's are now typically higher, often falling in the range allowing for education, training, and sometimes even employment. (Lerner, 1986:84 cited in Regoli and Hewitt, 1994:106)

The point Lerner is making is that the genotype responsible for creating Down's syndrome has not changed, but our responses to the condition have. As a result, the behavioural consequences of Down's syndrome are dramatically different today from those 30 years ago.

In their review of contemporary literature on genetics and criminal behaviour, Cloninger and Gottesman (1987) conclude, "there is no evidence that genetic factors are important in pre-pubertal delinquency as a class" (106). The authors maintain that environment and heredity may interact to produce criminal or delinquent behaviour, but they insist that, on the basis of the evidence, biological influences are limited or minimal. Not surprisingly, most modern biological theorists are a bit more positive about their work. They tend to take the position that "no specific criminal behaviour is inherited or physiologically preordained, nor is their any single gene that produces criminal acts." Rather, all behaviour is the result of biology interacting with the social and physical environment. Hence, modern biological theorists speak of behavioural "potentials," "susceptibilities," and "probabilities" rather than "causes" (Akers, 1994:76–77).

Psychological Positivism

Psychological theories did not develop until the 20th century. Essentially, these theories focus on the development of antisocial characteristics to explain criminal and delinquent behaviour. Unlike biological theories, some of the psychological theories stress environmental impacts on the formulation of antisocial characteristics. There are six groups of psychological theories on criminal and delinquent behaviour: psychoanalytic theories stemming from the work of Freud, behaviouristic explanations (B.F. Skinner), social learning theory (Albert Bandura), moral development theory (Jean Piaget), personality theory, and antisocial personality theory.

Psychoanalytic Theories

According to psychoanalytic theories, crime and delinquency are symptoms of an underlying emotional abnormality or disturbance that stems from childhood. The major theorists in this area are Sigmund Freud and Erik Erikson. Both assume that individual development occurs in stages and that personality abnormalities occur when individuals fail to resolve conflicts that arise in these various stages.

The Underdeveloped/Overdeveloped Superego For Freud (1953), there are three parts to the personality: the id, ego, and superego. The id is present at birth and is the basic biological and psychological part of the individual. It is instinctual, biological desire and does not differentiate between fantasy and reality. Hence, a hungry child will suck her or his thumb. The ego is the part of the personality that is able to separate reality from fantasy. It is the rational part of the mind/self. The superego is the conscience. As the moralizing part of the self, it is responsible for generating feelings of guilt, shame, remorse, etc.

In Freudian theory, there are five stages of personality (psychosexual) development. First is the "oral" stage (up to 1 year), second is the "anal" stage (age 1–3), third is the "phallic" stage (3–6), next is the "latency" stage (which lasts until puberty), and fifth is the "genital" stage. Conflicts arise between the id, ego, and superego in these stages. If unresolved, these conflicts will result in abnormal personality development. Crime and delinquency are seen as behavioural manifestations of abnormal personalities. The most crucial stage is the phallic stage (the Oedipus/Electra complex), in which the child loves the opposite-sex parent and hates the same-sex parent. Resolving conflict in this stage requires the child to identify with the same-sex parent. It is the resolution of these conflicts that leads to the development of the superego. Serious personality disorders are believed to develop from a fixation at this stage.

Crime and delinquency can be the result of either an undeveloped or overdeveloped superego. If underdeveloped, the superego is not strong enough to control or curb the id drives. People with an underdeveloped superego will do what they want without concern for consequences or for the feelings of others. If overdeveloped, the ego will experience such intense anxiety and guilt that a person may engage in crime because she or he unconsciously wants to be punished (Friedlander, 1947; Shoemaker, 1990; Akers, 1994). Crime is sometimes attributable to a weak ego since such individuals have … "poorly developed social skills, poor reality testing, gullibility and excessive dependence" (Andrews and Bonta, 1994:74, cited in Bohm, 1997:55).

Some decades after Freud, Erik Erikson (1950; 1968) modified Freudian theory by identifying eight stages of personal and social development. In Erikson's theory, individuals face crises and conflicts at each stage of development throughout their lifetime. If conflicts are unresolved at the early stages, personality development will be affected at subsequent stages. In the first stage, infancy, the crisis to be resolved involves the struggle between trust and mistrust. If a child fails to learn to trust, this will carry through to later stages of life. The most important stage in terms of delinquency is the fifth stage, age 12–18. Here the adolescent person is struggling to develop an identity as he or she grapples with such essential questions as Who am I? What will I become?

According to Erikson, there are three possible outcomes when this struggle is not resolved: identity diffusion, identity foreclosure, or negative identity. "Diffusion" occurs when an individual has failed to develop a coherent sense of self. "Foreclosure" develops when individuals have a premature sense of self; such people will experience problems if they fail to meet their own expectations (e.g., "I will be a rock star"), since alternatives have not been considered. "Negative identities" are identities that are not accepted or approved by others, particularly parents. According to Erikson, negative identities usually occur only when important "others" have failed to respond positively to prior identities. In other words, for these youth receiving attention for "bad" behaviour is better than receiving no attention at all (Regoli and Hewitt, 1994:125).

A number of critiques of the psychoanalytic perspective have centred on the issue of causal connections. Psychoanalytic theories posit a causal connection between the mind—an internal entity that is not directly measurable—and some measurable delinquent behaviour. This causal connection is "virtually impossible to establish" (Regoli and Hewitt, 1994:126).

Behaviourism

Behaviourism is one of the most widely used explanations of crime and delinquency. Quite simply, it suggests that people break the law because they can do so and not be punished. This idea is reminiscent of the classical school notion that punishment must fit the crime if crime is to be stopped. Behaviourists have attempted to explain how people learn to behave in particular ways. Whereas psychoanalytic and biological perspectives argue that behaviour is driven by forces within the individual, the behaviourist argues that a person's environment shapes or conditions her or his behaviour.

While this school of thought began with Pavlov's experiments with dogs at the turn of the century, B.F. Skinner (1938, 1953) is credited with developing behavioural principles of human behaviour. Simply put, any organism, human, animal, bird, or mammal will repeat behaviour that is followed by pleasure (a reinforcement) and stop behaviour that creates pain (a punishment). Behaviour is **conditioned** by these rewards and punishments. Hence, reinforcement (reward) increases the probability of a given behaviour and punishment decreases its probability.

Behaviourism is the cornerstone of the law-and-order approach to young offenders. Its proponents argue that the justice system, parents, and schools are "too permissive," and that young people "get away with crime" (i.e., are not punished). If we toughen the justice system, then, young people will be punished and therefore conditioned to not commit crimes.

In spite of its massive influence, behavioural theory also has its share of critics. The most persistent critique is that it ignores the role of thought in learning. People do think about what they do and mental processes cannot be ignored as a factor in all behaviour.

Social Learning Theory

Some psychologists responded to shortcomings in behaviourism by formulating explanations of learning that involve mental processes. Notable among these psychologists is Bandura (1977), who believed the social environment was the most important aspect in learning and that the learning process is **cognitive** rather than behavioural. This approach allows for one to learn through imitation and through watching others be rewarded or punished.

Social learning theory provided the impetus for concern about what children see on television and movies. It also provides a theoretical basis for "copycat" explanations. There are also sociological and social psychological versions of social learning theory, which will be discussed in the next chapter.

The major criticism of social learning theory is its failure to account for differences in cognition. Why is it, for example, that only some of the children who watched Power Rangers, Mutant Ninja Turtles, or the WWF imitated what they saw in ways that were harmful or destructive?

Moral Development Theory

Part of the answer to the above question comes from **development theory**. Jean Piaget (1932), who was one of the first to study cognitive and moral developmental processes in children, documented two stages of moral development: constraint and cooperation. Kohlberg (1964, 1969) expanded this two-stage model to six stages. In development theory, delinquents are said to be at a lower stage of moral development than non-delinquents. Hence, they are not concerned with the rights or feelings of others, focus on behavioural consequences (whether they will be caught or punished), and act to avoid punishment.

A major critique of this perspective comes from the fact that the research focused on boys to the exclusion of girls. Gilligan (1982) examined moral development in girls and found a very different orientation. For boys, moral development focuses on justice issues; for girls, it focuses on caring and responsibility issues.

Personality Theory

Like biological "types of people" theories, personality theory explains delinquent behaviour on the basis of "who" one is as a person. This perspective assumes that a particular trait or set of traits produces delinquent behaviour.

As early as the 1930s, personality traits were linked to delinquent behaviour. Healy and Bronner (1936), for example, reported that delinquents were unhappy, discontented, emotionally disturbed, jealous, and had feelings of inadequacy and guilt. Later research identified other personality traits of delinquents, including passivity, aggressiveness, emotional instability, egocentricity, immaturity, suggestibility, and lack of inhibition (Bromberg, 1953). Interestingly, many of these traits are contradictory (e.g., passivity/aggressiveness), and they do not permit consistent differentiation between delinquents and nondelinquents.

The development and use of more objective personality testing methods in the 1950s and 1960s led to far more reliable test results. The most widely used of these tests is the Minnesota Multiphasic Personality Inventory (MMPI). Results from this test show that institutionalized delinquents score high on the asocial, amoral, and psychopathic scales (Hathaway and Monachesi, 1953). This is not to say that the MMPI is able to predict delinquency. Nor does it mean that personality traits cause delinquent behaviour. Once again, time priority is important in that some of these traits may develop as a result of a history of criminal or delinquent behaviour and/or processing through the justice system.

Antisocial Personality Theory

People who are said to have an **antisocial personality** are sometimes referred to as "psychopaths" or "sociopaths." Hans J. Eysenck (1977) developed a theoretical scheme to explain the psychopathic personality. For Eysenck, personality is what causes certain behaviours to develop. Moreover, personality is determined physiologically and is possibly inherited. A psychopath is prone to criminal behaviour largely because of an inability to develop emotional attachments and to feel remorse or shame. The biological aspect of this theory comes from Eysenck's assumption that defects in the autonomic nervous system lead to the development of psychopathic emotional characteristics. Others have suggested that childbirth delivery complications, or birth trauma, may be responsible for the antisocial personality (Kandel and Mednick, 1991).

Clinical definitions of the terms "psychopath," "sociopath," and "antisocial personality" include the following traits: impulsiveness, an inability to relate to others or to learn from experience, insensitivity to pain (either one's own or that of others), and a lack of guilt or remorse. According to Shoemaker (1990), there is no agreement as to whether psychopathy or sociopathy applies to juveniles. While the MMPI measures psychopathology in delinquents, clinical definitions of sociopathy apply to adults. Children with these characteristics are generally referred to clinically as having an "impulse-ridden personality" or a "tension-discharge disorder" (Shoemaker, 1990:68–69).

One last "type of person" measure worthy of discussion because of its popularity in correctional settings is the Interpersonal Maturity Scale (I-Level). This scale developed from the work of Sullivan, Grant, and Grant (1957) and was applied in California as a focus for treatment plans in the 1970s (Palmer, 1974; Warren, 1970). It was also used along with the Conceptual Level Matching Model in Ontario youth correctional facilities in the 1980s (Leschied, Jaffe, and Stone, 1985; Leschied and Thomas, 1985). Similar to other developmental theories, the I-Level identifies a person's interpersonal development in stages. More specifically, it measures level of maturity in social and interpersonal skills through seven stages. Ninety percent of official delinquents are found in levels 2 to 4. Level 2 delinquents are asocial, aggressive, and power-oriented. Delinquents in level 3 are passive conformists and those in level 4 are neurotic. With this scale, delinquents may have combinations of traits, such as "passive-aggressive" or "neurotic-asocial."

According to Akers (1994:89), personality theories are more testable than psychoanalytic theories, but, unfortunately, the results are inconsistent. Shoemaker's (1990) review of psychological theories and empirical research leads to the conclusion that "the search for a unique set of personal, psychological antecedents of delinquency continues and remains unfulfilled" (73).

Sociological Positivism

While biology and psychology offer some explanations for crime and delinquency, sociology is responsible for most of the theorizing and research in this area. Sociology did not develop as a discipline in its own right until the latter part of the 1800s. While 19th-century sociological theorists like Émile Durkheim (1933, 1951) addressed crime in their writings, most did not consider delinquency as something distinct from crime that needed to be explained.

In North America in the 1920s and 1930s, delinquency theory was developed by a group of sociologists at what became known as the Chicago School of Urban Sociology. With few exceptions, their work was positivistic in nature and focused on the study of social problems. Like the biological positivists, these early sociologists were trying to develop explanations by examining the differences between delinquents and nondelinquents. However, their main concern was to discover what it is about the environment that affects an individual's behaviour. In addition, sociologists were among the first to develop explanations of delinquency and not just criminal behaviour. Because of its focus on the environment, sociological theory has had a considerable influence on social policy, delinquency prevention projects, and the manner in which young offenders are processed through the justice system. Psychology, with its focus on the individual, has had more impact on how we work with young people once they have been convicted or apprehended by the police.

Social Disorganization and Strain Theory

Social Disorganization Modern theories of delinquency began with the work of Clifford Shaw and Henry McKay at the Chicago School. Although some 19th-century thinkers had recognized that various social problems were associated with crime and poverty, Shaw and McKay (1931, 1942) were among the first to test this idea by looking at the distribution of delinquency by area—in their case, in the city of Chicago. This method of analyzing the spatial distribution of social problems and their relation to the physical environment is known as **human ecology**. What Shaw and McKay found from their comparisons of three different periods—1900–1906, 1917–23, and 1927–33—was a consistent pattern of delinquency in the city. Rates of delinquency were always higher in the area surrounding the centre of the city (zone in transition) and decreased as one moved out to the suburbs. The "zone in transition" was characterized by urban decay, poverty, high rates of adult crime, mental disorders, physical diseases, high dependency on social welfare, unemployment, and low rates of home ownership. For Shaw and McKay, who referred to this area as "socially disorganized," the social environment of delinquents—not their personality or physical characteristics—was the factor that distinguished them from nondelinquents.

As defined by Shaw and McKay, social disorganization describes a condition in which

- controls that would prevent delinquency are absent;
- parents and neighbours may actually approve of certain delinquent behaviours;
- opportunities for delinquency are numerous; and
- there is little opportunity for or encouragement toward employment (cited in Bohm, 1997:74).

One of the major criticisms directed toward social disorganization theory is that it fails to recognize that differences in social organization do not necessarily imply the negative; in other words, any form of organization other than that of the dominant group is viewed as disorganization. The Chicago School has also been criticized for failing to acknowledge the role that city planners and politicians play in the development of certain areas of cities at the expense of others (Bohm, 1997:76–77). Some have pointed to the reality of "defended neighborhoods" where stable organized communities will encourage delinquency or gang activity, consciously or otherwise, to protect the community from external threat (Suttles, 1972; Heitgerd and Bursik, 1987).

In the early 1930s, Shaw and McKay established a delinquency prevention project known as the Chicago Area Project (CAP). The objective of CAP was to rebuild disorganized neighbourhoods through schools, churches, clubs, businesses, and educational programs designed to increase public awareness of delinquency, to provide crime-prevention activities, and to foster community involvement in dealing with neighbourhood problems. The program met with mixed results (Akers, 1994:143; Lundman, 1993). A recent version of CAP is the Chicago Beethoven Project. Initiated in 1988, this program focuses on pregnant women and ways of breaking the cycle of welfare. Women receive prenatal care throughout their pregnancy, children receive health care, and mothers are taught how to care for their children (Regoli and Hewitt, 1994:147–48).

Anomie   Closely related to social disorganization is **anomie**, a concept that was first formulated by Durkheim. Anomie refers to a state of normlessness in which rules and regulations are no longer sufficient to control social behaviour. Robert Merton (1938) used the concept of anomie to develop a theory of deviance that forms the core of a group of theories that have come to be known as **strain theory**. Strain theory assumes that children are basically good and engage in delinquent activity only when faced with undue pressure or stress. Thus, conformity is the normal state of affairs; what needs explaining is why people would deviate or why children would be delinquent.

According to Merton, all people in North American society are socialized to aspire to the same culturally mandated goals—a good job, marriage, home ownership, children, two cars in the driveway, a dog and a cat, etc. However, the legitimate means for achieving these goals are limited by the social structure. The educational system is an example of a legitimate institutionalized means of goal achievement. Nonetheless, because of the cost of postsecondary education, among other things, it is difficult for people with low incomes to avail themselves of this means of goal attainment. Merton argued that such contradictions or discrepancies between cultural goals and structural means—anomie—are created and reinforced by a class system of reward distribution. The anomic conditions create "strain" or pressures to find other means to success, some of which may be illegal. While this strain can affect people from all social classes, individuals from lower-class backgrounds are more likely to experience it.

While there is disagreement among contemporary scholars as to whether Merton's theory allows us to make predictions about individual crime and delinquency or whether it is instead a structural theory (Bernard, 1987), Merton did offer explanations of different types of deviance. He did so by viewing them as adaptive responses to strain. In response to strain, there are five "modes of adaptation": conformity, innovation, retreatism, rebellion, and, ritualism.

If people accept cultural goals, but reject institutionalized means of goal achievement—that is, cannot get a university education, or finish high school, or get a job in order to obtain the things that they want—then they are likely to innovate to achieve their goals. *Innovation* results in various kinds of white-collar crime, theft, and, perhaps, drug dealing, or any other type of criminal behaviour that provides material gains. On the other hand, some people will accept institutionalized means of goal achievement, but lose sight of or abandon their original goals. *Ritualism* occurs when people reject or alter cultural goals and focus instead on the means of goal achievement. People who reject both institutionalized means and cultural goals through lack of interest are engaged in *retreatism*, a mode of adaptation that may lead to drug addiction, alcoholism, or a life on the streets. *Rebellion* occurs when people reject institutionalized means and cultural goals, but do so not for their own gain or for personal reasons. Rather than adopt a stance of passive rejection, these people will try to change the means and/or goals so that everyone can benefit. Merton maintained that this response was nonconformist and not in the same category as deviant behaviour for personal gain. Most people, however, will just simply conform to a state of anomie, meaning that they will try harder to achieve their goals by conventional means. Merton called this mode of adaption *conformity*.

Merton's general theory of deviance provided a context for his discussion of the structural impediments to success experienced by those from lower-class backgrounds.

Other theorists followed Shaw and McKay's lead and focused their attention exclusively on lower-class youth, particularly those living in poor areas of cities. While such a focus might seem unreasonable today, in the 1930s and 1940s only official statistics provided "facts" on delinquency. That lower-class youth were overrepresented in delinquency statistics from official sources was seen at the time as the most salient fact that needed to be explained. Theorists who focused on lower-class youth to develop explanations of delinquency included Cohen, Miller, and Cloward and Ohlin.

The Delinquent Subculture Albert Cohen's (1955) study of lower-class youth was chiefly concerned with gang delinquency. Cohen modified Merton's anomie theory, added a psychological dimension, and argued that delinquent behaviour is a "reaction formation" to the frustration of being a lower-class youth in a middle-class world. In this regard, delinquent behaviour is a group activity that offers a solution for lower-class youth. The **delinquent subculture** (gang) is a group solution to the frustration of being unable to achieve middle-class goals.

Like Merton, Cohen argues that lower-class youth aspire to the same goals as middle-class youth. However, lower-class youth and middle-class youth do not share the same social values, lifestyles, or skills. Hence, when lower-class youth find themselves in a middle-class education system, they are ill equipped to achieve success. After experiencing repeated failures in school, lower-class youth are led to not only reject the school and the middle-class values that it espouses, but to seek out others like themselves. This subculture affords a means of achieving success through the status it provides members who engage in delinquent activities. The delinquent subculture is hostile toward middle-class values and standards, and expresses this hostility by engaging in so-called senseless behaviour such as destroying school libraries. Not all lower-class boys, Cohen points out, resort to this kind of behaviour. Some will adopt a "college boy" response and continue to strive to achieve middle-class goals. Others become "corner boys" and resign themselves to life in the lower-class world.

Differential Opportunity Richard Cloward and Lloyd Ohlin also saw delinquency as a lower-class urban behaviour and developed differential opportunity theory to explain delinquent behaviour. Like Merton and Cohen, Cloward and Ohlin (1960) argued that pressures to achieve success combined with an inability to achieve success cause delinquent behaviour. However, while Merton focused on legitimate opportunities for achievement and success, Cloward and Ohlin recognized that some youth have access to "illegitimate" opportunity structures. If young people are denied access to legitimate opportunity structures or are unable to achieve success in legitimate ways, they will try to gain access to illegitimate opportunity structures. The extent to which illegitimate opportunity structures are available will depend on the neighbourhoods in which young people live.

According to Cloward and Ohlin, there are three types of delinquent subcultures found in lower-class neighbourhoods: the criminal gang, the violent gang, and the retreatist gang. Some lower-class neighbourhoods are relatively stable in that they have organized adult criminal activities and young people have an opportunity to become involved in illegitimate opportunities that are provided through adult criminal activities. Stability is achieved because the community or neighbourhood provides adult role models and ways of making money, albeit criminal and/or illegitimate. As was indicated by Shaw and McKay, however, some neighbourhoods are disorganized, and because of this there are no stable adult criminal activities. Any youthful criminality in this type of neighbourhood fosters conflict and violence between youth—hence the violent gang. Retreatist gang activities occur when youth are "double failures." As characterized by Cloward and Ohlin, retreatist gangs consist of young people who have not been able to achieve success in either legitimate or illegitimate ways. These are the youth who give up and retreat to a world of drugs and alcohol.

In the 1960s, an ambitious anti-poverty program was implemented in New York City. Following opportunity theory, the Mobilization for Youth Project was designed to improve living conditions and opportunities in high-delinquency neighbourhoods. This project was followed up in the United States by federal government policies that declared "war on poverty" and implemented community action programs, job corps programs, and Head Start programs. Despite the billions of dollars spent on those and other initiatives, the problem of poverty remains (Regoli and Hewitt, 1994:170–71).

Classical anomie and strain theories have been criticized for their focus on social class. Merton's theory primarily attempts to account for class differences in official crime rates, while Cloward and Ohlin focus on lower-class male subculture delinquency (Akers, 1994:54–55). Nonetheless, Merton maintains that strain can affect all classes. Some argue that this criticism is irrelevant because strain theories were never intended as an explanation for middle-class delinquency (Shoemaker, 1990:141).

Strain theories are limited because of their focus on educational and occupational sources of strain. Agnew (1985b, 1992, 2001) developed a general strain theory that extends the strain concept to include other sources. These include (1) failure to achieve goals; (2) removal of positive stimuli, such as the death or loss of a family member; and (3) confrontation with negative stimuli (e.g., child abuse).

Culture and Learning Theory

Class Culture   Walter Miller focused on cultural factors as he tried to identify characteristics of lower-class life that gave rise to delinquent behaviour. According to Miller (1958), the problems experienced by lower-class youth begin with the family structure—primarily a female-headed household. This arrangement forces boys to join all-male peer groups, or "one-sex peer units" (14). It is within these peer groups that boys learn the characteristics, or "focal concerns," of lower-class culture that generate delinquent behaviour.

The focal concerns of lower-class culture, Miller maintained, are trouble, toughness, smartness, excitement, fatalism, and autonomy. It is these focal concerns that lead lower-class boys to break the law. *Trouble* refers to the sense that getting into confrontational situations with police or people in authority is not something to be ashamed of and may even be encouraged and rewarded by the peer group. *Toughness* refers to a preoccupation with being physically strong or "macho." *Smartness* refers to an ability to outsmart or "con" other people, as opposed to being smart in an academic sense. *Excitement* refers to a desire for adventure, thrill, and risk-taking. *Fatalism* is believing that one has no control over the future, that things just "happen." *Autonomy* refers to a desire to be independent and in control, as opposed to bowing to authority. Adherance to focal concerns confers status on members of a peer group, but it is also likely to lead to delinquent behaviour. Hence, in Miller's view, delinquency was "normal" behaviour for lower-class boys rather than a reaction or adaptation to strain.

Miller's theory has two clear limitations. It cannot explain why many lower-class boys are not delinquent. Nor can it explain female delinquency.

Differential Association Edwin Sutherland added a new dimension to the issue of delinquency through his theory of differential association. According to Sutherland (1939), delinquent behaviour is learned behaviour, or behaviour that is learned by interacting with others who are delinquent. What is learned are the techniques, motivations, attitudes, and definitions that permit people to break the law. Sutherland took issue with Shaw and McKay's notion of disorganized communities by pointing out that these communities are not necessarily disorganized, but rather are organized in a manner not evident in mainstream communities.

Sutherland presented his theory of differential association through a series of principles. Of the nine principles, two are of particular significance:

1. A person becomes delinquent because of an excess of definitions favourable to violation of law over definitions unfavourable to violation of law.
2. While criminal behavior is an expression of general needs and values, it is not explained by those general needs and values, since noncriminal behavior is an expression of the same needs and values. (Sutherland & Cressey, 1974:75–77)

Like Cohen and Merton, Sutherland suggests that what distinguishes people from one another is the means that they choose to acquire what they want. For Sutherland, people's behaviour patterns are created by "differential association." This proposition is the core of Sutherland's theory, and it is reflected in the first principle above. According to this principle, people become criminal because they have more contact with criminal patterns than with noncriminal patterns. In other words, people who have learned how to lie, cheat, or steal will act on this knowledge if they have not also learned how to be law-abiding citizens.

With regard to the second principle listed above, it is commonly assumed within the positivistic tradition that delinquents and nondelinquents have different value systems. Sutherland argued that delinquents and nondelinquents have the same needs and values. Delinquent behaviour cannot be explained by those needs and values because they are shared by people who do not engage in such behaviour.

Drift and Delinquency An extension of Sutherland's principle that criminal and non-criminal behaviours are expressions of the same needs and values is found in David Matza's theory of drift and delinquency. Like Sutherland, Matza (1964) argued that delinquents are not much different from nondelinquents in terms of their values; hence, they are not firmly committed to delinquent behaviour. Unlike Sutherland, Matza argued that delinquent behaviour is situational rather than learned; in other words, it is particular situations and circumstances that lead to delinquent behaviour.

Matza's ideas are also different from those of Cohen and Miller. According to Matza, groups might encourage delinquent behaviour in particular circumstances, but group membership per se is not sufficient to drive youth toward delinquent behaviour. Young people are not likely to develop a set of values totally opposed to that of adults because their status in society makes them far too dependent on adults. Rather, delinquency is something that juveniles drift in and out of as situations, circumstances, and opportunities present themselves. However, if delinquents are not any different from nondelinquents with regard to their values, why are some juveniles involved in delinquent behaviour while others are not? Borrowing from Freud's notion of defence mechanisms, Matza's answer is that delinquent behaviour occurs when young people are able to rationalize their delinquent behaviour (Bohm, 1997:53).

Techniques of Neutralization Sykes and Matza (1957) suggest that there are five defence mechanisms, or "techniques of neutralization," that young people use to rationalize, justify, or excuse the negative aspects of their delinquent behaviour. *Denial of responsibility* occurs when young people refuse to accept any responsibility for their behaviour and blame others instead. *Denial of injury* occurs when a youth insists that no one was hurt in any way (e.g., "The store owner is too rich to notice a loss of money"). *Denial of the victim* occurs when a young person argues that the victimization was deserved in some way (e.g., "He was a bully and I had to put him in his place"). *Condemnation of the condemners* refers to the argument that those in authority—for example, police, parents, and teachers—are hypocrites. *Appeal to higher loyalties* occurs when a young person argues that his or her motivations were essentially honourable (e.g., "I was protecting my friends").

In *Go-Boy!*, Roger Caron (1978), a Canadian who spent most of his adult years in federal prisons, uses this neutralization technique when he says that one of the robberies he committed was motivated by his father's inability to make a mortgage payment; in committing the crime, he was "helping" his father.

For Shoemaker (1990:157, 167), the most serious shortcoming of both differential association and drift theories relates to problems of measurement. In order to test the theories, it would be necessary to assess a person's motivations, intentions, and attitudes toward crime and delinquency prior to the commission of a criminal or delinquent act. Of course, such an assessment can realistically occur only after the act has been committed.

Control Theory

The majority of theories we have discussed to this point fit into a category sometimes referred to as **consensus theory**. An implicit or explicit assumption in these theories is that most people are essentially law-abiding. Given this assumption, what needs to be explained is why some people are involved in criminal or delinquent behaviour. The answer, of course, varies by theory: reaction formation, anomie, differential opportunity, and so forth.

Other theories are driven by a different assumption about human nature. For some theorists, it is equally plausible to assume that unless people are constrained in some way they will behave on the basis of self-interest; hence, the likelihood of delinquent or criminal behaviour will be fairly high. Given this assumption, what needs to be explained is why most people are not involved in criminal or delinquent behaviour. The answer is, quite simply, that they are constrained from doing so. Those who begin with this assumption produce theories that fit in a category referred to as **control theory** because they seek to explain how it is that some people's behaviours are controlled while others' are not. Two theorists who made major contributions to this perspective are Walter Reckless, who developed containment theory, and Travis Hirschi, who produced the theory of the social bond.

Containment   Why don't all boys in high-crime neighbourhoods get into trouble? Reckless (1953) grappled with this question and concluded that "good boys" have a positive self-concept. According to Reckless, four factors influence delinquent behaviour. Pulling or pushing young people into delinquency are "outer pulls," or environmental factors such as poverty or unemployment, and "inner pushes," which are psychological or biological factors such as psychosis or hostility. Mitigating against push and pull factors are external and internal "containment" factors. External containments are outer controls (such as community ties) that protect young people from delinquent behaviour. Internal containments, the most important of which is a positive self-concept, also protect young people from pull and push factors. According to Reckless, a pro-social self-concept is the best defence against delinquent temptations.

The Social Bond The question "Why do they do it?" is simply not the question … The question is "Why don't we do it?" (Hirschi, 1969:34).

To answer the above question, Hirschi (1969) began with the notion that most young people will engage in delinquent behaviour unless there is something to prevent them from doing so. Hirschi called this "something," which forms the basis of his theory, the **social bond**. The social bond consists of four elements that bind a person to a conventional lifestyle: attachment, commitment, involvement, and beliefs. Young people with *attachments* to parents, schools, and other agents of socialization are less likely than those without such attachments to become delinquent. Unlike Cohen and Miller, Hirschi argued that attachment to peers is a deterrent to delinquent behaviour; delinquents, he believed, tend to be socially isolated.

Commitment refers to successes, achievements, and ambitions and the extent to which one has invested in these things. The greater the investment, the more one has to lose by engaging in delinquency. So, for example, those who are achieving success in school or are highly motivated to achieve are less likely to be involved in delinquent behaviour. *Involvement* refers to activity and the extent to which young people are engaged in productive activities. Those who are bored and have too much time on their hands are more likely to be involved in nonproductive activities, including delinquent behaviour. With regard to *beliefs*, Hirschi argued that a person who is committed to or believes in a conventional value system will be constrained from getting involved in criminal or delinquent activities. This is particularly the case when the person believes that rules and laws are morally correct and should be obeyed.

More recently, Hirschi collaborated with Michael Gottfredson and developed the General Theory of Crime (1990). This theory refines Hirschi's original control theory by focusing on self-control. They argue that there are important elements of self control: gratification, excitement and risk, long-term benefits, planning and skill, pain or discomfort to victims—an absence of which leads to low self-control and a greater propensity toward "criminality." People with low self-control tend toward impulsivity, short-sightedness, insensitivity, with a lack of verbal skills and orientation toward physical risk-taking (89–91, 157–58). From this theory, crime prevention is a simple matter of child-rearing, an idea to be pursued further in Chapter 7.

As we will see in the next chapter, social control theory is one of the most influential theories of youth crime. It is intuitively persuasive, readily lends itself to seemingly simple crime prevention strategies, and has more empirical support than many other theories of crime and delinquency. Nonetheless, it has not escaped criticism. Bohm (1997:106), for example, points out that control theory cannot account for "maturational reform"—the fact that most youth abandon criminal activities as they mature to adulthood.

SUMMARY

This chapter traces the development of academic thinking about delinquent and criminal behaviour from the 18th century to the 1960s. (For students interested in pursuing the theories discussed in this chapter, one of the most comprehensive books on delinquency theory, critiques, and research is Donald J. Shoemaker's *Theories of Delinquency: An Examination of Explanations of Delinquent Behaviour.*) In the next chapter, we discuss how some of these theories have been revised or integrated to create more comprehensive explanations of delinquency.

Theories are ideas that are developed as explanations for events and behaviour. They are made up of interrelated propositions which themselves are statements about the relationships between concepts. Research is a process whereby the empirical validity of theories or beliefs is tested. Statistical testing is a common method of establishing relationships between concepts. Causal relationships are the most difficult to establish because three criteria must be satisfied: a statistical relationship such as a correlation, time priority of the concepts in the "cause–effect" statement, and nonspuriousness.

The scientific approach to crime began in the 18th century and is known today as the classical school of criminology. By the 19th century, positivism was gaining a stronghold and scholars were trying to understand the differences between criminals and noncriminals. Early theorists focused on biological and physiological factors in their search for the causes of criminal behaviour. "Types of people" explanations of crime and delinquency included theories of the born criminal, feeblemindedness, tainted life blood, and the dangerous class.

Twentieth-century biological positivism has focused on twins and adopted children, body type, chromosomes, intelligence quotient, learning disability, and, most recently, attention-deficit hyperactivity disorder in its attempts to explain crime and delinquency. Research suggests that environment and biology may interact to produce criminal or delinquent behaviour. As a result, modern biological theorists speak of behavioural "potentials," "susceptibilities," and "probabilities" rather than "causes."

Psychological theories fall into six groups: psychoanalytic theories, behaviouristic explanations, social learning theories, moral development theories, personality theories, and antisocial personality theories. Most of these theories posit a causal connection between the mind and behaviour. Since the workings of the mind are not directly observable, it is impossible to establish these relationships empirically.

Sociology is responsible for most of the theorizing and research on the subject of crime and delinquency. Delinquency theory began with the work of sociologists at the Chicago School of Urban Sociology in the 1920s and 1930s. Until the 1960s, sociological positivism offered three theoretical perspectives: social disorganization and strain theory, culture and learning theory, and control theory.

Social disorganization and strain theory includes the work of Shaw and McKay on social disorganization, Merton on anomie, Cohen on the delinquent subculture, and Cloward and Ohlin on differential opportunity. Social disorganization theory has been criticized for exhibiting a middle-class bias toward urban core areas of cities. Strain theories are limited because of their focus on lower-class youth and only educational and occupational sources of strain.

Miller's culture theory identifies six focal concerns of lower-class culture that give rise to delinquent behaviour, but it cannot explain why many lower-class youth are not delinquent. Early learning theories included Sutherland's theory of differential association, Matza's drift theory, and Sykes and Matza's techniques of neutralization. These theories are impossible to measure because to do so would require knowing what a person was thinking before he or she engaged in criminal or delinquent behaviour.

The most important and influential control theory is Hirschi's theory of the social bond. The social bond consists of four elements: attachment, commitment, involvement, and belief. Hirschi's theory has more empirical support than many other theories of crime and delinquency. Hirschi and Gottfredson (1990) have developed a new version of control theory that focuses on the elements of self-control and its role in producing criminality.

CHAPTER 6

New Directions in Theorizing about Youth Crime and Delinquency

CHAPTER OBJECTIVES

1. To discuss labelling theory, the liberal and radical traditions of conflict theory, and the critical perspective in criminology.

2. To review types of integrative theory.

3. To discuss androgyny and sexism in theories of crime and delinquency from the 19th century to the present.

4. To discuss the position of girls in classical and contemporary theory.

5. To discuss new theories of delinquency.

6. To provide a feminist critique of new theories.

7. To discuss feminist theorizing about girls and delinquency.

KEY TERMS

Critical
Decarceration
Social order
Power
Criminalization
Social learning theory

Interactional theory
Oppression
Criminal event
Role theory
Androgynous
Chivalry hypothesis

Liberation hypothesis
Power-control theory
Patriarchy
Care ethic

INTRODUCTION

Prior to the 1960s, most explanations of crime and delinquency were positivistic in orientation and attempted to explain why an individual would behave in a criminal or delinquent manner. By the late 1950s and early 1960s an entirely new perspective was taking root in criminology. This perspective, labelling theory, moved thinking away from a positivistic approach by asking questions about crime rather than about the person. Labelling theory eventually had a significant impact on social policy and our responses to criminal and deviant behaviour. This new way of thinking contributed to the emergence of a **critical** perspective on crime. In contrast to positivistic theories, which seek to discover the "cause" of deviant behaviour, the critical perspective focuses more on power relations and social control, tends to be less concerned with statistical testing of theories, and relies less on official data for analyses.

This chapter begins with a discussion of labelling theory and critical perspectives on delinquency, and moves to a discussion of recent developments in the positivist tradition—namely, integration theories. Some of the movement toward integration was stimulated by a feminist critique of criminology theory. We will examine this critique along with recent feminist theorizing about girls and delinquency.

CRITICAL CRIMINOLOGY

Labelling Theory

While it was through the work of Edwin Lemert and Howard Becker that the labelling perspective became a major force in sociology, the origin of this perspective can be traced to Frank Tannenbaum and, more specifically, his book *Crime and the Community*.

Play and Delinquency

Tannenbaum (1938) rejected the positivist supposition that delinquents are somehow different from nondelinquents and that in order to understand delinquent behaviour it is necessary to determine what those differences are. Instead, he argued that children engage in delinquent behaviour without knowing that others view it as delinquent or bad. As Tannenbaum (1938) describes the process,

> there is a gradual shift from the definition of the specific act as evil to a definition of the individual as evil, so that all his acts come to be looked upon with suspicion ... [T]he young delinquent becomes bad because he is not believed if he is good. (17–18)

For Tannenbaum, the best adult response to delinquent behaviour is to do nothing. In his view, it is the conflict that develops between a child's play group and the community that turns play into delinquent or criminal behaviour. More specifically, adults in the community become annoyed or angered by what children are doing. They respond by trying to control or stop the activity. If children come to resent adult inter-ference and start to act in a defiant manner, adults will define them as bad. Being so defined will isolate these children from the community and from other children. In their isolated state, they will come to accept themselves as different and be encouraged to engage in more delinquent behaviour. This process, in which "the person becomes the thing he is described as being" (Tannenbaum, 1938:21), was later elaborated upon by Edwin M. Lemert (1951, 1967) and Howard Becker (1963).

Secondary Deviance

Lemert (1951) argued that there are two types of deviance: primary and secondary. *Primary deviance* is the initial act. Anyone is potentially a "primary" deviant if he or she does things that would likely be considered deviant if they were known about by others. *Secondary deviance* refers to all the behaviours that a person develops as a result of societal responses to her or his primary deviance. In other words, once discovered, a person may find it very difficult to behave or be seen as anything other than deviant precisely because his or her deviance is known to others. Hence, it becomes increas-ingly difficult for a secondary deviant to not be deviant in the eyes of the community. The person may begin to develop a self-concept as a deviant and act accordingly. The transition from primary to secondary deviance involves a lengthy interactive process between the person and societal reactions to both the person and her or his behaviour. According to Lemert (1951),

> the sequence of interaction leading to secondary deviation is roughly as follows: (1) pri-mary deviation; (2) social penalties; (3) further primary deviation; (4) stronger penal-ties and rejection; (5) further deviations, perhaps with hostilities and resentment beginning to focus upon those doing the penalizing; (6) crisis reached in the tolerance quotient, expressed in formal action in the community stigmatizing of the deviant; (7) strengthening of the deviant conduct as a reaction to the stigmatizing and penalties; (8) ultimate acceptance of deviant social status and ... the associated role. (76)

Like Tannenbaum, Lemert maintains that official responses to juvenile delinquency are more likely to increase delinquent behaviour than to prevent it from occurring again.

Societal Response

Becker (1963) began his work with the intriguing notion that acts are not deviant until they are so defined. According to Becker, deviance is not inherent in an act, but rather is created by our responses to the act. Consider the act of murder. We may define this act as "killing someone in cold blood," but there are circumstances in which killing someone in such a manner is not legally prohibited. Soldiers are trained to kill on com-

mand. Capital punishment also involves killing people in extremely cold-blooded circumstances. In both of these examples, killing someone does not constitute murder.
Moreover, killing in the context of war or capital punishment is not even considered
morally wrong by many people. This is the reasoning behind Becker's argument that
there is nothing inherent in any act that makes it deviant, delinquent, or criminal.

Becker also considered the process whereby people become delinquent. Like
Lemert, he maintained that this process begins with attaching a label to a person in
response to his or her behaviour. Once attached, the label is generalized to attach to
everything that the person does. In other words, deviance is a "master status," meaning
that no matter what her or his other qualities, a person who has been labelled will be
seen and responded to as a deviant. For example, before their crimes are discovered,
serial killers are often described by their neighbours as "nice people." Subsequent to the
discovery, the same neighbours will begin to view and respond to the person as a "serial
killer." Edwin Schur (1973) called this aspect of the labelling process "retrospective
interpretation." Once a person's deviance is discovered, we reinterpret all of his or her
past actions in light of the new information.

By the early 1970s, labelling theory was influencing social policy. "Least possible
interference" was the prevailing philosophy as **decarceration** policies were implemented, for better or worse, across North America. People were released from psychiatric hospitals and left to fend for themselves. Halfway houses and group homes were
opened to get adult and juvenile offenders out of institutions. (As we will see in
Chapter 7, the principle of "least possible interference" is a major component in the
Young Offenders Act.) In recent years, we have seen the emergence of an approach
that runs counter to the one suggested by labelling theory. The idea behind "reintegrative shaming" is that public shaming of a person's behaviour followed by community
forgiveness and attempts at bringing the person back into the community, will decrease
the likelihood of future criminality (Braithwaite, 1989).

Conflict Theory

Like labelling theory, conflict theory focuses on questions concerning the creation and
application of crime and deviance rules. In conflict theory, however, the emphasis is on
law rather than labels. In contrast to theories that assume **social order** is based on social
consensus, conflict theories begin with the assumption that conflict is the natural state
of affairs in society and order is possible only because one group has the **power** to
impose its view, interests, values, or culture on another. According to conflict theory,
power is an important component in society, and one that must be considered in any
attempt to explain criminal or delinquent behaviour. This perspective leads to a focus
on laws, lawmaking, the administration of law, and the impact of law on various groups
of people. Some conflict theories have been influenced by Weber (liberal conflict
theory), while others draw upon the ideas of Marx (radical conflict theory).

Liberal Conflict Theory

In keeping with a critical perspective, conflict theory has focused more on law, the application of law, and the administration of justice than on the etiology of criminal behaviour. Elements of conflict theory are apparent in some of the theories discussed in Chapter 4.

The theories of Shaw and McKay, Merton, and Sutherland focused on cultural and normative conflict and argued, albeit in different ways, that people behave according to what they have learned and what is considered normal in their own groups. Sometimes this behaviour is in conflict with learned behaviours that are considered normal in other groups.

Thorsten Sellin (1938) referred to the rules governing a cultural group as "conduct norms." He argued that since each culture has its own set of conduct norms, heterogenous societies, which have more than one culture, will have more group conflict than homogeneous or single-culture societies. For Sellin, heterogeneous communities, such as urban core areas of cities, will have higher rates of delinquency than more homogeneous suburban communities. The dominant cultural group in a homogeneous community will be the group with the most power and resources. When the normative behaviour of one group violates the normative behaviour of a group that has the power and resources to codify its conduct norms into law, the result is **criminalization** of the weaker group.

Two theories within the liberal conflict tradition more typical of a criminal perspective were developed by Austin Turk and George Vold. Turk (1969) argues that value conflicts perceived as threatening to those in authority will lead to less powerful groups being identified as criminal or delinquent. Hence, juvenile "gangs" who openly appear in conflict with police will have their behaviour defined as criminal or delinquent. In his book *Theoretical Criminology*, Vold argues that

> groups come into conflict with one another as the interests and purposes they serve tend to overlap, encroach on one another and become competitive ... [W]hichever group interests can marshal the greatest number of votes will determine whether or not there will be a new law to hamper and curb the interests of the opposing group. (Vold and Bernard, 1986:272–73)

Those groups least likely to be able to influence legislation, such as the poor, minorities, and young people, will find their behaviour viewed as threatening and thus more likely to be criminalized than the behaviour of more powerful groups.

Radical Conflict Theory

Although Marx and Engels wrote very little about crime, and even less about delinquency, their work forms the theoretical basis of radical conflict theory. According to radical conflict theory, capitalism is the root cause of crime. Capitalist society is composed of two major classes: the bourgeoisie, who control the means of production; and the proletariat, who sell their labour to the bourgeoisie. In capitalist society, conflict is inherent between the two major classes, and the criminal justice system is but one means used by the bourgeoisie to control the proletariat.

One of the first contemporary theorists to apply Marxist ideas to an explanation of delinquent behaviour was David Greenberg. Greenberg (1977) argues that young people are at greater risk of being involved in criminal activities because the age structure of capitalist society forces them into economic dependency. Particularly at risk are working-class youth who are excluded from all but the most degrading and low-paying jobs. As a result of their economic dependency, young people are particularly likely to commit property crime. As we will see in the next chapter, Greenberg linked these ideas to the school experiences of adolescents.

Herman and Julia Schwendinger (1979), who also see delinquency as a product of capitalist society, argue that delinquency is created by a drive for the profit on which capitalism depends. Profits are increased through technology or the introduction of machinery. Since young people are the least skilled or experienced workers, they are more likely than older workers to be displaced by new technology or machinery. Once out of the labour force, young people become increasingly dependent on school and family; they become *prototypic marginals*. Those young people who are not supported by their families, or who are unable to adapt to school life, are at particular risk of becoming involved in delinquent behaviour.

INTEGRATIVE THEORY

You may have gathered from the last chapter that many theories are similar and/or complementary. Some criminologists came to the same conclusion. By the 1980s, one of the "new directions" in theorizing was to develop more general explanations of crime and delinquency through an integration of existing theories. Some scholars, such as Hirschi (1989), have questioned the feasibility of integrating theories. Others have argued that theories can be integrated by absorbing similar concepts, by integrating common concepts, or by integrating propositions in different theories (Akers, 1994:183–87).

Social Learning Theory

Differential Association–Reinforcement Theory

In the late 1960s, Burgess and Akers (1966) reformulated Sutherland's theory of differential association by specifying the mechanisms whereby people learn criminal behaviour. Sutherland's eighth principle had merely stated that criminal behaviour is learned. Burgess and Akers used learning principles from behaviourist psychology to explain how criminal behaviour is learned. They referred to their integrated theory as "differential association–reinforcement theory." This theory maintains that a person's voluntary actions, including criminal actions, are "conditioned or shaped by rewards and punishments" (Akers, 1994:95). Akers revisited the theory in later works (1973, 1977, 1985) and referred to his modifications as **social learning theory**. This theory applied to delinquent and deviant behaviour as well as criminal behaviour.

Akers (1994:96–99) borrowed from neutralization theory and Bandura's (1977) work on imitation in developing his theory's key concepts: differential association, definitions, differential reinforcement, and imitation. *Differential association* refers to one's exposure to behaviour and norms for learning. *Definitions* refer to "attitudes or meanings that one attaches to given behavior" (97). Hence, people might believe it is wrong to steal, but rationalize doing so by saying things like, "This person is so rich, he'll never miss the money." The actual commission of a crime depends on actual and anticipated rewards and punishments—*differential reinforcement. Imitation* helps to explain the initial or "novel" behaviour.

Hence, according to Akers (1985),

> principle behavior effects come from interaction in or under the influence of those groups with which one is in differential association and which control sources and patterns of reinforcement, provide normative definitions, and expose one to behavioral models ... [D]eviant behavior can be expected to the extent that it has been differentially reinforced over alternative behavior (conforming or other deviant behavior) and is defined as desirable or justified when the individual is in a situation discriminative for the behavior. (57–58)

Social Control and Social Learning

Self-Derogation Theory

Howard Kaplan was one of the first to develop an integrated theory using a number of theories and perspectives. His self-derogation theory focuses on self-esteem and combines elements of social learning theory, control theory, strain theory, and labelling theory. Kaplan (1975) argues that we are all motivated to maximize our self-esteem and that our motivation to conform will be minimized by family, school, and peer interactions that devalue our sense of self. If these interactions are self-defacing, then the social control usually exercised in these groups will be ineffective. To the extent that a young person becomes aware of delinquent activities and feels that this behaviour will be self-enhancing, he or she will be attracted to delinquent groups. Involvement in delinquency will continue as long as the deviant group continues to meet the individual's need for positive self-evaluation.

Integrated Theory

Delbert Elliott and his associates David Huizinga and Suzanne Ageton (1985) developed a theory that integrates strain theory (anomie and social disorganization), social bonding, and social learning theory. Simply put, their theory argues that anomie, combined with social disorganization and inadequate socialization, sets the stage for weak bonds with social institutions. These weak institutional bonds lead to stronger bonds and greater associations with delinquent peer groups within which the learning of delinquent behaviour is enhanced.

Interactional Theory

Terrence Thornberry (1987) and Thornberry et al. (1991) also integrate social bonding and social learning theory. However, they incorporate aspects of social structure in their **interactional theory** by arguing that social class, race, and community and neighbourhood characteristics affect the social bond and social learning variables. While weakened bonds are the key to delinquent behaviour, the bonds themselves are not enough to produce or prevent delinquency. Rather, delinquency has to be learned and reinforced. Thornberry et al. (1991) refer to their model as "interactional theory" and maintain that it differs from other integrated models in three ways:

> First, it does not assume, as many control-based theories do, that variation in the strength of the bond just happens. This variation is systematically related to structural variables such as social class position and residential area. Second, it does not assume that causal models are stable over the life course. Causal influences vary at different developmental stages and at different stages of criminal careers (i.e., at initiation, maintenance, and termination). Third, it does not assume that causal influences are overwhelmingly unidirectional and that delinquency is merely an outcome variable. Many effects are bidirectional, and delinquency may contribute to the weakening of social bonds as well as being a consequence of weakened social bonds. (9)

As will be discussed in the next chapter, Thornberry and his associates tested their theory on self-reported delinquency and found that low levels of commitment to school and attachment to parents lead to delinquency, but also that delinquent behaviour affects commitment and attachment. Moreover, their research indicates that delinquency has a greater effect on attachment and commitment than commitment and attachment have on delinquency (1991:29–30).

Radical Conflict, Social Control, and Social Learning

Mark Colvin and John Pauly developed a theory that integrates radical conflict theory, social control theory, and social learning theory. Like other Marxian theorists, Colvin and Pauly (1987) argue that social control in capitalist society is coercive and is designed to support the class structure. However, with regard to understanding delinquency, they point out that these coercive control patterns are reproduced both at home and at school, and that one reinforces the other. Hence, very authoritarian family structures and the use of physical punishment (*coercive control*) are characteristic of homes headed by parents who have jobs without any autonomy or authority and who are monitored and regulated by superiors or supervisors. Coercive control is not conducive to strong bonds between parents and children.

Schools reproduce coercive control through mechanisms and structures that include such things as IQ tests, aptitude testing, and tracking. These mechanisms affect lower- and working-class youth in proportion to the strength of their family bonds. Colvin and Pauly argue that children with weak family bonds are more likely to be identified as potential problem students. As a result of this identification, a self-fulfilling prophecy is set in place. Further, schools that lack the resources to reward students will rely more on coercive controls as well as punishment.

In short, Colvin and Pauly's theory postulates that parents' class position is negatively associated with coercion in the workplace and that this enhances the development of coercive family control structures. Children in this type of family control structure have weak or *"alienated" family bonds* and are more likely to be placed in a coercive school control structure. Coercive school control in turn leads to increased association with similar peers, thereby predisposing some youth to an involvement in community and neighbourhood opportunities for delinquent behaviour.

Social Control Theory, Strain Theory, and Liberal Conflict Theory

Theory of Differential Oppression

The theory of differential oppression, developed by Robert Regoli and John Hewitt (1994), integrates strain theory, social control theory, and liberal conflict theory. Instead of viewing social control as always a positive force, Regoli and Hewitt view some aspects of social control as oppressive. They define **oppression** as the unjust use or misuse of authority, which "often results from attempts by one group to impose its conception of order on another group" (1994:206). People who are subject to oppressive measures of control are made into "objects" or are viewed as "things." As a result, they come to view themselves as objects rather than subjects; they become passive and accepting rather than active subjects who exercise autonomy and control over their own lives.

According to Regoli and Hewitt (1994), "children, like women, exist in a socially ordered world created by adults and are defined as 'objects' relative to the adult subject" (207). Just as women as objects are viewed as inferior to men, children as objects are viewed as inferior to adults. Moreover, they lack any power to change their situation. As Regoli and Hewitt (1994) state, compared to parents and teachers, children are relatively powerless and must submit to the power and authority of these adults. When this power is exercised to prevent the child from attaining access to valued resources or to prevent the child from developing a sense of self as a subject rather than an object, it becomes oppression. (208)

While all children are oppressed because of their status relative to adults, their oppression is a "matter of degree, not of kind." Some children are only "minimally oppressed," others experience severe oppression.

Regoli and Hewitt (1994) describe the theory of differential oppression in terms of the following four principles:

1. Adults emphasize order in the home and school. Children are continually forced to abide by the rules of those in authority and these rules are determined by adults' views about how children should behave.
2. Adults' perceptions establish children as inferior, subordinate, and troublemakers. It is assumed by adults that children must be controlled and that it is being done "for the child's own good." Seldom do adults acknowledge that if children are not controlled they may not necessarily be a threat to themselves, but they are certainly a threat to adult order, or order as it is defined by adults. A child who refuses to obey orders given by an adult is defined as "a problem," "a troublemaker," or "out of control." Children are inferior to the extent it is believed that they are incapable of knowing what to do "for their own good."
3. The imposition of adults' conceptions of order on children often becomes extreme to the point of oppression. While the general oppression of children, through laws and customs, limits their opportunities for autonomy and sense of value, the most destructive oppression is that which occurs on the individual level. Here the most destructive are those that involve force "as a result of relational coercion." Children most at risk are those who are "obedient out of a fear of losing approval, or of the adult withdrawing affection." When coercion and force become abuse or neglect, children often generalize this abuse of authority to other adults, such as the police or school authorities or shopkeepers.
4. Oppression leads to adaptive reactions by children (209–10).

Borrowing from Freire (1990:153), Regoli and Hewitt (1994) argue that children who are made to feel impotent and powerless by the oppressive acts of adults will adapt in four ways:

1. *Passive acceptance.* Children who are obedient out of fear behave much like slaves, prison inmates, and battered women. They are "fearful of freedom" and often learn to hate. Their hatred is repressed, which makes them susceptible to low self-esteem, alcoholism, drug addiction, and the like.

2. *Exercise of illegitimate, coercive power.* The child attempts to demonstrate power over adults by engaging in the illicit use of drugs or alcohol, crime, or sexual misbehaviour.
3. *Manipulation of peers.* The child tries to gain power through control of her or his peers. This strategy gives the child a feeling of empowerment.
4. *Retaliation.* Here children try to strike back at the people and the institutions that oppress them. School vandalism is one way; assault and murder of teachers or parents is an extreme response. Some children will become depressed or commit suicide (210–11).

No matter what the child's chosen mode of adaptation, the typical response of adults is to enhance his or her oppression, thereby escalating the problem. According to Regoli and Hewitt (1994), solutions to youth crime will not come from justice system reforms. Rather, they will come from changes to the social structure and existing social arrangements that will permit adults to see children as "equally valuable, autonomous, and independent human beings" (211).

OPPORTUNITY THEORY

Another new approach to understanding crime distinguishes between the characteristics of individuals as "causing" crime and the crime itself. This view looks at crime as an event connected to situational factors. Rather than asking why a person committed a crime, the question becomes why a particular **criminal event** happened. This perspective represents something of a move away from positivism and a return to the classical school in that it is based on the assumption that people operate on the basis of free will and make rational choices about engaging in criminal activity. One of its most important contributions is the notion that there is not one explanation for crime, but rather that different explanations may be required for different types of crimes. Hence the decisions or situations that lead to a property crime may be quite different from those leading to an assault. This approach also leads to the recognition that it is as, or more important to understand why a person stops his or her involvement in criminal activity as it is to know why she or he began. It is a perspective that provides a rationale for those who would advocate stiffer penalties as a means of deterring criminal activity.

Routine Activity Theory

Cohen and Felson (1979) began the work in this tradition from their observation that there had been an increase in crime rates following WWII contrary to expectations that these times of prosperity should reduce criminal activity. They reasoned that this was likely due to changes in *routine activities* brought about by structural changes.

Therefore, the more people who have cars that allow them to travel, have jobs that require them to travel, and have money to spend on activities outside the home, the more opportunities they have for criminal activity, and the more vulnerable they are as targets of criminal activity. The convergence of three components are required for a criminal event: *motivated offenders, suitable targets,* and the *absence of a capable guardian.* Crime could increase, they argued, if all three of these components remained the same, but there was a change in routine everyday activities (589). So for example, youth walking home from school rather than being bussed (a change in routine) increases the chances of "motivated offenders" coming into contact with "suitable targets." Cook (1980) expanded this "opportunity theory" by arguing that motivated offenders are also selective in their choice of targets. Ideal targets are those offering "a high payoff with little effort or risk of legal consequence."

Rational Choice Theory

Cornish and Clarke (1985) and Clarke and Felson (1993) developed opportunity theory further by combining all aspects of the criminal event, the offender, her/his motivation, and situational factors. They argue that offenders rationally assess all information about the potential crime and make a rational choice based on an assessment of consequences. This involves a process that is sometimes very complex where an individual is making decisions about "criminal involvement," either initially, or to continue, or to desist. Other situations involve less complex decision making. These refer to "criminal event" decisions which are tied more specifically to particular situations and/or circumstances. Hence, deciding to deal drugs at school is likely to involve a more complicated decision-making process than shoplifting snacks in a variety store on a "dare" while out with a group of friends.

THE FEMINIST PERSPECTIVE AND CRITIQUE

Early criminology theorists tended to ignore female behaviour in their efforts to explain crime and delinquency. It was not until women began entering the field of criminology that gender issues began to be seriously addressed. In this section of the chapter, we will review early theoretical efforts at explaining female crime and delinquency, examine the feminist critique of this work, and present recent research and theorizing about girls and crime.

The Invisible Girl

Frederic Thrasher's (1927) study of gangs in the 1920s identified about six female gangs. Using **role theory** to explain the rarity of female gangs, Thrasher argued that socially acceptable female behaviour is antithetical to gang activity. Girls who are involved in gang activities are not "girls" but rather "tomboys" who have taken on a male role. Shaw and McKay, who examined more than 60,000 male delinquents, have little to say on the subject of female delinquency. Merton's theory also ignores crime and delinquency among girls in that he does not apply his typology of adaptations to women.

In an early attempt to offer an explanation for female crime, Ruth Morris rejected Merton's assumption that everyone aspires to the same goals by arguing that the fundamental goals of women are different from those of men. According to Morris (1964), women are concerned with *relational goals* such as love, marriage, family, and friends, whereas men are concerned with material goals. She argues that since women's goals are more easily attainable than men's goals, we will find lower rates of crime and delinquency among girls and women. On the other hand, Alison Morris (1987) maintains that women do have the same material goals as men. In applying Merton's typology of adaptations to women, she points out that since women don't occupy the same status in society as men, they have fewer opportunities to achieve material success. Hence, Merton's theory would hypothesize that women and girls should actually be more delinquent than boys and men. We know from Chapter 3 that this is not the case.

Eileen Leonard (1982) offers a critique of Miller's (1958) argument that delinquency is created by the focal concerns of lower-class culture. If it is the focal concerns of lower-class culture that "cause" crime, she asks, then how do we account for the lower crime rates among girls and women who occupy lower-class positions?

Albert Cohen regarded delinquency and the delinquent subculture as specifically male phenomena. According to Cohen, the delinquent subculture is an adaptive response to the problems faced by boys. While boys are interested in achievements and in being "male," girls are interested in boys. When Cohen (1955) envisions girls as delinquent it is specifically in relation to sexual behaviour: "Sex delinquency is one kind of meaningful response to the most characteristic, most central and most ego involved problems of the female role: the establishment of satisfactory relationships with the opposite sex" (147).

On the subject of male delinquency, he has this to say: "However it may be condemned by others on moral grounds, it has at least one virtue: it incontestably confirms, in the eyes of all concerned, his essential masculinity. The delinquent is the rogue male" (139–40).

Chesney-Lind and Shelden (1992) respond as follows: "Cohen's comments are notable in their candor and probably capture the allure that male delinquency has had for at least some male theorists and the fact that sexism has rendered the female delinquent irrelevant to their work" (65).

Cloward and Ohlin not only focused on male delinquency, but they also assigned blame to mothers, particularly female-headed households. According to Cloward and Ohlin, in the absence of male role models, boys will have trouble developing a masculine image. This creates a source of strain for male adolescents:

Engulfed by a feminine world and uncertain of their own identification, they tend to "protest" against femininity. This protest may take the form of robust and aggressive behavior and even of malicious, irresponsible and destructive acts. Such acts evoke maternal disapproval and thus come to stand for independence and masculinity to rebellious adolescents. (Cloward and Ohlin, 1960:49)

As Regoli and Hewitt (1994) comment, "The fact that some girls do become delinquent was apparently of no interest to Cloward and Ohlin" (345).

Sutherland's differential association theory also ignores female delinquency. Sutherland simply attributes the different rates of delinquency for boys and girls to differential associations based on "different standards of propriety and supervision" for boys and girls. As for social control theory, Hirschi tested his theory by administering self-report surveys to some 4,000 boys. Early labelling theories ignored girls and women, but Rosenblum (1980) applied Lemert's theory in her study of prostitution. She showed that the lives of adult female prostitutes are "reorganized around deviance" (115), or what Lemert defined as secondary deviance. Chesney-Lind and Shelden (1992) suggest that "the same processes are likely to be at work in the lives of juvenile prostitutes who resort to 'survival sex' while on the run from home" (69).

Lest we think that the tendency to ignore gender is a thing of the past, a recent article by Gary Brayton (1996) uses gender-neutral or **androgynous** terms in referring to adolescent sex offenders and their victims. Brayton consistently refers to adolescent sex offenders as "adolescents," "perpetrators," or "offenders." What is so insidious about these gender-neutral terms is their implication that boys and girls are equally likely to be offenders or victims. O'Brien and Bera's typology of adolescent sex offenders (see Box 2.1 on page 38) suggests otherwise. Boys are more likely offenders and girls are more likely victims.

The Less than Perfect Girl

An absence of concern about female crime and delinquency in many theories does not mean that there were no explanations of female crime. While the early biological theories of crime and delinquency discussed in the preceding chapter may seem ludicrous by contemporary standards, they did not ignore women. Unfortunately, their perspectives on women and girls are at best stereotypical, and at worst misogynous. Yet, these theories continued to be used as explanations of female crime and delinquency well into the 1970s.

Early positivist criminology, as we saw in the last chapter, focused on biology in its search for the causes of crime and delinquency. Most of these early theories shared the assumption that males and females are inherently different. An extension of this assumption was that female crime would be different from male crime. Among the early explanations of female criminality, Lombroso's was perhaps most influential in that we see many of his ideas reflected in today's taken-for-granted and some scholarly views of female crime.

Biology and Physiology

Lombroso and Ferrero (1895) maintain in *The Female Offender* that female criminals are lower on the evolutionary scale than noncriminal females and that women as a whole are lower on the evolutionary scale than the general male population. According to Lombroso and Ferrero, women are weaker than men, as well as more childlike, more maternal, and less intelligent. Further, women's moral sense is inferior to that of men. As described by Lombroso and Ferrero, women are "revengeful, jealous, inclined to vengences of a refined cruelty ... [t]heir evil tendencies ... more varied than men's" (151). Nonetheless, they warn that female criminals, precisely because they are female, are less visible than male criminals:

> Very often, too, in women, the type is disguised by youth with its absence of wrinkles and the plumpness which conceals the size of the jaw and cheek bones, thus softening the masculine and savage features. Then when the hair is black and plentiful ... and the eyes are bright, a not unpleasing appearance is presented. In short, let a female delinquent be young and we can overlook her degenerate type, and even regard her as beautiful; the sexual instinct misleading us here as it does in making attribute to women more of sensitiveness and passion than they really possess. And in the same way, when she is being tried on a criminal charge, we are inclined to excuse, as noble impulses of passion, an act which arises from the most cynical calculations. (Lombroso and Ferrero, 1895:97)

The themes of male versus female biology and women's sexuality continued to dominate theories of female crime and delinquency after the turn of the century. Freud (1924) argued that female crime and delinquency stemmed from *penis envy*. During the oedipal stage of development, children must learn to repress their sexual love for their opposite-sex parent. For girls, the result is an *Electra complex*. Girls who are unable to deal adequately with this complex will exhibit not only penis envy but also a desire for revenge that will cause them to act out in various ways. In Freud's view, promiscuous sexual behaviour and prostitution were the consequences of girls' failure to cope with the Electra complex.

In 1923, W.I. Thomas published *The Unadjusted Girl*. The book, which was based on his study of case records from the Cook County Juvenile Court and the Girl's Protective Bureau in Chicago, was one of the first attempts to analyze female delinquent behaviour. Like Lombroso before him, Thomas focused on girls' sexuality, but his explanation was far more sociological in that he emphasized gender roles as a source of female delinquency. According to Thomas, much of human behaviour is driven by wish fulfilment, which in turn is driven by biological instincts. One important biological difference between men and women, Thomas argued, is that women have a greater need for love. Their need to both give and receive love is a source of delinquency (particularly sexual delinquency) for girls because they use their sex to fulfil other more basic needs. As Thomas put it, "[sex] is their capital" (1923:109).

Whereas Freud had maintained that sexuality was a source of female problems, Thomas argued that girls' problems stemmed from inadequate families, demoralization, and frustration stemming from social rules and moral codes. "Sexual passion," he wrote, "does not play an important role, for the girls usually become 'wild' before the development of sexual desire, and their casual sexual relations do not usually awaken sex feelings" (1923:109).

The early biological explanations of female crime are most reflected in the work of Otto Pollak (1950). Pollak attributed women's criminal behaviour to their physiology, and he used this same physiology to explain why women have lower rates of crime than men. According to Pollak, women are as criminal as men but use their physiology to hide their criminality.

Women are deceitful, Pollak maintains, and they are deceitful for three reasons: they have less physical strength, they lack a penis, and they menstruate. These physical differences from men require women to take a passive role in sexual relations and enable them to conceal their sexual arousal, while social norms force them to conceal not only menstruation, but sexual activity. All these factors encourage women to be deceitful, and a consequence with regard to crime is that women are "instigators" while men are "perpetrators." These same factors, referred to as *precocious biological maturity*, were used by Pollak to explain female sexual delinquency:

> The male has to be active while the female has to be passive. In the active attempt to find satisfaction for the sex urge, physiological precocity does not seem to help the boy very much, but for the girl who has to wait until she is 'propositioned,' the appearance of sexual maturity furnishes the opportunity for sex delinquencies that do not come the way of her normally developed age mates. (Pollak, 1950:125)

Anticipating what is now known as the **chivalry hypothesis**, Pollak attributes low rates of female delinquency and crime to women's lesser likelihood than men to be caught and processed; he maintains that this is because men and boys who are victimized by women and girls are reluctant to report, and because men in the criminal justice system, (e.g., police officers, prosecutors, judges, and juries) are reluctant to prosecute women and girls.

Not all early criminologists accepted biological explanations of crime. Bonger (1916) argued that the low rate of female crime was a result of women's position in society:

> Her smaller criminality is like the health of a hothouse plant; it is due not to innate qualities, but to the hothouse which protects it from harmful influences. If the life of women were like that of men their criminality would hardly differ at all as to quantity, though perhaps somewhat as to quality. (478)

Contemporary Theory and the Sexual Girl

The theoretical emphasis on female biology and sexuality as an explanation of crime and delinquency continued well into the 1960s and 1970s. As Chesney-Lind and Shelden (1992) point out, "most authors of the early works [1960s and 1970s] on female delinquency assumed that most female delinquency is either 'sexual' or 'relational' rather than 'criminal' in nature, and [were] convinced that social intervention administered by sensitive and informed individuals could help young women with their problems" (61).

Gisela Konopka (1966) posited that sexual behaviour causes girls to get into trouble. Like Freud, she maintained that problems begin in the family with conflicts between mothers and daughters. The emotional instability, loneliness, and low self-esteem girls experience as a result of these conflicts impels them into abusive and sexually exploitive relationships with boys. Those relationships, in turn, enhance family problems, reinforce low self-esteem and loneliness, and increase sexual delinquency.

The sexuality theme was reiterated by a group of British researchers, John Cowie, Valerie Cowie, and Eliot Slater (1968), who argued that dysfunctional families are the source of female delinquency, which they also saw as primarily sexual. However, their view of female delinquency was far less sympathetic than that offered by Konopka. Reminiscent of Lombroso, Cowie et al. contend that delinquent girls have more psychiatric and health problems than delinquent boys. Moreover, they are "oversized, lumpish, uncouth, and graceless with a raised incidence of minor physical defects" (Cowie, Cowie, and Slater, 1968:166–67). In their book *The Delinquent Girl*, the American researchers Clyde Vedder and Dora Somerville state, "when a girl is unable to gain a sufficient degree of acceptance from her home and peers, she seeks to deny this rejection by engaging in sexual acts which she fantasizes to be an expression of another's love" (Vedder and Somerville, 1975:109). Perhaps characteristic of the attitudes toward women and girls in the 1960s and 1970s, both Cowie et al. and Vedder and Somerville acknowledge the existence of sexual abuse and incest in the lives of the girls they studied, but fail to pursue its connection to girls' behaviour. Cowie et al. (1968:112) merely note that "a disconcerting number of [the girls] say they ran away from home because of sexual advances made by near relatives," while Vedder and Somerville (1975:154) suggest that girls run away because "they fear the incestual consequences of [their] own impulses."

Girls and Their Hormones

The most recent purely biological explanations maintain that hormones have something to do with delinquency. Male delinquency rates are understood to be higher than female delinquency rates because testosterone levels in boys are six times higher and androgen levels twice as high. This argument is further supported by studies reporting that violent female offenders have higher levels of testosterone than nonviolent women (see, for example, Dabbs et al., 1988). Premenstrual syndrome (PMS) has also been posited as a cause of aggressive behaviour (particularly criminal behaviour) among women (Ellis and Austin, 1971). However, Karen Pugliesi (1992) and Jessica McFarlane and Tannis Williams (1990) argue that PMS is a socially constructed label and yet another example of the medicalization of problems women experience as a result of their oppressed status in the family and society.

The Liberated Girl

By the 1970s, the women's movement was having an impact on public thinking about the "naturalness" or biological foundations of gender roles. People were beginning to accept the notion that "being a boy" or "being a girl" was a product of the socialization process. Not surprisingly, as attitudes changed so too did the thinking of some theorists on the subject of female crime.

Two works in particular had a major impact on our thinking about women and crime. Rita Simon's *Women in Crime* and Freda Adler's *Sisters in Crime*, both published in 1975, presented what has come to be known as the **liberation hypothesis.** According to this hypothesis, women are becoming more like men in their criminality as a consequence of the women's liberation movement. While Adler and Simon agreed that the spread of liberated attitudes was affecting criminal behaviour among women, they had different views of how these new attitudes were affecting women. Simon argued that liberated attitudes led to greater numbers of women working outside the home, which in turn increased opportunities for women to commit offences that were traditionally male activities, such as fraud, forgery, and embezzlement. Her argument was supported by figures showing that the most dramatic increase in women's crime was in the area of property crime. Adler, on the other hand, argued that liberated attitudes encouraged women to imitate male competitive behaviours, resulting in their growing involvement in masculine types of criminal activity such as gang activities, robberies, and muggings.

Neither argument has been supported by research or statistics on female crime and delinquency since the 1970s. As we saw in Chapter 3, girls are still less involved in delinquency than boys, and their crimes are less serious. Research in the United States on self-reported and official statistics has shown that rates of female delinquency increased throughout the 1960s and into the 1970s, but actually decreased after 1975. Moreover, according to studies comparing delinquent and nondelinquent girls' attitudes, delinquent girls are more traditional in their thinking about "women's place" (Chesney-Lind and Shelden, 1992:11, 79).

On the basis of this evidence, Chesney-Lind and Shelden (1992:11) suggest that the increases observed by Simon and Adler are likely better explained by the introduction of the baby boomers into the age of delinquency. They and others have argued that if liberated attitudes gave rise to behaviour changes among women during the 1960s and

1970s, then the behaviour of people in the criminal justice system was also affected. More specifically, the traditional attitude of paternalism and chivalry (described by Pollak, 1950) gave way to a law-and-order approach and a more gender-neutral treatment of male and female offenders.

Sorting Out What Needs to Be Explained

By the 1980s, the feminist critique of positivistic theories of crime and delinquency was in full swing. As we have seen, these theories were shown to be negative, sexist, and stereotypical in their view of girls and women. In addition, two important issues surfaced from feminist discourse: (1) the "generalizability problem," which concerns whether or not theories based upon the crimes and delinquencies of men and boys apply to women and girls; and (2) the "gender ratio problem," which concerns the ability of existing theories to explain gender differences in crime and delinquency (Daly and Chesney-Lind, 1988:514). Feminist criminologists thus sought to determine if specific theories of female crime need to be developed or if existing theory can be altered, modified, or integrated in some way that will explain both male and female crime.

According to Eileen Leonard (1982), certain parts of some theories, such as anomie, social control, differential association, conflict, Marxist, labelling, and social learning, may be useful in explaining both female criminality and male/female differences. Alison Morris (1987) suggests that while biological, psychiatric, and women's liberation theories are clearly wrong, "differential opportunity structure, associations, socialization, and social bonding can aid our understanding of crimes committed both by men and women and can take account of differences in the nature and extent of their crimes" (76). For their part, Chesney-Lind and Shelden (1992) maintain that

> if a theory of female delinquency is to emerge, it must draw on the best of a flawed heritage. Theories of boys' delinquency cannot be completely rejected, but their uncritical grounding in male behaviour must be recognized and corrected. Theories of female delinquency must get past common sense constructions of femininity to a broader appreciation of the role of girls' situations and lives in their troubles with the juvenile justice system. (79)

Delinquency and Patriarchy

In 1985, John Hagan, A.R. Gillis, and John Simpson (1985, 1987, 1988) introduced their "**power-control theory** of common delinquent behaviour," which combines conflict and control theories to explain differences in boys' and girls' delinquency.

Power-control theory contrasts gender roles and control mechanisms in patriarchal families with those in egalitarian families. In the patriarchal family, fathers work outside the home, mothers are restricted to the home and are responsible for socializing and controlling children. In egalitarian families, by contrast, roles inside and outside the home (including child-rearing) are shared equally by mothers and fathers, and boys and girls receive the same amount of supervision. According to Hagan et al. (1987), "positions of power in the workplace are translated into power relations in the household and the latter, in turn, influence the gender determined control of adolescents, their preferences for risk taking, and the patterning of gender and delinquency" (812).

A key difference between patriarchal families and egalitarian families is that in the former boys are encouraged to be risk-takers and girls—because they are controlled more rigorously—are raised to be risk-aversive. Hagen et al. (1987) tested their theory through a self-report study of 436 parents of high-school students in the Toronto area. They found that the delinquency rates of girls from patriarchal families were considerably lower than those of boys in patriarchal families. In egalitarian families, delinquency rates for girls and boys were closer.

Tests on larger samples in the United States have failed to support the power-control theory of delinquency (see, for example, Jensen and Thompson, 1990). Morash and Chesney-Lind (1991) found that boys were more delinquent than girls in both types of families, and that the most important predictor of delinquency was the quality of a child's relationship with the mother. The authors also found that

> in some types of families, boys were controlled more than girls. Specifically, if the mother was alone and unemployed, she controlled more of the decisions about boys than about girls, and was more punitive towards boys. A family with an unemployed mother alone also differs from other types in that the children identify less with their mother. (Morash and Chesney-Lind, 1991:371)

Some argue that power-control theory is feminist because it considers power relations and **patriarchy** in developing an explanation for differences in male and female crime and delinquency (Akers, 1994:174). Chesney-Lind and Shelden (1992) suggest otherwise:

> Although it is intriguing, this [theory] is essentially a not-too-subtle variation on the "liberation" hypothesis. Now, mothers' liberation or employment causes daughters crime ... Hagan and his associations are, however, to be commended insofar as they focussed on the importance of gender and patriarchy in the shaping of both male and female behaviour. (96–97)

Chesney-Lind and Shelden (1992:97) also point out that, despite increases over the past decade in both the number of female-headed households and women's participation in the labour force, female delinquency, whether measured by self-report data or official statistics, has either remained the same or declined.

Girls and Oppression

Messerschmidt (1986) offers a socialist-feminist explanation of the nature and low incidence of female crime and delinquency. According to Messerschmidt, in capitalist society the owners and managers of capital control workers; in patriarchal society men control women's labour and their sexuality. Hence, in a patriarchal capitalist society, women experience *double marginality* in that they are controlled not only by capital but also by men.

Regoli and Hewitt (1994) have applied their differential oppression theory to explain the gender differential in crime and delinquency as well as the nature of girls' crimes. If children are oppressed in society and viewed by adults as inferior, subordinate, and troublemakers, girls in patriarchal society are *doubly oppressed*. Making use of social learning concepts, Regoli and Hewitt argue that girls are socialized to be dependent and caring, to value themselves through others, and to refrain from risk-taking—all of which means they are less likely to engage in troublesome behaviours. Furthermore,

> adult conceptions in patriarchal societies of the *Girl as Female* (passive, relational, and nurturing) leads to oppression reinforcing her traditional gender role and, subsequently, to the girl's identity as "object." Treated as an "object," a girl may adapt by developing an identity through relationships with boys: she does not have to "prove" her own worth as long as she is "related" to a proven person. Consequently, her delinquencies may be indirect and relational. Being defined as a female "object" may also reinforce the identity of the girl as a "sexual object." In this case, adaptations may take the form of sexual delinquencies and prostitution. (Regoli and Hewett, 1994:348–49)

While recognizing the double oppression of girls, Regoli and Hewitt fail to develop the implications of masculine control of the sexuality and labour power of girls. Two feminist theories of female delinquency elaborate upon these relations and identify more specifically what it is about being a girl that leads to delinquency.

Feminist Theorizing about Girls

Ethic of Care

According to Morash and Chesney-Lind (1989), research suggests that women are "predisposed" to nurturing relationships with their children. The strength of mother–child relationships is the key to delinquent behaviour. In other words, strong bonds created through nurturing will reduce delinquency for both boys and girls. Morash and Chesney-Lind refer to this nurturing as an *ethic of care* and argue that children raised in an ethic of care will develop identities that involve a concern for others (75). Moreover, this **care ethic** need not be restricted to women and girls; any child, male or female, raised by a nurturing parent, mother, or father, will more likely be prosocial in their behaviour.

Female delinquency, according to Chesney-Lind and Shelden (1992; 1998), is a consequence of the fact that girls are more likely than boys to be victims of family-related sexual abuse. Hence, girls do the caring and are not cared for or about. Further, because women and girls are viewed as sexual objects in patriarchal society, girls are more vulnerable to physical and sexual abuse by male relatives. Girls who attempt to escape this abuse are vulnerable to apprehension by the justice system. If they fail to conform there, or if they "run away," they are then vulnerable to victimization on the streets where their survival depends on petty crime and often prostitution.

Resistance to Care Lessons

The development of the care ethic in girls is well documented in Reitsma-Street's (1991b) study of 26 pairs of sisters. In each pair, one sister was convicted for delinquency, the other was not. Reitsma-Street's work documents how girls learn to care, the costs of this caring, and how girls are policed to care. One of the most significant findings from Reitsma-Street's research centres on what she calls the sisters' *core commonalities*. She states that "of most relevance to women and caring were the core commonalities, which revolved around how the sisters learned to care for themselves and for others, the cost they bore for caring and how they were policed to conform to expectations about caring" (1991b:111). Further, "besides being less connected to their fathers and more ambivalent about their mothers, I could not see strong patterns in the sisters' relationships—or anything, for that matter, that could be argued to contribute either to delinquency or conformity" (118).

In learning the lessons of caring, girls are not permitted to develop a range of caring ways, but rather are pressured to care in three particular ways. Girls must

1. learn to be the major and primary providers of love and nurture;
2. learn to restrict caring for themselves to "looking nice and being nice," and, above all, learn to "not make a fuss"; and
3. learn "to make a boyfriend their primary object of caring" (119).

Whether girls learn these lessons or not, there are costs to bear: they restrict their interests, they neglect their bodies, and they risk poverty and dependence. Girls who do learn the lessons of caring learn to forfeit their physical, psychological, social, and material health to caring for others. There is an inherent paradox in the economic dependence caring brings: "while focusing care on a boyfriend is a source of economic vulnerability, continuing such care is critical because a relationship with a male who earns a satisfactory income is the major hope girls have for minimizing the impact of that vulnerability" (123).

Further, in learning to not care about her own needs, girls pay a "bodily cost":

> Suddenly her body is no longer at her own disposal but has become a zone where others have competing interests—parents and boyfriends and social workers and ad

agencies—a territory liable to a whole series of catastrophes: diseases, pregnancy, rape, abortion. (Kostash, 1987:175, cited in Reitsma-Street, 1991b:121)

Citing Donzelot (1979:8), Reitsma-Street argues that lessons of caring involve far more than mere socialization. Rather, girls are policed to learn their lessons through various *techniques of regulation* (1991b:123). There are levels to this policing, each one more intrusive than the last. The first level involves judgments of a girl's reputation, "slut" being the most deadly and effective. The second level involves physical force, or the threat of it, from the men and boys in the girl's life. The third level involves the justice system. The more a girl resists these lessons—the more she struggles against caring for others more than herself—the greater the personal cost. Thus, Reitsma-Street found that delinquent girls were more likely to report having fought against prioritizing "looking nice" or "being nice." They would avoid wearing dresses, they would swear or be loud, and they would often resort to physical fighting as a way to meet their needs. They were also more likely to be sexually active, to want to travel, and to pursue exciting and fun activities.

None of these resistances are "seen in the context of a society that limits the ways that girls can care for themselves and their loved ones and restricts avenues of protest against these limitations" (Reitsma-Street, 1991b:125). Rather, acts of resistance are interpreted by parents, teachers, and others in authority as signs of disturbance. The girls who undertake them are seen as needing help, protection, or correction—anything that will enable them "to act more like a normal girl" (126). Thus, judges tend to be far more lenient with girls who have committed common sorts of delinquencies like theft and burglary (especially if they have done so as accomplices of boyfriends) than with girls who show independence, especially when this independence involves running away from home, a treatment/correctional centre, or foster/group home.

SUMMARY

This chapter documents new directions in thinking about crime and delinquency. Some of the theories discussed have taken a critical perspective, while others have moved positivistic theories in new directions. Among these new developments are the integrative theories. Social learning and social control theories have received more empirical support than strain theory. As a result of the feminist critique of traditional positivistic approaches to explaining crime and delinquency, attempts have been made to develop theories that explain the crimes of girls as well as boys, and that contribute to an understanding of girls' delinquency from a feminist perspective.

Labelling theory moves sociological theorizing away from a positivistic approach to crime by asking questions about crime rather than about the person. Once we have accepted one of the central tenets of labelling theory—that no act is inherently deviant—we then have to ask questions about why some acts are defined as deviant, who defines them as such, how we respond to those who are labelled, and the impact of labels and definitions.

Critical theory in criminology focuses more on the effect of power relations in the production of crime and delinquency than on attempting to explain the "root causes" of an individual's behaviour. Conflict theory belongs in this tradition. Liberal conflict theory (Sellin, 1938; Turk, 1969; Vold & Bernard, 1986) focuses on value or cultural conflict, while radical conflict theory (Greenberg, 1977; Schwendinger and Schwendinger, 1979) focuses on the various ways in which capitalist forces of production contribute to delinquency.

Integrative theory combines or integrates concepts and propositions from a number of theories to create more general explanations of delinquency. Akers's (1985) social learning theory combines differential association theory and differential reinforcement theory to explain criminal and delinquent behaviour. Other theories that focus on social control and social learning theory include Kaplan's (1975) self-derogation theory; Elliott, Huizinga, and Ageton's (1985) integrative theory; and Thornberry's (1987) interactional theory. Colvin and Pauly (1987) combine radical conflict theory with social control and social learning, while Regoli and Hewitt (1994) combine strain, social control, and liberal conflict theory in their theory of differential oppression.

Another new approach to understanding crime that moves away from a strictly positivist tradition is opportunity theory. This approach looks at crime as an event connected to situational factors. Rather than asking why a person committed a crime, the question becomes why a particular criminal event happened. Routine activity theory, Cohen and Felson (1979), and rational choice theory, Cornish and Clarke (1985), begin with the assumption that people operate on the basis of free will and make rational choices about engaging in criminal activity. This approach leads to the recognition that it is as or more important to understand why a person stops his or her involvement in criminal activity as it is to know why she or he began.

Most criminology theory that emerged from the positivist tradition between the 1930s and 1960s is androgenous in that it purports to be a general theory of crime and delinquency, but explains only the behaviour of boys and men. Classical theory that did address female criminality tended to sexualize or pathologize women and girls, a tendency that carries through to some contemporary theory and research.

Feminist criminologists agree that theories must be able to account for differences in male and female crime rates (the gender ratio problem) and question whether theories based on the experience of men and boys can be applied to girls and women (the generalizability problem). Some feminist critics believe that old theories can be revised to account for both male and female criminality. Others argue that theories devoted to female crime exclusively need to be developed.

Some new theories of crime and delinquency have attempted to account for the behaviour of boys and girls. Theories that have emerged from the conflict perspective include Messerschmidt (1986), which focuses on patriarchy and capitalism and the double marginality of women; and Regoli and Hewitt (1994), which addresses the oppression of children by adults and the double oppression of girls. Hagan, Simpson, and Gillis (1985, 1987, 1988) combine conflict theory with control theory in their power-control theory of delinquency.

Feminist theorizing about girls' crimes focuses on patriarchy and the process by which masculine control of women, their labour, and their bodies translates into female criminality. Reitsma-Street (1991b) argues that girls are both taught and policed to care. Girls who resist the lessons of caring are subject to sanctions that vary in intensity from name-calling to physical force or the threat of apprehension by social agencies and/or the juvenile justice system.

The Influence of Family, School, and Peers on Youth Crime and Delinquency

CHAPTER OBJECTIVES

1. To determine the effects of family structure and family relationships on youth crime and delinquency.

2. To discuss individual, organizational, and structural factors that link school performance to youth crime and delinquency.

3. To present a critique of research linking IQ and tracking to school performance and delinquency.

4. To test Cohen's theory by examining the relationship between social class, school performance, and delinquency.

5. To discuss how attachment to friends affects youth crime.

6. To introduce social capital and lifecourse developmental theory and discuss how they incorporate family, school and friends into an explanation for youth crime.

7. To examine data on gangs and offer some explanations for gang membership.

8. To discuss the similarities and differences between gangs in Canadian and American cities.

9. To emphasize the political nature of gang definitions and images.

KEY TERMS

Microscopic	Tracking	Social capital theory
Family structure	Social class	Near group
Meta-analysis	Lifecourse developmental	Androcentric
Criminalize	theory	
Etiological		

INTRODUCTION

As we saw in the last two chapters and in the historical discussion in Chapter 1, some factors have consistently emerged in both taken-for-granted understandings and scholarly theorizing about crime and delinquency. The family has been a concern throughout Canadian history, and youth gangs and peer influences have been linked to crime and delinquency for at least 100 years. In addition, schools have been viewed as a source of youth problems for at least 40 years. Nonetheless, in spite of this consistency, there is little agreement as to what is problematic about these factors.

Control theory explanations such as Hirschi's make intuitive sense—children not attached to parents will be more delinquent than children who are attached. Yet, whether this explanation is confirmed empirically depends on how one defines "attachment": is it supervision or affection? In addition, many theories are contradictory. Control theory, for example, argues that strong attachments even to delinquent friends will decrease delinquency, while differential association theory implies that strong attachments to delinquent peers will increase delinquent behaviour. Attempts have been made by criminologists to develop models that sort through some of these contradictions and theoretical gaps, and that specify some of the links between social factors associated with delinquency. Over the last ten years, two new and not unrelated theories have been gaining prominence in criminology, social capital and lifecourse developmental theory. This chapter introduces this work and reviews recent research on and theorizing about family, school, gang, and peer influences on youth crime.

FAMILY

Most research examining the relationship between family and youth crime has looked at either the structure of the family or family relationships. These studies have taken a **microscopic** perspective and have examined **family structure** in terms of whether the family is broken (divorced or separated) or whether both parents are working. Family relationship studies look at such things as parenting skills, parental supervision of children, parenting styles, and young people's attachments to parents.

Family Structure

There are strong intuitive explanations as to why one-parent families may be more likely than two-parent families to produce delinquent children. First, of course, is the reality that children in one-parent families, particularly female-headed families, are considerably poorer than those in two-parent families. Mavis Hetherington (1977), who compared broken families with intact families, identified three major effects of divorce on women that *may* influence their children's behaviour: (1) single mothers are overburdened from working in the labour force and caring for children; (2) single mothers experience considerable financial stress in that female-headed households earn less than half the income earned in male-headed households; and (3) single mothers experience social isolation, which means they have fewer social and emotional supports. This of course does not mean that children from divorced homes *are* more problematic than other children.

Wallerstein and Kelly (1980) and Wallerstein and Blakeslee (1989) looked at the long-term effects of divorce on children and found that negative effects such as anger and depression can last as long as 15 years. A major problem with their research is that it did not incorporate, for comparative purposes, a comparison group of families not divorced. Some studies that did use comparison groups are equally flawed in that they relied on official data. In so doing, they may have measured the effect of police and judicial attitudes toward single-parent and female-headed households. Little research has examined the positive effects of single parenting on children. For example, it could be argued that these children are more independent and have a stronger sense of responsibility than children from two-parent homes. Recent Statistics Canada surveys report that parenting styles have more impact on children's behavioural patterns than income levels or family structure. More specifically, children from two-parent homes with "ineffective" or hostile parents are five times more likely to have "persistent behavioural problems" than children with an "effective" single parent (Philip, 1998:A9; Dauvergne and Johnson, 2001).

Edward Wells and Joseph Rankin (1991), who conducted a **meta-analysis** of the research on the impact of broken homes, found that the relationship between broken homes and delinquency is weak at best, that this relationship has been empirically demonstrated consistently for more than 50 years, that the relationship is stronger for minor crimes than serious ones, and that broken homes have more negative effects on boys than girls.

In addition, there is very little evidence that working mothers produce more delinquency. Less time spent with children does not necessarily mean less quality time. According to Melville (1988), "when working mothers derive satisfaction from their employment and do not feel guilty about its effects, they are likely to perform the mother's role at least as well as non-working women" (352). Thus, the bulk of the evidence suggests that single "moms" and working mothers do not "cause" delinquent behaviour. Where research has found a weak relationship, this may be due to parenting skills and parenting styles rather than family structure.

Parenting

Dianna Baumrind (1978, 1991) suggests that two important aspects of parenting behaviour are (1) the extent to which parents are supportive of their children's needs (*parental responsiveness*), and (2) the extent to which parents are demanding of appropriate behaviour from their children (*parental demandingness*). Hence, parents may be authoritative (i.e., supportive and demanding), authoritarian (rejecting and demanding), indulgent (supportive and not at all demanding), or indifferent (rejecting and not at all demanding). *Authoritative* parents set standards and have expectations that are consistent with their child's age. Such parents discuss and explain disciplinary matters with their children. *Authoritarian* parents value obedience and conformity. These parents tend to restrict children's autonomy and to favour the use of punitive disciplinary measures. *Indulgent* parents allow children considerable freedoms, are opposed to control or disciplinary measures, and see themselves more as resources for their children than as disciplinarians. *Indifferent* parents spend little time with their children, know little about their children's activities, and tend to put their own needs above those of their children. In extreme cases, indifferent parents neglect their children. Delinquent behaviour is most likely to be found among the children of indifferent parents (Baumrind, 1991). Canadian research shows that children are involved in far more aggressive behaviour when their parents are highly punitive (Baumrind's authoritarian type) and where parents are limited nurturers or tend to reject their children (Baumrind's indifferent type)(Sprott, Doob and Jenkins, 2001:7).

Gerald Patterson's (1980) research indicates that there is a connection between children's delinquency and parental tolerance. In other words, what parents tolerate is what children will do. He states:

> many ... parents maintain that since they had never actually seen their child steal, they could not prove that their child had stolen, and therefore, could not punish the child. In numerous instances, someone else had actually seen the child steal but the child's "story" would be accepted by the parents, who would then rise to the child's defence and accuse others of picking on the child. (82)

Patterson, who teaches parenting classes at the Oregon Social Learning Center, has established a program that is based on "seven rules of parenting" (see Box 7.1). According to Hirschi (1983), Patterson's rules would not be effective for all parents:

> The parents may not care for the child (in which case none of the other conditions would be met); the parents, even if they care, may not have the time or energy to monitor the child's behavior; the parents, even if they care and monitor, may not see anything wrong with the child's behavior; finally, even if everything else is in place, the parents may not have the inclination or the means to punish the child. (55)

Indeed, data from the U.S. National Crime Victimization surveys suggest that adults who have been abused and assaulted in the home, most often mothers, have a reduced capacity for supervising and monitoring their children (Mitchell and Finkelhor, 2001:946).

BOX 7.1

Patterson's Seven Rules of Parenting

1. Notice what the child is doing.

2. Monitor the child over long periods.

3. Model social skill behavior.

4. Clearly state house rules.

5. Consistently provide sane punishments for transgressions.

6. Provide reinforcement for conformity.

7. Negotiate disagreements so that conflicts and crises do not escalate.

Source: Patterson (1980:81).

Although parenting styles are important, so too are other factors. Differential association theory suggests that the children of criminal parents are more likely to engage in criminal or delinquent behaviour. Notwithstanding Hirschi's contention that "parents with criminal records do not encourage criminality in their children and are as 'censorious' toward their criminality as are parents with no record of criminal involvement" (1983:59), some studies have found a correlation between parent and child criminality. According to West and Farrington (1977), boys with criminal fathers are four times more likely than boys with noncriminal fathers to be involved in delinquent behaviour. Laub and Sampson (1988) found higher rates of delinquency among children of mothers and fathers who are deviant. What seems like a contradition here may be a result of research limitation in that it is difficult for us to know if such children are actually more delinquent than other children. It may be that police and courts are more likely to **criminalize** the misdeeds of these children because their parents have criminal records.

Structure and Relations

Most research on family influences on youth crime has focused on family structure and relations. Very little has addressed the overall social structure and its impact on particular families. One exception (discussed in the preceding chapter) is Hagan, Gillis, and Simpson's (1985) study of power relationships in the larger social structure. Their power-control theory looked at how structural power relations are reflected in control mechanisms in the home. They found that family control structures are influenced by whether or not both parents work and whether in their employment they occupy positions of power and authority. Differences in degree of delinquency, and between boys' and girls' delinquency, are based on whether families are structured as patriarchal or egalitarian. Delinquency—especially boys' delinquency—is more strongly correlated with a patriarchal structure.

Steven Cernkovich and Peggy Giordano (1987) attempt to ascertain whether structural factors or relationship factors are more important in children's delinquency. Their analysis, which is based on a sample of 824 adolescents, considers seven family interaction factors: control and supervision, identity support, caring and trust, intimate communication, instrumental communication, parental disapproval of peers, and conflict. In comparing the impact of these factors on behaviour with the impact of a broken family, they find that "internal family dynamics are considerably more important than family structure in affecting delinquency" (Cernkovich and Giordano, 1987:316).

In 1987–88, Thornberry et al. (1991) tested for interactional effects between family and school experiences. A total of 987 seventh and eighth graders enrolled in Rochester City public schools were interviewed three times and asked to report on their delinquent behaviour. In the first interview, they were asked about delinquency over the previous six months; in subsequent interviews, they were asked about delinquency since the first interview. The researchers found that the relationship between parental attachments and delinquent behaviour is not a simple one. The first stage of testing revealed that low parental attachment increases delinquency and, as expected, that delinquency worsens attachments to parents. However, the last two stages of testing indicated that while delinquency negatively influences attachment to parents, attachment does not have a significant effect on delinquency. According to Thornberry et al., "parental influences in accounting for delinquency diminished considerably over time as adolescents gain independence. Indeed, by middle adolescence attachment to parents is viewed as an effect of delinquency rather than a cause of it" (1991:30). Thornberry et al. elaborate upon the delinquency–attachment relationship and suggest its implications for how we respond to delinquent behaviour:

> Because of its reciprocal relationships with the bonding variables, delinquent behaviour contributes, in a very real sense, to its own causation. Once exhibited, delinquency causes a deterioration in attachment and commitment, which, in turn, leads to further increases in delinquency. Treatment agents need to be aware of this causal pattern and should design intervention strategies that reduce or mitigate the negative consequences of delinquency on family and school. If this is not done, then the adolescent's contin-

uing delinquency may simply "undo" the success of intervention programs in improving attachment to family and commitment to school. (1991:31)

Their model and results also suggest the need for "holistic treatment strategies," family interventions that start early in a child's life, school programs that "break the cycle of alienation from school," and, for older youth, programs that "provide for a smooth transition from school to work" (1991:32). These strategies will be discussed more fully in later chapters.

The Meaning of Family Attachment

Research on children's attachment to parents suggests that this attachment reduces rates of delinquency when it is measured as "affect," or emotional ties, rather than as supervision. Positive emotional attachments tend to be most effective in reducing delinquency. Children who feel loved, who identify with their parents, and respect their wishes, are less likely to be delinquent than children who come from homes where there is conflict or neglect, or where discipline is lacking, or erratic, or extreme.

Since low attachment seems to start the delinquency process, it is important to know just what it means. In measuring parental attachment, Thornberry et al. (1991) used an 11-item scale that measured, among other things, children's perceptions of warmth, liking, and feelings of hostility between themselves and their "primary care-taker." Thornberry et al. indicate that in 85 percent of the cases in their sample, the primary caretaker is the mother, while in 10 percent of the cases it is a stepmother. Only 5 percent of the cases involved a caretaker other than a mother or stepmother, such as father or grandparent (1991:17).

More often than not, mothers are the focus of research on family relationships. Interestingly, ethnographic studies of young offenders often indicate that fathers are particularly disruptive to family life, and that children's "bad" relationships with mothers are frequently due to larger problems in the family setting stemming from the fathers' violence. Elliott Leyton (1979), for example, interviewed young people incarcerated in juvenile facilities in Newfoundland. The following three accounts (from Tyrone, Mercedes, and Lucien respectively) focus on fathers' destructive behaviours:

> Father used to come home late in the night drinking. He was cracked, like somebody gone mental. Once he came home and he took off his belt and he hit my sister across the leg for no reason, leaving a great mark. He was drunk, right. He got arrested three or four times up at the house. One Christmas he even caught the place on fire, the fire started in the wardrobe upstairs. He got my mother—she's got false teeth now—and he knocked all her teeth out and he took the phone and ripped it off the wall; and he had a bottle of liquor there, he smashed it and pushed us all around. I, we, told him to get out of the house ... I don't talk to my father. Sometimes I talk to him. I talk to him any time I want to—my mother won't say nothing—but the rest of my family don't talk to him. He's nice to me all the time. (Leyton, 1979:42–43)

When I was younger, my parents fought a lot. Their fights were usually about money or something stupid like that. I didn't like being at home. As I got older I started to drink, I'd come home drunk and I'd usually end up being whipped [by my father] next morning. A couple of times I got locked out of the house. Once I was so cold I wanted to come in, so mom had to phone the police on dad so he'd let me in. Another time I slept in the car because he wouldn't let me in. I almost froze. (66–67)

Dad didn't abuse me so much when he was drinking; he was better to me when he was drunk than when he was sober—he was cranky then, you couldn't look at him. Me and him couldn't get along together. He'd always be fighting with me when I was 13 and 14, and when mom would go to work I'd go out and I wouldn't come home 'til she came home because we'd be fighting. We'd fight about any old thing. I'd get in trouble in school or around our neighbourhood. If I was hanging around with a hard bunch, he didn't want me hanging around with them: he was always fighting me about that. They were fist fights. He'd hit me and I'd hit him back or kick him. Then I wouldn't be able to go home. When mom would come home, nothing would be said. He'd only have a fight with mom. (123)

Virtually all of the young people Leyton interviewed tell of violent, angry, and destructive fathers. To focus on attachments to mothers, or even attachments to parents, is to miss the most important **etiological** question about delinquency—namely, what factors are responsible for weak attachments to parents? It is only through ethnographic studies that we can begin to understand why some young people have weak attachments to parents. Mark Le Blanc (1992), based on his work with families and young offenders in Quebec, recognizes that "marital variables" have direct links to delinquent behaviour. Children exposed to physical fighting and violence in the home are more likely to behave aggressively, exhibit emotional disorders and be involved in property crime (Dauvergne and Johnson, 2001). Schissel (1997) finds marital discord and parental problems with alcohol and drugs are associated with young offenders' substance abuse and legal problems, such as time spent in custodial facilities and various administrative charges (96–100). McCarthy and Hagan's (1992) work with homeless youth in Toronto indicates that abusive homes will often force youth onto the streets where crime is necessary for survival.

A national survey of runaway youth in Canada found various patterns of parental neglect, family conflict and violence, school problems, and abuse as reasons for running. Hagan and McCarthy (1998) found 60 percent of Toronto and Vancouver street youth had been physically abused and 14 percent of girls and 6 percent of boys reported sexual abuse (23–24). Canadian studies report anywhere from 18 to 32 percent of runaway street youth became involved in prostitution (Fisher, 1989; Kufeldt and Nimmo, 1987, McCarthy, 1990, Hagan and McCarthy, 1998:116). Schissel and Fedec (1999) found that Saskatoon and Regina young offenders who had experienced childhood neglect, sexual, physical, or psychological abuse were more likely to be involved in prostitution. Among these factors, all were highly significant for Aboriginal youth, but only childhood sexual abuse was a significant predictor for non-Aboriginal youth involved in prostitution (43).

Those writing from a feminist perspective are well aware of the impact of poor parenting and violence on girls and they also recognize the connection between relationships and social structure. Chesney-Lind and Shelden (1998, 1992), for example, argue that a feminist perspective on female crime will not only account for patriarchal social structures, but will contain an explicit concern about physical and sexual abuse of girls:

> Unlike young men's victimization, young women's victimization and their response to it is shaped by their status as young women. Hence, young women are much more likely than their opposites to be the victim of sexual abuse ... more likely to be victimized by a relative, and more likely to be abused over a long period ... [T]heir vulnerability is heightened by norms that require that they stay at home, where their victimizers have greater access to them. Moreover, ... females' victimizers (usually males) can invoke official agencies of social control ... [A]busers have traditionally been able to utilize the uncritical commitment of the juvenile justice system to parental authority to force girls to obey them ... [M]any young women on the run from homes characterized by sexual abuse and parental neglect are pushed by the very statutes designed to protect them into life on the streets ... [Y]oung girls are seen as sexually desirable ... [which] means life on the streets and survival strategies are shaped by patriarchal values. (1992:91)

In other words, one cannot understand the crime and delinquency of girls without accounting for the status of women in patriarchal society and the consequent victimization of women and girls not only in the home but also in the justice system. Similarly, one cannot talk about attachments or commitments to family and parents without recognizing that, for some youth, there is good reason for weak attachments. In these cases, one would be reluctant to say that the "cause" of delinquency is weak attachments to mothers or parents.

THE SCHOOL AND DELINQUENCY

If commitment to school is related to delinquency and attachment to parents, the question remains as to what it is about school that may lead to low commitment levels. Both Albert Cohen's subcultural theory and control theory suggest that school is a determinant of delinquent behaviour. Canadian research has shown that both self-reported delinquency and official rates of delinquency are strongly correlated with school failure (Le Blanc, 1983; Gomme, 1985). Cohen (1955), in his version of strain theory, indicated that the delinquent subculture stemmed from *reaction formation*, wherein lower- and working-class youth responded to the frustrations they experienced in a middle-class school system. Control theory simply posits that low levels of commitment will lead to delinquency. Colvin and Pauly (1987) combine these two ideas and argue that *coercive controls* in working-class families combine with similar controls in schools to increase the chances of failure among working-class youth in the school system. Hence, some explanations focus on the organization of schools and classrooms, others on the role of school in the larger social structure and its impact on particular class and minority groups, and still others focus on an individual's short-comings.

Individual Failures

IQ

Reminiscent of early biological understandings of criminality as a function of "feeble-mindedness" are modern claims that a low IQ is predictive of school failure and sub-sequent delinquent behaviour. This is the view presented by James Q. Wilson and Richard Herrnstein (1985). Based on their studies in the United States and Great Britain, they report that the IQ of nonoffenders is some 10 points higher than that of offenders. They argue that IQ has a direct effect on delinquency in that young people with low intelligence tend to be impulsive, lacking in moral reasoning, and inclined to think only in terms of immediate gratification. For these youth, school failure encour-ages delinquency:

> A child who chronically loses standing in the competition of the classroom may feel justified in settling the score outside, by violence, theft, and other forms of defiant ille-gality. School failure enhances the rewards for crime by engendering feelings of unfairnes. (Wilson and Herrnstein, 1985:121)

Hirschi (1969) argues that IQ is related to delinquency indirectly through its effect on grades. IQ affects grades, which in turn affect one's attachment to school. Attachment to school affects one's tolerance of school authority, and tolerance of authority affects one's involvement in delinquency. Although research in the 1960s and 1970s indicated that grades are better predictors of delinquency than IQ, more recent research challenges Hirschi's argument. Liska and Reid (1985), for example, argue that

> street delinquency may be correlated with troublesome school behavior in classrooms, school halls and school yards ... [A]lso, adolescents involved in delinquency simply have less time for school; thus, delinquency, independently of teacher reactions, may decrease school attachment. (557)

Of course, none of the IQ research addresses the cultural bias inherent in IQ tests and its negative effects on students from minority groups. Box 7.2 presents an example of a question from the WISC-R, an IQ test used in California. The scores for this ques-tion are (a) two points, (b) two points, (c) one point, and (d) no points. What makes the question culturally biased is the high probability that children who have experienced racial prejudice or police harassment will choose (d) based on the assumption that picking up the wallet would make them vulnerable to accusations of theft (Regoli and Hewitt, 1994:263).

Tracking

One of the consequences of IQ tests and other forms of testing is that schools "streamline" or "track" students into different types of classes. Students can be tracked into vocational programs, college prep programs, remedial programs, or special ed programs, to name a few. Studies have shown delinquency to be more strongly correlated with **tracking** than with gender or **social class** (Kelly, 1975; Gamoran and Mare, 1989). Based on his Montreal studies, Mark Le Blanc (1993) reported a number of school experiences, including tracking, to be predictors of delinquency. Nonetheless, it is not necessarily IQ or grades that determine students' tracks. Tracking decisions are often made by counsellors, teachers, and parents, and they are often made on the basis of race and class. Regoli and Hewitt (1994:262) report that African-American students are two times more likely than white students to be tracked into special education classes. However, as the proportion of African-American teachers increases in schools, the number of African-American students in special ed programs decreases.

In a longitudinal study conducted in the United States, a group of high-school students were interviewed four times over the course of their school experience. The results provided little evidence that delinquency was related to tracking at either the

---

BOX 7.2

An Example of an IQ Test Question

What should you do if you find a wallet in a store?

(a) Find out whom it belongs to and return it.

(b) Give it to the store owner or a police officer.

(c) Try to find the owner.

(d) Make believe you didn't see it.

Source: Adapted from Regoli and Hewitt (1994:263).

beginning or the end of the high-school career (Wiatrowski et al., 1982). For Tanner (1996), an important finding is that 87 percent of the students said they were satisfied with their track allocation. This finding suggests to Tanner that tracking may be related to delinquency only when students are negatively labelled because of it and come to resent being tracked. Given the contradictory research evidence on tracking, Tanner argues that "a reasonable conclusion might be that a sense of fairness about appropriate track allocations reduces delinquency" (1996:102).

School Failures

School Organization

Another way of looking at tracking and IQ testing and their impact on delinquency is to consider them as part of the organization of the school rather than as factors related to the young offender. Many people today are of the opinion that youth are problematic because of the school system itself. In his book *The Literacy Hoax*, Paul Copperman (1980) outlines a number of problems associated with schools that he thinks contribute to delinquency. Simply put, he argues that school delinquency is created by a lack of teacher authority. This lack of teacher authority is a function of the organization of the school, particularly with respect to school principals. According to Copperman, a school cannot teach students in the absence of a strong principal who is able to exercise authority and concentrate on curriculum and teaching (including the firing of incompetent teachers). Similarly, a lack of parental support for school systems and teachers reduces teachers' authority in the classroom. If parents don't support and respect teachers, neither will children. Copperman also views open classrooms with flexible schedules, electives, and light course loads as problematic. A lack of structure in classrooms translates into teachers' loss of control over students. It is precisely this loss of control, Copperman maintains, that leads to violence, disruption, and drug use in contemporary schools. Others take an opposite position. Schissel (1997), for example, is of the view that rigid, authoritarian school systems exacerbate youth problems, particularly for those individuals who are marginalized, "at risk," or simply have not had the advantages others have (120–26). He advocates more flexibility in schools to meet youth needs and a "human rights approach" to youth education (121).

Structural Failures

Social Class

A question lurking behind all of the research regarding, tracking, IQ, and loss of teacher authority is whether or not these factors are related to delinquency because of the class structure of Western society. Greenberg (1977) argues that the regimentation of schools causes delinquency and that regimentation is more likely to be resented by working-class youth. Students who are doing well academically, or who participate in extracurricular activities, may find school rules to be mere annoyance because they find rewards in the school system. However, students who are not actively involved in school life, or who are not doing well academically, will find the same rules to be oppressive because they are not being rewarded by the school system. Further, Greenberg argues, working-class youth are more affected than middle-class students by worsening job conditions because such conditions force them to stay in school longer than they normally would. Students forced to remain in school will find the school experience particularly degrading and will strike out against teachers and school property in an effort to regain their self-esteem. Perhaps the strongest support for this argument comes from American and Canadian research showing that delinquency declines after young people graduate from or drop out of school (Elliott, 1966:307–14; Elliott and Voss, 1974a, 1974b).

Davies (1994b), in a survey of high-school students in Ontario, challenges the notion that resistance to or rebellion against school systems is a working-class behaviour. Davies found that resistant attitudes and behaviours, such as drug and alcohol use and disrespect toward police, are associated with tracking and academic problems but unrelated to class background. Rather, the school "stands on its own" as a causal factor in delinquent behaviour among high-school students. On the other hand, there is evidence that school problems and resentment of school have a racial component. Solomon (1992), who documented through ethnography the resistance of black male students in a Toronto high school, argues that this resistance is race based. For black students, school resistance is a consequence of a conflict between schools' cultural assumptions and rules and their own cultural backgrounds and experiences.

A classic study by Arthur Stinchcombe (1964) puts an interesting twist on Cohen's idea of status frustration. While he agrees with Cohen that status frustration generated by the school system is a source of delinquency, Stinchcombe maintains that it is not working-class students but rather middle-class students who are most likely to be frustrated. Students who are most pressured to do well in school (i.e., middle-class students) are the ones who will be most likely to experience status frustration if they do not meet expectations. These are the students most at risk of delinquency. Based on his study of a California high school, Stinchcombe found (1) that poor grades were related to rebellious behaviour, and (2) that the most rebellious students were male middle-class students with poor grades.

According to Davies (1994a), school failure is related to male delinquency, not female delinquency. Girls leave school not because they are frustrated with school or are failing, but because they have placed "domestic" concerns above academic concerns. Whereas boys leave school as a form of resistance and rebellion, girls leave school because of marriage and motherhood. Neither response is related to class position.

In his review of the literature on school rebellion, Tanner (1996) concludes, "regardless of whether it is called rebellion or resistance, anti-school behaviour has its origins in factors and experiences located inside the school yard gates rather than in the wider world beyond them" (116).

PEERS: FRIENDS AND GANGS

Friends

The single most important predictor of "official" delinquency is delinquent friends. Moreover, research has firmly established that peer group experiences are also predictors of the seriousness of delinquency (Morash, 1986). Importantly, other research confirms that youth crime is more a function of "companions" than group behaviour such as gangs (Regoli and Hewitt, 1994:277).

Explanations of the relationship between peer relations and youth crime come from variations of Sutherland's theory of differential association, such as social learning theory (Akers, 1985). Here it is argued that criminal behaviour is learned through group affiliations, such as delinquent friends, that reinforce nonconforming behaviour. Brownfield and Thompson (1991) add elements of Hirshi's control theory to this argument and ask how attachment to friends affects an individual's involvement in criminal behaviour. Based on an analysis of self-reported delinquency data from the Seattle Youth Study of male youth, they found support for both social learning and social control theories. Although the strongest relationship was between peer association and self-reported delinquency, "trust in friends and respect for friends [was] negatively associated with self-reported delinquency" (Brownfield and Thompson, 1991:57). In other words, boys who trust and respect their friends are less likely to be involved in crime and delinquency; stated conversely, boys engaged in crime and delinquency are less likely than nondelinquents to trust or respect their friends.

How gender is related to peers and youth crime was examined by Morash (1986). Here, a sample of youth in two Boston communities were interviewed about their criminal activity. Morash found that gender effects on crime operate through types of friends. Quite simply, one reason for lower rates of self-reported crime among girls is that their friends are less likely than the friends of boys to be delinquent.

Finally, there is the question of how family and friends combine to affect the likelihood of youth crime. According to Warr's (1993) analysis of data from the U.S. National Youth Survey,

> the amount of time spent with family is indeed capable of reducing and even eliminating peer influence. By contrast, attachment to parents (the affective relation between parents and offspring) apparently has no such effect. Instead, it appears to affect delinquency indirectly by inhibiting the initial formation of delinquent friendships. (247)

Making Sense of the Connections

As the above discussion implies, family, school, and friends all interconnect with each other in a variety of ways in the creation of youth crime. Over the last decade, criminologists have begun to recognize these connections and two new theoretical approaches are developing that offer explanations not only of how youth get involved in criminal activity, but also incorporate the important fact of why most eventually desist. **Lifecourse developmental theory**, as it is applied to crime, takes a contextual approach. It looks at criminal behaviour in the context of the course of life, which is characterized by *transitions* (short-term changes), and pathways or *trajectories* (long-term trends or patterns). Sociological lifecourse theory views these trajectories and transitions as embedded in social institutions (Elder, 1985). Pregnancy, for example is a life transition, something that changes the course of one's life, the effect of which sets in motion a particular trajectory depending on the age and sex of a person. The consequence of pregnancy on a career is radically different for women and girls than for boys and men and equally different for a woman with an already established career than a teen-age school girl. Some criminologists have integrated control theory and strain theory with lifecourse theory to explain crime. Sampson and Laub (1993), for example, argue that crime is the product of the amount of informal social control associated with life transitions. Therefore, it is not marriage or employment that increases social control, but emotional and mutual ties that increase both social and self-control, thereby reducing criminality.

Lifecourse developmental theory connects family, friends, and school to youth crime by integrating aspects of **social capital theory** (Elder, 1988, 1990). Social capital refers to investments in institutional relationships such as family, work, and school. "Social capital is productive making possible the achievements of certain ends that in its absence would not be possible" (Elder, 1988:98). Hence Sampson and Laub argue that weak social bonds mean a lack of social capital and explaining crime involves identifying the characteristics of social relations that facilitate or impede the development or accumulation of social capital. Hence, to use our earlier example, teenage pregnancy occurring in the context of substantial social capital such as a supportive family network, adequate income, educational, and employment opportunities is not likely to result in problematic behaviours. On the other hand, very different results would be expected in the absence of social capital, that is a girl with an abusive family, no marketable labour skills, inadequate income, and little to no education (Matsueda and Heimer, 1997).

Hagan and McCarthy define social capital as

> originating in the socially structured relations between individuals, in families, and in aggregations of individuals in neighborhoods, churches, schools, and so on. These relations facilitate social action by generating a knowledge and sense of obligations, expectations, trustworthiness, information channels, norms, and sanctions. (1998:229)

Social capital and life course development theory explain how young people get involved in crime while others do not, and why some become uninvolved while others continue to be involved into adulthood. Hagan and McCarthy (1998) use these concepts to explain the behaviour of street youth in Toronto and Vancouver. The youth in their study not only had limited social capital, but they came from families with limited social capital. Their families are the ones described earlier in the chapter, those with poor parenting, violence and abuse, neglect, and that are economically marginalized. The youth themselves have had poor experiences in school with teachers and low grades. It is thus the lack of social capital that leads them into the transition to the street and a continued erosion of social capital. This in itself propels street youth toward the justice system and a further reinforcement, as well as erosion, of low social capital. In other words, without a major event or transition out of this situation, a criminal trajectory is in the making for many street youth, particularly if their low social capital leads them to an organized criminal network.

Gangs

Some researchers contend that police are the best source of information on gang activities (see, for example, Maxon, Gordon, and Klein, 1985). Others point to the political nature of gang definitions in suggesting that much gang information reflects the interests of researchers and the agendas of law enforcement, politicians, and the media (Conly, 1993; Spergel and Curry, 1991). As discussed in Chapter 1, Zatz (1987) connects the discovery of a gang problem in Phoenix with "the acquisition of federal funds to create and maintain a gang squad within the Phoenix police department" (153). More important, a growing body of research reports that the identification of young people as gang members has a negative impact on their processing through the justice system (Chambliss, 1973; Werthman and Piliavin, 1967; Morash, 1983; Pearson, 1983; Zatz, 1985).

Although many police departments and members of the public see youth gangs as a growing threat, scholars who have attempted to measure and explain gang activities have not found it to be an easy task. The first challenge in studying gangs is to determine what constitutes a gang and what behaviours constitute gang activity. In addition, until recently, most of our information about gangs came from research conducted in the United States; Canadian criminologists are now questioning the applicability of this information to the Canadian scene. Finally, as with general delinquency, much has been assumed and little known about the involvement of girls in gang activity.

Definitions of Gangs

As we know from Hollywood Westerns, gangs used to refer to desperadoes, adult outlaws who spread havoc and violence throughout the American West as they carried out robberies of banks, stagecoaches, and eventually trains. After the turn of the century, gangs began to be associated with inner cities in the United States. In his book *The Gang: A Study of 1,313 Gangs in Chicago*, Frederic Thrasher (1927) focused on youth groups, presenting them as localized and organized by territory. Walter Miller's (1980) definition of gangs is closer to police and public conceptions of gangs:

> A youth gang is a self forming association of peers, bound together by mutual interests, with identifiable leadership, well developed lines of authority, and other organizational features, who act in concert to achieve a specific purpose or purposes which generally include the conduct of illegal activity and control over a particular territory, facility, or type of enterprise. (121)

Ruth Horowitz (1990) challenges these views by pointing out that research on youth gangs indicates that not all such gangs are involved in illegal activities; moreover, only some gangs claim a territory, and not all are highly organized with identifiable leadership. Most important, research on U.S. gangs throughout the 1960s and 1970s indicated that gang members are more likely to wile away their time than spend it engaging in criminal activities (Klein, 1971). Hagedorn (1988) reports that the primary gang activity in Milwaukee involved "partying and hanging out." With regard to turf, Krisberg's (1975) study of African-American gangs indicated that some members never leave their section of the city. According to Hagedorn (1988), turfism among urban gang members has been reduced because of frequent relocations of residences. Also accounting for the decline of turfism was urban renewal throughout the 1970s and the increased availability of cars (Regoli and Hewitt, 1994:281).

On the question of gang cohesiveness and commitment, gang members observed by Klein (1971) were "dissatisfied, deprived, and making the best of an essentially unhappy situation" (91). Organization and leadership has been found to vary by gang. Keiser (1969) found the Vice Lords, a Chicago gang, to be highly organized. Muehlbauer and Dodder's (1983) analysis of a suburban gang, the Losers, showed an organization with a nucleus of 10 to 12 members around which all other members revolved. Yablonsky (1959) suggests that most gangs would be better conceptualized as a **near group**. Near groups have ill-defined membership, limited cohesion, minimal consensus regarding norms and rules, and vague leadership. Mathews (1993) work with youth gangs in Toronto suggests that "gang/group" is a more accurate term to describe youth groups and that they should be viewed along a continuum of friends who spend time together and occasionally get involved in criminal activity, on the one end, to organized criminal groups on the other.

Measuring Gang Activity

The increases in gang activity reported in the media are problematic given the difficulty of defining what constitutes gang activity. Hence, there is also some debate as to what should constitute gang activity. Maxon and Klein's (1990) analysis of police departments' definitions of gang activity in Los Angeles and Chicago points to considerable variation in definitions. What is considered gang violence in Los Angeles would not be considered as such in Chicago. Chicago police require a gang-related motive before they will consider an incident to be gang activity, whereas both the Los Angeles Sheriff's Department and Police Department require only that victims or accused are known to be gang members.

Fagan (1991) compared self-report data on crime (serious incidents involving harm, injury, property damage, or selling drugs) from youth living in low-income neighbour-hoods in Chicago, San Diego, and Los Angeles. Not surprisingly, he found that criminal activities were more prevalent among male gang members than nongang youth. However, when he compared the average number of reported acts, Fagan found that gang members were more involved in nonviolent offences while nongang youth were more involved in assaults (major and minor), robberies, and extortion. Chesney-Lind et al. (1994), who conducted their research in Honolulu, Hawaii, compared youth identified as gang members by police with delinquents not identified as gang members. They found that the offences of youth not identified by police as gang members were no different in severity or frequency from those of youth identified as gang members. The most common offences of identified gang members were property-related offences and "status" offences. Where the two groups differed was in their racial com-position. "Groups most commonly labeled by police as gang members are Filipino and Samoan males" (Chesney-Lind et al., 1994:201). According to the researchers' survey of self-reported gang members, 42 percent were Hawaiian/part Hawaiian, compared with 9 percent in the police-identified group (219).

Canadian Gangs

Studies of gangs in Canada are rare. Rogers (1945) studied street gangs in Toronto in the 1940s, and little research was done after that until Joe and Robinson (1980) looked at immigrant gangs in Vancouver's Chinatown in the 1970s. Joe and Robinson's find-ings seem to confirm most of what we know about gangs in American cities—that is, they are short-lived and not highly organized. Joe and Robinson report that most of the gangs they studied were no longer in existence within five years. Nor are gangs new to Canadian cities. Young's (1993) historical analysis of gangs in Vancouver shows periods of heightened activity. During the late 1920s, there were what newspapers referred to as "corner lounger gangs." The late 1940s and 1950s were the period of "zoot suit" and "hoodlum" gangs. The late 1960s and early 1970s were dominated by "park gangs."

Based on studies of gang members serving terms in British Columbian prisons, Gordon (1995) offers a method of categorizing gangs and gang activities, as well as data on the incidence and volume of gangs in Vancouver. According to Gordon, five different groups have frequently been referred to as gangs: youth movements, youth groups, criminal groups, criminal business organizations, and street gangs. *Youth move-*

ments refer to distinctive modes of dress and activities that serve to set one group of young people apart from another. Thus in the 1950s we had "zoot suiters," in the 1960s "mods and rockers," in the 1970s "hippies," and in the 1980s "punk rockers." *Youth groups* are "small clusters of friends" who hang out together in public places. *Criminal groups* are groups of friends who are together specifically for the purpose of committing a crime and who may consist of young people, adults, or a combination of the two. A *criminal business organization*, by contrast, is a "consortia of adults who ... engage in crime for profit" (Gordon, 1995:313). All of these groups are different from *street gangs*, which Gordon defines as "groups of young people and young adults who have banded together to form semi-structured organizations, the primary purpose of which is profitable criminal activity" (313). Street gangs differ from youth groups and criminal groups in that members identify themselves as a gang, adopt a name for themselves, and wear distinctive clothing or tattoos.

Interestingly, as with research in the United States, Gordon (2000) reports that some of the Vancouver "gangs" were figments of the imagination of media and police. One group discussed in a newspaper as the gang "Back Alley Boys" referred simply to a small group of young offenders who had been bullying high school students for cash and possessions. Another group of eight youth and young adults were involved in a series of bank and store robberies over a four month period and were referred to by police and media as the "626 gang" because they used Mazda 626 cars in their heists. Not only had this group not chosen this name, but they did not perceive of themselves as being a "gang" (47).

According to Gordon, recent active street gangs in Vancouver are similar to Canadian gangs in the 1950s (the Alma Dukes and the Vic Gang) and the park gangs of Vancouver in the 1970s (Clark Park Gang and Riley Park Gang). Like earlier gangs, today's gangs are made up of males aged 14–26 who are interested in lucrative property crime and whose activities tend to involve violent offences such as assault and weapons offences. Some gangs are involved in activities related to drugs and prostitution. As with the findings in American studies, Gordon reports that street gangs tend to be short-lived. In the spring of 1991, there were about 10 street gangs in Vancouver (including the Bacada Boys, Los Diablos, Mara Latinos, and Patook); by the fall of 1993, most of these gangs had disappeared and six new gangs had formed (e.g., Los Cholos and East Van Saints). Groups disband for a number of reasons, including arrest, convictions, and simply loss of interest. It would appear that street gangs in Canada today are not much different from those studied by Joe and Robinson in the 1970s. Gordon states,

> whatever the causes of street gangs, the regularity of the cycles of activity suggests that the current wave in Greater Vancouver will eventually diminish and disappear, only to reappear at some future date, probably in a similar form. This may be a gloomy prospect for some, but it is probably indicative of the health, rather than the distress

of Canadian cities. Unlike the situation in many American cities, street gangs have not become an entrenched feature of the Canadian urban landscape, and the chances of them doing so are still fairly slim. (1995:318)

Explaining Gang Membership

Recent theorizing about male crime focuses on masculinities and differences between men in terms of their access to power and resources (Connell, 1987; Messerschmidt, 1986). According to these theories, young men create different cultural ideas of dominance, control, and independence—*hegemonic masculinity*—based on their class and race position in the social structure. Young minority males in economically impoverished communities choose public and private displays of aggressive masculinity (intimidation and gang violence) as a source of status and respect because they are "typically denied masculine status in the educational and occupational spheres" (Messerschmidt, 1993:112). Katz (1988) refers to the public aggressiveness of these males as "street elite posturing," while Connell (1987) calls it "doing gender." Horowitz (1987), who studied a Chicano community in Chicago, suggests that in such communities gang violence is understood and "articulated within the cultural framework of honor" (437).

Gordon (1995) offers psychological and interpersonal explanations for youth involvement in gang activities. On the psychological side are "pull" factors such as the opportunity for material rewards (money, cars, etc.) not readily available through conventional means. Other "pull" factors include the psychological rewards stemming from friendship networks such as relief of boredom and a sense of independence and autonomy from the adult world. Unfortunately, there are also the "push" factors involving negative school experiences and extremely problematic home lives that propel young men toward gang membership. Gordon reports that 40 percent of gang members in British Columbian prisons had experienced "unstable and extremely unpleasant domestic conditions" characterized by drug and alcohol abuse and physical and sexual abuse. Moreover, gang members' home lives were "compounded by extreme problems in school—truancy, fighting, and academic failure." Recent ethnographies of gang members in low-income neighbourhoods in Honolulu reveal that these youth also come from neighbourhoods and families "scarred by violence ...; 55 percent of the boys and three quarters of the girls interviewed were victims of physical abuse, and 62 percent of the girls were the victims of sexual abuse or sexual assault" (Joe and Chesney-Lind, 1993:12). Enriquez (1990) presents similar findings and reports that the Honolulu youth gang he studied had come into existence for "security reasons." He maintains that the current panic about youth gangs is a "red herring" intended to divert attention from the socioeconomic problems experienced by low-income youth (54).

Girls and Gangs

In keeping with the spirit of the liberation hypothesis, the North American media have implanted the notion that "girl gangs" are a growing phenomenon and that their activities are as violent as those of male youth gangs (Vincent, 1998). Not surprisingly, most gang research is **androcentric** (i.e., male-centred), so that what little we do know about girls and gang activities is stereotypical, sexist, and/or simply incorrect. Gang activity on the part of males is presented as a "normal" response to their "abnormal" circumstances. On the other hand, girl gang members

> typically are portrayed as maladjusted tomboys or sexual chattel, who in either case, are no more than mere appendages to boy members of the gang. Collectively they are perceived as an "auxiliary" or "satellite" of the boy's group, and their participation in delinquent activities (e.g., carrying weapons) are explained in relation to the boys. (Joe and Chesney-Lind, 1993:8)

According to Joe and Chesney-Lind, recent research either continues this trend (as in Martin Jankowski's (1991) *Islands in the Streets*), or shifts to the "liberated woman" theme. As an example of the latter, Carl Taylor (1993) in *Girls, Gangs, Women and Drugs* states, "we have found that females are just as capable as males of being ruthless in so far as their life opportunities are presented. This study indicates that females have moved beyond the status quo of gender repression" (cited in Joe and Chesney-Lind, 1993:9). Similarly, in a recent *Globe and Mail* article, a police detective, said to be an expert on youth crime, is quoted as saying, "we shouldn't be surprised by what's happening ... [W]hat we're looking at is ladies coming of age in the 1990s, and girls are taking on a much more aggressive, violent role" (cited in Vincent, 1998).

A few studies go beyond stereotypical notions of girls (see, for example, Quicker, 1983; Campbell, 1984, 1990; Fishman, 1988; Harris, 1988; Lauderback, Hansen, and Waldorf, 1992; Moore, 1991). What these studies indicate is (1) that girls often form gangs after being abandoned by their children's fathers and/or after living in abusive and controlling relationships; and (2) that gang membership provides a source of support for girls, sometimes financial, but mostly familial and emotional. Joe and Chesney-Lind (1993), who interviewed 48 self-identified gang members in Honolulu, identified four common themes that cross gender and ethnic lines:

1. *Gangs provide a social outlet.* Girls like to dance and sing, boys like to cruise in cars; both like to drink and fight, but boys more so than girls.
2. *Gangs serve as an alternative family.* Both boys and girls use the gang as a replacement for deceased or absent parents.
3. *Gangs help members to deal with family problems and family violence.* Both boys and girls experienced physical abuse at home, but for different reasons—the girls for being away from home too much or too late, the boys for their crimes and delinquencies.

4. *Gang activities compensate for impoverished community life.* Both boys and girls use the gangs to escape the "boredom" of their impoverished lives.

These findings are very similar to conclusions drawn from Canadian studies of youth crime on Native reserves (York, 1990; Shkilnyk, 1985).

Joe and Chesney-Lind (1993) argue that in order to understand girls' participation in gangs, we must place that participation

> within the context of the lives of girls, particularly young women of color on the economic and political margins. Girl gang life is certainly not an expression of "liberation," but instead reflects the attempts of young women to cope with a bleak and harsh present as well as a dismal future. One fifteen year old Samoan girl captured this sense of despair, when in response to our question about whether she was doing well in school she said, "No, I wish I was, I need a future. [My life] is jammed up." (35)

SUMMARY

The family, school, friends, and gang membership have been consistently identified by academics and through public discourse as sources of youth crime and delinquency. This chapter reviews some of the recent research on the impact of these factors on crime and delinquency.

Family structure, measured as a broken home or a home with a working mother, has consistently been identified, theoretically and empirically, as a factor in delinquency. However, the evidence suggests that parenting styles, the quality of family relationships, and internal family dynamics are far more important factors than family structure. According to power-control theory, differences in degree of delinquency, and between boys' and girls' delinquency, are based on whether families are structured as egalitarian or patriarchal. Tests of interactional theory have shown that low parental attachment increases delinquency, which in turn worsens attachments to parents. However, as adolescents age, parental influences diminish; delinquency lessens parental attachments, not vice versa.

Research has demonstrated that grades and low commitment to school are better predictors of delinquency than IQ scores. However, while low commitment leads to delinquency, delinquency also reduces commitment to school. The organization of schools and classrooms and the class structure of Canadian society are also seen as a source of delinquency. Contrary to Cohen's (1955) suggestion that a middle-class school system creates status frustration for working-class boys, research has shown that middle-class boys with poor grades are more likely to be delinquent and to rebel against schooling. Race is also a component in school resistance. According to Solomon (1992), school resistance on the part of black students is a consequence of a conflict between schools' cultural assumptions and rules and these students' own cultural backgrounds and experiences.

The single most important predictor of "official" delinquency is delinquent friends. Morash (1986) attributes the lower rates of self-reported crime among girls to the fact that girls are less likely than boys to have delinquent friends. According to Warr (1993), the amount of time spent with family can reduce peer influence, while attachment to parents can reduce delinquency indirectly by inhibiting the initiation of attachment to delinquent friends. Brownfield and Thompson (1991) found that boys who trust and respect their friends are less likely than boys who do not trust and respect their friends to be involved in crime and delinquency.

Lifecourse developmental theory as it is applied to crime looks at criminal behaviour in the context of the course of life, which is characterized by transitions (short term changes), and pathways or trajectories (long term trends or patterns). Sociological lifecourse theory views these trajectories and transitions as embedded in social institutions. Crime, therefore, can be seen as the product of the amount of informal social control associated with life transitions. Social capital refers to investments in institutional relationships such as family, work, and school. Social capital and lifecourse developmental theory is able to explain how some young people get involved in crime while others do not, and why some become uninvolved while others continue to be involved into adulthood.

Information on gangs varies depending on how "gang" is defined and how gang activity is measured. Both are politically motivated activities that reflect the interests of researchers and the agendas of law-enforcement agencies, politicians, and the media. Research on youth gangs indicates that not all such gangs are involved in illegal activities, that members do not spend much time on criminal activities, that their activities are no more severe or frequent than those of nongang youth, that only some gangs claim a territory, and that not all gangs are highly organized with identifiable leadership.

Gordon's (1995) research indicates that street gangs in Canada today are not much different from those in the 1970s. Canadian street gangs tend to be short-lived and composed of males aged 14–26 who are primarily interested in lucrative property crime. Boys and girls seem to join gangs for the same reasons. Gang membership provides a social outlet, escape from an abusive or neglectful family life, and compensation for an impoverished community life.

CHAPTER 8

First Contact: Police and Diversionary Measures

CHAPTER OBJECTIVES

1. To examine the initial stages of youth involvement in the youth justice system.

2. To detail factors and issues associated with police discretion in decision making.

3. To outline principles and rules regarding diversion and extrajudicial measures under the YCJA and discuss how these compare to diversion under the YOA.

4. To examine provincial differences in the administration of diversionary measures and in types of programs.

5. To identify and discuss issues associated with diversionary programs.

KEY TERMS

Diversion	Stigmatization	Reconciliation
Discretion	Alternative measures	Mediation
Surveillance	Principle of least	Restitution
Extralegal	possible interference	Net widening
High-risk youth	Extrajudicial measures	

INTRODUCTION

In this chapter, and in the next two chapters, we discuss the various stages of the youth justice system, focusing particular attention on how the stages are organized, how decisions are made, and which factors affect decision making at each stage. A youth's involvement with the justice system begins with a police investigation to determine whether or not an offence has taken place. The police or the Crown have the option in most provinces (not Ontario) to divert youth from the courts through YOA provisions for alternative measures. These diversionary provisions have become more formalized with the YCJA. As well as providing for diversionary programs, the YCJA encourages police to consider issuing a warning for first-time offenders involved in non-violent offences. This has created an additional level to diversion from the YOA. As a result of these diversionary provisions, if a youth successfully completes an alternative/extrajudicial measures program, his or her involvement with the justice system ends. Under the YOA, youth who failed to complete such programs were sent to court (except in British Columbia) with their original formal charge. While there are a number of justifications and benefits to **diversion** for both the young offender and the

---

BOX 8.1

Joey: "Police Apprehension"

Joey and his friends headed off to Sussex, New Brunswick. After they arrived at their destination, Dale took the truck out for a run. Joey was shooting paint balls at [his] friend's little brother when he learned that Dale had rolled the truck. By the time he arrived at the scene of the accident, an RCMP auxiliary officer was just pulling up ... The boys told the police officer that they stole the truck in a panic after the owner tried to molest Dale ... Both boys recanted later the next day ... They thought that they would be charged with auto theft, assault, and possession of stolen goods ... "But all he (the truck owner) wanted back was his tools." ... Joey and Dale were charged with possession over 1,000 dollars ... Because Joey was arrested in New Brunswick he was remanded to the Kingsclear reform school in Fredericton for two weeks.

Source: Adapted from MacDonald (1994a).

justice system, the concept and the practice is not without its critics. This chapter discusses the structure and process of diversion as well as current issues.

POLICE CONTACT AND DECISION MAKING

A young person's involvement in the justice system may begin with police contact in a public setting or with a complaint laid by parents, school authorities, or someone who has been victimized. Police have a considerable amount of **discretion** in making decisions about how to proceed with suspicious or accused youth. The YCJA requires a police officer to consider if warning or cautioning a youth is sufficient (see Box 8.2), but section 6(2) clearly suggests that it is not a violation of youths' legal rights if the police fail to do so. Sections 7 and 8 allow provinces to formalize these warnings and cautions. Nova Scotia, for example, has a formal letter that is issued to all youth so warned by police. Therefore, an individual officer has the power, freedom, and autonomy to choose from a number of courses of action including,

1. issuing a warning (formal or informal) to the young offender about his or her behaviour and then letting the person go;
2. taking the young person home for a talk with parents or guardians;
3. taking the young person to the police station for questioning before releasing her or him;
4. writing up a report on the young person before release;
5. charging the young person with an offence;
6. (in some provinces) referring the young person to a diversionary program or youth justice committee; or
7. holding the young person in detention for further judicial processing.

Police officers can have a significant impact on young people's futures depending on how they choose to exercise their discretionary power. Ontario police statistics for 1992 indicate that 26,412 young people were in police records who had not been charged with an offence; this amounted to almost one-third the number of young people charged by police that year (Doob, Marinos, and Varma, 1995:94). In 1993, informal police processing of apprehended youth ranged from one-half to less than 20 percent, depending on jurisdiction (Report, 1996). Canadian and British studies of policing indicate that police **surveillance** of youth is disproportionately high compared to surveillance of adults. This discrepancy does not necessarily translate into high rates of criminalization. Rather, most criminal cases involving young offenders are handled informally (Ericson and Haggerty, 1997; Loader, 1996; Meehan, 1993). Nonetheless, the YOA did result in dramatic increases in the formal charging of young offenders (Schissel, 1997, 1993), which suggests a substantial decrease in the use of discretion by police with youth. Whether the provisions in sections 6 through 8 of the YCJA

BOX 8.2

YCJA Guidelines for Police

Section 6(1) of the YCJA requires police officers to consider if a warning is sufficient response to a youth's behaviour:

Section 6(1) A police officer shall, before starting judicial proceedings or taking any other measures under this Act against a young person alleged to have committed an offence, consider whether it would be sufficient, having regard to the principles set out in section 4, to take no further action, warn the young person, administer a caution, if a program has been established under section 7, or, with the consent of the young person, refer the young person to a program or agency in the community that may assist the young person not to commit offences.

Section 6(2) The failure of a police officer to consider the options set out in subsection (1) does not invalidate any subsequent charges against the young person for the offence.

---

result in reductions of formal charges will only be known after the legislation has been in effect for a few years.

This raises the question as to why some youth are charged and others are not. Research has shown that there are legal and **extralegal** factors associated with police discretion. Legal factors refer to legal requirements or to things generally considered relevant or pertinent in criminal justice matters. Extralegal factors are those factors not necessarily or usually considered legitimate or relevant in justice decision making. For example, it would be considered discriminatory or even illegal to hold someone in pretrial detention because of the colour of his or her skin; doing so because of the seriousness of the offence would not be considered as such. In this example, skin colour is an extralegal factor and offence seriousness is a legal factor.

Legal Factors Affecting Police Discretion

Research on police discretion, most of which has been done in the United States, began more than 20 years ago. This research confirms what we might expect—that the seriousness of an offence and prior arrest records influence police decisions to lay a charge (Piliavin and Briar, 1964; Krisberg and Austin, 1978; Lundman, Sykes, and

Clark, 1978). However, this does not mean that police discretion is not operative in serious offences. Sellin and Wolfgang (1964), in an examination of Philadelphia police records, found that in cases where youth were involved in offences that led to the hospitalization or death of a victim, only about half resulted in arrests or charges. It is also important to recall from Chapter 3 that the majority of youth offences resulting in charges are not serious offences. Therefore, relying solely on the serious-ness of the offence would not take us very far in understanding the factors that lead to police charging.

Another important factor affecting the use of discretion is prior police contact. Cicourel (1968) argued that simply being in contact with police was often enough to increase the probability of police charging a youth. He suggests that having police attention drawn to oneself would lead to being known by the police. This contact would be remembered, thereby increasing the chances of arrest in future encounters. Similarly, the tendency of police to arrest certain "types" of youth helps to create a police record for some youth, which in turn increases the chances of future arrest and processing through the system. Terry (1967) showed that offenders without police records made up 38 percent of police arrests and only 7 percent of court referrals. On the other hand, youth with extensive records made up 20 percent of arrests and 60 percent of referrals to court.

Extralegal Factors Affecting Police Discretion

Race

While there is considerable evidence that legal factors have an effect on police charging, it is extremely difficult to separate some of these factors, particularly prior record, from extralegal factors. Recent research has shown that both legal and extralegal factors are related to race. Minority youth are more likely to be arrested by police and to have a record. This suggests that race may very well be a more important factor than police record (Dannifer and Schutt, 1982). In other words, if police are more likely to keep records on minority youth, we should not be surprised to find that minority youth are more likely than white youth to be processed by police (Smith and Visher, 1981; Huizinga and Elliott, 1987).

While the race differential in police processing is clear, the reasons for it are not. It is easy to conclude that police may be biased, but other factors may also be at work. Black and Reiss (1970), for example, found that whether or not a case proceeds to court has a lot to do with complainants and their wishes. Based on their finding that police complied in every case in which a complainant requested that a youth not go to court, they suggest that African-American youth may have higher arrest rates because complainants are less likely to ask for leniency in their cases. Doob and Chan

(1995) found that the victim's request was an important factor in police charging in Canada. Others have argued that racial bias in the justice system is the most important factor in explaining differences in police arrest and charging (Dannifer and Schutt, 1982; Fagan, Slaughter, and Hartstone, 1987).

Class

Evidence on social class is mixed. According to Sampson (1986), youth who live in poor neighbourhoods with high crime rates have higher arrest rates than youth living in middle-class neighbourhoods. On the other hand, Shannon (1963) and Bodine (1964) argue that differences in charge and arrest rates by neighbourhoods can be explained by type of offence and police records. Thornberry (1973), who questioned this argument, found that lower-class youth were treated more severely regardless of their offence and prior record; he also found that class differences in charges were greatest when the offence was more serious.

Based on research conducted in Toronto, Hagan, Gillis, and Chan (1978) found that police attitudes toward or perceptions of crime-prone areas, coupled with citizen complaints, were strong predictors of delinquency rates. They note that "actual class differences in the experience of juvenile crime are amplified by underclass housing conditions and complaint practices, and, in turn, even more so by police perceptions" (100). Sampson (1986:881) found that social class, race, and having delinquent friends accounted for roughly one-third of the variation in police responses to youth.

Age and Sex

Research on the effect of gender on police encounters generally shows that girls are treated more leniently (Elliott and Voss, 1974b; Armstrong, 1977; Chesney-Lind, 1970). However, other research shows that sex differences in charging depend on type of offence. Teilmann and Landry (1981) and Horowitz and Pottieger (1991) demonstrate that police are more likely to respond harshly to girls involved in minor offences, but less likely to arrest girls for more serious offences. DeFleur (1975) and Visher (1983) both found that police are reluctant to arrest female suspects who behave in stereotypical female ways such as crying. Girls who did not adhere to middle-class behavioural standards for a traditional female were not afforded leniency or chivalry by police officers. Age also has a bearing on police discretion in that younger girls seem to be treated more harshly. Visher (1983) found that police were more likely to arrest younger girls, but that age had no bearing on their use of discretion with respect to boys. According to Ericson's (1982) study of police patrols in Ontario, young men of lower socioeconomic status are disproportionately stopped, searched, questioned, and recorded; they are referred to in police culture as "pukers"—that is, people requiring "extra surveillance."

BOX 8.3

How Effective Is Police Contact?

Some interesting research on the issue of police contact comes from Carl Keane, A.R. Gillis, and John Hagan (1989) who surveyed 835 students from four high schools in Toronto. Keane and his colleagues set out to determine whether police contact deters or increases delinquent activities among young people. Students filled out a questionnaire in which they were asked about delinquent friends, police contact, and marijuana use, among other things.

The authors found that the students who reported being risk-takers—that is, those who responded positively to the statement "I like to take chances"— were more likely to increase their marijuana use as a result of police contact. On the other hand, those who were identified as "risk-aversive" because they did not agree with the statement about taking chances were more likely to be deterred by police contact.

Keane et al. found that boys were more likely than girls to report a willingness to take chances. Based on this finding, they concluded that police contact is more likely to deter girls—at least from using marijuana—than boys. More specifically, they argue that for risk-takers

> there is a positive relationship between being picked up by the police and reporting the use of marijuana. We suggest that whereas for risk-aversive juveniles police contact acts as a deterrent and generates an increase in control, for risk-takers it provides an opportunity for involvement and interaction with delinquent others [differential association theory] which may lead to further delinquent behaviour, such as using marijuana ... [M]ales are more likely to take risks, while females tend to be risk-aversive. Because of this, females are more likely to be deterred from delinquency as a result of police contact while male delinquent behaviour is likely to be amplified. (241)

The results from this research are important because they strongly suggest that we cannot merely assume that police contact will have a deterrent affect on all young people with respect to all types of offences. At the same time, it should be pointed out that gender differences may occur because police contact itself varies for boys and girls as much as its consequences. Whether boys are risk-takers and girls are risk-aversive is also debatable. Boys and girls may have very different ideas about what it means "to take chances."

Source: Adapted from Keane, Gillis, and Hagan (1989).

Demeanour and Race

One factor that has been consistently found to affect the outcome of youth encounters with police is a young person's demeanour. A youth's appearance and attitude, and how that youth behaves with a police officer, will influence how the officer will use her or his discretion (Cicourel, 1968; Hohenstein, 1969; Black and Reiss, 1970; Winslow, 1973; Smith and Visher, 1981; Morash, 1984). Youth who fit a stereotypical image of delinquents—that is, who exhibit a disrespectful, uncooperative, or defiant manner—are more likely to be arrested. The significance of demeanour depends on the seriousness of the offence (Piliavin and Briar, 1964), but also on race. According to Ferdinand and Luchterhand (1970), African-American youth expect the worst from police and therefore are more likely to behave in a defiant manner. Police, in turn, see African-American youth as more threatening and hostile than other youth.

A recent study of police–minority youth relations in Metropolitan Toronto and York Region illustrates and confirms the type of encounters described by Ferdinand and Luchterhand. Neugebauer-Visano's (1996) interviews with Toronto youth clearly indicate that young people, regardless of colour, believe that black youth are a focus of police harassment.

> It's like this. They hassle anybody who is young and looks out of place. With me they'll talk about me being on a joyride thing. But with blacks they call it car theft. No big deal. What sounds worse in court? Joyride is having fun. But stealing cars is breaking the law. (Georgette, white, 18:294)

> White kids are lucky. They can always pretend to be afraid of the police. Cops believe them. Cops see some bonds with them. All a white kid has to do is fake it. They can play better. My brothers and sisters can't play along. They don't know how. They're too hurt. Too suspicious of the cop. African Canadians are never trusted anytime. Even when they're innocent they're guilty. They are made to feel guilty. I'm not saying that white kids love the police or the cops like all the white kids. All I'm saying is that black kids have a hell of a time connecting with the cop. It's deep. Really deep. Cops don't get it. (Amanda, black, 17:295)

> What kind of dumb fucks do they think we are. Piss on us and then expect us to respect that shit [community policing]. Times are changing. I think that is what the cops want. They want us to declare war. They want me to be mouthy. They want something on me. Why give them an excuse to fuck you. Just be cool. Take the heat. (Manley, black, 16:300)

Citing a 1976 report on police attitudes toward visible minorities in Toronto, Neugebauer-Visano states, "in response to the police slogan 'to serve and protect,' the feeling among blacks is that the motto of some police officers may as well be 'to harass and oppress'" (1996:302).

Studies of Aboriginal youth in Canadian cities have shown similar kinds of problems. Native youth in cities tend to be located in areas where there are high levels of policing, thereby increasing their chances of arrest (Schissel, 1993). In addition, some police hold stereotypical views of Native peoples. Hylton (1981), who studied police and public attitudes toward Aboriginal youth in Regina, found a relationship between negative attitudes toward Native peoples and a fear of crime. The Aboriginal Justice Inquiry of Manitoba reports that Aboriginal youth have more charges laid against them, are more likely to be held in detention prior to court, and are more likely to be denied bail (Hamilton and Sinclair, 1991). According to Fisher and Janetti (1996):

> Aboriginal people perceive the justice system as discriminatory and culturally insensitive ... [A]boriginal people perceive themselves to be subjects of the system, rather than informed, empowered and accepted participants in the system. When the system is perceived as fundamentally unjust, the end products are lack of trust and alienation. A justice system that may be difficult to understand and that both in appearance and reality treats aboriginal peoples differently may not offer them justice at all. (247)

Aboriginal youth have been found to be overrepresented at every stage of the criminal justice system—arrests, convictions, detention, and in custodial centres (LaPrairie and Griffiths, 1982; Morin, 1990).

Family and Community

Both the family and the community have an impact on police discretion. When parents are interested in and concerned about their children's behaviour and appear cooperative with police, a warning is more likely to be given. Similarly, when a community has youth centres, safe houses, and other facilities offering programs or safe living space for young people, then police have choices. Community options are particularly important in cases where parents are less than interested in their children's behaviour or well-being. As we will see later in this chapter, extrajudicial measures programs affect police decisions to the extent that police have a choice other than total release or processing through the justice system. Unfortunately, this third choice may lead to more rather than fewer police charges.

Police Departments

The amount of discretion used by a police officer is sometimes limited by law, as in the case of extrajudicial measures policies that restrict these options to first time offenders. It is also limited by the policies of the departments and municipalities within which officers do their work, as well as by the attitudes and characteristics of individual officers. Wilbanks (1975), who looked at the relationship between departmental policy and police officers' decision making, found that the best predictor of police decisions was the personal views of police officers rather than department policy. However, other research (Wilson, 1968; Sundeen, 1972) suggests something more complex. The extent to which police officers are able to make decisions based on their personal views and beliefs depends on the organization of the police department—that is, on whether it is characterized by close supervision or centralized management. According to Wilson (1968), whether or not police officers send youth to court depends on how much they are expected to be involved in the case and whether they will have to appear in court. Goldman (1963) found that officers who were paid a fee for serving as witnesses in court were more likely to send youth to court than were those who were required to use their own unpaid time for court appearances.

Conly's (1978) study of Canadian cities in the 1970s showed considerable variation by city; for example, while 17 percent of youth were being charged by police in Hamilton, 96 percent were being charged in Calgary. Some Canadian police departments have adopted risk management programs for **high-risk youth** in their jurisdictions (Ericson and Haggerty, 1997). These programs involve intensive police supervision of a youth and his or her family which sometimes lasts as long as two years. When improvement is not apparent, the youth graduates to a more intrusive surveillance program, Police Attending Youth (PAY). The PAY program involves heightened investigation of the youth's activities, record keeping, and coordination of efforts toward criminal prosecution and "appropriate" sentencing (Ericson and Haggerty, 1997:170–271). When these youth are arrested, their files are stamped "PAY" and specialized investigations and prosecutors are brought in. In the words of one police officer,

> we can provide the information on that kid from day one, from the first time he was reported missing when he was aged eight all the way through the gambit. There's often twenty or thirty pages of information that we can provide the court. (Ericson and Haggerty, 1997:273)

Research Summary on Police Discretion

Regoli and Hewitt (1994) review the American research on police discretion with respect to juveniles. Their conclusions are listed below:

1. Police departments vary considerably in their policies and practices with respect to release or referral of people with whom they have contact.
2. Most juveniles apprehended are reported by citizen complaints, rather than on police initiative.
3. Police handling of serious offences is based chiefly on legalistic criteria, rather than upon social class or racial distinctions.
4. With less serious offences, decisions to arrest are based principally on complainant preference, but what is defined as offensive behavior is influenced by other, extralegal factors. (374)

Doob and Chan (1995), who studied factors affecting police decisions in Toronto, found that the four most significant of those factors were offence seriousness, previous contacts with police, young person's demeanour when apprehended, and victim's request.

DIVERSIONARY MEASURES

There were no specific provisions for diversionary measures under the JDA. Young people were kept out of the justice system solely through the exercise of police or prosecutorial discretion (Bala et al. 1994:77). During the 1970s, labelling theory raised concerns about the **stigmatization** that could result from formal processing in the justice system. One consequence of these concerns was the development of numerous programs whose objective was to divert young people from the formal justice system. In 1977, for example, Quebec passed the Youth Protection Act, which combined juvenile delinquency cases and child welfare cases in services designed to meet both needs. Diversion is a key component of this legislation. Police are required to refer all young people to an intake officer who decides whether to take further action through the court, divert the young person to another aspect of the system, or take no action (Bala et al., 1994:78).

As we saw in Chapter 2, the notion of diversion is expressed in s. 3(1)(d) of the Young Offenders Act, which states, where it is not inconsistent with the protection of the public, taking no measures or taking measures other than judicial proceedings should be considered for dealing with young persons who have committed offences." This principle, along with its resultant policies and programs, was referred to as **alternative measures** and was complemented by the **principle of least possible interference** contained in s. 3(1)(f) of the YOA. While diversion as alternative measures (AM) is not a formal principle of youth justice in the YCJA, both the principle of diversion and the concept and practice of AM have now been formalized to an even greater degree under the concept **extrajudicial measures**, which is defined in the YCJA as "... measures other than judicial proceedings under this Act used to deal with a young person alleged to have committed an offence." Extrajudicial measures are presented as a set of principles (s. 4) and objectives (s. 5) (see Boxes 8.4 and 8.5) with accompanying rules regarding sanctions (s. 10) and a formalized set of regulations regarding the police role in this process.

This is a significantly different approach to diversion than under the YOA in that it actively promotes the diversion of youth from formal police processing and the courts as well as provides a framework for the implementation of restorative justice principles. Section 4 establishes that diverting youth from police action in courts is not "doing nothing," but rather that it is an appropriate way of ensuring that young people are held accountable for their behaviour, if their offence is a non-violent one. It also

BOX 8.4

Principles of Extrajudicial Measures under the YCJA

Section 4. The following principles apply in this Part in addition to the principles set out in section 3:

(a) extrajudicial measures are often the most appropriate and effective way to address youth crime;

(b) extrajudicial measures allow for effective and timely interventions focused on correcting offending behaviour;

(c) extrajudicial measures are presumed to be adequate to hold a young person accountable for his or her offending behaviour if the young person has committed a non-violent offence and has not previously been found guilty of an offence; and

(d) extrajudicial measures should be used if they are adequate to hold a young person accountable for his or her offending behaviour and, if the use of extrajudicial measures is consistent with the principles set out in this section, nothing in this Act precludes their use in respect of a young person who

(i) has previously been dealt with by the use of extrajudicial measures, or

(ii) has previously been found guilty of an offence.

does not preclude diversion for repeat offenders or even for those who may already have gone through the courts for another offence.

Section 5 further provides for the realization of restorative justice principles and a more holistic approach to youth justice by recognizing that a criminal offence is a harm not only to a victim but also to the community. This section underscores the importance of victim, family, and community involvement in responding to youth. As we saw earlier, section 6 of the YCJA adds another level to diversion by encouraging police officers to offer warnings and cautions to youth or to refer them to community

---

BOX 8.5

Objectives of Extrajudicial Measures under the YCJA

Section 5. Extrajudicial measures should be designed to

(a) provide an effective and timely response to offending behaviour outside the bounds of judicial measures;

(b) encourage young persons to acknowledge and repair the harm caused to the victim and the community;

(c) encourage families of young persons—including extended families where appropriate—and the community to become involved in the design and implementation of those measures;

(d) provide an opportunity for victims to participate in decisions related to the measures selected and to receive reparation; and

(e) respect the rights and freedoms of young persons and be proportionate to the seriousness of the offence.

---

based programs rather than charge and process them through the formal system, including a more structured diversion program (extrajudicial sanctions).

Section 10(2) of the YCJA outlines the necessary criteria for using extrajudicial sanctions in a given case:

An extrajudicial sanction may be used only if

(a) it is part of a program of sanctions that may be authorized by the Attorney General or authorized by a person, or a member of a class of persons, designated by the lieutenant governor in council of the province;

(b) the person who is considering whether to use the extrajudicial sanction is satisfied that it would be appropriate, having regard to the needs of the young person and the interests of society;

(c) the young person, having been informed of the extrajudicial sanction, fully and freely consents to be subject to it;

(d) the young person has, before consenting to be subject to the extrajudicial sanctions, been advised of his or her right to be represented by counsel and been given a reasonable opportunity to consult with counsel;

(e) the young person accepts responsibility for the act or omission that forms the basis of the offence that he or she is alleged to have committed;

(f) there is, in the opinion of the Attorney General, sufficient evidence to proceed with the prosecution of the offence; and

(g) the prosecution of the offence is not in any way barred at law.

These rules and regulations regarding extrajudicial sanctions (ES) are identical to those for alternative measures (YOA s. 4(1)). The YCJA sections 10(3) through (6) are also identical to the YOA in the requirement that extrajudicial sanctions may not be used if a youth denies participation in the offence or prefers to have her/his case addressed by the court. Two additions to this part of the YCJA involve a requirement for ES administrators to notify parents that an ES has been undertaken (s. 11) and that victims have a right to be informed (if they so request) not only of an ES action, but also of the identity of the young person (s. 12).

After the YOA was implemented, all provinces eventually had alternative measures programs. Ontario was one of the last to do so. These programs varied in terms of how they were administered, who made the decision to refer a youth to alternative measures, and when this decision was made. Although programs were generally restricted to youth accused of minor offences who did not have prior records, Quebec and some Aboriginal communities operated alternative measures for more serious repeat offenders (Bala et al., 1994:79). Extrajudicial measures in the YCJA, given their similarity to alternative measures provisions in the YOA, are likely to follow the same practices.

Diversionary Programs

According to Schrader's (1994) analysis of alternative measures programs across the country, there are three types of programming. Under **reconciliation/mediation**, offenders and victims are brought together; apologies, either verbal or written, and the writing of essays or letters are among the program's elements. The second type of program, *retributive/restitutive*, is more punitive, involving **restitution** through such things as fines, financial compensation to (or actual work for) victims, or community service. The third type of program is *rehabilitative/educational* and is exemplified by the Stop-Lift Program in Saskatoon run by the John Howard Society. This anti-shoplifting program is for young people involved in petty theft. The program is designed

> to create an awareness in the young person of the effects of his or her actions on themselves, the victim, the community and society at large, and to provide an opportunity for the young person to reflect on his or her development, discuss values and focus on

issues such as self esteem, peer pressure and decision making skills. (JHS pamphlet on Stop-Lift, cited in Schrader, 1994:167)

The ALLY Project (Alternative Likable Literacy for Youth), offered by the Youth Alternative Society in Halifax (now the Community Justice Society), combined education and restitution. Youth who participated in the project did community service work (restitution) and in the process learned a new skill and improved their literacy levels (education). The ALLY Project required youth to engage in community service work with a local artisan, to undertake library research on the craft, and to keep a journal record of their learning as it unfolds. The program was designed to

1. instigate a new form of learning for youth in conflict with the law by connecting the arts community to them;
2. promote outreach and awareness for these youth to resources otherwise viewed as unattainable; and
3. foster growth in the areas of research and documentation skills and to assist youth in becoming skilled in an alternative area other than the academic realm, where many of them feel they have failed (Youth Alternative Society, 1997).

Usually, provincial governments, through either social services or correctional services departments, handle alternative measures programs and will likely do so for extrajudicial sanctions. In some cases, the programs are and will be implemented by social agencies or specially mandated agencies such as the Community Justice Society in Nova Scotia. In some provinces, administration is shared. In Alberta, correctional staff handle approximately 60 percent of referrals; the remaining are dealt with by either the Social Services Department in major cities or Youth Justice Committees, or through contracts with Native Service Providers (Schrader, 1994:136). Prince Edward Island and Quebec administer alternative measures programs through government, while Saskatchewan, British Columbia, Ontario, and Nova Scotia tend to contract to social service agencies, community agencies, and various service providers.

The manner in which diversionary measures are implemented varies by province. Young people suspected of offences may be brought into these programs before or after a charge has been laid. In Ontario, an application must have been made to the court in order for a youth to be considered for an alternative measures program.

In most provinces, referral to diversionary measures occurs before a youth is charged with an offence (he or she must first admit responsibility for the offence). Only Ontario uses a post-charge system whereby youth enter alternative measures after going to court. A majority of cases in the Yukon are also processed on a post-charge basis (Engler and Crowe, 2000:3). Saskatchewan and Nova Scotia use a pre- and post-charge method whereby the Crown prosecutor or the judge may make a referral to alternative measures after a young person has been formally charged by police. In most cases, the police initially make the referral for alternative measures. In Prince

Edward Island, the police determine whether a youth is eligible for alternative measures and the case is then referred to the Crown for approval.

In all other provinces, the Crown prosecutor is responsible for referrals to diversionary programs. In New Brunswick, for example, police prepare a report after they have investigated an incident involving a young person. The report is forwarded to the Crown, at which point the police officer may recommend that a young person participate in alternative measures. The Crown reviews the report and decides whether or not the young person will be charged or whether the case should be dealt with by

---

BOX 8.6

Essay by a Young Offender Who Participated in a Diversionary Program

Life's Too Short

Well, it has been a rough year for me. I imagine for teenagers like myself, there is nothing "unrough" about getting involved with drugs, alcohol, sex … and the list goes on.

During the last year of my life I have faced it all. I got into smoking dope and drinking every day. I started hanging around the wrong crowd and this was the major downfall of everything that went wrong in my life.

I started shop-lifting mainly because my friends were and at first I got away with it. That ended real soon. I was caught and charged. I received a punishment for it.

I've been living on my own for over a year, and believe me, don't be in a hurry to move out. It's hard worrying about a job and having money to live. I also haven't talked to my family in a year because of my mistakes.

I'm not saying I know it all because I don't. I've had to make some big changes in my life and because of it I've grown up a lot. I have some good people in my life now and I plan on keeping in the positive side of life! It's far too easy to let yourself fall back down.

"Life's too short to grow up too fast!" Enjoy life's good things! Take care!

Source: Youth Alternative Society Newsletter (1997: Jan/Feb).

alternative measures. Newfoundland differs from other provinces in that all police referrals must be authorized by both the Crown and a Youth Justice Committee. Ontario is the only province not to use police referrals.

British Columbia is unique in its adoption of a nonprosecutorial model for diversionary measures (see Box 8.7). British Columbian Youth who are referred to alterna-

---

BOX 8.7

Diversionary Measures in British Columbia

British Columbia's practice of not prosecuting youth for failure to complete diversionary measures agreements stems from a Supreme Court decision in a case where such a prosecution occurred. According to Chief Justice Anderson, prosecution in this context is illegal, contrary to the philosophy of diversion, and useless as a deterrent:

> Only the Courts have the right to impose sentence and the Crown cannot create an administrative program inherently coercive in nature, whereby the accused accepts "diversion" on terms fixed by the Crown, subject to its control, retaining the discretion to revive the criminal proceedings if the accused fails to adhere to the terms. The Crown cannot thwart the role of the law in this way ... [Such a] diversion agreement amounts to a pre-trial probation order. The exercise of such power by the Crown constitutes a direct and unlawful interference with the proceedings of the Criminal Courts and amounts to an abuse of process ...
>
> Even if I am wrong in respect of the conclusions I have reached, it would seem unwise to prosecute in cases of default. Some of the purposes of "diversion" are to avoid expense, publicity and legal entanglements. It is readily apparent that such purposes will not be achieved by proceeding against a defaulting accused on "revived" charges ... [V]ery little will be accomplished by the use of "default" sanctions. I do not think it cynical to say that the threat of sanctions will not deter those who are bent on a career of crime. An accused who violates his undertaking is likely to return to the courts in respect of some other offence in any event.

Source: *R. v. Jones* [1979] 4 C. R. (3D).

tive measures and subsequently fail to complete their agreements do not go to court. In every other province, youth who fail to comply with alternative measures agreements, contracts, or programs are referred back to court. In Ottawa, police may, at the pre-charge stage, refer 12- to 15-year-olds who are not involved in a violent offence to the Preventative Intervention Program (PIP). Charges are not laid if the young person fails to complete the program.

The Youth Justice Committee

The Youth Justice Committee concept was established by the YOA and is maintained by the YCJA Section 18(1):

> The Attorney General of Canada or a province or such other minister that the lieutenant governor in Council of the province may designate, or may establish, one or more committees of citizens, to be known as youth justice committees, to assist in any aspect of the administration of this Act or in any programs or services for young offenders.

The YCJA is more specific than the YOA about the role and function of the committee and, unlike the YOA, does not require youth justice committee members to perform their duties without "remuneration." Section 18(2) outlines the functions of the youth justice committee as

1. to give advice on appropriate extrajudicial measures;
2. to provide support to victims and facilitate reconciliation between young offenders and their victims;
3. to ensure community support is available to youth;
4. to help coordinate youth services with activities of the justice system;
5. to advise federal and provincial governments on the justice system's compliance with the act and various policies and procedures of youth justice;
6. to provide public information on the act and the youth justice system.

Youth Justice Committees are used in Manitoba, Alberta, New Brunswick, Newfoundland, and the Northwest Territories. In Manitoba, the Crown refers cases to probation officers who in turn refer them to Youth Justice Committees. These committees are responsible for providing diversionary measures programs. Of the 73 committees in Manitoba, 18 are Aboriginal. Each of the 73 committees has its own constitution and policies. As described by Ryant and Heinrich (1988),

> some committees meet directly with youth, while others maintain a more distant relationship. Some committees routinely include victim–offender mediation as part of the disposition, while others do not. Some committees meet as a group with the young offender, while others delegate the work ... to an individual member or subcommittee. (98)

In New Brunswick, a youth's case proceeds from the police to the Crown, who determines if the case will be dealt with through diversionary measures. The case is then forwarded to a probation office. A probation officer conducts an interview with the youth and his or her family. If the young person admits responsibility, a contract is worked out and the case is brought before an Alternative Measures Committee. The probation officer presents information regarding the offence to the committee and discusses the type of agreement developed with the offender. Upon the consent of the committee, the young person signs the contract. Alberta has 29 Youth Justice Committees. Three are directly involved in diversionary measures administration; the remaining committees, most of which are active in Aboriginal communities, act in an advisory capacity with respect to the sentencing of young offenders (Schrader, 1994:136).

British Columbia also has youth justice committees. In Nanaimo, the RCMP make recommendations to the Crown and approved cases are then referred to the John Howard Society. The society consults with a Neighbourhood Accountability Board, which assists in developing a young person's reparation agreement. The province's South Island Tribal Council program takes a more active role. Under this program, a young person meets with members of the Tribal Court and a diversion coordinator. The coordinator conducts an interview with the youth and makes recommendations to the Tribal Court. If the Tribal Court decides to accept the young person, it outlines a contract for the youth. The youth is then supervised and counseled by an elder from the community (Jackson, 1988).

In Newfoundland, Youth Justice Committees serve as a vehicle for creating a sense of ownership and empowerment among community members with respect to youth justice matters. The 25 committees in the province decide whether or not to proceed with cases using diversionary measures. The process begins with a committee conducting an intake interview with the young person, his or her parents or guardian, and the victim of the offence. On the basis of this interview, the committee determines how best to proceed (Newfoundland and Labrador, 1994).

Referral and Success Rates

Rates of referral to diversionary measures vary across the country. Nova Scotia's average referral rate, calculated as a percentage of numbers of youth apprehended from 1987 to 1995, is 24 percent (Montgomery, 1997). Quebec reports a five-year average of 36 percent; New Brunswick, 35 percent (1992–93); Saskatchewan, 22 percent (1991–92); Alberta, 17 percent (1992–93); and British Columbia, 16 percent (1993) (Schrader, 1994).

Diversionary measures programs are highly successful. Nova Scotia reported success rates ranging from 92.9 percent in 1992 to 98 percent in 1988 (Montgomery, 1997:109). Over a five-year period, Quebec reported an average success rate of 97 percent; Manitoba, 86 percent; Alberta, 94 percent; New Brunswick, 91 percent; British Columbia, 89 percent; and Saskatchewan, 80 percent (over a two-year period) (Schrader, 1994). The overall success rate across the country in 1998–1999 was 93 percent (Engler and Crowe 2000:11). The Department of Justice in Nova Scotia conducted a study comparing first-time offenders in alternative measures with those going through the courts for similar offences. First-time offenders going through court had a higher rate of recidivism than those going through alternative measures (Montgomery, 1997). There is every reason to expect that success rates will be just as high for extrajudicial sanctions even if they retain exactly the same structure and programs as under the alternative measures guidelines.

Diversionary Measures Issues

In this section, we consider three diversionary measures issues: net widening, mediation, and administration and control (O'Brien, 1984; Tobin, 1987; Schrader, 1994; Montgomery, 1997).

Net Widening

Supporters of diversion maintain that diverting offenders out of the youth justice system is in the best interests of both offenders and taxpayers. If nothing else, diversion prevents problems associated with reintegration after incarceration and provides an alternative to high-cost court proceedings and dispositions. Legislators have clearly attempted, through the YCJA, to increase the use of diversion by adding another level to diversion prior to that of diversionary programs and by insisting that this is an appropriate way for young offenders to be held accountable for their behaviour. One could reasonably assume that many minor offences that would have been processed through alternative measures under the YOA will now simply receive a warning and other offenders who might have gone to court will now receive an extrajudicial sanction.

Critics have long argued, however, that formalizing diversion results in more people going into the system, thereby effecting a "widening of the net" (Cohen, 1985). More specifically, it is argued that in the absence of diversionary measures, youth with a minor offence and no prior record would likely be "let go" with a warning. In this view, adding a warning letter amounts to formalizing procedures for those who would have been "let go." Others suggest that diversionary measures are not an alternative to court, but rather an alternative to police discretion. In other words, discretion is merely shifted from police to the Crown prosecutor (Montgomery, 1997). Since the YCJA specifies that extrajudicial diversionary measures may not be used if a youth denies participation in the offence or prefers to have her/his case addressed by the court, this particular type of net widening remains and may even be exacerbated by a more formal cautioning system. Ontario sidestepped these **net widening** issues by sending all cases to court before alternative measures would be considered.

BOX 8.8

Diversionary Measures and Mediation

Many diversionary measures programs include a mediation session involving the young offender, a parent, the victim, a police officer, and a trained volunteer mediator. The purpose of these sessions is to discuss the problem and arrive at an agreement whereby the young offender agrees to perform some act or service as a means of making amends and accepting responsibility for her or his behaviour. There are three stages in mediation: (1) exploring the conflict; (2) understanding the conflict; and (3) resolving the conflict.

1. *Exploring the conflict.* During this stage both parties to the conflict are given the opportunity to state their position. The opening position which is stated is often about obvious issues. The task of the mediator is to assist the parties in identifying the underlying issues which, more often than not, are far more significant. Each party is given the opportunity to make an uninterrupted statement.

2. *Understanding the conflict.* Part of the process is to try and sort out the major area of the conflict and deal with that in a systematic way. The role of the mediator is to keep focusing the task on resolving the major issues.

3. *Resolving the conflict.* During this stage, the mediator examines the goals of each party and identifies the various options for resolving the dispute. The intent is to produce a final agreement.

The Role and Skills of the Mediator

1. *A mediator must be able to create conditions for effective communication.* It is important that the mediator establish an environment for effective communications between the parties ... [T]he language that the mediator uses ... must not display any prejudgments of either party and not be parental in tone ... [T]he mediator must place himself [herself] in a position where he [she] can see both parties and observe what is going on ... [T]here has to be the reality of a balance of power.

2. *The mediator must be able to identify relevant and key issues as well as the needs and interests of the party.* The mediator must also maintain a problem-solving orientation ... [M]ediation is not therapy. One must ... guard against falling into the trap of just responding to feelings for the sake of responding and facilitating more exploration of that area.

3. *The mediator must have the skill to respond accurately to the feelings of the situation and the meaning of what the parties are saying.* One of the things that the mediator must be able to do is to communicate with immediacy—to be able to respond to exactly what is happening here and now in terms of the behaviour of one or both parties ... [T]he mediator must communicate what the specific behaviours are in a non-judgmental way so as to keep the interaction focussed ... [T]he solution is only meaningful when it comes from the parties themselves.

4. *The mediator must maintain a position of neutrality.* Neutrality means not taking sides, not only verbally, but even in body language. If it appears that the mediator is only listening to one of the parties, it may be perceived that he [she] is losing some of his [her] neutrality.

5. *The mediator must be able to confront the parties.* There are various levels of confrontation, going from mild to heavy.

6. *The mediator must be able to respond to the parties.* The skill of responding is one of the foundational pieces in mediation because without this the mediator will not have a basis to move in with any of the other skills. It is another word for communicating understanding. The mediator must communicate understanding. The skill of responding is based on listening. It is a response to the content of what has been said.

7. *The mediator must be a source of problem solving, not problem generation.* Frustrations can arise in all sorts of contexts, and for all sorts of reasons. The mediator must preclude a conflict being generated by the fact that he [she] is mediating. The mediator does not want to become part of the problem. Frustration occurs when an individual has a need which is not being met or fulfilled.

Mediation is clearly an alternative in resolving disputes. It is an alternative which gets away from the compulsoriness and the arbitrariness of the system, and it focuses on the individuals themselves. The notion is that two human beings are in conflict, one of whom has transgressed certain rules. Nonetheless, there is still a human interaction somewhere in all of this. Mediation tries to re-emphasize some of those values as opposed to strict judicial processing.

The focus in mediation is on generating new alternatives, new ways of doing things which will result in a "win-win" situation for both. In a mediation process, there is an expectation that they will be listened to and understood. If that does not occur, all the mediator is doing is increasing his [her] frustration level. The more conflicts that are unresolved, the more conflicts there will be in the future.

Source: Tobin (1987:118–23).

A related concern is whether diversionary programs can be truly voluntary when the consequence of nonparticipation is for a youth to go to court. Questionable too is the fact that, in most provinces, court proceedings result when a youth fails to fulfil any agreement reached through diversionary measures. British Columbia and the Ottawa-based Preventative Intervention Program (PIP) avoided charges of coerced participation by not proceeding with prosecution if a youth did not participate or did not successfully complete a diversion program.

Proponents of pre-charge and post-charge diversionary measures prosecution argue that there needs to be an incentive (or a threat) in order for diversionary measures to work. However, the success–failure rates that are available, as we have seen, do not suggest any difference in success between programs with or without sanctions for noncompliance. Nonetheless, the success rates reported for these programs are problematic because it is impossible to know if successes are due to the diversionary measures programs or the fact that mostly minor cases—that is, youth who would not likely reoffend after police contact and warnings—are processed through diversionary measures. Some provinces lobbied for changes to the YOA eligibility criteria so that more serious offences and offenders with prior records could be included in diversionary measures programs. The YCJA does not preclude using extrajudicial measures for repeat offenders or even for youth who have prior convictions, these decisions are left up to provinces. It does, however, restrict extrajudicial measures to non-violent offences.

Mediation

A major problem in mediation programs concerns the role of victims. Successful mediation requires the participation of both the accused and the accuser, but many victims of crime are reluctant to face the accused. Supporters of mediation argue that it is equally difficult for an accused to face her or his accuser and, further, that the most important part of the healing process is for both parties to come to see each other as people—to understand why the incident occurred and how they affected and continue to affect each other.

Although most diversionary measures programs report a high level of victim participation, there can be problems when the accuser is a business. Many businesses, particularly large department stores, will not participate in mediation programs. Some stores (Zellers and The Bay, for example) have even launched their own civil suits against offenders by sending a bill for their costs. Thus, offenders who have accepted responsibility and "paid" for their offence according to the justice system, face a potential civil penalty as a result of action by the stores. The legality of this practice has been successfully challenged in court by some adult offenders (Bell, 1995:20). In general, victims and offenders who have participated in mediation programs report a high level of satisfaction (78 and 74 percent, respectively), while negotiated arrangements were acceptable to both parties (92 percent) (Umbreit, 1995). Box 8.9 presents an example of the views of participants in mediation programs.

BOX 8.9

Participant Views on Diversionary Measures Mediation

A Parent

This is a marvellous intervention for first offenders. The non-judgmental and non-threatening attitude and atmosphere was very unexpected. The volunteer allowed us to verbalize our feelings and emotions and discuss whatever was on our minds while keeping us on track to meet the objective of the meeting. It even expedited the healing process between parent and child. I am sincerely thankful for a such a program. I wish more parents would take the interest in accompanying their child to such a meeting (JHS alternative measures Report, April 1994, cited in Schrader, 1994:183).

Youth and Victim: Before

Head bowed, voice lowered, eyes avoiding contact, she twists the corner of her jacket nervously. Across from the 15-year-old sits the security officer for the department store. He asks again, why did she try to leave the store without paying for the make-up? The question is asked directly, but not harshly. She hesitates, then shrugs. After a brief silence, a third person, seated between them, speaks. The mediator, a skilled professional, suggests that perhaps they can come back to that question a little later.

Youth and Victim: After

The 15-year-old smiles, stuffing her carefully-folded agreement into her back pocket as she heads for the door. She still can't believe that the security guard accepted her offer. He had seemed like kind-of-a-jerk the first time they met, but now she is almost looking forward to helping him on a Saturday afternoon.

The security guard sips his coffee, slowly shaking his head. The girl had been much more likeable and responsible than he had expected, and had offered to do three times more work to make amends than he ever would have expected. Although he had come to the meeting planning to demand an essay and an apology from the teenager, he likes the idea of her working for him. He wonders what the Saturday afternoon security tagging will be like (Pate and Peachey, 1988:105, 118–19).

Administration and Control

The issue of administration and control concerns the role of the community in deciding who is diverted and when, and how committed governments are to providing resources for diversionary measures programming. As we have seen, some provinces are firmly committed to community involvement in youth justice processes and have established Youth Justice Committees as active participants in diversionary measures programs; in some Aboriginal communities, the committees operate as a sentencing circle. However, only Newfoundland involves the committee in deciding what cases will actually be diverted to diversionary measures on a provincewide basis. Hence, the control and autonomy afforded community committees will vary not only by province, but also within provinces (Schrader, 1994; Report, 1996:52–54).

Tobin (1987) notes that mediation programs can be either community based or justice-system based. Only community-based mediation—in circumstances where disputes are handled by community committees before police involvement—is truly diversionary. An example of this type of mediation is the Community Boards Program in San Francisco; complaints are initiated by community people who contact the agency, report a dispute, and ask for assistance in reaching a resolution (Tobin, 1987:114).

The legal profession is the main opponent to community-based programs. Their opposition stems from concerns about people practising law who are not qualified to do so. On the other hand, a justice-based system of mediation has its own major weakness—namely, that program success depends on an acceptance of diversion philosophy on the part of individual police officers, Crown prosecutors, and their departments. According to Schrader's (1994) analysis of alternative measures programs across the country, there was considerable variation, within provinces, in diversion rates by police departments. There was also variation in diversion rates and programs by regions. Urban areas have far more resources to support diversionary measures programs than do rural areas. A related issue concerns the availability of resources for Aboriginal youth. Both Alberta and Saskatchewan have expressed concern about low rates of diversionary measures referrals for Aboriginal youth; they hope to address this inequity by increasing the number of Native service providers in their respective provinces (Schrader, 1994).

None of these issues are likely to change under YCJA provisions for extrajudicial measures because provinces maintain control of the administration of extrajudicial measures including its programs. Ontario, for example, initially resisted introducing alternative measures and eventually came to use courts rather than police as entry points for diversionary programs in many jurisdictions. Since Ontario has also repeatedly requested that the federal government move youth justice procedures and sentences closer to those found in the adult system, it is unlikely, with the vagueness of section 10 of the YCJA, that Ontario will change its diversionary practices in the near future. On the other hand, provinces currently working toward implementing restorative justice principles in the youth justice system, such as Nova Scotia and Prince Edward Island, have been provided more latitude to do so with the YCJA. Overall, unless more provinces change their prosecutorial models for youth who fail to comply with extrajudicial sanctions, little will change from YOA practices.

SUMMARY

A young person's involvement with the youth justice system begins with police contact. Except in cases involving the most serious offences, police have considerable discretionary power with regard to charging the youth with a criminal offence. A number of factors, both legal and extralegal, have been found to influence police decision making. In most provinces, the police or Crown are empowered under YCJA provisions for diversionary measures to divert young offenders from the courts. Diversionary measures programs vary across the country, both within and between provinces.

The most important legal factors influencing police discretion are offence seriousness and prior record of the offender. Minor offences offer more latitude for police discretion. Police contact in itself also increases the chances of future arrest.

Race, class, sex, age, demeanour, and complainant have all been identified as significant factors affecting police decision making. Other important extralegal factors include family, community, neighbourhood, and the structure and organization of police departments. The extent to which the personal views and beliefs of individual police officers affect their decisions depends on the organization of their departments.

Extrajudicial measures as expressed in the YCJA are based on the philosophy that diversion is the most appropriate and effective way to address non-violent youth crime. The YCJA requires that in every case an extrajudicial sanction should be proportionate to the offence and provide an effective, timely opportunity for young offenders to acknowledge and repair the harm their behaviour has caused for victims and communities. Diversionary measures programs are usually restricted to first-time offenders charged with minor offences. Some provinces are lobbying to follow Quebec's lead in including more serious offences.

Diversionary measures programming can be categorized as reconciliation/mediation, retributive/restitutive, or rehabilitative/educational. In most provinces, police make referrals to diversionary measures. Only Ontario uses a post-charge system, in which all youth are required to go to court before entering diversionary programs. Only British Columbia adopted a nonprosecutorial model for administrating diversionary measures. In some provinces, Youth Justice Committees made up of citizens participate in these decision-making processes. Province by province, anywhere from 16 to 36 percent of apprehended youth have been referred to diversionary measures; success rates range from 80 to 98 percent.

Critics charge that diversionary measures are a net-widening mechanism because programs are largely restricted to minor offences by youth with no prior record and because, in most provinces, failure to comply results in court processing. The usefulness and effectiveness of mediation is also questionable if victims are not willing to participate in the process. Most contentious of all is the question of who should control or administer diversionary measures. Some argue that to be truly diversionary, programs should be community-based and administered independently of the justice system. The closest any provinces have come to this model is by implementing Youth Justice Committees.

CHAPTER 9

Going to Court

CHAPTER OBJECTIVES

1. To provide a statistical profile of the youth court population and show how it has changed over time.

2. To examine pretrial procedures and decision making associated with bail, detention, and transfer to adult court.

3. To discuss the role of defence counsel and legal representation in youth court.

4. To review sentences allowable under the YCJA and the principles that support them.

5. To discuss sentencing principles under the YCJA and how they compare to those for adult sentencing.

KEY TERMS

Interim release
Pretrial detention
Presumptive offence
Legal advocate
Guardian

Sentencing conference
Retribution
Proportionality principle
Deterrence

Incapacitation
Rehabilitation
Gendered expectations

INTRODUCTION

In Canada, more is known about the youth court than any other aspect of youth justice. Because of the creation of the Youth Court branch of the Canadian Centre for Justice Statistics, information has been readily available for discussion and analysis since the inception of the YOA. Not all of this information is comparable over time because of the time delay in introducing 16- to 17-year-old youth to the system, because not all provinces initially participated in sending their court statistics to Ottawa and because of the introduction of the YCJA and important procedural and substantive changes. Nonetheless, researchers have been able to identify trends in the application of YOA principles and considerable debate accompanied these analyses, some of which influenced YOA reform and the resulting YCJA.

This chapter begins with a profile and analysis of the cases appearing before youth court and proceeds to a discussion of the various stages of court decision making, including judicial discretion. Pretrial decisions regarding bail, detention, and transfer to adult court are addressed, along with the associated issues of net widening, deterrence, and potential violation of due-process rights. The chapter moves on to a discussion of sentencing practices in youth court. Following a review of the allowable sentences and

---

BOX 9.1

Joey: "Court and Sentencing"

The accused don't come alone to Judge Deborah Gass's courtroom. They have to bring a lawyer's advice and their Mom and Dad. Joey appeared in youth court on July 14, 1993. He was sentenced to six months' probation and allowed to leave with his family, who were to take him to Hawthorne House, a group home ... All in all Joey was in court three more times after his first appearance in court [for new offences]. On every occasion he received some sort of custody order.

Some of the cases that are heard in youth court involve some pretty horrendous backgrounds. [Says Judge Gass]: "[T]hey're not all coming from nice middle-class backgrounds with all that middle-class kids would have going for them. So you have to weight that in."

Source: Adapted from MacDonald (1994b:6).

the principles that support them, we consider how relevant adult sentencing principles are to youth court sentencing; how race, class, and gender affect sentencing decisions in youth court; whether youth court sentences under the YOA amounted to anything more than a "slap on the wrist"; and we discuss how this will change under the YCJA.

THE COURT

A Profile

In 1999–2000, the youth court processed 102,061 cases, a 4 percent decrease from the previous year and an 11 percent decrease from 1992–93 (Sudworth and deSouza, 2001:2). The first year to show a decrease (5 percent) in court caseload since the YOA was implemented was 1994–95. Up until 1994, the court caseload had increased 20 percent since 1986–87 (Hendrick, 1997; Statistics Canada, 1998:i, xii). Most of this growth came from increases in charges for administrative offences. While the overall youth court caseload is declining, administrative charge cases continue to show increases. In 1999–2000, the rate of fail to appear cases had increased by 10 percent from 1992–93 and the rate of YOA charge cases had increased by 33 percent. Among these, the most common is failure to comply with a disposition (Sudworth and deSouza, 2001:3). Hence the significance of the net-widening discussion of prosecutorial diversion models in the last chapter.

With the exception of administrative offences, the rate of all other cases has been on the decline. The rate of property crime cases has decreased by 38 percent since 1992–93 and the rate of violent crime cases by 3 percent since 1998–99. These declines are likely due to increases in the use of police discretion and diversionary measures. Police criminal code charges, for example, have decreased by 31 percent since 1992. The most common youth court cases (40 percent) involve property offences (see Table 9.1). Of these offences, the most common is theft under $5,000 (14 percent of the total number of court cases). Half of all the cases were processed in two months or less; 19 percent take longer than six months (Sudworth and deSouza, 2001:3, 5, 10). The longest cases involve hearings for transfers to adult court; in 50 percent of these cases, it took four months or more to reach a decision about transfer (Doherty and de Souza, 1996).

Approximately 80 percent of youth court cases involve male youth; of these youth, 54 percent are 16- to 17-year-olds. The proportionate number of girls going to court increased from 18 percent in 1992–93 to 21 percent in 1999–2000, and they are younger than boys; 42 percent of the girls in these cases were between 16 and 17, and 15-year-old girls make up the largest category at 24 percent. Overall, younger girls are more likely in court than boys of the same age. While the number of cases going to court has decreased since 1992–93, the absolute number of girls going to court has increased from 20,775 to 21,507, and these are largely for administrative offences. Girls have increased from 21 to 26 percent of the YOA offence cases, from 21 to 25 percent of the other Criminal Code category and from 18 to 22 percent of the violent crimes category (Sudworth and deSouza, 2001:5–6). Since the YOA was implemented, the number of girls in court for failure to comply charges has continued to increase as a proportion of all girls' charges, from 6.1 percent in 1985–86 to 27.3 percent in 1995–96 (Reitsma-Street, 1999:338).

Repeat offenders make up a considerable portion of court cases. Thirty-five percent of the convicted cases in 1999–2000 were repeat offenders, about 10 percent of the convictions are "persistent" offenders, that is youth with three or more prior convictions. Repeat offenders are more involved in property crime (53 percent of all property cases) than in violent offences (25 percent). Persistent offenders make up 10 percent of the court caseload. More boys in court are repeat offenders than girls (37 percent vs. 29 percent) and 11 percent of the male cases are persistent offenders, while only 5 percent of the girls fall into this category (Sudworth and deSouza, 2001:10).

Pretrial Detention

Both the YCJA and Criminal Code provisions regarding judicial **interim release** apply to young offenders. The YCJA requires that young people held in detention prior to trial be detained separately from adults (s. 30(3)), unless no youth facility is available or it would be unsafe to do so (s. 30(3)(a) and (b)), and except for youth who are

TABLE 9.1

Number and Percentage of Cases in Youth Court, 1999–2000, by Type of Offence

Offence Category	Number of Cases	Percentage*
Property offences	41,122	40
Violent offences	22,937	22
Other Criminal Code	18,718	18
YOA offences	13,763	13
Drug offences	5,394	5
Other federal offences	127	1

*Does not add up to 100 because of rounding.

Source: Adapted from Statistics Canada (2001), *Juristat,* Cat. No. 85–002, 21(3), pp. 4 and 13.

between 18 and 20. The YCJA allows for a young person aged 18 to 20 to be held in adult provincial facilities (s. 30(4) and (5)). The judicial interim release provisions of the Criminal Code require that a young person be brought before a youth court judge or justice of the peace within 24 hours. At this hearing, the prosecutor must show why the accused should be held in custody. The Criminal Code provides two reasons for **pretrial detention**: primary grounds and secondary grounds. Primary grounds are invoked when the court is convinced that custody is necessary to ensure that the youth will appear in court. Secondary grounds are invoked when the court believes that custody is necessary for public protection (Doob, Marinos, and Varma, 1995:101; Bala et al., 1994:88).

An important difference for young offenders, created by the YCJA, is the required presumption in the YCJA that pretrial detention is not necessary under certain conditions. When considering secondary grounds for detention, that is whether detention is necessary for the protection of society (s. 515(10)(b) of the Criminal Code), section 29(2) of the YCJA requires the court to presume that pretrial detention is not necessary if, on a conviction, the young person could not be sentenced to custody because of YCJA restrictions on committal to custody (s. 39(1)(a)(2)(c), as discussed below). One of the important restrictions on committal to custody that is different from the YOA is on the grounds of social welfare considerations. In other words, the YCJA specifically prohibits placing a young offender in pretrial detention "as a substitute for appropriate child protection, mental health or other social measures" (s. 29(1)).

Pretrial facilities vary considerably across the country. Some youth are detained in group homes and detention facilities that offer school, recreational, and counselling programs. Some jurisdictions do not offer programs in detention facilities, while other jurisdictions do not even have detention facilities. Sometimes youth are detained in custodial facilities for young people serving sentences (Bala et al., 1994:89). Morin (1990) and Hamilton and Sinclair (1991) report that youth in Aboriginal communities are often removed from their communities because of a lack of detention facilities.

The number of young persons held in pretrial detention increased substantially under the YOA. Between 1986 and 1994, there was a 33 percent increase in the number of young people remanded in custody across the country (Foran, 1995). During this period, only Manitoba, the Yukon, and Prince Edward Island showed decreases in numbers of youth held in remand; all other provinces showed increases. In Ontario between 1985–86 and 1988–89, the number of 16- and 17-year-old youth in detention increased by 38 percent; there was a 71 percent increase in the number of bail hearings for 12- to 15-year-olds; and the number of pretrial detentions in 1989 was 30 percent higher than in 1985–86 (Kenewell, Bala, and Colfer, 1991:160).

In 1998–99, 24,061 youth were detained in pretrial detention, this amounts to 60 percent of custody admissions and only 23 percent were for violent offence charges. The majority of youth admitted to pretrial detention are 16 and 17 years of age, but there are more 14- and 15-year-old girls detained than boys of that age group (34 percent vs. 20 percent). Girls are also detained more often with minor offences (see Box 9.8). Similarly, Aboriginal youth are far more likely to be held in detention than non-Aboriginal youth and more likely held for minor offences, especially Aboriginal girls. Twenty-six percent of admissions to detention are Aboriginal youth and 36 percent of girls admitted are Aboriginal. The average length of stay is 21 days with one half being released in less than one week. Seventeen percent of youth in remand are there from one to six months (Statistics Canada, 2000:1–18).

The court may decide to release a young offender if it is satisfied that a responsible person is willing to assume responsibility and control of the youth. This responsible person, who could be a parent, some other adult relative, or a family friend, makes an application for release and is examined by the court to determine if he or she is a suitable alternative to custody for the young person. A youth may also be released if a responsible person agrees to forfeit money or some security if the young offender violates the conditions of release. The YCJA allows an accused youth to refuse this type of release. Release conditions may include such things as a curfew, a specified place of residence, requirements to attend school, and a list of persons with whom the youth is not to associate. A youth who does not follow the direction of the person into whose custody he or she has been released, or who fails to comply with the conditions of release, may be returned to the custody of the court (Hak, 1996:57–58). Overall, this alternative method of release has been highly underutilized (Report, 1996:178).

Widening the Net

Pretrial detention contributes to net widening by increasing the number of youth in custody, and by escalating charges for young people through rules associated with violations of release conditions. Gandy (1992), who examined transcripts of bail hearings in three Ontario cities, argues that bail hearings often set youth up for further offending, thereby assuring custodial dispositions for some. He found that, contrary to the rules (secondary grounds), most young people detained in pretrial custodial facilities were initially charged with nonviolent offences. According to Gandy,

> the courts have created a situation, through very restrictive conditions of release, in which "out of control" is an almost inevitable outcome. It may be that the court should consider imposing the fewest conditions that are compatible with the protection of the public. It would appear that in establishing the conditions of release some judges use a shotgun approach to try to anticipate all contingencies. (1992:75)

Some youth are adversely affected by the use of pretrial detention and the rules and regulations concerning bail release. The use of pretrial detention is particularly problematic for homeless youth, for Aboriginal youth, for those whose friends or relatives are not likely to be considered responsible by the court, and for those with poor parental relations. Many youth end up in custody not because they committed a serious crime, but because (1) they did not follow the direction of the court or their parents, or (2) they do not have parents, adults, or relatives who are willing or able to assume responsibility for them (Gandy, 1992). Section 31(2) of the YCJA addresses this issue by directing the court to attempt to find a responsible person in instances where a youth would be detained in custody if no such person is immediately available.

Transfer to Adult Court

For those committed to youth justice reform, one of the most contentious aspects of the YOA was s. 16, which allowed judges to transfer youth (over 14 at the time of their offence) to adult court for trial if they had been charged with a serious indictable offence. Transfer was not initially automatic and applications for transfer were made by the Crown or the young person. When the YOA was first implemented, the decision to transfer required the court to strike a balance between "the interest of society" and "the needs of the young person." In practice, there was considerable variation in how judges interpreted s. 16. Manitoba and Alberta, both with a relatively high transfer rate, placed a greater emphasis on the "interests of society." Ontario, Quebec, and Saskatchewan, on the other hand, placed a greater emphasis on the "needs of the young person," as reflected in their much lower rate of transfer (Bala et al., 1994:101–2). As a result of discrepancies such as these, the YOA, and the test for transfer, were twice modified—first in 1992 and again in 1995.

The first amendments specified more clearly what should be done if principles could not easily be balanced. As we see in Box 9.2, s. 16(2) required the court to consider a number of factors in making its decision. One of the most important of these factors was "the availability of appropriate treatment and correctional resources" in the youth system compared to available resources in the adult system. Thus, if the court decided that the protection of society and the rehabilitation of the young person could not be reconciled under the YOA, the youth could be transferred to the adult system for trial.

One young offender successfully argued to have his youth custody sentence changed to adult custody. Convicted of manslaughter in the stabbing of a cabdriver, the youth was sentenced in 1996. He was to serve one-and-a-half years at the Nova Scotia Youth Centre, two years in a provincial jail, and the remainder of his sentence in a federal penitentiary. At the original sentencing, Justice Hood expressed concern that the young offender would be "badly influenced" by an adult penitentiary culture. At the custody hearing, corrections officials maintained that the young offender, then 19, had successfully completed all the programming offered by the youth facility and that it would be a "recipe for disaster" to keep him there or move him to a provincial facility. Only the penitentiary system, they argued, could give the youth what he needed, that is, "more advanced educational programming and more intensive psychiatric counselling and addiction treatment" (Armstrong, 1997).

A major concern at transfer hearings therefore was whether the young person was likely to be rehabilitated within the duration of the sentence allowed in the youth court. Initially, the maximum sentence in youth court for first-degree murder was three years. In adult court, the choice for young offenders was a life sentence with a minimum of 25 years before eligibility for parole. Hence, judges or juries were reluctant to sentence youth in the same manner they would adults. Hak (1996) tells of the case of a young person who had been involved in a fatal driving accident: "[Given] the age of the young offender and the lack of a prior record, it was unlikely that the adult court would sentence the youth to more than three years. As that sentence was available in youth court, transfer to adult court would have had little meaning" (63).

The disparity between youth and adult sentences was reduced considerably in 1992. Amendments allowed the youth court to impose a murder sentence of five years less a day. For those transferred to and convicted in adult court, a life sentence meant eligibility for parole after five to ten years. Amendments also permitted adult courts to determine whether the young person would be sent to an adult federal penitentiary, an adult provincial facility, a youth custody facility, or any combination of the three. The second set of changes, in 1995, lengthened youth court sentences and shortened youth sentences in adult court thereby bringing the two closer together. Changes included the following:

- Youth court sentences for first- and second-degree murder were increased to ten years and seven years respectively.
- Young offenders charged with murder who were to be tried in youth court were given the choice of trial by judge and jury or trial by judge alone.
- For youth transferred to adult court, eligibility for parole was increased to ten and seven years respectively for first- and second-degree murder.
- Sixteen- and 17-year-old youth charged with murder, attempted murder, manslaughter, aggravated sexual assault, or aggravated assault were to be automatically transferred to and tried in adult court unless an application was granted for the young person's case to be heard in youth court (section 16(1.01).

With the latter change, another reverse onus situation was created. The onus was on a 16- or 17-year-old offender to demonstrate to a judge why she or he should be tried in youth court rather than adult court. In justifying this change, then–Minister of Justice Allan Rock stated,

> public protection is a primary concern and this is best achieved through community based crime prevention programs for children at risk and through rehabilitation, wherever possible. At the same time, we must ensure that young people understand that violence is not acceptable and that there are serious consequences for violent behaviour. (Minister of Justice, 1994)

BOX 9.2

YOA Provisions for Transfer

Section 16(2) of the YOA outlines the factors that the court was required to consider in making decisions about transfer. These factors were to be considered in the context of the principles laid out in s. 3 of the YOA:

(a) the seriousness of the alleged offence and the circumstances in which it was allegedly committed;

(b) the age, maturity, character and background of the young person and any record or summary of previous findings of delinquency;

(c) the adequacy of this Act, and the adequacy of the Criminal Code or any other Act of Parliament that would apply in respect of the young person if an order were made under this section to meet the circumstances of the case;

(d) the availability of treatment or correctional resources;

(e) any representations made to the court on behalf of the young person or by the Attorney General or his agent; and

(f) any other factors that the court considers relevant.

Under the 1995 revision, subsection 1.1 was added. It states,

> In making the determination referred to in Subsection (1), the youth court, after affording both parties and the parents of the young person an opportunity to be heard, shall consider the interest of society, which includes the objectives of affording protection to the public and rehabilitation of the young person, and determine whether those objectives can be reconciled by the youth being under the jurisdiction of the youth court.

Transfer Issues

Issues surrounding transfer include whether it will reduce youth crime (deterrence), whether it will increase the number of youth in the adult system (net widening), and whether it is "fair" to young offenders (due process). While there is no shortage of groups lobbying for more young offenders to be processed through adult courts, there

BOX 9.3

YCJA Provisions for Adult Sentences

Section 62 of the YCJA outlines the conditions under which the youth court has the power to impose an adult sentence on a young offender, and s. 72(1) outlines the factors that the court must consider in making a decision as to a youth's liability for an adult sentence:

Section 62. An adult sentence shall be imposed on a young person who is found guilty of an indictable offence for which an adult is liable to imprisonment for a term of more than two years in the following cases:

(a) in the case of a presumptive offence, if the youth justice court makes an order under subsection 70(2) (youth does not request a youth sentence) or paragraph 72(1)(b) (see below); or

(b) in any other case, if the youth justice court makes an order under subsection 64(5) (youth does not oppose an adult sentence) or paragraph 72(1)(b) (see below) in relation to an offence committed after the young person attained the age of fourteen years.

Section 72 (1). In making its decision on an application heard in accordance with section 71(hearing for adult sentence), the youth justice court shall consider the seriousness and circumstances of the offence, and the age, maturity, character, background and previous record of the young person and any other factors that the court considers relevant, and

(a) if it is of the opinion that a youth sentence imposed in accordance with the purpose and principles set out in subparagraph 3(1)(b)(ii) and section 38 would have sufficient length to hold the young person accountable for his or her offending behaviour, it shall order that the young person is not liable to an adult sentence and that a youth sentence must be imposed; and

(b) if it is of the opinion that a youth sentence imposed in accordance with the purpose and principles set out in subparagraph 3(1)(b)(ii) and section 38 would not have sufficient length to hold the young person accountable for his or her offending behaviour, it shall order that an adult sentence be imposed.

BOX 9.4

YCJA Definition of Presumptive Offence

The YCJA defines a presumptive offence as,

(a) an offence committed, or alleged to have been committed, by a young person who has attained the age of 14 years, or, in a province where the Lieutenant Governor in Council has fixed an age greater than 14 years under section 61, the age so fixed, under one of the following provisions of the Criminal Code:

  (i)   Section 231 or 235 (First Degree Murder or Second Degree Murder with—the meaning of Section 231),

  (ii) Section 239 (Attempt to Commit Murder),

  (iii) Section 232, 234, or 236 (Manslaughter), or

  (iv) Section 273 (Aggravated Sexual Assault),

(b) a serious violent offence for which an adult is liable to imprisonment for a term of more than two years committed, or alleged to have been committed, by a young person after the coming into force of section 62 (adult sentence) and after the young person has attained the age of 14 years, or in a province where the Lieutenant Governor in Council has fixed an age greater than 14 years under section 61, the age so fixed, if at the time of the commission or alleged commission of the offence at least two judicial determinations have been made under subsection 42. (9), at different proceedings, that the young person has committed a serious violent offence.

is little evidence to suggest that transfer will actually have a deterrent effect on youth crime. According to two American studies, changes that allowed automatic transfers in New York and Idaho did not result in a decrease in serious youth crime (Singer and McDowall, 1988; Jensen and Metsger, 1994). Notwithstanding this finding, young offenders in a study conducted in New York reported being more afraid of adult court than youth court (Glassner et al., 1983).

BOX 9.5

Maximum Penalty for First-Degree Murder under the YOA

In Youth Court:

- Ten-year sentence of six years' custody and four years' conditional supervision in the community.

- Custody term served in youth facility. Transfer to adult provincial facility possible at age 18.

In Adult Court:

- Mandatory life sentence with parole eligibility after 10 years.

- Sentence served in youth facility, provincial adult facility, federal penitentiary, or a combination of the three.

Two teens were recently transferred to adult court in Edmonton and convicted of fatally stabbing a mother of two. One was convicted of second-degree murder and sent to the federal penitentiary in Prince Albert, Saskatchewan, to serve a life sentence. He is not eligible for parole for seven years. The other youth was convicted of manslaughter and will serve four and a half months of a four-year sentence in the Edmonton Young Offenders Centre before being transferred to an Alberta adult penitentiary. He will be eligible for parole after two years.

Source: Teens Who Killed 1997:A18.

According to McGuire (1997:197–98) lengthy sentence provisions resulting from 1995 changes to the YOA (Bill C-37) are likely to result in fewer transfers to the adult system rather than more. McGuire bases this argument on the major differences between adult and youth facilities with respect to treatment and rehabilitation programs. She refers to *R. v. James Albert C.* (T) [1991], where the court noted,

> this phase I facility [Syl Apps Secure Custody Facility] has twenty treatment beds and is based on Milieu Therapy in which each part of the youth's day from the moment he wakes until the end of the day is focused on treatment … Warkworth Institution [adult

BOX 9.6

Maximum Penalty for First-Degree Murder under the YCJA in Youth Court

Section 42(2) ... if the offence is first degree murder or second degree murder within the meaning of section 231 of the *Criminal Code*, the court shall ...:

(q) order the young person to serve a sentence not to exceed

(i) in the case of first degree murder, ten years comprised of

(a) a committal to custody, to be served continuously, for a period that must not, subject to subsection 104(1) (Continuation of Custody), exceed six years from the date of committal, and

(b) a placement under conditional supervision to be served in the community in accordance with section 105, and

(ii) in the case of second degree murder, seven years comprised of

(a) a committal to custody, to be served continuously, for a period that must not, subject to subsection 104(1) (Continuation of Custody), exceed four years from the date of committal, and

(b) a placement under conditional supervision to be served in the community in accordance with section 105:

(r) make an intensive rehabilitative custody and supervision order in respect of the young person

(ii) that is for a specified period that must not exceed, in the case of first degree murder, ten years from the date of committal, comprising

(a) a committal to intensive rehabilitative custody, to be served continuously, for a period that must not exceed six years from the date of committal, and

(b) subject to subsection 104(1) (Continuation of Custody), placement under conditional supervision to be served in the community in accordance with section 105, and

(iii) that is for a specified period that must not exceed, in the case of second degree murder, seven years from the date of committal, comprising

(a) a committal to intensive rehabilitative custody, to be served continuously, for a period that must not exceed four years from the date of committal, and

(b) subject to subsection 104(1) (Continuation of Custody), a placement under conditional supervision to be served in the community in accordance with section 105;

If the youth is to receive an adult sentence, he/she would receive the same sentence as an adult.

---

federal penitentiary] has a mental health staff of four psychologists to deal with an inmate population of approximately 700, a ratio of 175:1. The only therapy that the psychologists provide is crisis management as the vast majority of their time is spent doing risk reports prior to parole hearings.

Justice Lucien Beaulieu (1994) raises some serious legal concerns about transfer provisions in the YOA. He points out that since the primary focus of transfer hearings is to determine the type of sentence that a young person would get in youth court versus adult court, a fundamental and "cherished principle of criminal common law" is compromised. Our justice system requires that an accused be presumed innocent until proven guilty in a court of law. However, in transfer hearings for young people, we are forced to "presume innocence but assume guilt." All of the information considered in a transfer hearing—predisposition reports, medical reports, psychological reports, and the like—reflects on assumption of guilt on the part of the accused. Beaulieu (1994:338–39) suggested that since some exceptional cases of young offenders might be better transferred to the adult court for sentencing, the legislation should be altered so that transfer to the adult system for sentencing would take place after a young person had been found guilty in youth court. Both the Federal-Provincial-Territorial Task Force and the Standing Committee on Justice and Legal Affairs recommended that the YOA be revised so that transfer provisions would be imposed after a finding of guilt (Report, 1996:305–6; Cohen, 1997:65).

BOX 9.7

Positions on Youth Incarceration in Adult Facilities

Clinical Social Worker at a YOA Transfer Hearing

The culture in a federal institution is based on physical power and intimidation, not on cooperation and earning good will such as is found in the community. A young offender who is not sufficiently tough will be abused physically, sexually ... [I]f he refuses the protection and homosexual advances from the tougher, older inmate, then he will be raped and abused until he accepts that protection.

The only protection which can be afforded a young offender is to place him in segregation ... Anyone who is put in segregation for reasons other than punishment is labelled, rightly or wrongly, as a possible informer and therefore life becomes very dangerous when he re-enters the general prison population.

Forensic Scientist at the Same Hearing

I can guarantee after ten years we'll have the worst frustrated and angry man. I can guarantee that the damage that the penitentiary system will do will be far worse than anything you've ever seen.

Source: *R. v. G.J.M.*, 21 April 1992, unreported (Alta. Q.B.):T.P. 33.

Adult Sentences and the YCJA

Legislators responded to these concerns by sidestepping the whole issue of a transfer hearing. The issue ei the YCJA is one of liability for an adult sentence. There are now provisions in the legislation giving youth court the power to impose adult sentences (see Box 9.3) rather than have to face the arduous task of deciding to transfer a youth to adult court. This was accomplished through the creation of the **presumptive offence** (see Box 9.4) in combination with new sentencing provisions for "serious offences" and "serious violent offences." Quite simply, whether a youth is liable to an adult sentence is largely determined by the nature of the offence and the youth's age. Basically, there are three situations where youth are automatically liable to an adult sentence. First, the YCJA requires an adult sentence for youth 16 and over who are found guilty of serious violent offences. The presumptive offence rule applies to youth aged 14 and 15, unless a province changes the minimum age to 15 for their jurisdiction. Section 64(i) further strengthens the court's ability to impose adult sentences by extending these powers to also include offences where "an adult is liable to imprisonment for a term of more than two years, that was committed after the young person attained the age of 14 years." Furthermore, s. 42(9) allows the youth court to determine that an offence is a serious one. In these instances, the onus is on the Attorney General to request an adult sentence and for the accused youth to challenge such a request, or for a young offender to apply for the court to order that she or he is not liable to an adult sentence and for the Attorney General to challenge.

These new provisions for adult sentencing have solved the legal dilemma raised by Justice Beaulieu, but they have also created new problems, the nature of which depends on which model of juvenile justice is adopted. Crime control advocates, particularly Alliance MPs are still advocating for the age of eligibility to be lowered from 14 (Hogeveen and Smandych, 2001:161–162), while welfare and restorative justice advocates are concerned that these new provisions will result in far too many 14- and 15-year-old youth in the adult system—a regressive return to pre-JDA years. Similarly, these same advocates foresee greater numbers of youth overall in the adult system thereby undermining the very reason for a youth justice system—to keep them out of the adult system. This too is a main reason for Bloc MPs' opposition to the YCJA; these automatic adult sentences effectively undermine the welfare and restorative justice aspects of Quebec's Youth Protection Act (Hogveen and Smandych, 2001:163–164). According to 1999–2000 court statistics, there were 7,103 youth charged with violent offences more serious than minor assault. Taking away the 15 percent that are 12 and 13 years of age, there were roughly 6,000 youth who could potentially be eligible for an adult sentence under YCJA rules. A significantly greater amount than the 52 cases that were actually transferred under the YOA rules (Sudworth and deSouza, 2001:7, 14, 16). As we will see later in this chapter, adult sentences also mean adult rules. Young offenders with adult sentences, some as young as 14, will now come under the jurisdiction of the Corrections and Conditional Release Act including the Parole Act and decision making powers of the Parole Board, legislation that governs adult federal corrections. Another question relates to the future of youth in the adult system—taking us right back to the issue addressed in Box 9.6 and by McGuire (1997)—whether adult facilities have programs and staff that can address the needs of young offenders.

The Reality of Transfer Decisions

A minority of youth court cases involve the most serious offences. In 1992–93, there were 547 cases heard in court of young persons charged with serious indictable offences. Fifty-four percent of these (292) involved 16- and 17-year-old youth and 10 percent were female youth (Statistics Canada, 1993:7). In 1994–95, there were 123 cases sent to adult court, 67 percent of which involved violent offences and 24 percent of which involved property offences. The highest rate of transfer occurred in Manitoba where 58 cases (47 percent of all cases) were transferred to adult court. According to youth court reports, young people in Manitoba are choosing to transfer to adult court as a means of avoiding a sentence to a youth custody facility (Doherty and de Souza, 1996:7). In 1995–96, 74 cases were transferred to adult court, 92 were transferred in 1996–97, and in 1999–2000, 52 cases were transferred. Of these latter cases, 60 percent involved violent crimes and 23 percent involved property crime. Seventeen-year-old youth accounted for 54 percent of these transfers. (Hendrick, 1997:6; Statistics Canada, 1998:vii; Sudworth and deSouza, 2001:7)

COURT PROCEEDINGS

Youth court trials begin with a plea. Most young offenders plead guilty. In 1999–2000, 67 percent of youth court cases involved a finding of guilt, a figure unchanged from the previous five years (Hendrick, 1997:6; Doherty and de Souza, 1996:7; de Souza, 1995:2; Sudworth and deSouza, 2001:7). Interestingly, since 1986 there has been a 40 percent increase in the number of girls found guilty in the court, compared with only a 10 percent increase for boys (Report, 1996:614). Although it is difficult to know from these figures how many youth actually plead guilty, studies of individual courts have shown high rates of guilty pleas (Bell, 1994b). If a young person pleads guilty, the court proceeds directly to sentencing; if she or he pleads not guilty, the case goes to trial. The youth court trial is the same as the adult court trial, with two exceptions. Initially, under the YOA there was no preliminary hearing and no jury trial in youth court, but the 1995 revisions (Bill C-37) allowed young offenders to opt for a jury trial in murder cases only. The YCJA changes these rules considerably.

The YCJA allows a youth to elect a trial when an application has been made for an order for an adult sentence, when a young offender is subject to an adult sentence, or when she or he is facing a murder charge. This is also the case in instances where the charge is one where an adult is entitled to a jury trial. In all these cases. Section 67(2) outlines the instructions that the judge must put to the young person:

> You have the option to elect to be tried by a youth justice court judge without a jury and without having had a preliminary inquiry; or you may elect to have a preliminary inquiry and to be tried by a judge without a jury; or you may elect to have a preliminary inquiry and to be tried by a court composed of a judge and jury. If you do not elect now, you shall be deemed to have elected to have a preliminary inquiry and to be tried by a court composed of a judge and jury. How do you elect to be tried?

Young offenders in Nunavut have the right to be tried by the Nunavut Court of Justice (s. 67(4)). Youth may not elect for a jury trial if they are subject to a youth sentence unless the charge is murder (s. 66).

Preliminary inquiries are also now required to be conducted in the same manner as they are for adults except where it might be inconsistent with the YCJA. In addition, s. 67(6) gives the Attorney General the power to require a young person be tried by a judge and jury even in cases where a young person elects to be tried without a jury.

Legal Representation

Only with the introduction YOA (s. 11) did young offenders have the right to legal representation. There are four types of representation available to a young offender: privately retained lawyer, legal aid lawyer, duty counsel (i.e., a lawyer on duty each day in the court), or a court-appointed/funded lawyer. Court-appointed lawyers are not available in adult court. Young offenders who are unable to retain the services of a private lawyer or a legal aid lawyer have the right to request that the court provide them with a lawyer—a policy that has been criticized for giving inexperienced lawyers an opportunity to learn on the job (Hak, 1996:54).

Under the YCJA, young people are still entitled to a lawyer, either private or legal aid, or to a court-appointed lawyer through s. 25. If the court has a sense that the interests of a young person and the interest of a parent are in conflict, the judge is then required to ensure that a young person is represented by counsel, independent of his/her parents (s. 25(8)). Subsection (10) allows provinces to establish a program that would recover the cost of a young person's counsel either from the young person or the parents of the young person.

Whether a young offender has a lawyer does seem to make a difference. A survey of major cities across the country just prior to implementation of the YOA indicates that the presence of a lawyer and type of representation have an influence on the likelihood of conviction and/or type of conviction. Duty counsel were found to be considerably less "successful" than private lawyers. In fact, duty counsel cases were comparable in outcome to cases with no legal representation. Private lawyers were found to be better than duty counsel at negotiating to have charges dropped and in defending not-guilty pleas (Carrington and Moyer, 1990:633). Both Bell (1994a) and Schissel (1993), who studied individual youth courts in 1986, report that type of representation makes a difference and that the effect of representation varies by race, class, and gender of the accused. As Box 9.8 indicates, Aboriginal youth do not benefit as much from private and legal-aid lawyers as do non-Aboriginal youth.

The Role of Lawyers

There is some debate over what role lawyers should play in youth court. Should they act in the best interest of the child, or should they merely offer legal representation?

In other words, should a lawyer assume a **legal advocate** role or a **guardian** role? The Law Society of Upper Canada advises lawyers to serve as advocates:

> There is no place ... for counsel representing the child to argue what is in his opinion in the best interest of the child. Counsel should not be deciding whether training school would be "good" for the child ... It is advice with respect to the legal rights of the child which is being provided, and that advice is being provided to the child, not to the parents, not to the court, and not to society, but to the child. (1981, cited in Bala et al., 1994:83)

Lawyers who assume a legal advocate role will advise young clients of their rights to remain silent, suggest that they not cooperate with police, provide a legal defence and try to prevent a conviction, and, in a case of conviction, try to get the most lenient disposition possible (Milne, Linden, and Kueneman, 1992:329).

Lawyers who assume a guardian role are primarily concerned about what they believe to be the "best interests" of the young offender. As one Manitoba lawyer puts it, "my attitude to the practice of law is not adversarial. I am aware of the legal issues and the fact that I am a lawyer, but I am concerned with rehabilitation. I do take the role of a stern parent" (cited in Milne, Linden, and Kueneman, 1992:333). In the event of a conviction, this kind of lawyer will be primarily concerned about what he or she thinks the young offender requires for rehabilitation.

Youth Understandings of Their Legal Rights

Abramovitch, Peterson-Badali, and Rohan (1995) compared a sample of Toronto high-school students aged 11 to 18 with a university student population regarding their understanding of their rights to silence and to legal representation. The researchers found that youth over 16 understand their rights better than younger youth and that older youth are more like university students in this regard. An important difference between the groups is that younger youth are more likely to assert their right to silence if they perceive strong evidence of guilt in the case and are more likely to assert their right to a lawyer if the evidence of their guilt is perceived as weak. The researchers conclude that university students are less naive than young high-school students in that, for them, the guilt or innocence of accused persons have no bearing on their assertion of their rights.

COURT SENTENCING

The YCJA makes sentencing a far more complex process than it is under the YOA by adding **sentencing conferences** to the process, providing general sentencing principles, restricting the use of custody and providing for a greater range of sentencing options. Section 19 of the YCJA allows for sentencing conferences to act as an advisory body with

BOX 9.8

Profile of an Edmonton Youth Court, Summer 1986

Detention on Arrest

1. Repeat offenders were detained more often than first offenders.

2. Natives are detained more often than other youth, particularly for non-serious offences.

3. With non-serious offences, girls are detained more often than boys.

4. Boys are detained more often than girls for serious offences.

5. Other young offenders (nonwhite or non-Native) are less likely to be detained on arrest.

Legal Representation

1. Male youth who are charged with serious offences and who have previous convictions are more likely to have private lawyers or legal-aid lawyers.

2. Female young offenders charged with serious offences and with previous convictions are less likely to have private lawyers or legal-aid lawyers.

3. The "other" racial group is more likely to be represented by private lawyers or legal-aid lawyers when charged with serious offences or when they have a previous conviction.

Plea

1. Youth with prior records are less likely to plead guilty than first offenders.

2. Youth with private counsel or legal aid are less likely to plead guilty than those represented by duty counsel.

3. Native offenders are less likely to plead guilty than whites or others when their parents are present in court and more likely to plead guilty when they do not have parental support.

Adjudication

1. Private lawyers or legal-aid lawyers are most beneficial for those charged with serious offences.

2. Private lawyers and legal-aid lawyers appear more successful in getting charges withdrawn for young offenders in the "other" racial group and least beneficial in this regard for Native young offenders.

Source: Schissel (1993:101–2).

regard to sentences and sentence reviews as well as extrajudicial measures, conditions for interim release, and reintegration plans. These committees are to consist of a youth court judge, the provincial director, a police officer, a justice of the peace, a prosecutor or youth worker. Before sentencing, the court is required to consider recommendations from a sentencing committee (if they have been established by the province), pre-sentence reports, and any other information submitted by parents or counsel.

In particular, before imposing a custodial sentence, s. 39(6) of the YCJA requires the youth justice court to consider a pre-sentence report and "any sentencing proposal made by the young person or his or her counsel" unless the young person or his or her counsel indicates a preference to not have a pre-sentence report (s. 39(7)). In these instances, the onus is on the court to ascertain if the report is not necessary. Section 40 of the YCJA outlines what should be contained in a pre-sentence report. These reports are generally prepared by a probation officer who seeks information about the youth's background including a history with the JDA, YOA, or alternative measures; results from an interview with the victim; the recommendation of a sentencing conference; and information from the youth's parents, extended family, social workers involved with the family, and school officials. The reports also often contain judgments about the emotional development, attitude, maturity, and character of the youth, as well as information about her or his insight into the offence, willingness to make amends, and plans for the future particularly with regard to changing her or his behaviour.

Sentencing Principles

There are four basic principles that govern sentencing in adult criminal cases: retribution, deterrence, incapacitation, and rehabilitation. **Retribution** is based on notions of moral accountability and the idea that persons who intentionally harm others should

---

| BOX 9.9 |

Excerpts from Predisposition Reports, Ontario Family Court, 1986

1. [This woman is] despondent and somewhat tired of the burden of raising adolescents.

2. In order to try to understand Paul better and to control him, his mother has attended several tough love sessions. Her attitude is "I've made up my mind I'm not going to let him beat me." ... It would appear Paul's position in the house is very precarious.

3. Before the court, your honour, is a twelve year old Native youth whose history of truancy problems surfaced [five years ago] and has not lost momentum since that time. George's truancy appears to be a symptom of an underorganized family system. It was earlier identified in [an] assessment that George's truancy arose as a result of increasing family disorganization as well as anger at his mother for her inability to take charge of the family. It would seem that interventions have had very little impact on helping to alleviate the multi-issues presented by the various members of this family ... Although a great deal of court and agency history has preceded ... [the] current court situation, it is important that its impact not cloud or colour the present need to continue and try to plan for this youth.

Source: Bell (1993).

---

suffer negative consequences so that wrongs can be righted. An additional component of this principle is the **proportionality principle**—the belief that justice is best served if the consequence is in proportion to the crime. So, for example, the death penalty would be an inappropriate sentence for car theft or shoplifting. For advocates of crime control, retribution is interpreted as punishment and the proportionality principle often means vengeance or "an eye for an eye."

Deterrence is a theory that originated in the 18th century. It is based on the assumption that people will not engage in certain activities if the potential costs of doing so are greater than the potential gains. Deterrence may be general or specific/individual, meaning that negative consequences directed at an individual may be designed to dissuade all members of a society from engaging in similar actions (general). Sanctions may also be designed to prevent a particular person from re-offending (specific/individual). **Incapacitation** refers to measures taken, such as a prison sentence, to deprive a person of the opportunity to commit an offence (Bala et al., 1994:30–34). **Rehabilitation** seeks to "change" or "reform" an individual. It may or may not involve particular treatment strategies or programs.

Restorative justice principles of restoration, reconciliation, and reintegration are new concepts just beginning to work their way into sentencing discourse. In Canada, they are appearing in youth justice reforms such as the YCJA. An important issue concerns the extent to which adult sentencing principles are appropriate in youth justice systems, a discussion we will return to at the end of this chapter.

TABLE 9.2

Juvenile Justice Models and Sentencing

Juvenile Justice Model	Sentencing Principle	Court Sentence	Correctional Programming
Welfare	Rehabilitation	Probation with conditions Treatment orders Community service order Conditional discharge	Treatment Rehabilitation
Justice	Retribution Proportionality	Range of sanctions proportional to offence	All sanctions proportional to offence Voluntary
Crime control	Punishment Incapacitation Deterrence	Fine or custody Lengthy sentence	Prisons Tighter security Longer sentences
Restorative	Reintegration Restoration Reconciliation	Mediation, conferencing Sentencing circle	Victim and community participation Reparation Crime prevention Promotion of responsibility for action

YCJA Sentencing Principles

Section 38 of the YCJA presents a significant change from YOA sentencing provisions in that it sets out the purpose and principles for youth sentencing along with factors to be considered in all sentence deliberations, something that did not exist under the YOA. While the general principles of s. 3 apply to youth sentences (as they did under the YOA), s. 38 principles are also to be used by the court in determining sentences. Under the YOA, the only directive provided to the court regarding disposition decisions is for the court to strike a balance between the interests of society and the needs of the young offender.

Interestingly, as with the s. 3 principles, there is no one justice model reflected in s. 38. An examination of these principles and requirements (Box 9.10) reveals an interesting combination and prioritizing of the different justice models (see Table 9.2 and Table 7.2). Justice principles of retribution (subsection (1)(2)(d)(iii) and (3)(a) and (b) and proportionality (subsection (2)(a)(b)(c)) are paramount. These sections make it clear that the purpose of sentencing is to hold a young person accountable and to impose "meaningful consequences." More importantly, from a justice perspective, these consequences must be proportional to other youth sentences for similar offences and not any more severe than an adult sentence for a similar offence and circumstance. The court is also required to look beyond the offence and consider the youth's intention, degree of involvement in the offence, and degree of harm caused by the action.

Nonetheless, subsection (1) also speaks of "protection of the public," a crime control objective and subsection (2)(a) speaks of punishment. While stated in the negative, that punishment should not exceed that appropriate for an adult, this subsection nonetheless explicitly presents punishment, rather than proportionate sanctions, as an important principle of juvenile justice. Welfare principles are also evident. Subsection (2)(d)(i) reintroduces the minimal interference principle of the YOA and applies it specifically to sentencing; subsection (d)(ii) incorporates the principle of rehabilitation from both the JDA and YOA, and subsection (1) presents rehabilitation as a primary objective of "just sanctions." In addition, restorative justice principles are introduced through subsections (1)(d)(ii) and (iii) as well as (3)(c). Reintegration is stated as a primary objective and guiding principle for sentencing decisions. However, while it might appear that this act, like the YOA before it, is establishing all the justice models as guiding principles, it does not. Section 38(1) includes all models in a manner that gives priority to accountability and protection of the public, and subsection (2)(d) clearly states that welfare and restorative justice principles apply only *after* consideration of proportionality and responsibility principles. Hence, justice and crime control principles are paramount with welfare and restorative justice principles as secondary.

BOX 9.10

The Purpose and Principles of Sentencing under the YCJA (Section 38)

Purpose:

(1) The purpose of sentencing under section 42 (youth sentences) is to hold a young person accountable for an offence through the imposition of just sanctions that have meaningful consequences for the young person and that promote his or her rehabilitation and reintegration into society, thereby contributing to the long-term protection of the public.

Principles:

(2) A youth justice court that imposes a youth sentence on a young person shall determine the sentence in accordance with the principles set out in section 3 and the following principles:

(a) the sentence must not result in a punishment that is greater than the punishment that would be appropriate for an adult who has been convicted of the same offence committed in similar circumstances;

(b) the sentence must be similar to the sentences imposed in the region on similar young persons found guilty of the same offence committed in similar circumstances;

(c) the sentence must be proportionate to the seriousness of the offence and the degree of responsibility of the young person for that offence; and

(d) subject to paragraph (c), the sentence must

(i) be the least restrictive sentence that is capable of achieving the purpose set out in subsection (1),

(ii) be the one that is most likely to rehabilitate the young person and reintegrate him or her into society, and

(iii) promote a sense of responsibility in the young person, and an acknowledgment of the harm done to victims and the community.

Factors to be taken into account:

(3) In determining a youth sentence, the youth justice court shall take into account

(a) the degree of participation by the young person in the commission of the offence;

(b) the harm done to victims and whether it was intentional or reasonably foreseeable;

(c) any reparation made by the young person to the victim or the community;

(d) the time spent in detention by the young person as a result of the offence;

(e) the previous findings of guilt of the young person; and

(f) any other aggravating and mitigating circumstances related to the young person or the offence that are relevant to the purpose and principles set out in this section.

Youth Sentences

Section 42(2) of the YCJA allows for a wide range of youth sentences from a reprimand to the most severe in terms of loss of freedom, intensive rehabilitative custody with community supervision. The youth court will have far more sentencing options than under the YOA (s. 20(1)) and can choose any one or combination of sentences for a convicted youth. It will be at least two years before data are available from the youth court on these new options and at least five years before any comparisons can be made with YOA sentences. The major sentencing categories from the YOA remain: absolute and conditional discharge, fine, community service order, probation, treatment order, and custody. They are discussed below with corresponding YCJA options.

Absolute Discharge

An absolute discharge is a sentence with no sanctions. The young person, even though found guilty, is free to leave the court with no penalty. This disposition is given most often for very minor offences when the young person has no prior record. In 1999–2000, 2 percent of court cases resulted in an absolute discharge (1,363 cases) (Sudworth and deSouza, 2001:16). The YCJA also allows the court to reprimand a youth as a sentence option.

Conditional Discharge

The 1995 YOA amendments, Bill C-37, introduced a new disposition—the conditional discharge, and it is retained by the YCJA. The conditional discharge has always been available as a sentencing option in the adult system, where it is generally viewed as similar to probation, but more lenient. The conditional discharge provides for conditions similar to those outlined in a probation order. After successful completion of the terms of the order, however, the person's criminal record is "erased"; in other words, the person is discharged without a conviction on his or her record. Such a person who applies for employment and is asked about any prior convictions can legally respond in the negative. In the youth system, a conditional discharge similarly erases a person's criminal record so that she or he can no longer be viewed as a convicted offender. It is most commonly used in combination with probation orders. In 1999–2000, less than 2 percent of sentences were conditional discharges (Sudworth and deSouza, 2001:8).

McGuire (1997:198–202) argues that the conditional discharge can work to a youth's disadvantage in some circumstances. Under the YOA, a conditional discharge may be revoked at any point if a young person is convicted of another offence. The court may then impose another disposition while denying the right to appeal with respect to the original sentence. In every other instance, courts are not permitted to impose a greater intervention for young offenders following original sentencing (i.e., when dispositions are reviewed). Because the conditional discharge allows for greater intervention with respect to young offenders, it should be viewed, McGuire suggests, as something more punitive than probation, but less intrusive and less punitive than custody.

Fine

The court may impose a fine not to exceed $1,000, but it must consider the youth's ability to pay. Under a fine option program, young people can elect to do community service work if they are unable to pay a fine. In 1999–2000, 6 percent of court cases resulted in a fine (4,091 cases). Fines are most common in motor vehicle offences (Sudworth and deSouza, 2001:8,16). Usually a majority of fines are for small amounts. In 1996–97, more than half of those fines (55 percent) were $100 or less, while 43 percent were between $101 and $500. Two percent of the sentences involved fines over $500 (Statistics Canada, 1998:x). The YCJA maintains the fine option, but offers the court an additional range of similar sanctions: compensation to be paid for loss of property, income, or support (with different rules in the Province of Quebec); restitution, an order to restore or replace stolen or damaged property; restitution that encompasses an order to pay someone who may have purchased stolen property from the young offender; and, compensation in kind for loss, damage, or injury caused by the young offender.

Community Service Order

The court may order young people to perform supervised community service for a period not to exceed 240 hours. Community service orders (CSO) are often operated through probation offices. Arrangements are made for young people to work, without compensation, for food banks or other charitable or nonprofit organizations such as the Society for the Prevention of Cruelty to Animals. Most commonly, a CSO is attached to another more serious sentence. In 1999–2000, 27 percent of all convictions received a CSO while only 7 percent of the court dispositions were for community service orders alone (total of 4,772 cases) (Sudworth and deSouza, 2001:8).

BOX 9.11

Court Transcript of Discussions Preceding Sentencing

Young offender, Susan, was found guilty of shoplifting and has a prior record of similar offences. Susan lives in a very impoverished section of the city and is supported by her mother, a "single mom" on welfare.

Judge to Susan:

J.   Susan, why do you take these things?

S.   [pause] Well, 'cause I want the stuff.

J.   Because you want the stuff, well is that a good reason?

S.   No.

J.   Pardon?

S.   No.

J.   No? OK so you went out and stole in March and got caught. Why didn't you stop then? A month later, you were out stealing again. Why?

S.   I don't know.

J.   You don't know? We'll have a family court clinic assessment [psychiatric assessment] and this case will be adjourned for a month.

Judge's questioning of Susan's mother:

J.   Mother, what would you like to say please?

M.   Well, I certainly don't want her to be taken out of her home. Other than her shoplifting she doesn't cause any problems. She is handable.

J. She is what?

M. She is [pause]—I can handle her and when she was brought home by the police it was a total surprise to me.

J. Why should it be such a surprise to you? She's been out of control ... now as long as I can remember, hasn't she? How many times have you been here with your two daughters, especially Susan?

M. Yeah, well I [pause] I think she is making progress.

J. Is she?

M. At this new school like I don't think that if the program was interrupted it would be very good for Susan, maybe open custody or—

J. Well for all I know they probably will put her in open custody. That's the way they do it these days.

M. I know she was very depressed and frustrated when she wasn't keeping up in the normal school in the Grade 8 because she was going to the general learning disability class where she wasn't supposed to be in. I placed her in the special school. Ever since then she has been more happier, the depression has ceased. So I thought that maybe, well, that was one thing I did, placing her in this special program and other than that—

J. And that seems to be working more or less?

M. Yes.

Later, the Judge resumes his discussion with Susan's mother and says:

J. What I am thinking of is six months' open custody followed by a year's probation. Mrs. C., do you want to comment on that?

M. Mmmmm, it just seems like a very long time, half a year.

J. Well, you know she has been in trouble over and over again, hasn't she?

M. I don't really—

J. Just say it, whatever is on your mind.

M. I (pause) I don't really know if she'll respond to that, maybe she will (pause) she's not responding right now. She doesn't seem to realize—

J. In truth, she hasn't responded to anything favourable, has she?

M. (no response)

J. Has she?

M. Well ...

J. How long have you been looking up and seeing her in front of me?

M. That's true, that's true.

J. Isn't that right?

M. Mmmmm—

J. It's always the same story. She's back again with more offences, doesn't cooperate with probation. Isn't that right?

M. I don't know if she will stay if she goes to open custody.

J.   If she doesn't stay she will get locked up. Maybe that is what she needs is some control. She has no control—she does what she wants.

M. She is rather hard to handle right now.

J.   Yes, and her sister is not a very good influence on her, is she?

M. No.

J.   All right, please sit down. If there is anything else you'd like to say you will be given a chance.

At sentencing the Judge says:

... six months' open custody, followed by 12 months' probation, concurrent. What are you crying for, Susan? This is the best thing that ever happened here. We should have done this a long time ago.

Source: (Bell, 1993).

Probation

The most common sentence or disposition in youth court is probation and it is most commonly administered for sexual offences, minor assault, drug offences, theft, and arson. In, 1999–2000, 48 percent of court cases with a guilty finding resulted in a probation disposition (Sudworth and deSouza, 2001:8). A probation order is a means of controlling and supervising a young person's behaviour while he or she is in the community. There are sanctions for noncompliance with the conditions of probation. Two conditions are mandatory in all probation orders. All probationers are required to "keep the peace" and "be of good behaviour," and to appear in court as required. The YCJA adds two new mandatory conditions: prohibition from possessing or purchasing weapons, ammunition, and explosive substances, and any other conditions necessary to "secure the young person's good conduct" and prevent further criminal activity. In addition, young people may be required to report to a probation officer on a regular basis, maintain employment, go to school, reside at a particular residence, report any change in address, or/and remain within the court's jurisdiction. The court often orders a youth to not associate with certain people and to avoid certain neighbourhoods, obey a curfew, abstain from drugs/alcohol, or attend treatment or counselling programs. Prohibition orders can also be imposed under the YCJA independently of a probation order.

A failure to comply with conditions of probation can result in a new charge—failure to comply—and a return to court for sentencing on this charge. Community service orders are often included as a condition of probation. The maximum term for probation is two years. In 1999–2000, 33, 028 cases resulted in probation. Slightly more than half (56 percent) of these probation orders ranged from 7 to 12 months: 22 percent were for 6 months or less, and 22 percent were for more than 12 months. Generally, the more serious the offence, the longer the term of probation (Sudworth and deSouza, 2001:9).

Treatment Order

Section 22 of the YOA allowed the court to order youth detained in a hospital or other facility for the purpose of treatment, providing he or she gave consent. The requirement of consent for treatment was a contentious aspect of the YOA (Leschied and Jaffe, 1991), and the 1995 amendments to the YOA (Bill C-37) repealed sections 22 and 20(1)(i) of the act. Treatment as a disposition was no longer allowed under the YOA after that date. Fetherstone (2000) argues that the YCJA principles move the youth justice system even further from a welfare model by requiring similar sentences for similar offences and sentences proportionate to the offence (111–112). Nonetheless, it does promote rehabilitation as a sentencing principle and provides new sentencing options that are potentially rehabilitative: intensive support and supervision program (if provided by provinces); attend a non-residential program for up to 240 hours; and intensive rehabilitative custody. In so doing it sidesteps the issue of consent to treatment. Provisions for the use of these sentences by the court will be discussed in the next chapter.

Custody

Under the YOA, custody sentence options are limited to two choices. The court could sentence a young offender to one of two levels of custody—open or secure—which differ in terms of restrictions on freedom of movement, level of supervision, and access to the community. The YCJA has considerably expanded these choices perhaps because, as we will see in the next chapter, the use of custody under the YOA was a contentious issue. Those advocating a crime control or justice model wanted more and longer custody sentences for some young offenders, while welfare and restorative justice model advocates expressed alarm over an excessive use of custody by the courts. The YCJA has addressed this issue in a number of ways. First, s. 39(1) of the YCJA specifies that a young person cannot be sentenced to custody unless she or he has committed a violent offence, has already received a non-custodial sentence and failed to comply with that, has committed an indictable offence for which an adult would receive a federal prison term, or has committed an indictable offence. In this latter case, the court is required to argue that there are aggravating circumstances that justify a custody sentence and that a non-custodial sentence would violate the sentencing principles of s. 38.

Secondly, s. 39(2) specifies that when any of the conditions in subsection (2) are met and a custody sentence is allowed, the court must then consider all non-custodial alternatives and determine that there is no reasonable alternative before imposing a custodial sentence. Section 39(3) outlines the factors that the court must consider regarding non-custodial alternatives including the availability of alternatives to custody, the likelihood based on previous experience and sentences that the young person will comply with a non-custodial sentence, and whether alternatives have already been used or what alternatives have been used with people who have committed similar offences under similar circumstances. The court is also prohibited from using custody "as a substitute for appropriate child protection, mental health or other social measures" (s. 39(5)), and is not prohibited from using a non-custodial sentence in circumstances where a young offender is a repeat offender (s. 39(4)). Importantly, these provisions do not preclude a non-custodial sentence in convictions for violent offences, nor is a custody sentence for non-violent offences.

Finally, in all cases where a judge imposes a custody sentence, the court must state the reasons why a non-custodial sentence was not appropriate, and if a case and circumstances are considered exceptional, the court is required to state why a non-custodial disposition is not appropriate for a non-violent offence and also state the reasons why a case is considered an exceptional one (s. 39(9).

Type of custody sentences have also changed. Judges no longer make determinations about level of custody; rather, they have choices about types of custody, which include custody with supervision in the community, custody with conditional supervision, a deferral of custody and supervision (except for presumptive offences), and intensive rehabilitative custody and supervision. All custody sentences are now accompanied by some type of supervision order. These will be discussed further in the next chapter.

Although the Criminal Code provides for mandatory minimum custody sentences for certain types of offences committed by adults, the YOA did so only for first- and second-degree murder. The YCJA keeps these same minimums (see Box 9.6) and specifies a two year maximum for all other youth sentences except where the offence would warrant a life sentence for an adult, or is a presumptive offence. These carry a three year maximum youth sentence.

Since 1992–93, the use of shorter custody sentences has increased annually. In 1999–2000, slightly more than three-quarters of custody dispositions were for three months or less (77 percent) up 6 percent from eight years ago; only 6 percent of the custodial sentences were for more than six months and 33 percent were for less than one month. In total, there were 23,215 cases sentenced to custody; 17 percent of cases were sentenced to open custody and 17 percent to secure custody. Serious offences such as attempted murder, murder, and manslaughter are highly likely to receive custody sentences but beyond these, administrative offences are most likely to result in a custody term (Sudworth and deSouza, 2001:8,9,17). Again, there have been dramatic increases for girls. Over the last four years, the number of girls committed to custody has increased by 26 percent, while male committals have increased by only 4 percent. Many of these committals stem from a higher rate of charges against girls for breach of a community order (Report, 1996:614). The reasons for this discrepancy will be considered in Chapter 11.

Review Order

There are no changes in the YCJA from the YOA regarding review orders. All custody sentences of greater than one year in length must be reviewed each year and the youth or a parent may request a review after six months. When the custody term is less than one year, the youth or parent may request a review after one third of the sentence (minimum 30 days). Reviews may also be requested for non-custodial sentences as well as the level of custody imposed Q12 (s. 87.(1) and s. 94). Section 94(6) of the YCJA outlines the grounds for reviewing a young offender's sentence: the youth has shown progress with respect to rehabilitation; that the circumstances that lead to the youth's sentence have changed materially; that new services or programs are available that were not available at the time of the youth's sentences; that the opportunities for rehabilitation are now greater in the community; or any other ground that the youth justice court considers appropriate.

In this review, the court has three options, all of which involve a lesser sentence: (1) transfer the young offender to a less secure custody level, or from custody to conditional supervision or probation; (2) release the youth from a non-custodial disposition or vary the disposition in some way (e.g., the court might omit a curfew or change a condition in a probation order); or (3) confirm the existing disposition and make no change.

Sentencing Issues

In this section, we consider three sentencing issues that have been addressed by academics and practitioners: (1) the extent to which adult sentencing principles are relevant to the youth justice system; (2) the extent to which extralegal factors—race, class, and gender—affect court dispositions; and (3) the severity of youth court sentencing relative to adult court sentencing and sentencing under the Juvenile Delinquents Act.

Relevance of Adult Sentencing Principles to Youth Court

Retribution and Incapacitation As we have seen in this and the last chapter, the principle of retribution, viewed as moral accountability, is an integral aspect of youth justice under the YCJA. However, given that young people lack the moral development, intellectual and emotional capacity, and judgment of adults it would be unreasonable to apply an adult standard in making them accountable for their actions (Bala et al., 1994:30–31). Those who advocate transferring youth to adult court and subjecting youth to adult sentences do in fact hold youth to an adult standard of accountability. A position at odds with the spirit of a youth justice system.

Incapacitation refers to removing offenders from the community—generally by putting them in an institution—so that they can no longer pose a threat (Bala et al., 1994:34–35). While most would agree that young offenders who have committed serious violent crimes should be removed from the community, there is no agreement as to where they should be held in custody, for how long, and under what conditions. Some people maintain that youth facilities are "holiday camps" and should be more like places of punishment. Others think ahead to the time young offenders will be released back into the community and worry that custodial institutions may be "schools of crime" or a "recipe for disaster." This latter view is expressed by Chief Judge Lilles of the Yukon Territorial Court:

> Affording protection to the public is not synonymous with incarceration. In the long term, society is best protected by the successful rehabilitation of the offender. Society is not protected if a youth emerges institutionalized from a federal penitentiary, or having learned additional criminal skills that would make him more dangerous. Unnecessary or unproductive incarceration of a youth or young adult in the federal system will rarely be in the interests of society. (*R. v. M. T.*, April 15, [1993] Yukon Territorial Court, cited in Bala et al., 1994:35)

The YCJA attempts to resolve this dilemma by allowing the court to decide who goes where.

Rehabilitation Rehabilitation attempts to "change" the offender through the use of various types of programs such as behaviour modification or group therapy. The ultimate goal is to reintegrate the offender back into society. Rehabilitation is viewed as particularly attractive for young offenders because "it is assumed they will be more amenable to rehabilitation than adults" (Bala et al., 1994:36).

The problem with applying the principle of rehabilitation to youth sentencing is that it can be viewed as counter productive to the proportionality principle also contained in the YCJA. This was also an issue under the YOA. A 1993 Supreme Court decision upheld a two-year open-custody sentence because of concerns about the youth's "depressing home conditions." In his decision, Justice Cory addressed the issue of proportionality as follows:

> It is true that for both adults and minors the sentence must be proportional to the offence committed. But in the sentencing of adult offenders, the principle of proportionality will have a greater significance than it will in the disposition of young offenders. For the young, proper disposition must take into account not only the seriousness of the crime but also all the other relevant factors ... Intolerable conditions in the home indicate both a special need for care and the absence of any guidance within the home.

The situation in the home of a young offender should neither be ignored nor made the predominant factor in sentencing. Nonetheless, it is a factor that can properly be taken into account in fashioning the disposition. (*R. v. J. J. M.* [1993], C. S. J. 14.)

In a case heard before the Ontario Court of Appeal in 1985, the judge reduced a youth's sentence from two years' secure custody to 18 months. In doing so, he took a position opposite to Justice Cory's by arguing that proportionality is more important than rehabilitation. He states,

the fact that this young offender may require some long-term form of social or institutional care or guidance if there is to be any real prospect of his rehabilitation does not mean that the vehicle of the Young Offenders Act can be employed for that purpose. Here, as under the Criminal Code, it is a cardinal principle of our law that, within the limits prescribed by Parliament, the punishment should fit the crime but should not be stretched so that it exceeds it, even where that might be thought desirable by some in the interest of providing some extra protection for the public. (*R. v. Richard I.* [1985], 17 C.C.C. (3D) 523, 44 C.R. (3D) 168 (Ont. C.A.))

Deterrence On the issue of general deterrence—which is based on the assumption that one young offender's sentence will deter others from engaging in similar crimes— judges were clearly divided with the YOA. In the Alberta Court of Appeal, Justice Stevenson wrote,

in any event, deterrence to others does not, in my view, have any place in the sentencing of youth offenders. It is not one of the principles enumerated in the catalogue in section 3 of the Act which declares the policy for young offenders in Canada. Indeed, I note that in regard to secure custody, section 24(5) prohibits committal unless necessary for the protection of society. (*R. v. G. K.* [1985], 21 C.C.C. (3D) 558 (Alta. C.A.))

One year later, Justice Brooke of the Ontario Court of Appeal disagreed with this decision. In *R. v. O.*, he wrote,

with the greatest deference, we do not agree with that statement. We think it is too broad. The principles under section 3 of the Young Offenders Act do not sweep away the principle of general deterrence. The principles under that section enshrine the principle of protection of society and this subsumes general and specific deterrence. It is perhaps sufficient to say that in our opinion the principle of general deterrence must be considered but it has diminished importance in determining the appropriate disposition in the case of a youthful offender. (*R. v. O.* [1986], 27 C.C.C. (3D) 376 (Ont. C.A.))

The principle of individual deterrence is based on an assumption or belief that people make decisions on the basis of rational choice. The rational choice model of decision making requires that a youth who is considering engaging in criminal activity will

1. think about the consequences of his or her behaviour;
2. give some thought to the chances of getting caught;
3. know what the penalty is for the offence;
4. take the chances of apprehension into account; and
5. weigh the cost of the sanctions/penalty against what can be gained from the offence.

Doob, Marinos, and Varma (1995) maintain that contemplation of all these things is highly unlikely, particularly on the part of adolescents. They cite the work of Weagant and Milne (1992) who argue, on the basis of their direct contact with young offenders, that

> teenagers seldom contemplate the consequence (i.e., punishment or sanction by the court) when they intentionally engage in criminal behaviour. This is because of one basic principle which we have learned through our experience: teenagers willingly engage in criminal behaviour when they think they are going to get away with it. If they think they are going to be apprehended they don't do it. The last thing the teenage girl thinks before pocketing that cassette tape is what happened to a friend who got caught and went to youth court. The only thing running through that girl's mind is: where is the security guard. (cited in Doob, Marinos, and Varma, 1995:63)

Deterrence is still not a stated principle of youth justice in Canada and will likely continue as a contentious issue.

Race, Class, and Gender

Research conducted in the United States indicates that race, class, and gender characteristics affect what happens to young offenders in the justice system. The effect of these factors is not always straightforward, since they usually interact with each other and with legal variables such as prior record. Unfortunately, there has been very little Canadian research on this subject. Some work has been done on the experiences of First Nations and Aboriginal youth in the justice system. Beyond this, Schissel's (1993) work in an Edmonton court (see Box 9.8) and Bell's (1994a) work in a southwestern Ontario court shed some light on the effects of race, class, and gender in Canadian youth courts.

With regard to race, Aboriginal youth are more likely than non-Aboriginal youth to be convicted and more likely to receive a custody sentence or probation. In addition, without a parent or guardian in court, Aboriginal youth are more likely to receive more severe dispositions (Schissel, 1993:99–102). A lack of resources or detention facilities in Aboriginal communities also means that more Aboriginal youth will be removed from their communities (Morin, 1990; Hamilton and Sinclair, 1991). To the extent that justice officials define and assess "responsible parents or guardians" in non-Native terms, Aboriginal youth are also less likely to be released either without charges or on bail (LaPrairie, 1983; Stevens, 1990).

Generally, most girls in court are two years younger than boys (age 15 vs. 17) (Schissel, 1993:37–38). As Duffy (1996) puts it, "it appears that courts are most offended by young girls (15 years of age) who are 'already' in trouble with the law and by older boys (17 years old) who are 'still' in trouble. The harshest sentences go to older males and younger females" (Duffy, 1996:214). Bell's (1994a), Schissel's (1993), and Duffy's (1996) findings on gender elaborate upon the complex ways in which gender, class, and family factors influence court outcomes. According to Bell, girls are treated more leniently than boys only if their offences are the traditional criminal offences of property crime and crime against the person. Girls charged with administrative offences and with mischief or disturbing the peace are treated more severely than are boys. Both boys and girls are treated leniently if their only parent is a single mother—provided that she is not a professionally employed mother. When parents (particularly mothers) are professionals, and when fathers appear in court, young offenders are treated more severely (Bell, 1994a:45–54). Thus, for girls, sentencing is something of a "double whammy." Not only are they judged in terms of their ability to conform to the stereotype of the "good daughters," but they are judged by their parents' ability to conform to **gendered expectations** of "good parenting." (See Box 9.11.)

Is Youth Court Sentencing a "Slap on the Wrist"?

The majority of those who have studied or worked in the youth justice system do not believe that youth sentences amount to a "slap on the wrist." There are a number of reasons they take this position. As we will see in the next chapter, a major reason is that, from 1986–87 to 1993–94, there was a 41 percent increase in the number of custody dispositions meted out in the youth courts (Foran, 1995:7). Of course, various interest groups who lobby for tougher sentencing measures take a very different view of the youth justice system. For them it is too lenient.

Bala (1988) suggests that how one views the YOA-based justice system depends on the object of comparison. If the YOA-based system is compared with the adult justice system, and with sentencing guidelines of the Criminal Code, a different view emerges than if it is compared with the Juvenile Delinquents Act. As Bala describes,

> the YOA [and the YCJA] does not have a single, simple underlying philosophy; there is no single, simple philosophy that can deal with all situations in which young persons violate the criminal law. When contrasted with the child welfare oriented philosophy of the JDA, the YOA emphasizes due process, protection of society, and limited discretion. In comparison to the adult criminal code, however, the YOA emphasizes the special needs and limited accountability of young persons. (1988:15)

Compared with the JDA, then, the YOA and the YCJA look tough. Compared with the adult system, however, the YOA appears lenient. The YCJA with its added emphasis on diversion and non-custodial sentences looks even more lenient than the YOA, but its creation of the presumptive offence and automatic adult sentences make it far tougher than the YOA. As we will see in the discussion that follows, comparisons of legal provisions and sentencing practices for specific offenders suggest that the issue is more complex.

What Is Being Compared? It is fairly clear that the youth justice system is more lenient than the adult system for youth under age 14 with respect to particularly violent offences (including murder). Such is not always the case when it comes to other offences. For example, while adults are eligible for parole and may be released after serving one-sixth of their sentence, or are entitled to statutory release after serving two-thirds of their sentence, young offenders lack the benefit of these provisions. In lieu of parole or early release, the young offender has conditional supervision and even this is not automatic.

Doob, Marinos, and Varma (1995) compared custody dispositions from youth court in 1992–93 with disposition from six adult provincial courts. They found that the percentage of cases resulting in custody are roughly the same for youth and adults charged with mischief offences, theft under $1,000, failure to comply with a disposition or probation order, and assault. Offences for which adults are more likely to receive a custodial sentence include failure to appear in court, robbery, and sexual assault (Doob, Marinos, & Varma, 1995:65). Bell and Smith (1994), who compared median sentence length for Nova Scotia youth and adults sentenced to custody during the period 1992–94, found that for some offences, young offenders get longer custody terms than adults. Their comparison of broad categories of offences, and some specific offences, revealed that the median sentence length (in days) is longer for young offenders (see Tables 9.4 and 9.5). With respect to offenders with no previous record, young offenders receive longer or equal custody terms for theft, mischief, serious assault, and common assault. With respect to offenders with a previous custody record, young offenders receive longer sentences than adults for theft, mischief, sexual assault, and common assault (Bell & Smith, 1994). Similarly, a recent Statistics Canada comparison of youth and adult custody sentences for the entire country found that in 1998–1999, youth received longer custody terms than adults for theft, serious and minor assault, break and enter, mischief, drugs, weapons charges, and failure to appear (Sanders, 2000:11).

These comparisons are suggestive rather than conclusive (Doob, Marinos, and Varma, 1995). Given that different sentencing principles underlie the youth and adult justice systems, we should not expect—or even want—outcomes to be the same. The fact that adults have parole means that while their sentences may be longer than those of youth, their time served may be shorter. It may also be the case that adult offences and youth offences are viewed differently by courts. A break and enter or a robbery committed by an adult may be seen as a professional activity and more as experimentation if engaged in by a juvenile. Such differences aside, the evidence suggests that youth court sentencing cannot be easily dismissed as a "slap on the wrist." Conversely, for those who would argue that more youth should receive adult sentences, it cannot be assumed that stiffer penalties would be the end result. As we saw earlier in this chapter, young offenders in Manitoba were opting for transfers to the adult court as a way out of the youth justice system. Whether the YCJA's provision for less severe youth sentences than adult sentences will be achieved remains to be seen.

TABLE 9.3

Length of Custody, Adult and Youth Offenders, Nova Scotia, 1992–1994

Median Custody Sentence Lengths (Days) for Offenders with No Previous Custody Terms, Nova Scotia, 1992–93 and 1993–94

Offence Type	Adult	Young Offender
Property	122	122
Person	120	120
Public order	30	61
Administration of justice	51	61
Morals	68	137
All	87	94
Break and enter	244	150
Theft	90	91
Mischief	45	61
Serious assault	120	120
Common assault	60	74
Sexual assault	303	122
Robbery	1095	122

Source: Bell and Smith (1994).

TABLE 9.4

Length of Custody, Repeat Adult and Youth Offenders, Nova Scotia, 1992–1994

**Median Custody Sentence Lengths (Days) for Offenders
with Previous Custody Terms,
Nova Scotia, 1992–93 and 1993–94**

Offence Type	Adult	Young Offender
Property	183	184
Person	183	184
Public order	61	122
Administration of justice	60	61
Morals	30	122
All	106	151
Break and enter	375	213
Theft	122	151
Mischief	61	122
Serious assault	242	153
Common assault	90	150
Sexual assault	383	441
Robbery	1095	548

Source: Bell and Smith (1994).

SUMMARY

The first year to show a decrease in youth court caseload since the YOA was implemented was 1994–95 and the caseload has decreased every year since then. Most youth court cases involve male youth. The most common offences are property crimes. Girls going to court tend to be younger than boys. Under the YOA, there was an increase in the number of youth held in pretrial detention, which critics charge is a net-widening mechanism. YCJA provisions requiring the court to assume that pretrial detention is not necessary may halt this increase and reduce the numbers of youth in detention.

Transferring a youth to adult court was one of the most contentious, complicated, and legally problematic aspects of the YOA because the transfer occurred before a finding of guilt. The YCJA has sidestepped many of these problems through the creation of the presumptive offence, requiring an automatic adult sentence for any youth aged 14 or older convicted of these offences, as well as other "serious" offences committed by youth aged 16 and 17. Youth facing adult sentences also have adult legal rights that are not available to those receiving youth sentences—they can elect a jury trial and are entitled to a preliminary hearing.

Private lawyers have been found to be more successful than duty counsel in defending clients. Lawyers who assume a "guardian" role are primarily concerned with the "best interests" of their clients. Lawyers who assume a "legal advocate" role are more concerned with their clients' legal rights. The YCJA allows the court to order young offenders or their parents to pay for court appointed representation.

The most common sentences in youth court are probation and custody. Custody rates skyrocketed under the YOA in spite of restrictions and provisions for diversion. The YCJA strengthens these restrictions by requiring a conviction for a violent offence for custody to be considered and a justification for a custodial sentence for a non-violent offence conviction.

Sentencing principles from all juvenile justice models have been incorporated in the YCJA. Nonetheless, justice principles of proportionality and retribution along with the crime control principle of punishment take precedence over the welfare principle of rehabilitation and restorative justice principles of reintegration and reparation. The general principles governing adult sentencing are retribution, deterrence, incapacitation, and rehabilitation, all except deterrence have been established by the YCJA. There has been no consensus among youth court judges regarding the application of rehabilitation and deterrence principles. Retribution and incapacitation are generally seen as appropriate in the youth justice system as long as they are not applied in the same way they are applied in the adult system.

Race, class, and gender characteristics affect what happens to young offenders in court. Aboriginal youth, girls charged with nontraditional offences, and youth with professional parents (especially professional mothers) are treated more harshly than other youth.

Juvenile justice under the YOA appears tough when compared with juvenile justice under the JDA and "lenient" when compared with the adult system. However, actual comparisons of adult and youth sentences suggest that sentencing in the adult system is not always tougher than sentencing in the youth system. Given the different philosophy underlying the youth justice system, we should neither expect nor desire identical outcomes in the two systems.

CHAPTER 10

Youth Corrections: Going to Jail

CHAPTER OBJECTIVES

1. To trace the history of juvenile institutions in Canada from prisons to industrial training schools and correctional centres.

2. To examine YCJA provisions for custody.

3. To discuss reasons for increases and variations in the use of custody under the YOA.

4. To discuss different types of correctional programs along with their objectives and philosophies.

5. To examine issues associated with treatment and rehabilitation.

6. To discuss aftercare programs and their importance in successful youth corrections.

KEY TERMS

Remand
Training schools
Secure custody
Open custody
Conditional supervision
Intensive rehabilitative
    custody and
    supervision

Aftercare
Corrections
Correctional
    programming
Cognitive skills
Life skills

Boot camps
Treatment
Rehabilitation
Indeterminate sentences
Determinate sentences

INTRODUCTION

In 1998–99, close to 2 percent of the Canadian youth population between the ages of 12 and 17 were in custody or on probation. Overall, 10,698 boys and 2,292 girls were sentenced to a term in custody, with an average daily count of 4,600 youth in custody or .2 percent of Canada's youth population. Only 707 of these youth were under age 14, but slightly more than one-fifth were young girls (21 percent). A disproportionate number of these youth were Aboriginal. Twenty-two percent of the male youth sentenced to custody were Aboriginal as were 27 percent of the female youth (2,370 and 626). On any given day there were 836 youth held in **remand**. In the same year approximately, 33,713 youth were under supervision in the community on a probation order (Statistics Canada, 2000:22, 23, 25, 30, 32, 35, 48–51).

Custody is an expensive undertaking. It costs an average of $80,000 per year to keep a young person in custody. Actual costs vary depending on the facility's level of security. Community-based residential custody expenses range from $8,000 to $12,000. The average costs of low and high security facilities are $70,000 and $120,000 respectively. Supervising a young offender in the community through programs such as

---

BOX 10.1

Joey: "Custody"

Joey didn't want to go back to Hawthorne. His parents insisted, so at a red light Joey jumped out of the car. He was caught two days later and taken to Hawthorne House for a few weeks ... [H]ere he picked up another charge ... assault ... Joey returned home and to his local school ... [A] month later he was back in court to be sentenced to Shelburne Youth Centre for a week, 30 hours community service and a year probation ... In November Joey skipped his court date for the assault charge ... Joey was charged with four counts of breaching probation and an undertaking to return to court ... The judge sentenced him to three and a half months in Shelburne Youth Centre ... Joey was very active while in Shelburne ... He joined air cadets ... [W]hen Joey was released he went job hunting. In a few days he found a job at a fast food restaurant ... He plans to repeat grade ten in the fall.

Source: Adapted from MacDonald (1994b, 1994c).

probation is considerably cheaper, at approximately $600 to $700 per person (Newfoundland and Labrador, 1994 October:1).

The practice of keeping adults and young people in separate correctional facilities began about 140 years ago. This chapter begins with a discussion of the history of youth corrections in Canada. Next, it examines YCJA provisions for youth custody followed by a discussion of contemporary facilities and programs. A discussion of some of the critical issues in corrections today rounds out the chapter.

HISTORICAL FOUNDATIONS

The foundation for the practice of institutionalizing Canadian youth separately from adults was laid in 1857 with the passage of the Act for Establishing Prisons for Young Offenders. The first institution was opened at Isle aux Noix on the Richelieu River in October 1858, and the second at Penetanguishene on Georgian Bay in August 1859. Both institutions had formerly been used as army barracks. The intention was to provide a better environment for youth than was to be found in adult penitentiaries. While both boys and girls were sent to Isle aux Noix, only boys were detained at Penetanguishene (Carrigan, 1991:405–6). Notwithstanding all the good intentions, both institutions reportedly "fell short of expectations" and became "primarily institutions of work and punishment" (Carrigan, 1991:406).

From Reformatories to Industrial Schools

In 1867, J.M. Langmuir was appointed Ontario's first Inspector of Prisons, Asylums, and Public Charities. He began with a campaign to change correctional philosophy and policy regarding youth. His efforts were instrumental in changing Penetanguishene from a "reformatory prison" to a "reformatory for boys," with a mandate to foster the "education, industrial training and moral reclamation of juvenile delinquents" (Langmuir, cited in Carrigan, 1991:407).

Meanwhile, efforts were under way in other parts of the country to provide institutions that would serve as places of reform for all children in need—the poor and the neglected, as well as the delinquent. Children in need would be prevented from becoming criminals, it was argued, if they received care and education, and were taught a trade through industrial training. Halifax was one of the first cities to develop an institution that provided those things. The Halifax Protestant Industrial School (est. 1864) and the St. Patrick's Industrial School for Catholic Boys (est. 1865) were followed by the Monastery of the Good Shepherd, an Industrial School for Roman Catholic Girls. Ontario's first industrial schools were the Victoria Industrial School for Boys (est. 1887) and the Alexandra Industrial School for Girls (est. 1892).

By 1927, there were 24 industrial schools spread across the country: nine in Quebec, five in Ontario, four in Nova Scotia, two in British Columbia, two in Manitoba, and one each in Saskatchewan and New Brunswick (Carrigan, 1991:422). All had similar routines. Half a day was spent in school and half in learning a trade. Boys typically received training in carpentry, shoemaking, cooking and baking, and farm and garden work; girls were taught sewing, knitting, crocheting, dressmaking, shoemaking, and domestic science (Carrigan, 1991:422; Sutherland, 1976:137).

Training Schools

Officially designated as "industrial training schools" at the turn of the century, these institutions came to be known as **training schools.** Not surprisingly, as more industrial schools were built, their use increased. In 1922, 8.5 percent of children convicted in juvenile court were sentenced to industrial schools. That figure rose to 11.5 percent in 1932, 13.1 percent in 1945, and 14.4 percent in 1949 (Carrigan, 1991:426; Hackler, 1978:104). Thereafter the numbers declined. By 1968, the number of youth sentenced to training school had dropped to 8 percent; by 1973, custody sentences made up 2.3 percent of convictions (Hackler, 1978:104–6). A Canadian criminologist writing in the late 1970s reported that "there has probably been no increase in the use of training schools in the last few years … [T]here is a general indication that the juvenile justice system in Canada has not been opting for an increased use of institutional care" (cited in Hackler, 1978:105–8).

One of the major reasons for declining rates in the use of training schools was that provinces began to restrict their use. In the early 1970s, British Columbia abolished the use of secure custody and then, as if anticipating the YOA, reintroduced it in 1977; this reintroduced custody was to be used only for "hard core" offenders and for the purpose of "protection of society." Ontario also restricted the use of training schools; only youth who had committed an offence for which an adult would be sentenced to prison could be sentenced to custody. The development of community programs and group homes in the 1970s further reduced the use of training schools (Markwart, 1992:232).

Youth Centres

Corrections for young people underwent both structural and procedural changes with the introduction of the YOA. Two levels of custody were established, **secure** and **open,** and the court was required to set the level of custody at sentencing. When sentenced for a murder conviction in youth court, a set period of community supervision was also required after a youth was released from custody. While the court established level of custody, provinces were given the power to designate which of their facilities would classify as open (limited restrictions on movement) or secure (maximum restrictions on movement). Hence, there was considerable variation in facilities across the country.

BOX 10.2

A Young Person's Thoughts about Detention

I went to court
all dressed up
in high heeled shoes
and a deadly suit
for the whole four days
Sitting in that court room
knowing I was guilty
and lying through my teeth
—only made it harder
The threat of their time
—too much to bare
I wish for death
but each morning
when I wake
I'm pleased
and stay pleased until night hits
But left alone I feel like
a beast that can't sleep
& bang my head against the wall
pacing up and down
like a tiger
Knowing I'm really
a cub
that's been deserted.
n.g.

From *Heroes and Villains* an anthology of poems by young people in detention. Via Magenta, Adelaide, Australia, 1994.

In Newfoundland, for example, the Department of Social Services Division of Youth Corrections was responsible for carrying out the sentence of the court. This department has two divisions—Community Correctional Services and Secure Custody and Remand Services. Community Correctional Services is responsible for alternative measures, non-custodial supervision programs, and open-custody services and facilities. Newfoundland's open-custody facilities consisted of eight group homes, three assessment centres, and foster homes. There were two facilities for secure custody and remand—the Newfoundland and Labrador Youth Centre in Whitborne and the Pleasantville Youth Centre in St. John's. In 1994–95, funding was allocated for an additional regional youth centre in Cornerbrook (Newfoundland and Labrador, 1996).

In British Columbia, youth institutions and other young offender programs such as probation and alternative measures come under the jurisdiction of the Ministry for Children and Families. British Columbia had five secure-custody centres—one on Vancouver Island, one in Vancouver, one in the Fraser Valley, one in the Interior, and one in the North Region. There were seven open-custody facilities, one in each region and three in Vancouver. There were also three community-based residential centres (CBRCs) in the province.

Ontario and Nova Scotia are unique in that the implementation of the YOA created a split jurisdiction over young offenders, such that 12- to 15-year-olds were processed differently from 16- to 17-year-olds. In both provinces, 16- to 17-year-olds remained under the jurisdiction of adult corrections and 12- to 15-year-old youth under the jurisdiction of the youth system. Courts were also operated separately. Youth under 15 were processed under the Family Court, as they had been under the JDA. Youth aged 16–17 were processed in adult court under YOA restrictions; the court was referred to as "youth court" when young offender cases were heard. Both provinces have since moved to have all young offenders processed through the family court.

While both provinces maintain jurisdictional distinctions, there have been other changes. Since August 1994, all youth corrections in Nova Scotia are under the jurisdiction of the Department of Justice. Youth institutions continue to be separated by age and/or sex. All secure-custody sentences for males aged 16–17 were served in the Nova Scotia Youth Centre, while 12- to 15-year-olds served their sentences at the Shelburne Youth Centre. All female young offenders sentenced to secure custody were held at Shelburne regardless of age. Nova Scotia also has the Cape Breton Youth Resource Centre, a facility that provided temporary detention and open custody for male offenders.

Ontario continues to divide young offenders into Phase I (12–15) and Phase II (16–17). Phase I youth are under the jurisdiction of the Ministry of Community and Social Services, while Phase II youth are under the jurisdiction of the Ministry of the Solicitor General and Correctional Services. As in Nova Scotia, jurisdictions have been combined in some areas for female offenders. For example, in Hamilton, Brantford,

Niagara, and Haldimand-Norfolk regions, the Ministry of Community and Social Services provides detention for Phase II female youth. This change resulted from (1) the closing of secure-custody/detention facilities for 16- to 17-year-old female youth at the Hamilton-Wentworth Detention Centre in June 1995, and (2) recommendations contained in the Women's Issues Task Force Report (Ontario Ministry of the Solicitor General and Correctional Services, 1995b).

The YCJA, on the other hand, does not require the youth court to specify a level of custody for young offenders. Rather, s. 85(1) requires only that provinces have at least two levels of custody for young persons and that levels be distinguished by the degree of restraint of the young persons in them. It is still the Lieutenant Governor in Council who determines facility custodial levels, but it is now the provincial director who determines the level of custody to be served by each young person rather than the court. Where custody was addressed in the YOA in terms of two levels of security (open and secure), the YCJA paves the way for individual custodial sentences and provincial facilities to be differentiated by multiple security levels and a variety of programs and intervention methods. Provinces are not likely to change YOA facilities in any major ways in the foreseeable future. What did change is the concept of custody and its lack of links with community corrections.

Custody Provisions under the YCJA

The whole concept of custody, as a sanction for the criminal offences of youth, changed under the YCJA. With the YOA, custody was mostly perceived and used as an end in itself leading to a number of after care issues to be discussed later in the chapter. With the YCJA, custody is no longer an entity unto itself, but rather exists as part of a larger system of programs and community supervision designed to rehabilitate and reintegrate young offenders back into the community as law abiding people. This represents a whole new shift in emphasis regarding the purpose of custody. The YCJA refers to custody as "the custody and supervision system" and it is clear that its purpose is a welfare and restorative one: to carry out the sentence of the court and assist the reintegration and rehabilitation of youth. Still, the ultimate objective is one of crime control: to "contribute to the protection of society" (see Box 10.3). Interestingly, these are also the purposes of the adult correctional system as mandated by the Corrections and Conditional Release Act.

New sentencing options under the YCJA created two new aspects of youth correctional programs: the conditional supervision order and intensive rehabilitation custody and supervision. As we saw in the last chapter, youth serving a custody sentence are required to serve the latter portion of their sentence in the community under supervision. Section 105 of the YCJA outlines the regulations regarding the conditions of a **conditional supervision** order and the powers of the provincial director regarding required and discretionary conditions. Under this section, the provincial director is

Purpose of Custody and Supervision

Section 83 outlines the purpose and limitations of the custody and supervision system.

   (1) The purpose of the youth custody and supervision system is to contribute to the protection of society by
      (a) carrying out sentences imposed by courts through the safe, fair and humane custody and supervision of young persons; and
      (b) assisting young persons to be rehabilitated and reintegrated into the community as law-abiding citizens, by providing effective programs to young persons in custody and while under supervision in the community.

   (2) In addition to the principles set out in section 3, the following principles are to be used in achieving that purpose:
      (a) that the least restrictive measures consistent with the protection of the public, of personnel working with young persons and of young persons be used;
      (b) that young persons sentenced to custody retain the rights of other young persons, except the rights that are necessarily removed or restricted as a consequence of a sentence under this Act or another Act of Parliament;
      (c) that the youth custody and supervision system facilitate the involvement of the families of young persons and members of the public;
      (d) that custody and supervision decisions be made in a forthright, fair and timely manner, and that young persons have access to an effective review procedure; and
      (e) that placements of young persons where they are treated as adults not disadvantage them with respect to their eligibility for and conditions of release.

required to bring a young person to the youth justice court before the custodial portion of her or his sentence expires for the court to set the specific conditions of the youth's conditional supervision.

The necessary conditions of the conditional supervision order include the following:

- to keep the peace and be of good behaviour;
- to appear before the youth justice court when required;
- to be under the supervision of the provincial director or designate;
- to inform the provincial director when arrested or questioned by the police;
- to report to the police as instructed;
- to advise the provincial director of any change in address, employment, vocational or educational training, volunteer work, family or financial situation, and any changes that might affect the young person's ability to comply with the conditions of the order;
- to not own, possess, or have the control of any weapon, ammunition, prohibited ammunition, prohibited device, or explosive substance; and,
- to comply with any reasonable instructions that the provincial director considers necessary.

In addition, the court may impose any number of additional conditions regarding where the youth will live, including who with; what efforts the youth will make to get a job, attend school or other place of training or recreational program; restrictions on moving out of the court's jurisdiction; and any other conditions the court considers appropriate to promote the youth's reintegration.

The **intensive rehabilitative custody and supervision** order is reserved for youth convicted of the most serious violent offences, murder, attempted murder, manslaughter, aggravated sexual assault, or is a repeat offender and has been convicted of a serious violent offence that an adult is liable to a prison term of more than two years. In addition, s. 42(7) of the YCJA also requires the court to establish three other conditions:

(b) the young person is suffering from a mental illness or disorder, a psychological disorder or an emotional disturbance;

(c) a plan of treatment and intensive supervision has been developed for the young person, and there are reasonable grounds to believe that the plan might reduce the risk of the young person repeating the offence or committing a serious violent offence; and

(d) the provincial director has determined that an intensive rehabilitative custody and supervision program is available and that the young person's participation in the program is appropriate.

Two other aspects of the YCJA compliment and strengthen the rehabilitative and reintegrative mandate of s. 83(1): youth workers and reintegration leave. Under the

YOA, youth workers duties and functions were connected to community dispositions such as probation and conditional supervision. The YCJA (s. 90) requires that a youth worker be assigned to every youth sentenced to custody. This worker is responsible for developing plans for the youth's reintegration into the community that would set out the most effective programs for the young person as well a supervising and providing support to the youth when she or he is released from custody and is under supervision in the community.

The YOA allowed for temporary absences and day release (escorted or unescorted) from custody for a period of up to 15 days. These releases were granted by the provincial director for medical, compassionate, humanitarian, or rehabilitative reasons, or to allow a youth to attend school, find a job or work, or participate in training or treatment programs. The YCJA refers to this type of release (s. 91(1) and (2)) as reintegrative leave, allows release for the same reasons as the YOA, and extends release to a 30 day period that can be renewed any number of times.

YOUTH CUSTODY ISSUES

Of the 40,205 youth admitted to custodial facilities in 1998–99, 19 percent were sentenced to secure custody and 21 percent to open custody; the remaining 60 percent had been remanded to custody to await trial or sentencing (Statistics Canada, 2000:10). Although property offences predominate among cases sentenced to secure custody, their proportion declined from 46 percent in 1991–92 to 42 percent in 1999–2000. Over the same period, the proportion of secure-custody sentences for YOA administrative offences increased from 12.2 percent to 19 percent, while the proportion of secure custody sentences for violent offences increased from 16 percent to 22 percent (St. Amand and Greenberg, 1996:9; Statistics Canada, 2000:20-21).

Increased Use of Custody

One of the interesting effects of the YOA is that its implementation reversed the declining JDA trend in the use of custody. Most research comparing the uses of incarceration under the JDA and the YOA has concluded that the YOA created an increase in the use of custody for young offenders (Leschied and Jaffe, 1987, 1988, 1991; Markwart and Corrado, 1989; Leschied, Jaffe, and Willis, 1991). Some of this research is problematic because it has not considered age differences before and after legislative change. Nonetheless, when age is considered, the results are even more astounding. Between the last year of the JDA and the third year of the YOA, custody sentences in British Columbia increased by 85 percent; at the same time, adult admissions to custody in British Columbia decreased by 12 percent. In Manitoba, the youth population sentenced to custody increased by 148 percent. Further, from 1984–85 to 1989–90, virtually every province increased its use of custody (Markwart, 1992:236–38, 242).

Leonard, Smandych, and Brickey's (1996) research confirms this trend reversal over a 20-year period in Manitoba. Viewed over the period 1968 to 1990, admission rates, discharge rates, and daily population rates in Manitoba show an increased use of custody since implementation of the YOA. From 1968 to the mid-1970s, custody rates declined and then increased dramatically in 1984. According to the authors, the average daily rate of incarceration under the JDA was 4.7 youth per 10,000 in custody, while the YOA average is 10.3 youth per 10,000—a 219 percent increase (Leonard, Smandych, and Brickey, 1996:132–33).

Remarkably, this trend continued through to the mid-1990s and for both levels of custody. From 1991–92 to 1993–93, there was a 10 percent increase in the average daily count of youth in Canadian custodial facilities, and a 5 percent increase each year after that, up to 1994–95 (Foran, 1995:9). From 1990 to 1995, there was a 15 percent increase in the number of youth in secure custody and a 24 percent increase in the number of youth in open custody (St. Amand and Greenberg, 1996:5). Daily counts and rates of incarceration did not begin to show consistent decreases until the latter part of the 1990s (Statistics Canada, 2000:48–49).

TABLE 10.1

Distribution of Custodial Admissions by Offence Type, 1998–1999

Offence Type	Secure	Open	Remand
	% of Cases	% of Cases	% of Cases
Violent	22	22	23
Property	42	43	37
YOA[1]	19	22	18
Other CC[2]	12	8	18
Other[3]	3	3	2
Drugs	2	2	3

1. YOA offences include failure to comply with a disposition, failure to comply with an undertaking, contempt against youth court, and other YOA dispositions.

2. Other Criminal Code offences include impaired operation of a motor vehicle, escape from custody, being unlawfully at large, failure to appear, failure to comply, and disorderly conduct/nuisances.

3. Other offences include Narcotics Control Act offences, Food and Drug Act offences, and other federal statute offences.

Source: Statistics Canada (1996), *Juristat*, Cat. No. 85–002, 16(5), p. 8; Statistics Canada (2000), Youth Custody and Community Services Data Tables, 1998-99, p. 20-21, 30-31, 12-13.

Provincial Variation

While custody trends were fairly consistent across the country, there were and are provincial variations. All provinces showed increases between 1990 and 1995 in the number of youth in custodial facilities (the Yukon and Northwest Territories were exceptions). Increases ranged from 3 percent in Prince Edward Island to 58 percent in Newfoundland and Labrador. Alberta showed a 39 percent increase and British Columbia a 29 percent increase, while increases in other provinces ranged from 8 percent to 18 percent (St. Amand and Greenberg, 1996:6). Youth court statistics for 1994–95 show that Saskatchewan and Manitoba at 37.4 and 31.7 percent respectively, had the highest overall custody rates, while Quebec at 10.5 percent had the lowest. In fact, Quebec is consistently low (St. Amand and Greenberg, 1996:9).

As Table 10.2 shows, by 1998–99, many provinces were showing decreases in their incarceration rates that had been consistent for five years. Alberta declined consistently from a rate of 26.8 per 10,000 youth in 1994–95 to 17.8 in 1998–99, New Brunswick from 31.3 to 23.2 and British Columbia declined from 1995–96 with a rate of 13.4 to 11.3 in 1998–99. Ontario's declines were less dramatic from 23.4 1994–95 to 22.2 in 1998–99. Among the provinces, Saskatchewan and Manitoba have maintained the highest rates. Manitoba's rate was 31.6 in 1994–95 and 31.2 in 1998–99. Saskatchewan on the other hand continued to increase its rate throughout this period with an incarceration rate of 36.8 in 1994–95 and 41.2 in 1998–99.

The Yukon and Northwest Territories have extremely high rates of incarceration, a majority of which are Aboriginal youth. The same is true of Saskatchewan and Manitoba. In 1998–99, 74 percent of youth admitted to custody in Manitoba were Aboriginal youth and 90 percent of the girls admitted were Aboriginal. In Saskatchewan, 70 percent of youth were Aboriginal and 71 percent of girls were. For the Yukon and Northwest Territories, the figures are 51 percent youth, 69 percent girls, and 76 percent youth and 83 percent girls respectively (Statistics Canada, 2000:24, 34). We will return to a discussion of these figures in the next chapter.

Explaining Increases and Interprovincial Variation

When increases in the use of custody were first noticed, they were largely understood as a result of the new philosophy of the YOA. It was argued that judges were favouring crime control principles over welfare principles (Leschied and Jaffe, 1991). This interpretation was supported by the fact that more youth were going to custody for shorter periods of time, with the greatest increases occurring for sentences of three months or less—a trend that is also reflected in more recent statistics (Statistics Canada, 1998:ix). It seemed that judges were shifting toward a "short, sharp, shock" style of sentencing. However, Leonard, Smandych, and Brickey (1996) suggest that these increases are due more to changes in sentencing practice and the consequence of this change than to the adoption of a new philosophy. They argue that shorter sentences ultimately give youth more opportunity to commit crimes; the result is an increase in the number of offenders, some of whom are being committed to custody three times or more in a single year.

The other problem requiring explanation is the variation in rates across the country. In spite of reporting consistent increases, not all provinces are using custody at the same rate. According to Doob and Sprott (1996:411), we "need look no further than the court house door" for explanations of provincial and jurisdictional variation. It is not youth behaviour that is different across the country, but rather "the behaviour of provincial criminal justice personnel" (411). It appears that type and length of sentence is fairly consistent for serious offences. Where inconsistencies in sentencing arise is in regard to less serious charges. Variation may be a function, then, of the number of less serious charges being brought to court by police and Crown prosecutors. Similarly, Carrington and Moyer's (1994b) research suggests that interprovincial variation can be explained by the "level of police activity" and by judicial "decision as to length of custodial sentence" (288). Once the YCJA has been in effect for a few years, we should expect reductions in the amount of provincial variation in rates of incarceration.

TABLE 10.2

Provincial Incarceration rates per 10,000 youth: 1994–95 and 1998–99

Province	1994–95 %	1998–99 %
Newfoundland	27.1	23.0
Prince Edward Island	29.7	19.0
Nova Scotia	22.5	19.5
New Brunswick	31.3	23.2
Quebec	11.2	10.5(1995–96)
Ontario	23.4	22.2
Manitoba	31.6	31.2
Saskatchewan	36.8	41.2
Alberta	26.8	17.8
British Columbia	14.0	11.3
Yukon	49.2	48.3
Northwest Territories	79.7	64.1

Source: Statistics Canada (2000) Youth Custody and Community Services Data Tables, 1998–99. Cat. No. 85-226-XIE, pp. 48–49.

Youth Serving Adult Sentences

As with the YOA, the YCJA requires young people who are sentenced to custody to be held separately and apart from adults, but it does not require this for youth with adult sentences and youth sentenced to adult facilities. When a youth has been sentenced to youth custody and reaches the age of 18, the provincial director has the power to request that the remainder of the youth sentence be served either in a provincial correctional facility for adults or in a penitentiary, if the court considers it to be in the best interest of the young person or in the public interest, or the youth has two years or more remaining on his or her custodial sentence (s. 92(2)). This section essentially allows the youth justice court to authorize a provincial director to place a youth serving a youth sentence in a federal penitentiary.

More specifically, subsection (5) of s. 92 allows for young persons committed to custody under a youth sentence, who may also have an adult sentence, to serve this sentence in a youth custody facility, in a provincial correctional facility for adults or, if the unexpired portion of the sentence is two years or more, in a penitentiary. For youth serving a sentence in a youth custody facility who reach age 20, s. 93 also allows for the young person to be transferred to a provincial correctional facility for adults or to a penitentiary if the court considers it to be in the best interests of the young person or the public interest and there are two or more years of the sentence to be served. When a young person is transferred to the adult system to serve the remainder of a youth sentence, s. 93(3) requires that the Prisons and Reformatories Act and the Corrections and Conditional Release Act (legislation regulating adult corrections) be applied, except for the protection that youth have in the YCJA regarding publication of records and information.

YCJA requirements for a portion of a youth's custody sentence to be served in the community makes the custody sentence similar to adult parole entitlements. As in the adult system, a youth who violates the conditions of his or her supervision may be returned to custody to serve the remainder of the sentence. The difference is that, in the youth system, the court sets the length and conditions of custody and supervision rather than a parole board and the Attorney General (YCJA s. 98(1)) may apply to the court to keep a youth in custody for a longer period of time (see Box 10.4).

CORRECTIONAL PROGRAMS

Correctional programs are a vital aspect of youth justice since they are an important component in the rehabilitation and reintegration process designed to prevent future criminal behaviour when a youth completes his or her sentence. Correctional programming involves institutional programs as well as **aftercare** or follow-up programming that assists in reintegrating young offenders back into their homes and

BOX 10.4

Extending a Period of Custody

Section 98(4) outlines the factors to be considered by the youth court in deciding if a youth should remain in custody for a longer portion of her or his sentence. These factors include

(a) evidence of a pattern of persistent violent behaviour and, in particular,

(i) the number of offences committed by the young person that caused physical or psychological harm to any other person,

(ii) the young person's difficulties in controlling violent impulses to the point of endangering the safety of any other person,

(iii) the use of weapons in the commission of any offence,

(iv) explicit threats of violence,

(v) behaviour of a brutal nature associated with the commission of any offence, and

(vi) a substantial degree of indifference on the part of the young person as to the reasonably foreseeable consequences, to other persons, of the young person's behaviour;

(b) psychiatric or psychological evidence that a physical or mental illness or disorder of the young person is of such a nature that the young person is likely to commit, before the expiry of the youth sentence the young person is then serving, a serious violent offence;

(c) reliable information that satisfies the youth justice court that the young person is planning to commit, before the expiry of the youth sentence the young person is then serving, a serious violent offence;

(d) the availability of supervision programs in the community that would offer adequate protection to the public from the risk that the young person might otherwise present until the expiry of the youth sentence the young person is then serving;

(e) whether the young person is more likely to reoffend if he or she serves his or her youth sentence entirely in custody without the benefits of serving a portion of the youth sentence in the community under supervision; and

(f) evidence of a pattern of committing violent offences while he or she was serving a portion of a youth sentence in the community under supervision.

communities. It also involves programming for youth who have been given a community sentence such as probation or community service.

Many low security custodial facilities are operated through contractual arrangements with private organizations such as the Salvation Army and the John Howard Society. Specialized programs for offenders in this type of facility are often provided through contracts with community-based professionals. In Nanaimo, British Columbia, for example, the Salvation Army runs the Weisman House Program, which provides academic life skills training and counselling. Also in British Columbia, the John Howard Society runs the Discovery Centre (in Campbell River), which provides services for sex offenders, while the Sliammon Native Council provides services for Native sex offenders at Powell River through the Coast Salish Youth Cultural Program. Many facilities offer in-house programs such as recreational programs, education, employment, life skills, and substance abuse (British Columbia Ministry of the Attorney General, Correction Branch, 1995).

High-level security facilities provide programming developed by in-house professional staff and youth workers. Often a multidisciplinary team will develop a case management plan for each youth based on an assessment of his or her individual needs. All custodial facilities begin the correctional process with an initial assessment to determine the needs and appropriate management strategies for each youth. In Ontario, this assessment must be completed within 72 hours of admission for Phase II youth. All custodial facilities rely on volunteer-based programs for some services (Ontario Ministry of the Solicitor General and Correctional Services, 1995b). So, for example, the Elizabeth Fry Society in Vancouver provides various recreational and social programs, as well as creative pool programs, for all security levels at the Burnaby Youth Correctional Centre (British Columbia Ministry of the Attorney General, Corrections Branch, 1995).

Types of Programs

The YCJA sets the parameters for juvenile **corrections**. However, since the provinces are responsible for implementation, there is considerable variation in philosophical orientations to **correctional programming**. Some provinces have adopted a punitive crime control stance. In Ontario, for example, the solicitor general has introduced boot camps and a disciplinary approach to programming in other custodial facilities. Other provinces, including Newfoundland, are developing programs to minimize the use of custody. Although provincial correctional philosophies do change (particularly when there is a change in the governing political party), there is a certain amount of consistency in the types of programs offered to young offenders, both in custodial facilities and in the community.

BOX 10.5

The Ottawa-Carleton Young Offenders Unit: A Facility for Secure Detention and Short-Term Custody

The Ottawa-Carleton Young Offenders Unit is a facility for 16- to 17-year-old offenders that is contained within an adult correctional facility.

Accommodating Young Offenders

Over the years, the Ottawa-Carleton Young Offenders Unit has been transformed into a secure and structured setting ... The unit has a 24-bed capacity, [and] the number of young offenders "in residence" often exceeds that number. There is a high turnover, with an average length of stay being approximately one month. Most of the unit's young offenders are awaiting bail, trial, sentencing, transfer or review hearing.

Upon sentencing, residents receiving a long-term sentence (three months to three years) are transferred to a secure-custody setting ...

In the young offenders unit, all offenders (regardless of gender or admission status) are housed together. They eat together, participate in programs together and spend idle time in the same day room. Female sleeping quarters, however, are far removed from the male quarters. Each unit has a high ratio of specialized staff to residents. Staff develop supervision and intervention strategies to deal with "offender blending" problems as they arise.

An internal classification system (each offender is assessed by security and clinical staff) is also used to prevent victimization in the unit. Young offenders likely to prey on others share accommodations with similar offenders, to minimize the chances of housing potential victims with "predators."

A reward system also encourages the young offenders to perform 16 pro-social behaviours each day. Youth officers tally the offenders' weekly point totals and, depending on their total, the offenders are placed in one of three "levels." Young offenders at the highest level receive the most privileges (such as contact visits with parents or late day-room time). On the other hand, misconduct punishments can result in level downgrading, cell confinement (for a specified time period, not to exceed three days) or extra cleanup duty.

Offender-Management Procedures

Upon admission to the unit, the offender undergoes an intake needs assessment and a psychological evaluation. Each young offender's criminal history (such as circumstances of present and past offences), attitudes, family background, peer associations, education, employment, substance abuse, emotional and physical health and unit adjustment (such as problems with peers and staff) are evaluated systematically.

Once program needs are identified, offenders are referred to appropriate service providers (such as the school program for academic upgrading). A "plan of care" is developed for each young offender, detailing the duration and intensity of [his or her] required services ...

Offender case reviews are held regularly to discuss escorted passes (for recreational or community outings) and to discuss passes for regular home visits. This process usually considers

- outstanding charges (if any);
- prior record of escapes (if any);
- type of offence(s);
- family support (ability to control and supervise);
- the results of a meeting with parents (before release);
- feedback from the supervising probation officer;
- overall unit behaviour.

Service Provision

Within the unit, a multi-disciplinary team (consisting of a social worker, a psychologist, a chaplain, two teachers, a recreational officer, a unit manager, two operational managers and twelve youth officers) provides services to the young offenders.

The unit social worker prepares youth court reports for sentence reviews and transfer hearings. Other duties include chairing weekly case review meetings and completing discharge summaries—to another secure custody facility, open custody or the community (probation). Aside from this administrative role, the social worker also provides individual and group counselling, covering such areas as anger management, social and inter-personal skills, family counselling, job preparation and discharge planning.

Clinical services are also provided by a chaplain who delivers spiritual, substance abuse, and family counselling, and by a psychologist who specializes in the areas of sexual abuse, psychotic disorders, suicidal ideation, and depression.

Academic upgrading is offered through correspondence courses (with the assistance of two teachers), and leisure activities are coordinated by a recreational officer.

Source: Motiuk (1995:28–30).

BOX 10.6

Newfoundland's Division of Youth Corrections: Mission and Guiding Principles

Mission

All young persons who are in conflict with the law are to be afforded opportunities, appropriate to their needs and characteristics, to participate in a full range of programs and services designed to enhance their self-esteem, to promote law abiding behaviour, and to foster self-development aimed at assisting them to live successfully in the community.

Principles for Administration of Service Delivery

(a) Each youth has unique needs, which must be assessed and responded to in an individual manner.

(b) The assessment of a youth's needs must be viewed in the context of each individual's family, community, and cultural system, and parents or guardians should be involved at all stages of the Youth Corrections process.

(c) While programs for groups of young offenders will be developed, there must remain a commitment to individual case planning for each young person, whether in a custodial or community setting. The young person should be involved to the maximum extent possible in the development of an individual case plan.

(d) As the community has both the right and responsibility to respond to the phenomenon of youth crime, community involvement in both the management of Youth Corrections Programs and in the mobilization of resources and services for young offenders should be maximized to the greatest extent possible. The provision of services through a partnership between Government and the community maximizes the efficiency and effectiveness of the service.

(e) Where it is not absolutely necessary to do otherwise for the protection of society, young offenders should be provided with rehabilitative services and effective supervision in their home and community settings, rather than be placed in a custodial setting.

(f) Where custodial care is deemed necessary, young persons should be placed in the least restrictive environment that is consistent with their needs and level of social functioning, and should be regularly assessed for their suitability for return to a community setting as early as possible.

Source: Newfoundland and Labrador, Division of Youth Corrections.

BOX 10.7

Differing Views of a High Level Custodial Facility for Young Offenders

Administration

Most of the boys have gone through probation, alternative measures, they've been before the court two, three, four times and this is the last alternative … Sometimes the first time a kid comes in he may have been in trouble for a serious offence, the next time it may have changed to more of a property-related offence. It's a small gain. We don't look for miracles.

Basically, [facility programming involves] making a person stop and think rather than reacting emotionally, and understanding why they think the way they do and understanding the consequences of their actions, understanding they have choices … When [young offenders] go from there to an environment where their old peer group exists, they don't have the controls any more … the slippage can be considerable.

Victims

You take them and you put them in this [facility] that is like a hotel—there's swimming pools, I guess there's nothing that they could want … [A]re they really being punished?

Young Offenders

1. *Convicted of Break and Enter:*

   [In the first institution] you'd sit around, smoke cigarettes and watch TV ... [In this facility, the programs] help me, like, stop and think about problems before I do things. Before I didn't care. I always thought about myself, not other people. I was self-centred ... but now I think about other people and what I did to them. The people I stole from, I wouldn't want to feel what they would feel.

   Your freedom's gone. It's a jail because when you're in your room, your door's locked at night.

2. *Convicted of Murder:*

   I feel remorse for what I did. But I've gotta work on myself while I'm here, so I won't repeat things I've done in the past and be back in a place like this.

   In some ways [this facility is] the best thing to happen to me. Not how I got here but what it did for me, because if I hadn't come here, things probably would have just got worse. I know I hurt my family and a lot of other people with what I did, so I don't want to be like that. I don't want to be the way I was anymore. I want to change.

3. *Involved in Drugs, Convicted of Break and Enter:*

   [About leaving the facility] I'm kind of worried about that. I'm scared to get into the same old areas. It'll be a good chance to see how much willpower I got.

4. *Suicidal Youth Convicted of Theft:*

   Drugs change the way I'd relate to my folks, the way I'd talk to them. I just wanted to run away. I have flashbacks now of everything bad I did.

5. *Convicted of Assault and Break and Enter:*

   [About drug treatment] I resisted it a bit because I didn't really want it, but I needed it and I didn't get enough of it, especially at the Centre. [It] was more or less volunteer and you could do pretty much what you wanted. [At this facility] they teach us to stop and think about the consequences, how to say no and stick to your word. They give you a lot of help here, a lot more than the other places. They teach us this is the last stop here. It's the Big House next time ... [About being a crook] It's not really worth it, because I was just robbing myself, wasting my life. You might not wake up and realize it until you're thirty, sitting in a jail. That's not gonna be me ... I'm not going back to crime. You may as well realize it while you're young.

Source: Dorey (1996).

There are three types of correctional programs: general, offence specific, and offender specific. General programs usually apply to all offenders and include such things as life skills, education, recreation, and counselling programs. Offence-specific programs target specific offences, examples are the Stoplift Program for shoplifters and sex offender programs. Offender-specific programs target the offender's problems and behaviours and are exemplified by substance abuse programs, leisure time programs, and anger management. Some facilities are specifically designed to provide programming for special needs. Examples of low security level facilities in Ontario that provide for the special needs of Phase II youth include Portage, which provides substance abuse programming for 42 youth; Eagle Rock, which has five beds for Native youth; and the Terry Fox Centre, which provides ten beds for detention (Ontario Ministry of the Solicitor General and Correctional Services, 1995b).

Programs are also offered to youth serving sentences in the community. Community programming is often provided through services contracted by governments. So, for example, the Pacific Legal Education Association contracts with the Province of British Columbia to provide volunteer supervision for young offenders accused of sex offences and intensive supervision for youth serving probation sentences. The organization also provides support in employment, independent living, anger management, and other special-needs services. The Changes Program in British Columbia assists male young offenders with life skills, educational upgrades, and job placements. The Exodus Program run by the Governing Council of the Salvation Army provides a residential treatment program for youth with codependency or substance abuse problems (British Columbia Ministry of the Attorney General, Corrections Branch, 1995).

Most institutions offer programming in the area of education, counselling, life skills, and recreation. In most cases, programs are developed on an individual basis to meet young offender needs. Behaviour modification programs, or a token economy system, are most often used as a method of reinforcing program objectives. With behaviour modification, offenders are rewarded or punished through earning or losing points toward various privileges (See Box 10.5).

Some newer high security level youth centres are designed to facilitate small-group living arrangements and interaction. Living areas consist of a group of small cottages, and youth are responsible for cleaning, cooking, and laundry—activities that are viewed as part of life skills training. Facilities such as Waterville in Nova Scotia assign youth to cottages on the basis of programming needs. While some cottages focus on academic education, others emphasize vocational training or substance abuse.

Education

Educational programming is an important part of correctional programming because many youth have experienced failure in the regular school system and are poorly motivated with respect to academic studies. Educational programs aim to address self-esteem, motivation, and overall reading and writing skills, as well as academic subjects and vocational training. Some students work on academic credits through correspondence courses. Others are granted an Educational Temporary Absence for the purpose of attending local schools. Some institutions offer computer classes in which young offenders are able to learn basic word processing and some software applications. Youth facilities sometimes arrange with local community colleges to provide instruction in specialized vocational studies.

Life Skills and Cognitive Skills

Many young offenders are seen to have failed to acquire the **cognitive skills** that are essential to effective interpersonal relations. Problems in the area of interpersonal relations stem from a lack of parental guidance, poor home environments, and negative peer group influences. Life and social skills programs attempt to provide young offenders with an opportunity to develop appropriate cognitive skills and self-esteem, and to replace anger, hostility, and aggression with prosocial attitudes and behaviour.

Cognitive skills programming focuses on self-analysis, self-control, reasoning, critical thinking, and problem solving.

1. *Rational self-analysis*. The objective is to teach the offender to pay attention to and critically assess his or her own thinking.
2. *Self-control*. Involves teaching offenders to stop, think, and analyze the consequences of their behaviour before they act.
3. *Means/End reasoning*. The aim is to teach youth to think about appropriate prosocial means of satisfying their needs before they act.
4. *Critical thinking*. Requires teaching young offenders how to think logically, objectively, and rationally as opposed to externalizing blame and overgeneralizing or distorting facts and information.
5. *Interpersonal cognitive problem solving*. The objective is to teach youth how to analyze interpersonal problems, how to recognize how their own behaviour affects other people and why others respond to them as they do, and how to understand and consider other people's values, behaviour, and feelings. (Nova Scotia Department of Corrections, 1994)

Working through the development of cognitive skills provides an avenue for addressing more specific problems such as anger management, employment strategies, stress management, and decision making. **Life skills** programs focus on communication skills, family and peer relationships, sex education, and personal hygiene.

Substance Abuse

A first step in programming for many young offenders is to successfully work through a substance abuse program. These programs are designed to provide the resources, encouragement, and support that a young person will need to overcome physical, emotional, and/or psychological addictions to alcohol and/or drugs. Substance abuse programs are seen as a starting point for youth to learn how to overcome their addictions. An important part of substance abuse programming is to involve community support systems and groups (such as Narcotics Anonymous and Alcoholics Anonymous) so that these first steps can be followed through when young offenders are released into the community.

Recreation

Recreational facilities and programs, particularly those that feature pools and gymnasiums built into youth facilities, are viewed by some public interest groups as bringing a "holiday camp" atmosphere to youth corrections. Those responsible for administrating youth facilities and programs have a different view. They see recreational programs as an integral part of the rehabilitation process and emphasize the therapeutic benefits of recreation. Many facilities offer arts and crafts programs in addition to their sporting and physical fitness programs. All of these programs are designed to teach young offenders to make productive use of their leisure time and to assist youth in improving their interpersonal and communications skills and ability to work cooperatively. Other program objectives include providing youth with a sense of accomplishment and well-being, and giving them an opportunity to explore their individual talents and interests.

Some facilities offer wilderness survival programs. DARE in Northern Ontario and the Challenges Program in the South District of British Columbia are based entirely on an Outward Bound philosophy. These programs are designed to enhance self-awareness, foster a sense of self-reliance and trust, and help youth develop goal-setting and problem-solving abilities. Some programs, such as aquatics, are run as a vocational training program. Temporary absences are often granted to allow youth to attend and/or participate in community-based recreational activities.

Work Activities and Incentives

Daily work routines are another part of institutional programming. These programs are designed to meet institutional needs (e.g., cleaning the facility) and at the same time give young offenders opportunities to develop good work habits. Institutions usually offer an allowance program as a positive behavioural incentive. For example, under the Incentive Allowance Program, the Nova Scotia Department of Correctional Services pays one dollar per day to all youth in custodial facilities. The allowance, which is not automatic, but must be earned, is credited to a trust account held for each youth (Nova Scotia Department of Corrections, 1994).

Boot Camps

Two provincial governments (Ontario and Alberta) implemented **boot camps** for young offenders. Boot camp refers to facilities or programs that emphasize military-style discipline, physical conditioning, and teamwork in their attempts to

BOX 10.8

Treatment Program for Sex Offenders in Young Offender Institutions

Adolescents who commit sexual offences are believed to be caught in a cycle that is self-perpetuating. Adolescent sex offenders have often been victims of emotional, psychological, and sexual abuse and their offending behaviour is a repeat of the kinds of things that have been inflicted on them. It is believed that without intervention and therapy they will continue to compensate for what has been done to them by sexual offending and re-offending. (Ryan and Lane, 1991)

The Nova Scotia Youth Centre for 16- and 17-year-old male offenders offers an adolescent sex education and resocialization treatment program (ASERT). This is a 16-week program designed to follow the cycle of sexual assault and relapse prevention. The program involves group therapy, an abused-person recovery program, cognitive/social skills, health/sex education, one-to-one counselling, and family training.

The purpose of the program is to assist young offenders who have committed sexual offences. Assistance is in the form of (a) recognition, (b) comprehension, and (c) lessening the risk of offending again. Program objectives are

- to help young offenders who have committed sexual offences not to re-offend;

- to teach young offenders cognitive skills that will assist them in making decisions;

- to teach young offenders social skills that will enable them to function as a group;

- to set up a system of support in order to assist young offenders as they re-enter the family and the community; and

- to educate young offenders about relevant health/sex education topics.

Source: Nova Scotia Department of Justice, Corrections Branch (1994).

rehabilitate young offenders. People who believe that youth today lack discipline and respect for authority tend to be attracted to the idea of boot camps. For governments, boot camps offer a cheap alternative to incarceration. It would appear that these programs are being adopted for political, financial, and ideological reasons, not because of any demonstrated success.

In 1992, the U.S. Department of Justice implemented the first boot camp programs for juveniles—one in Cleveland, Ohio; one in Denver, Colorado; and one in Mobile, Alabama. The programs involved a three-month residential program for youth followed by six to nine months' community programming. The primary motivation for the camps was financial; the diversion of "less serious" youth offenders from institutions to boot camps provided a cheap solution to overcrowded juvenile institutions (Bourque et al., 1996).

Each of the three U.S. boot camps was evaluated over a two-year period. They were found to be cheaper (at an average per resident cost of $26,000 (U.S.) per year) than other types of institutions, but no more effective than probation or custody in reducing recidivism rates. In Cleveland, recidivism rates were actually higher for boot camp participants than for youth in state correctional facilities (Peterson, 1996). Importantly, boot camps produced cost savings only when compared with secure custody; a 90-day stay in boot camp cost as much as the same length of stay in open custody. Completion rates for the boot camp part of the program were very high (80 to 94 percent). In contrast, completion rates for community aftercare ranged from 26 to 49 percent. The major reason for youth not completing the community aftercare part of the program was arrest for a criminal offence (20 to 33 percent) (Bourque et al., 1996:5).

While evaluation of any program is a difficult undertaking and results are often difficult to interpret (Zhang, 1998), these evaluations revealed a number of problems with boot camps that are useful for future endeavours. These included community resistance to the location of the boot camps, aftercare facilities, and programs, and the fact that aftercare program locations were not always accessible by public transportation. Other problems included inappropriate placements, tensions between military-minded staff and staff operating rehabilitation programs, high staff burnout and turnover; an overly abrupt transition from boot camp structure to aftercare supervision, and lack of consistent philosophy between staff and between different phases of the program.

Peterson (1996) and Bourque et al. (1996) argue that a militaristic discipline and structure can be useful for some youth. Youth who need a highly structured and controlled environment can benefit if boot camp is combined with rehabilitative programs designed to meet their educational, psychological, and emotional needs. They provide the following recommendations with respect to future boot camp programs:

1. There should be community acceptance of boot camp, combined with a commitment and involvement in aftercare facilities and programs.

2. Given that recidivism rates were highest for youth who had been held in custody in the past and for those involved in the least serious offences, boot camps
   would be more successful for young people involved in moderately serious
   offences who have not been in custody in the past.

3. There should be careful screening and selection of staff at the beginning of the
   program, as well as ongoing staff training. Activities of staff in all phases of the
   program must be coordinated, as should program philosophy.

4. The transition between boot camp and aftercare should be less abrupt. At least
   in the beginning, aftercare should be more structured and disciplined and should
   also provide some form of required participation.

5. There should be coordination among the various community agencies involved
   in aftercare, as well as an understanding and commitment to the program philosophy and procedures of the boot camp aftercare.

6. All staff and all agency participants should have a clear understanding of the
   rationale for the various aspects and activities of the program (Peterson, 1996;
   Bourque et al., 1996:7–9).

Scared Straight

Scared Straight is another program with widespread public appeal. Numerous Scared
Straight programs were implemented throughout the United States in the late 1970s
and early 1980s, and many people are still intrigued by the idea. A well-known and
highly publicized Scared Straight program was implemented at the New Jersey
Rahway State Prison 20 years ago. The purpose of the program was to expose young
offenders to the "realities" of life in adult prisons by having them participate in confrontation sessions with adult male prisoners. Between 1976 and 1981, over 13,000
young offenders attended confrontation sessions at the Rahway State Prison, a max-
imum-security prison for men. According to the 1978 film documentary *Scared
Straight*, 90 percent of the youth who participated in the program did not become
involved in further delinquency (Bortner, 1988: 295–96).

Scared Straight is a disturbing film that documents how participating youth were subjected to intensive verbal abuse and threats of physical abuse and assault. Contrary to the
documentary's claims of success, later assessments of Scared Straight suggest that the program does not deter young people from delinquency. Finckenauer (1982:135) found that
41.3 percent of the juveniles who attended the Scared Straight sessions committed new
offences within six months after their visit to the prison; comparable juveniles who had
not attended or participated in these sessions had a recidivism rate of only 11.4 percent.

Programming Issues

Two important issues in youth corrections today concern the location of youth correctional institutions and the efficacy of treatment or rehabilitation programs. The

effect of institutional programming on Aboriginal youth and girls is an issue we will examine in the next chapter.

Location

Controversy over the location of youth facilities is sometimes based on the NIMBY (Not In My Back Yard) syndrome. While community residents or homeowners will sometimes object to a facility in their town or neighbourhood, community business leaders and politicians will often vie for custodial facilities because of the money and jobs they bring to a community. Correctional facilities contribute to local economies through the dollars that are spent on food and other maintenance costs for prisoners; more indirectly, they contribute through salaries paid to employees. In addition, some facilities provide community access to their pools and gymnasiums. Institutions may also organize projects to raise money for volunteer organizations within the community, thereby helping to ensure good public relations. Low security custodial facilities are often more contentious than high level security facilities because—with the exception of wilderness camps and facilities located in other rural settings—they are intended to be located in residential neighbourhoods.

Treatment and Rehabilitation

No discussion of correctional programming would be complete without a consideration of the issues associated with the very idea of **treatment** or **rehabilitation**. These concepts tend to be used interchangeably as both refer to the objectives of correctional programs. The term "treatment" is often used to refer to psychiatric and psychological programs that involve individual or group counselling or psychotherapy and whose purpose is to change a person's behaviour or attitudes. The term "rehabilitation" also refers to programs designed to affect change; these programs may involve educational and vocational training, as well as various types of life skills programming. Most treatment programs are geared toward a particular type of offender, as exemplified by sex offender treatment programs. Rehabilitation usually refers to a philosophical approach to correctional programming. The variety of programs through which it seeks to correct or change stands in contrast to programs that are based on the principles of retribution or incapacitation. With respect to both treatment and rehabilitation, the most important issue is whether programs are successful.

Does Treatment Work?

The question of whether or not treatment programs are effective is difficult to answer because most correctional programs have not been rigorously evaluated using a scientific testing model with control groups. Rather, programs tend to be evaluated by the people running them. Seldom is follow-up information available regarding how people have fared over time after leaving correctional programs. Most evaluation studies report relatively low success rates; it would appear that more people are not changed by correctional programming than are changed (Ekstedt and Griffiths, 1988).

One classic study published in the 1970s had a profound impact on attitudes and thinking about correctional programming. Robert Martinson (1974) examined all the research that had been done to evaluate treatment programs and concluded from the results that "nothing works." Not surprisingly, correctional workers and treatment providers took issue with this finding. Some treatment advocates scrutinized Martinson's work and concluded that he was wrong. When Martinson (1979) later re-examined his earlier work, his critics reported that he had retracted his "nothing works" conclusion (Gendreau and Ross, 1987). However, Doob and Brodeur (1989) argue that Martinson's critics had misrepresented both his original and later work. Although Martinson conceded in his re-examination that some programs have a modest success rate, his most significant finding—and one ignored by his critics—was that some programs had negative consequences for participants.

The important lesson to be learned from Martinson's findings is that we cannot assume that because our intentions are good, or because we want to help a person, that in the end the person will actually benefit from treatment. There are many reasons why programs may not have the positive effects that are intended. The most important of these is that an institutional setting may not be conducive to rehabilitation (Rothman, 1980). It may be unreasonable to expect that removing people from their communities and subjecting them to a variety of programs will somehow equip them for reintegration back into their communities. Equally important is the fact that short sentences afford limited time in which to affect change.

The treatment issue underscores the need for intervention before young people find themselves in conflict with the law. Given the general lack of success with treatment programs, many observers fear that institutions are serving as warehouses for young people rather than as agents of positive change.

BRIDGING THE GAP: AFTERCARE

A major stumbling block exists for young offenders and any correctional efforts at rehabilitation or reintegration when youth reach the end of their sentences. In a welfare/rehabilitation-oriented justice system with **indeterminate sentences**, as we had under the JDA, youth were not released into the community until it was decided they were ready for release. Under the YOA and the current system, with its **determinate sentences**, there is a predetermined time frame in which to work in a rehabilitative manner with youth. A short sentence may serve to disrupt school programming for youth who are in school, and may allow only a minimal exposure to institutional programs. Whatever positive behavioural/attitudinal changes may occur can be quickly undermined when youth return to their homes, neighbourhoods, friends, and "old" ways. Youth who made some progress in their programs may have nowhere to go on release, but back to the streets or families that have been a major source of their problems. In order to effect lasting change, both time and a continuation of programs and support services are required after young people are released from an institution or come to the end of their community sentence. The YCJA's requirement of community supervision after a term in custody is a step in the right direction toward aftercare, but the sentence ends regardless of the likelihood that a youth's needs for support and supervision may continue.

A lack of aftercare can be particularly damaging to the success rate of Outward Bound wilderness programs. These programs are intended to affect change in urban youth by removing them from their familiar urban settings. Chesney-Lind and Shelden (1992:197) report that, after five years, there was no difference in recidivism between a group of boys who participated in an Outward Bound program and a matched group who went to training schools.

While there is a general consensus on the need for aftercare, there is debate over which branch of government (if any) should pay for it. Some jurisdictions have developed aftercare programs, but others are less likely to do so, particularly in light of government cutbacks on social spending.

Aftercare Programs

Stop and Think, a program run by trained staff from the YWCA in the urban core of Halifax, involves working with youth in correctional facilities before they are released and then continuing the programming after release. A case management plan is developed for each youth, and programs are offered over a six-week period in the areas of sexuality, drugs, family relations, leisure education, self-analysis, motivation/goal setting, and the criminal justice system. Having completed the initial phase, youth enter an academic upgrading program for school preparation or literacy instruction, a career planning program, and a pre-employment training program that involves work placement. The program also includes supervision of youth who return to school or employment during and after custody. On completion of the program, youth are linked to support systems in the community, such as alcohol and drug counselling groups. Following its first year in operation, Stop and Think reported that two-thirds of the youth who successfully completed the program did not engage in further criminal activities. Despite the result, the provincial government failed to renew funding for the program.

Another program involving intensive supervision and aftercare is the Intensive Intervention Program. Designed by the Government of Newfoundland and Labrador, the program is a joint effort of the government's Child Welfare and Youth Corrections branches. It is grounded in an understanding of the characteristics of young offenders, the reasons for youth crime, and the current overuse of custody by the justice system. The overall goal of the Intensive Intervention Program is to reduce the number of committals to remand and custody, to encourage earlier release from custody, and to provide youth with residential arrangements other than custody. Other objectives include the following:

1. To reduce the incidence and seriousness of criminal offences.
2. To provide a more effective approach to the problems that contribute to criminal behaviour.
3. To improve planning regarding individual and family needs.
4. To provide opportunities for positive social and emotional development.
5. To increase the amount of support and services provided to families of young offenders.
6. To provide increased levels of supervision and structure on a day-to-day basis.
7. To have the courts recognize Intensive Intervention as a viable alternative to custody (Newfoundland and Labrador 1994:6).

In order to maximize short-term benefits, the program is aimed at youth considered to be at immediate risk of custody. Referrals to the program have been prioritized as follows:

- *First priority level.* Youth currently in custody or recently released from custody.
- *Second priority level.* Youth currently under community supervision.
- *Third priority level.* New cases entering youth court.
- *Fourth priority level.* Referrals from outside the justice system. This might include youth already involved in the child welfare system who are identified as at risk of offending or a sibling of a young offender already in serious conflict with the law.

The Intensive Intervention Program is based on the belief that the underlying causes of youth crime are rooted in family and personal circumstances—hence the family involvement in programming. The intervention program has seven components: family intervention and support, supervision of the young offender's activities, crisis planning, individual or group counselling, community integration, advocacy of and support for essential services and programs for youth and their families, and residential assistance and housing. In all cases, families are required to be a part of the intervention program. For young people who are not living with parents, or who are in need of a placement away from their families, residential accommodation is provided as part of the program; in these cases, parents are still involved in the program.

SUMMARY

The groundwork for the practice of institutionalizing Canadian youth separately from adults was laid in 1857 with the passage of the Act for Establishing Prisons for Young Offenders. The first institution was opened at Isle aux Noix on the Richelieu River in October 1858, and the second at Penetanguishene on Georgian Bay in August 1859. Both institutions were looked upon as "reformatories"—places offering education and industrial training. Within a decade, industrial training schools were opening across the country. With the YOA came a change in terminology. Youth institutions are now referred to as detention centres, youth correctional centres, or community-based residential facilities. The YCJA made youth corrections more like the adult system by adding conditional supervision to all custody sentences. The purpose of youth corrections under the YCJA is rehabilitation and reintegration in order to protect society.

Admissions to industrial training schools as a percentage of children convicted in juvenile court increased in the decades leading up to the Second World War, but declined thereafter. The introduction of the YOA reversed the declining trend. Between 1990 and 1995 alone, there was a 15 percent increase in the number of youth in secure custody and a 24 percent increase in the number of youth in open custody. By the end of the 1990s, custody rates were on the decline again in most provinces. The YCJA restrictions on the use of custody should continue this trend.

Some attribute the increase in the use of custody to a shift among judges to a "short, sharp, shock" style of sentencing. Others suggest that shorter sentences give youth more opportunity to commit crime, resulting in an increase in the number of repeat offenders, who are more likely than first-time offenders to receive custody sentences. Interprovincial variations in the use of custody stem from differences in levels of police activity and judicial discretion.

It costs anywhere from $80,000 to $120,000 per year to keep one young offender in custody. Actual costs vary depending on the facility's level of security. Overall, .2 percent of the Canadian youth population is currently serving a custodial sentence—an average daily count of 4,600.

There are three types of correctional programs: general, offence specific, and offender specific. Most institutions offer programming in the area of education, counselling, life skills, and recreation. Behaviour modification programs are most often used as a method of reinforcing program objectives. Some newer secure-custody facilities are designed to facilitate small-group living arrangements.

Boot camps are cheaper to maintain than secure-custody correctional institutions, but about the same as open-custody facilities in terms of cost. Boot camps have been found to be no more effective in reducing recidivism than probation or other forms of custody.

Treatment and rehabilitation have been contentious issues since the implementation of the YOA. Of particular concern is whether or not young people should have the right to refuse treatment and whether or not treatment programs are effective. One reason programs do not always have the intended positive effects is that institutional settings may not be conducive to rehabilitation.

More important than treatment or rehabilitation programs is the aftercare that occurs when youth are released into the community or finish serving their community sentences. Institutional programs such as boot camps often fail because there is no continuity of support and programming in the community.

CHAPTER 11

Perpetuating Social Injustice

CHAPTER OBJECTIVES

1. To document how and why correctional programs fail girls and Aboriginal youth.

2. To discuss why equal treatment perpetuates social injustice.

3. To discuss new ways of thinking about correctional programming for girls and Aboriginal youth.

4. To discuss examples of correctional programs designed specifically for girls and Aboriginal youth.

KEY TERMS

Reintegration	Minorities	Sentencing circles
Eurocentric	Social injustice	Reconciliation
Equality	Monolithic	
Reverse discrimination	Healing	

INTRODUCTION

Section 3(1)(b) of the YCJA establishes that the youth criminal justice system must be separate from the adult system and while accountability is an integral part of this system, s. 3(b)(ii) makes accountability contingent on "the greater dependency of young persons and their reduced level of maturity." In other words, they are not adults, and as such must be treated differently from adults in criminal justice matters. This is a fundamental principle of juvenile justice which implicitly acknowledges that justice would not be served if youth received the same justice as adults. The YOA did not acknowledge that in some ways the needs of Aboriginal youth and girls differed from the needs of Euro-Canadian boys, the dominant group in the juvenile justice system. Section 3(c)(iv) acknowledges that there are important sociohistorical, cultural, gender and other differences between young Canadians and instructs that within the youth justice system, all measures taken should "respect gender, ethnic, cultural and linguistic differences and respond to the needs of aboriginal young persons and of young persons with special requirements." The YCJA also recognizes that the special circumstances of Aboriginal youth should be acknowledged in decision making.

As we saw in earlier chapters, theories of youth crime and delinquency developed with boys in mind failed to explain girls' offences. The same is true of law, the administration of justice, and correctional programming. To the extent that these things are not developed with girls or Aboriginal youth in mind, justice is not served for many of these youth. For them, in particular, youth justice is an injustice. This does not mean that the youth justice system has a positive impact on all boys, but rather that we need to critically examine how the system affects girls and Aboriginal youth precisely because of their status in Canadian society. Professor Patricia Monture-OKanee, in her submission to the Royal Commission on Aboriginal Peoples, argued that the oppression of youth of all races will continue until the contradictions of colonialism, racism, and sexism are exposed (1993:118).

This chapter focuses on correctional programming and its impact on Aboriginal youth and girls. It discusses how corrections under the YOA failed to meet the needs of many youth from these groups and how we might rethink correctional responses to Aboriginal youth and girls. Examples of programs designed specifically for these groups are presented.

ABORIGINAL YOUNG OFFENDERS

Correctional Problems

One of the most comprehensive analyses of Aboriginal people and the justice system comes from a public inquiry undertaken by the Manitoba provincial government. In their report on the results of this inquiry, Associate Chief Justice A.C. Hamilton and Associate

Chief Judge C.M. Sinclair identify two correctional problems: (1) the overuse of custody for Aboriginal youth, and (2) inappropriate programming. They state that "the present system of dealing with Aboriginal young offenders, by removing them from their communities, warehousing them and then returning them to their communities, is both ineffective and inconsistent with the principles of the YOA" (Hamilton and Sinclair, 1991:566). A more recent Royal Commision on Aboriginal Peoples also identified difficulties in detaining Aboriginal youth separately from adults in remote locations (1996).

Overuse of custody means two things: Aboriginal youth are disproportionately sentenced to custody or held in remand, and they are disproportionately held in secure custody. High rates of pretrial detention are due in part to the criteria used by judges in determining whether to grant bail. These criteria include whether the youth has a job, or is going to school, has family stability, and whether or not the youth's parent(s) are employed, or drug or alcohol problems have been experienced by the youth or her or his family. All of these factors are directly linked to the economic and social marginality of Aboriginal peoples in Canadian society. For this reason, Hamilton and Sinclair (1991) argue that decision making based on such criteria constitutes discrimination against Aboriginal youth.

Interestingly. 718.2(e) of the Criminal Code, introduced in 1996, directs judges to consider alternatives to prison for aboriginal offenders. It states that

> all available sanctions other than imprisonment that are reasonable in the circumstances should be considered for all offenders, with particular attention to the circumstances of Aboriginal offenders.

What is interesting about this section of the Criminal Code is that it only applies to adults. In spite of numerous revisions to the YCJA and specific submissions recommending that such a provision be included in the YCJA, by the summer of 2001, no such clause had appeared in the YCJA, only a promise by the justice minister to introduce amendments (Roach and Rudin, 2000:381–383). This essentially amounts to a form of age discrimination. Aboriginal youth have not received the same standard of fairness from the courts as Aboriginal adults and may not unless they are charged with a serious or presumptive offence and are subject to an adult sentence. Hence, the over-representation of aboriginal youth in prisons, particularly for minor offences, not be addressed. A last-minute amendment to the YCJA by the senate in January 2002 requires similar considerations for Aboriginal youth.

A lack of young offender facilities and programs in Aboriginal communities has been cited as another reason for the overuse of custody for Aboriginal youth. In addition, because Aboriginal youth are most often sent from their communities to serve custody sentences, successful community **reintegration** is undermined. When Aboriginal youth return to their communities after serving their sentences, they do so as "outsiders"; this alienation from culture can contribute to an escalation of legal problems (Fisher and Janetti, 1996:248). Hamilton and Sinclair (1991) sum up the problem:

> The fact that existing correctional facilities are situated far from aboriginal communities is a problem. Successive governments have refused to consider establishing appropriate facilities for youth who reside in Northern Manitoba. Most young people from the north have no contact with their family or friends during their incarceration. Because of distances and cost, these young people do not have the opportunity to visit their homes and to prepare for their eventual release. This is a lesser problem for aboriginal families in the south, but even they have trouble visiting family members who are in custody. (566–568)

Hamilton and Sinclair also express concern about inappropriate programming for Aboriginal youth in custodial facilities. They are especially critical of Agazziz and the Winnipeg-based Manitoba Youth Centre (MYC). Although both institutions are used as open and secure custody, Hamilton and Sinclair suggest that there is little differentiation between custody levels and that the MYC in particular "is a jail" (1991:566). At the time of the inquiry, neither institution offered culturally relevant programming for Aboriginal youth, nor were Aboriginal youth counselled "by people from their own culture" (568).

Rethinking Correctional Responses to Aboriginal Youth

At the core of the correctional system's failure with respect to the treatment of many Aboriginal youth is a justice system whose philosophies and practices serve as a reflection of the wider **Eurocentric** society. Central to Liberal Canadian thinking about what is fair and just is the notion of **equality**—the belief that everyone should be treated equally and that to do otherwise is to discriminate. These arguments were heard in the House regarding s. 718.2(e). Both Reform members and the Bloc Québécois argued that Aboriginal offenders should be treated the same as non-Aboriginal offenders—to do otherwise is **reverse discrimination** (Roach and Rudin, 2000:379–380). Hence, the importance of the Supreme Court's interpretation in *Gladue*. It argued that

> the fact that a court is called upon to take into consideration the unique circumstances surrounding these different parties is not unfair to non-aboriginal people. Rather, the fundamental purpose of s.718.2(e) is to treat aboriginal offenders fairly by taking into account their difference.

Herein lies the problem with correctional responses to female and Aboriginal young offenders. To the extent that Canada fails to specifically acknowledge—through its laws and their administration, and through correctional policies and practices—that the life experiences of **minorities** differ from those of the dominant group, then **social injustice** is perpetuated, and particularly when peoples are oppressed, marginalized, and dispossessed. In the case of Aboriginal youth, injustice is also perpetuated when Canadian laws, social policy, and practices fail to recognize fundamental cultural differences that separate Aboriginal young offenders from the principles that form the basis of Canada's justice system.

This is not to suggest that Aboriginal culture is unified or **monolithic**. Aboriginal societies are culturally diverse in a variety of ways. Nonetheless, certain common aspects of Aboriginal culture and their clashes with the dominant Euro-Canadian legal system have been identified by a number of scholars and reports (see, for example, LaPrairie 1988, 1983; Law Reform Commission of Canada, 1991; Hamilton and Sinclair, 1991; Ross, 1992, 1994; Schissel, 1993; Crow, 1994; Goff, 1997). The most important commonality is Native spirituality—this lies at the heart of cultural differences that differentiate Aboriginal societies from non-Native society.

There are four particular aspects of Aboriginal cultural difference that are of significance to justice administration and correctional programming: a principle of not burdening others with one's problems, an orientation to the present and future rather than the past, a focus on the collective rather than the individual, and an emphasis on **healing** rather than punishment. As we have seen, therapy and counselling are common ingredients of correctional programs. They involve talking about one's problems and, in particular, dwelling on one's past experience and the behaviour that led to criminal charges and sanctions. According to Ross (1992) and others, these activities are culturally unacceptable to some Aboriginal peoples (see Box 11.1 and Box 11.2).

The two points of cultural difference—not wanting to burden others and an orientation to the present and future—are suggestive of reasons why Eurocentric programming may be unsuccessful with many Aboriginal offenders. The other two points of difference—a focus on the collective and an emphasis on healing—suggest ways in which correctional programming might be made more positive for some Aboriginal youth. As we will see in the next chapter, these ideas are beginning to infiltrate the justice system as a whole and are presenting serious challenges to retributive principles of justice.

Positive Directions in Programming for Aboriginal Youth

There is a general acceptance that programming for Aboriginal youth must be culturally appropriate if it is to be useful and effective rather than counterproductive. Policymakers have two choices, first, to create separate programming for Aboriginal youth within the existing system, or, second, to develop mechanisms that will allow the development of youth programming as part of a separate Aboriginal justice system. Governments are divided on this question.

The federal position, which was first presented by former Justice Minister Kim Campbell, rejected the notion of a separate Aboriginal justice system in favour of an incorporation of Aboriginal values into the broader legal system. The Liberal government under Jean Chrétien has recommended that Aboriginal peoples play a more central role in sentencing Aboriginal offenders and in developing alternatives to prison (Goff, 1997:84). In 1993, Manitoba adopted a system that would "combine Aboriginal methods of conflict resolution with rules and procedures of the existing system." Aboriginal judges and paralegals would handle summary convictions and youth cases. On the other hand,

BOX 11.1

Different Views on Therapeutic Intervention

On Burdening Others

A young Native offender was brought into court one day to be sentenced on a number of serious charges ... It was clear that this young man had many unresolved emotional problems, for he had been constantly in trouble with the law and had already been placed in a number of different institutions. That formed part of the court's dilemma, for we wanted to find a place that showed the greatest promise of involving him in some successful therapy. We spent a considerable amount of time talking about what he needed when he suddenly interrupted our discussion. He said that he'd been through different kinds of therapy already but that it didn't work. Therapy would fail, he said, not because he was embarrassed to talk about [his problems] but because it wasn't right to talk about them. It wasn't right to "burden" other people in that way ...

In the mainstream culture we are virtually bombarded with magazine articles, books and television talk shows telling us how to delve into our psyches, how to explore our deepest griefs and neuroses, how to talk about them, get them out in the open, share them, and so on. At times it seems as if the person who can't find a treatable neuroses deep within himself must for that reason alone be really neurotic!

The Native exhortation, however, seems to go in the opposite direction ... It forbids the burdening of others. It is almost as if speaking about your worries puts an obligation on others to both share and respond, an obligation difficult to meet, given the prohibition against offering advice in return.

Even the act of concentrating privately on your feelings seems to be discouraged. Such self-indulgence seems to be viewed as a further source of possible debilitation which poses a threat to the survival of the group.

I suspect that the number of psychiatric misdiagnoses must be staggering, for we cannot see their behaviour except through our own eyes, our own notions of propriety. To us, the person who refuses to dig deep within his psyche and then divulge all that he sees is someone with serious psychological problems. At the very least, he is someone who, we conclude, has no interest in coming to grips with his difficulties, no interest in trying to turn his life around ... Unable to see beyond our own ways we fail to see that there are others, and we draw negative conclusions about the "refusal" or "failure" or "inability" of other people to use our mode of behaviour.

Source: Ross (1992:32–34).

BOX 11.2

Different Views on Correctional Philosophy

On Orientation to the Present and Future

Could it be that we view people as being defined not by essential strength and goodness but by weakness and, if not outright malevolence, then at least indifference to others? Our judicial lectures and religious sermons seem to dwell on how hard we will have to work not to give in to our base instincts. Is that how we see ourselves, and each other?

... The Elders of Sandy Lake (and elsewhere) certainly do not speak from within that sort of perspective. At every step they tell each offender they meet with not about how hard he'll have to work to control his base self but instead how they are there to help him realize the goodness that is within him.

In short, the Elders seem to do their best to convince people that they are one step away from heaven instead of one step away from hell. They define their role not within anything remotely like the doctrine of original sin but within another, diametrically opposed doctrine which I will call the Doctrine of Original Sanctity ...

The freely chosen responses to criminal activity illustrate the differences which flow from adopting each of the two perspectives. If it is your conviction that people live one short step from hell, that it is more natural to sin than to do good, then your response as a judicial official will be to use terror to prevent the taking of that last step backward. You will be quick to threaten offenders with dire consequences should they "slide back" into their destructive ways. In fact, a Band Councillor once asked me directly why our courts came into his community when all we wanted to do was, in his words, "terrorize my people with jail and fines." If, by contrast, it is your conviction that people live one step away from heaven, you will be more likely to respond by coaxing them gently forward, by encouraging them to progress, to realize the goodness within them. The use of coercion, threats or punishment by those who would serve as guides to goodness would seem a denial of the very vision that inspires them. And that, I suggest, is how Elders see it.

Source: Ross (1992:168–69).

Saskatchewan has moved in the direction of a separate, parallel system by establishing a Justice-of-the-Peace Program on northern reserves (Goff, 1997:84). Nova Scotia has adopted a similar approach on some reserves by establishing Aboriginal **sentencing circles**. Alberta has developed "community sentencing panels" in a number of communities (Price and Dunnigan, 1995). The model of community members convening to determine appropriate action for convicted offenders will be discussed in the next chapter.

BOX 11.3

The Origins of Sentencing Circles in Sentencing Practice

The practice known as community peacemaking circles has its roots in innovative sentencing decisions. An early example involved a 1978 case heard in British Columbia by Judge Cunliffe Barnett ... The case involved a 14-year-old boy who committed armed robbery after a string of other offences. The boy was clearly becoming more threatening and dangerous, and there seemed little choice but to impose a prison sentence. However, community members felt the boy had much to contribute if his energies could be rechannelled, and knew that potential would be lost if he went to jail. So his uncle and other community leaders asked Judge Barnett to sentence the boy instead to a period on a remote island within the band's reserve (and where his uncle went regularly in his work, so the boy was not abandoned). Judge Barnett had long been dissatisfied with the legal system's limitations, and gladly ordered the recommended sentence ... [In the end] the community was right. The boy came back from his experience transformed and was never in trouble again. He became a leader in British Columbia's Aboriginal communities, and helped many other young persons stay out of trouble with the law (Cunliffe Barnett, 1996, as cited in Sharpe, 1998:37

...Territorial Court Judge Barry Stuart saw in 1981 that the system he represented was hindering local communities from solving the problems in their midst. So he began asking the community to help him find meaningful sentences that might encourage rehabilitation in the community. He sat with community members in a circle, following native custom, and the term "circle sentencing" stuck. The term gained official legal status in 1991 (Sharpe, 1998:37).

To be consistent with Aboriginal cultural values, correctional programming, as it is currently practised in the criminal justice system, may not be appropriate for many Aboriginal youth. Hamilton and Sinclair (1991) argue that

> young offenders should be left in their home communities, except in the most extreme situations. Efforts should be directed to determining the reason for their unacceptable conduct, and at helping the youth and the parents to deal with the reason for the offence and to avoid any repetition of it. The main objective should be to restore harmony in the community ... (566)

For those youth who may require more structure, Hamilton and Sinclair recommend open-custody homes that would allow them to find or keep employment and continue schooling. They also recommend the establishment of wilderness camps—particularly in Aboriginal communities—that would provide various programs such as education, recreation, counselling, and instruction in Aboriginal culture and life skills; work programming in these camps would be designed to provide skills training useful for future employment (Hamilton and Sinclair, 1991:569). For serious offenders who may require secure custody and some form of institutional programming, the following recommendations have been proposed:

1. a focus on dispute resolution, healing wounds, and restoring social harmony (Dickson-Gilmore, 1992);
2. an emphasis on spiritual ceremonies to assist in healing processes;
3. a recognition that people must be viewed as "participants in a large web of relationships" rather than as isolated individuals (Ross, 1994:262);
4. a central place for community elders as both teachers and healers; and
5. the hiring of facility or program staff who can speak Aboriginal languages (Hamilton and Sinclair, 1991:588–89).

Aboriginal Programs

Cultural Rediscovery

Rediscovery camp programs for Aboriginal youth have been developed in British Columbia. Fashioned along the lines of the Outward Bound philosophy, they are intended to reconnect Aboriginal youth with the land and their cultural roots. Sometimes used to introduce youth to traditional hunting and fishing, these programs usually involve the teaching of traditional skills, dances, legends, and songs, as well as the provision of environmental education (Fisher and Janetti, 1996:251–52). As a measure of their success, the Rediscovery International Foundation was established in 1985; its purpose is to expand the programs to Aboriginal communities around the world (Henley, 1989).

Education and Skills Training

The Ma Mawi Chi Itata Centre in Winnipeg is a community-based Aboriginal youth program designed to keep Aboriginal youth out of detention through the provision of bail supervision. In addition, the program encourages Aboriginal youth to further their education and skills training and provides assistance in finding jobs. Hamilton and Sinclair (1991:569) recommend that the Ma Mawi Chi Itata Centre program be expanded to provide supervision and educational employment programming in a day program in order to keep Aboriginal youth out of custodial facilities altogether.

Education and Healing

Also in Manitoba, the Interlake Reserves Tribal Council proposed that the Native Harmony and Restoration Centre at Pineimuta Place be used as a centre for developing healing and **reconciliation** programs. The programming at the centre would provide schooling and vocational training along with instruction in traditional tribal customs and values. The goal of the program would be to return people to their home communities "healed and reconciled." The centre's proximity to a number of Aboriginal communities would facilitate victim-offender reconciliation and make it possible for family members to live at the centre with the accused (Hamilton and Sinclair, 1991:579).

Community Healing

Ross (1994) compares three programs in Manitoba that have taken different approaches. The Hollow Water Reserve has chosen to modify the existing Western justice system in developing its Community Holistic Healing Program. This program for sex offenders is staffed by a team made up of volunteers from the community and officers with the RCMP. The process begins with disclosure of the abuse to the community team. Criminal charges are laid, but the offender has the option of participating in the healing program or proceeding with the charge in a court of law. In either case, the charge goes to court. However, if the offender agrees to participate in the healing program, the community team will, at sentencing, present to the judge a report detailing the person's progress in the healing program. The community team is in principle opposed to recommendations for prison sentences.

At Sandy Bay, a panel of elders from the community works with a judge or justice of the peace to determine an appropriate sentence for offenders. The sentences are most often community work or restitution. If the Aboriginal offender fails to fulfil the terms of the community sentence, the panel of elders "banishes" him or her to the judgment of the Western legal system.

In the Atawapiskat community, a panel of elders, independent of the justice system, hears cases and determines sentences. If an offender fails to abide by a community-imposed sentence, his or her case is turned over to the provincial court (Ross, 1994:249).

GIRLS AND CORRECTIONS

Correctional Problems

Like Aboriginal youth, girls are processed through a youth justice system that is designed to address the needs of Euro-Canadian boys and there are a disproportionate number of First Nations girls and young women of colour in the justice system (Chunn, 1998; Bourne, McCoy and Smith, 1998; Canadian Association of Elizabeth Fry Societies and Correctional Services of Canada, 1990; Leah, 1995; LaPrairie, 1995). More to the point, girls in the correctional system generally find themselves even housed with boys. There are a few exceptions, such as Vanier Centre in Ontario. As with women in the adult system, girls are "too few to count" (Adelberg and Currie, 1988) for governments to warrant facilities and programs that are appropriate for girls. As the Federal-Provincial-Territorial Task Force on Youth Justice states,

> to some extent, young female offenders suffer from the greater degree of social con-
> formity of their female peers—if they offend, their minority representation in the
> youth justice system inhibits the development of specialized programs, especially in
> respect of custody and alternatives of custody ... [S]imply put, there are numerous
> financial and practical obstacles to developing specialized programs, precisely because
> of small numbers. For example, it would be impractical, or prohibitively expensive, to
> develop a specialized alternative program for females in a small or mid-sized town.
> (Report, 1996:617)

The girls themselves are well aware of this injustice. As one young incarcerated women states, "women [girls] are placed in jail without any choice. They're forced to be with men [boys]. It doesn't make sense that there's ... only one [system] for youth" (Totten, 2000:47).

If we knew little about female crime and delinquency prior to the 1980s, we know even less about girls in correctional settings. We do know, from statistics reviewed in earlier chapters, that girls are more likely than boys to be confined for less serious offences, and at younger ages. There is also some evidence that girls are more likely than boys to be sentenced to custody for breach of probation or community service orders and administrative offences (Report, 1996:615). A survey of all incarcerated girls in British Columbia over an eighteen month period, from April 1998 to October 1999, found that almost one-half (44.8 percent) were serving time for breaches of court orders. Only one-quarter (27 percent) had committed a violent offence. Even more striking was that a one-year follow-up of the girls revealed that two-thirds had been returned to custody, 80 percent for non-violent offences and almost 80 percent of these (78.3 percent) were charged with administrative offences within three months of their release (Corrado, Odgers, and Cohen, 2000:196–198).

This tendency to use custody as a response to noncriminal behaviour is generally understood to stem from a paternalistic desire to protect girls for "their own good," as well as from chauvinistic attitudes about "bad girls" who need to be controlled. Corrado et al. (2000) also found this to be the case. One probation officer, for example, offers this rationale for charging a young woman with breaching her probation.

> ... I breach her for her safety ... her probation runs out in September and we are worried that she will become street entrenched ... what else can we do? ... she won't leave the streets, and she is in some very real and immediate danger. (203)

And again, the girls are aware of this. One 14 year old says, "I'm here because of drugs ... the judge wants me off the streets ... he thinks that I am a danger to myself" (Corrado et al. 2000:200). Hence the dilemma raised by Justice McCully in Box 11.4, is protecting girls from their own choices a violation of their constitutional rights? The two main issues regarding girls in the juvenile justice system then are paternalism and gender-appropriate correctional programming.

Rethinking Correctional Responses to Girls

It is now generally recognized that one of the most important programming needs for girls is to receive the skills training necessary for economic survival and independence. This need is a continuing one because girls are still being taught that their economic survival and well-being depends on marriage and motherhood (Chesney-Lind and Shelden, 1992). Surveys of poor youth in Hawaii exemplify this point. While pregnant and parenting teens were primarily concerned about medical care, finances, and child care, their social workers saw parenting classes, child care, family planning, and vocational training as most important for them (Yumori and Loos, 1985:16–17). A survey of girls in custody in Nova Scotia revealed that 15 percent of the respondents were mothers (Nova Scotia Department of Community Services, 1993:14) and in British Columbia a majority of girls in prison had been on their own from a very early age. Almost 90 percent of the girls in custody had been kicked out of their family home or had left of their own volition. Only 37 percent were living at home at the time of the offence that brought them to prison (Corrado et al. 2000:196).

Programming for girls needs to reflect a recognition that many young female offenders have been victims of abuse at the hands of those in positions of trust—parents, male relatives, friends, neighbours, and boyfriends. The Nova Scotia survey indicated that 63 percent of the girls in custody had been abused; one-third reported sexual abuse and another third physical abuse (Nova Scotia Department of Community Services, 1993:5). Unfortunately, these findings are fairly typical. In the British Columbia survey, 67 percent of the girls had been physically abused and 52 percent had been sexually abused (Corrado et al. 2000:199). Chesney-Lind and Shelden (1992) state that programming for girls should address a variety of needs,

---

BOX 11.4

A Judge's Point of View on Girls in Detention

Protective detention seems to be utilized more often for girls than for boys in the juvenile system, reflecting the paternalistic traditions of juvenile justice. Most juvenile court judges, including women, are unwilling to let girls be used, abused, and subjected to numerous indignities on the streets. While I share those concerns, and I personally abhor ingrained attitudes and traditional roles of our society which subject women in general to such atrocities, I cannot justify subjecting girls to yet another loss of personal control and liberty by placing them in secure correctional facilities to protect them from their own choices ... [A]lternatives must be developed to assist courts in releasing such girls to placements outside secure correctional settings. We are stretching the bounds of constitutional acceptance by using detention as a holding facility for promiscuous, prostituting, street-walking juvenile girls.

Source: McCully (1994:17).

---

including "dealing with the physical and sexual abuse in their lives (from parents, boyfriends, pimps, and others" (184–85). This is not to say that boys have not also experienced abuse, or that some boys don't need similar programs. Rather, because of the status of women and girls in Canadian society, the effectiveness of programming— particularly that which stresses economic independence—may depend on programs that address abuse issues.

A question arising from the small numbers of girls in corrections is whether to provide separate programming for girls or include girls in programming designed for boys. As suggested earlier, considerable resources would be required to provide separate facilities and separate programs for girls. Nonetheless, Hamilton and Sinclair (1991) maintain that designing programming and facilities for young offenders on the basis of economic factors is "abhorrent"; in their view, "young people should not be mistreated by the justice system because of a lack of resources" (567). A recent national survey of institutionalized girls indicated that they too see this as problematic and that it is a source of injustice. One young woman summarizes the problem when she poignantly states,

> the first time I was [institutionalized] with boys, they used to harass me and everything
> ... I was the only girl ... Like, (they said) I'll see you in your bedroom tonight, and stuff
> like that. *I stayed scared* (Totten, 2000:41) (italics mine).

As we will see in the next chapter, there are new initiatives that are capable of addressing specialized programming needs for individuals without incurring exorbitant or "new" costs.

Correctional Programming Effects

The first steps in developing appropriate gender programming are to recognize how girls and boys differ in terms of their needs and to acknowledge differences in the effects that specific programs have on boys and girls.

Chesney-Lind and Shelden (1992) review various types of treatment programs and make recommendations regarding their applicability to services and programs for female youth. One of their findings is that case work and group therapy undertaken by social workers has been less effective in reducing recidivism than some programs not run by juvenile justice agencies. Davidson and Redner (1988) have developed an intervention model that provides a trained "family worker" to work with a youth at risk and his or her family. This is similar to what is being proposed in Newfoundland in that the family worker would be involved in behavioural change programs, community resources development, and advocacy work in the schools and other institutions. Chesney-Lind and Shelden (1992) maintain that all case work approaches must be sensitive to "gender issues [as well as] culturally aware" (186).

Group counselling for girls must address problems associated with physical and sexual abuse. This type of therapy is likely best conducted in groups of girls with the same histories rather than in general groups or coed groups. Evaluation studies have found individual counselling to be the least effective type of intervention program (Lipsey, 1990). Especially problematic are programs based on psychotherapy models that draw upon Freudian development theory (Chesler, 1972; Hare-Mustin, 1983). Such programs tend to exhibit a "blame the victim" attitude and an overreliance on developmental theories based on boys' lives and experiences (see, for example, Piaget (1932) and Kohlberg (1964), discussed in Chapter 3). It is also problematic for girls when counsellors are male. One female youth states,

> ... there was not ... ever one woman psychologist for us. It was always these men psy-
> chologists ... When you are just coming off the street, and you're dealing with pimps
> and johns and stuff like that, the last person you want to talk to is some guy about it.
> (Totten, 2000:47)

Much family therapy and counselling is based on the notion that keeping families intact is all-important. This view is especially problematic with respect to boys and girls who have been physically and sexually abused by family members. In such cases, family therapy is not a positive approach to take unless the young person is provided with programs and services that allow her or him to live separately from the family (Herman, 1981; Chesney-Lind and Shelden, 1992:192–93).

Foster care is often used as a means of getting children out of their homes. All too often, though, children have been abused and/or neglected in these placements. Although group homes seem to be less problematic than foster homes, and are generally viewed as more desirable than institutional sentences, it is not clear that they are a positive experience for girls. A study of three group homes in Ohio found that girls in these placements had less success than boys. This is not to say that girls cannot benefit from an application of the group home concept, but rather that group home programming must be assessed for its appropriateness for girls. Similar problems can be seen with Outward Bound wilderness programs. The question here is whether or not counsellors and workers in these programs "rely on male models of physical challenge and risk taking as metaphors for success in life ... [and whether] the programs explicitly [are] enforcing traditional gender scripts" (Chesney-Lind and Shelden, 1992:198).

Academic, vocational, and work programs are particularly vital for girls. Research has shown that school failure is as likely to result in delinquency for girls as it is for boys. More important, recent studies have suggested that the problem is not so much the school failure as it is the link between problems at home and problems at school; in other words, for girls, it is problems at home that lead to school problems and subsequent delinquency (Chesney-Lind and Shelden, 1992:189).

Vocational programs are generally less successful than work programs in reducing delinquency. This is likely because vocational programs do not offer what many youth want and need most—real employment experience. The programming challenge for female youth is to provide nontraditional vocational and employment programs and to convince staff and potential employers that girls are as capable as boys when it comes to performing nontraditional jobs. In the survey of girls in Nova Scotia institutions cited earlier, respondents reported being offered vocational programming in a number of areas, including babysitting, woodworking, computers, hospitality management, cooking, and driver's education. Although the report which resulted from the survey recommends that girls be offered male programming such as work and life skills training, as well as some academic programs only accessible to male youth, no consideration is given to nontraditional vocational programming (Nova Scotia Department of Community Services, 1993).

Positive Directions in Programming for Girls

With respect to gender-appropriate programming, an important question is whether to provide coeducational programming or separate programming for boys and girls. There are strong arguments for both positions. Past experience indicates that the institutional experience and its programming has benefitted boys more than it has girls, which lends strong support to the argument for programming designed specifically for girls. On the other hand, it has been argued that coeducational programming better reflects everyday life, brings a "degree of normalcy" to institutional life, and improves social skills (Nova Scotia Department of Community Services, 1993:12). The comments of one girl in Totten's (2000) study gives cause for reflection on the benefits of exposure to "everyday life":

> ... Guys would be fighting over girls ... I would see guys whacking off ...they'd sit there and fart and spit .. Some guys would fight with girls ... It's a big time tease. I felt like people were fucking with my sexual emotions. (40)

A middle-of-the-road position might be to assess all programs in terms of their gender-appropriate nature and to offer some programs only for girls. One institution in Nova Scotia offers a program called So He Says He Loves You. This eight-week program addresses abuse survival and victimization and is restricted to girls, although a similar coed program is also offered. Other needs-specific programs might address such topics as pregnancy, parenting, and date rape.

A related issue is whether staff in female institutions should include men. According to the Nova Scotia report on female offenders, there should be male staff in female institutions because "it is unhealthy ... to foster a perception amongst the female residents that men are present only when physical containment or discipline is necessary" (Nova Scotia Department of Community Services, 1993:18). The report further recommends a partner approach whereby male staff would be paired with female work partners. It also recommends that female young offenders be given the right to request female doctors, psychologists, or psychiatrists (19). On the other hand, Faith (1993) points out that women and girls who have been physically and sexually abused do not feel comfortable with men who have institutionalized power over them. Rather, they are more likely to benefit from other women who have shared experiences and have "subsequently learned to forgive, honour and love themselves" (164). The girls themselves seem to agree:

> When you are involved in a restraint ... to have a bunch of men jump on you and drag you somewhere ... You see your friends being jumped by men and they're screaming ... (Totten, 2000:47)

And,

> When I was on my period I asked the [male] guards for something and they wouldn't get me anything, they told me to use toilet paper. (Totten, 2000:41)

Chesney-Lind and Shelden (1992) offer the following suggestions on how appropriate programming for girls might be designed:

1. A number of programs are now adopting family intervention or counselling strategies. These programs need to be very carefully thought out and assessed precisely because of the "gendered nature of family life and the unique problems that girls experience within family units."

2. Counselling programs are not found to be as effective with girls, but might be more productive if they are "sensitive to the abuse backgrounds of street youth," and are not used as a substitute for "educational and realistic employment programming."

3. Group counselling may be more effective with girls if it occurs outside institutional settings. Counselling within institutions has not been found as effective for either girls or boys. An important aspect of special programming for girls is "to address their victimization and their relationships with deviant street networks."

4. Where counselling is part of programming, it must be part of programs that address housing and employment needs as well as being "sensitive to issues such as sexual abuse, rape, date rape, violence in teenage sexual relationships."

5. Advocacy programs are far more critical for girls than generic counselling programs because many problems encountered by girls seem to be aggravated by "traditional juvenile justice practices."

6. Programs that provide independent living for young people in combination with ongoing 24-hour support services are an important component of successful programming for young people. With regard to some girls it is important to recognize that independent living programs also need to take into account their need to live with their children. Support in mothering and daycare is required along with skill and employment training to accompany independent living.

7. All programs should recognize that many young people, particularly girls, are unable to safely return to their homes and families (198–208).

New Correctional Programs for Girls

Chesney-Lind and Shelden (1992:200–7) discuss three innovative correctional programs for girls: community outreach, addictive love, and independent living. Some of these programs also include boys.

Community Outreach

The Children of the Night Program in Southern California, similar to many programs now operating in Canadian cities, offers services and assistance to homeless youth. It provides a 24-hour hotline, and a walk-in centre that offers medical aid. Clothing, crisis intervention, referrals for housing, drug counselling, and employment are also provided. Professional counselling is free and includes an outreach component—volunteer street workers who go into the community and offer "on-the-spot" counselling.

Addictive Love

The New Directions for Young Women Program in Seattle, Washington, is designed to address abusive relationships. It focuses on "addictive love," an important component of battering relationships. This type of relationship is potentially very destructive and puts women and girls at great risk of being abused. As NiCarthy (1983) notes, "if only one thing or person is of importance or gives the whole meaning to life, if the addicted woman will do anything to be allowed to have the beloved object, she places herself at his mercy" (122).

Independent Living

A particularly innovative program is CHILD, Inc. Initiated in the state of Delaware, CHILD provides an independent-living program and a foster-care program for youth being released from young offender institutions. It was designed as an alternative to institutionalization for girls (Dell'Olio and Jacobs, 1991). The foster-care aspect of this program provides specialized training and 24-hour support services for foster families working with high-risk boys and girls. The specialized training, combined with the high salaries paid to foster parents, contributes to the willingness of foster parents to provide homes for girls as well as young mothers and their children. Compared to 54 percent of the boys, only 37 percent of the girls in the foster-care program were rearrested. The corresponding rearrest rates for matched institutionalized youth were 65 percent for boys and 50 percent for girls (Dell'Olio and Jacobs, 1991:19).

SUMMARY

Aboriginal youth in the justice system are disproportionately held in remand, sentenced to custody, and placed in secure custody. Girls who find themselves in court are more likely than boys to be sentenced to custody for less serious offences, and at younger ages. Because Euro-Canadian boys constitute the majority of youth in the justice system and custodial institutions, programming is most often devised to meet their specific needs. For those Aboriginal youth who are sent from their communities to serve custody sentences, successful community reintegration is undermined. Governments have justified these inequities on the grounds that it would be too expensive to provide separate programming and facilities for Aboriginal youth and girls. The juvenile justice system thus perpetuates the inequities already experienced by these two groups of youth.

Central to the Canadian justice system is the notion that "equality" is the cornerstone of fairness and justice. However, treating people who are already oppressed and marginalized as equal before the law, or failing to recognize important aspects of cultural and social diversity, only serves to perpetuate social injustice. The Supreme Court of Canada has argued that treating Aboriginal peoples differently in the justice system does not constitute reverse discrimination. Nonetheless Aboriginal youth facing youth sentences may not be afforded the same special considerations in sentencing as are Aboriginal adults.

Four aspects of Aboriginal cultural difference are of significance to justice administration and correctional programming: a principle of not burdening others with one's problems, an orientation to the present and future rather than the past, a focus on the collective rather than the individual, and an emphasis on healing rather than punishment. Recommendations for achieving more positive correctional programming for Aboriginal youth include a focus on dispute resolution, an emphasis on spiritual ceremonies, a central role for community elders, and the hiring of staff who speak Aboriginal languages.

Girls are more likely than boys to be confined because of a paternalistic desire to protect them "for their own good" and because of chauvinistic attitudes about "bad girls" who need to be controlled. Girls are usually confined in male facilities and denied gender-appropriate programming because they are seen as too few in number to justify separate facilities.

Programs that tend to be least effective for girls include individual counselling, family therapy, and group counselling in institutions. Effective programming for girls will explicitly recognize the gendered nature of family life and the unique problems this creates for girls. It will also recognize that many female young offenders have been abused by parents, boyfriends, and others in positions of trust. More than anything, many girls require female staff and professionals as well as gendered programming that will provide employment and skills training, advocacy, and ongoing support systems. Independent-living programs that allow young mothers to live with their children are an example of innovative programming for girls.

CHAPTER 12

A Century after the Fact: Where Do We Go from Here?

CHAPTER OBJECTIVES

1. To discuss a holistic approach to youth issues.

2. To examine how reform proposals in law, structure, philosophy, and policy will affect youth justice in practice.

3. To outline new and positive directions in youth justice reform initiatives.

KEY TERMS

Holistic solutions
Law reform
Structural change
Prevention
Restorative justice

Peacemaking circles
Sentencing grid
Community-based
  intervention

Family conferences
Reintegrative shaming

INTRODUCTION

A century ago, Canadians thought poverty, neglect, and poor parenting were the sources of youth crime. The creation of the juvenile justice system was their solution. Family courts were the cornerstone of this system, and they were supported by probation, supervision, and institutions that would teach morals and trade skills to neglected and delinquent children. Today, many academics, policymakers, and members of the public still think that the family is the source of youth crime, and we still rely on probation and institutions to solve the problem. While some things have not changed, others have. An important structural change came with the YOA and the introduction of alternative measures, a change that is maintained and strengthened with the extrajudicial measures of the YCJA. And, as we saw in previous chapters, there have been some innovations in correctional programming. Unfortunately, the YCJA also introduced a structural change with provisions for adult sentences that serve to erode the fundamental precept of a juvenile justice system—its separateness from the adult system. Where we go from here in creating a system that responds positively to youth crime issues depends on how we use the wealth of theoretical and research knowledge that has been accumulated over the past century. If we are to move ahead in positive directions, we need to consider what we know about youth crime and our responses to it, and we need to learn some lessons from the past in order not to repeat mistakes.

RETHINKING JUVENILE JUSTICE

A theme that runs throughout this book is that youth crime is not as widespread as its presentation in the media would suggest. Another theme—and lesson we should have learned from the past—is that our system is failing our youth. As a society, we are failing to provide young people with the care and protection they need, and should be entitled to, in the family, in the schools, and in the justice system. One of the most important lessons to be learned from the past is that supervision and institutionalization are not the solutions to youth crime. These are piecemeal efforts that focus on individuals as the source of problems. For new directions, what is required are **holistic solutions**—a package that focuses on *all* aspects of youth issues, not just criminal activity.

   We also need to adopt a coordinated approach to youth problems. More specifically, change requires that we consider **law reform** and **structural change** of the sort that will combine child welfare and juvenile justice initiatives. While welfare and justice were once combined through the Juvenile Delinquents Act, the Young Offenders Act brought about their separation and the YCJA seems to be reuniting the two, but only for youth involved in minor offences. Perhaps it is time to revisit the vision of the

19th-century child savers and recognize once again that youth crime is merely one aspect of a larger social issue. In moving forward, we should recognize that child welfare and juvenile justice are also a public health problem and that children and youth are victims as well as victimizers (Krisberg and Austin, 1993:182).

A holistic approach to youth crime addresses "the whole child" and requires a coordination of the welfare, health, education, employment, and justice branches of government. It also requires that young people be included in and with community-developed proposals for solutions. It also demands that we think about doing something before the fact of crime as well as after. We need, in other words, to think in terms of **prevention** as well as appropriate justice system responses. One of the reasons reintegration after the fact of crime is so difficult is that many young people are economically and socially marginalized and not integrated as productive young members of society. Poverty, poor health, poor schooling, lack of employment opportunities, and poor family relationships place them on the periphery of mainstream Canadian society.

BOX 12.1

Youth Reflections on the Consequences of their Criminal Actions

On Theft

When I was caught stealing … I was going through many different emotions, embarrassed to be in front of everyone at a time like that. I kept thinking, God help me, I really didn't mean to do it … I was mad at myself for putting this situation on me. I hurt my family, friends and especially myself.

If anybody ever reads this essay, and is thinking about stealing, take my advice and don't bother. Just walk away … I hope I never get into this kind of trouble again because it is not very nice to be worried all the time about dealing with the police, especially when you are 14 years old.

On Assault

If anybody ever tells me or dares me to do something I know isn't right, I'm not going to do it and neither should anybody else because you could get arrested, you could be sent to a home away from your family, you could get charged, you could lose your friends and might have a criminal record and won't get a very good job because people would be afraid of you ... [T]he kid you beat up could have been a very good friend until you hurt him. I know now that I will never hurt anybody on purpose again ... [W]hen I think of how the boy must have felt, I really get upset at myself ... [N]obody likes to feel pain and somebody like me who gets beat up a lot should know that. Maybe I thought if I beat somebody else up instead of the other way around, it would make me feel tougher, but instead I felt stupid ... I just take it a day at a time and wait for him to forgive me for what I did to him. I am really sorry for what I did to him and his parents and wish that it would never have happened.

To Victims

I am writing to you to apologize about the incident which occurred in your home. I feel extremely bad for what I did. I wish I had thought about what I was doing. I hate carrying around this guilt. I guess it's part of my punishment. I hate thinking about what I did. The more I think about it, the worse I feel. I'm trying to put myself in your shoes. I now realize how both of you must have felt, having a stranger come into your home and take something belonging to you. If ever anybody were to do something like that to me, I would find it extremely hard to forgive them for what they did. Nothing gave me the right to take something not belonging to me. I would understand if you cant forgive me. But I hope one of these days, you will find it somewhere in your hearts to accept my apology.

I am very sorry for all the pain I have caused in your life. Please forgive me!!! I have learned my lesson in all of this. I have changed my life right around. I spent time with my grandparents, my family and I am hanging around with a very good crowd. I would like to give a special thanks to the Y.A.S. [Youth Alternative Society] for giving me a chance, and most of all GOD.

Source: Excerpts from youth letters, Youth Alternative Society files, Halifax/Dartmouth, Nova Scotia (n.d.).

In thinking about post-crime solutions, we need to consider not only corrections, but every aspect of the justice system. This involves thinking about the law itself, about the structure of the justice system, about the philosophy underlying both the law and institutional policy, and about how all of these things affect correctional programming. Whether thinking about law or programs, we need to be sensitive to gender, race, class background, culture, and the impact of our policies and procedures on female youth as well as Aboriginal and other minority youth.

Proposed solutions to youth problems and youth crime abound. The most recent is the YCJA, and a variety of other initiatives including **restorative justice** are in the design or early implementation stages. Some changes are more promising than others. Many proposals offer little to change the status quo (Rothman, 1980). Other proposals are regressive in that they threaten to worsen the situation rather than improve it. Proposals that are neutral or regressive ignore the lessons of the past. On the other hand, there are creative and positive proposals in that they have the potential to improve the lives of young people and in the process may reduce youth crime.

Positive and Negative Directions

Philosophy

Many new programs, policies, and proposals for law reform are based on a "get tough" philosophy that places emphasis on deterrence, punishment, or a "short, sharp, shock." The Scared Straight program and boot camps are based on this philosophy, as are electronic monitoring programs and "house" arrest. Just as programs based on rehabilitation models have been shown not to have created large-scale changes, so, too, programs based on a get-tough philosophy are not likely to produce any new or positive results. The entrenchment of "protection of society" as the primary objective of the youth justice system by the YCJA is clearly aligned with a get-tough philosophy that is a major point of contention among political parties and interest groups.

A new philosophy, which has its roots in Aboriginal cultures, is that of healing. According to Western views, at least since the 19th century, a person perpetrates a crime against a victim or "society" and therefore must be punished or rehabilitated. In keeping with a holistic approach, the healing philosophy recognizes that harm has taken place and attempts are made to restore a sense of balance between the victim, offender, and the community. All parties affected by the offence—including families and friends of both the accused and the victim—become involved in a healing process whose main objective is to restore balance and harmony to the lives of individuals and to the community as a whole.

Peacemaking circles are a key mechanism of healing philosophy. They are grounded in the belief that the responsibility for crime rests partly with the community and not solely with the offender and his or her family (Sharpe, 1998:37). There are three types of peacemaking circles currently in practice in Canada (mostly in Aboriginal communities): the healing circle, the sentencing circle, and the community peacemaking circle (Stuart, 1997:12). Healing circles bring people together to solve problems before criminal incidents occur and provide support for people already serving sentences. Sentencing circles bring justice officials and other concerned parties together to consider and make decisions about sentences (Sharpe, 1998:39). The community circle is used in reference to criminal offences and at many stages of the judicial process, from police apprehension to sentencing. It too involves the offender and victim, and their supporters, as well as court officials and other professionals, in a process that is open to the whole community (Sharpe, 1998:40–41). In lieu of a hierarchical structure, peacemaking circles are structured such that all participants "share equal responsibility for the process and its outcome ... [and] outcomes are decided by consensus" (Sharpe, 1998:40). An important challenge for peacemaking circles is to ensure that "vulnerable" individuals or groups are not subject to the tyranny of more powerful community individuals and groups (Griffiths and Hamilton, 1996:188).

A philosophy of healing is also reflected in restorative justice policies, an example of which has been implemented by the Genesee County Sheriff's Office in Batavia, New York (see Box 12.2), and is currently being considered for adoption by some provincial justice departments in Canada. Nova Scotia, for example, began implementing a restorative model of youth justice on a limited basis in 1999. Their slogan is "Crime HURTS ... Justice HEALS." Similarly, a fundamental belief of the Genesee Justice group is that crime is a peace issue.

> There are several sayings about time. "Time is of the essence." "Time is on your side." "There is a time and place for everything." "Timing is everything." These statements are also true when it comes to doing justice. When it comes to Restorative Justice there is a time for offenders and victims and the community to come together. There is a time for peace. There is a time for healing. There is a time to forgive and to ask for forgiveness. There is a time for internal and external reconciliation.
>
> Make time for making crime a peace issue. (Genesee Justice, 1995:48)

Canadian policymakers are beginning to recognize potential benefits of programs based on restorative justice principles. These benefits stem from the core values of restorative justice programs: equal support to all parties, equal power in decision making for all concerned parties, and the fostering of individuals' capacities for productive participation in the community. Sharpe (1998:93) cautions, however, that any potential benefits can be undermined by a number of factors, including net widening, shaming, professional domination, routinization, overreaching the skill base, and sustaining injustice:

- *Net widening*. Net widening can occur if programs based on restorative justice principles extend the scope of criminal justice rather than transform the administration of justice. Since it is intended to be a nonpunitive response, it should be used for minor offences, but also more serious offences. To do otherwise is to simply "add on" to the existing punitive system of justice.
- *Shaming*. While it is essential to convey a clear message to offenders that their criminal acts are not acceptable, this does not mean explicitly shaming a person (i.e., making her of him feel like a "bad" person). This is "disintegrative shaming,"

whereas the goal of restorative justice is "reintegrative shaming"(see discussion later in the chapter).

- *Professional domination.* Because of the training, skills, and experience of professionals, it is relatively easy for them to dominate conferencing or mediation sessions, or for them and others to think that the professional "knows best."
- *Routinization.* Because professionals will be involved in conflict resolution on a regular basis, the uniqueness of each case can be lost, making it difficult for professionals not to respond in routine ways.
- *Overreaching the skill base.* Some cases such as sexual assault or domestic violence will require specialized skills and training to avoid traumatizing victims further or putting them at additional risk.
- *Sustaining injustice.* Without careful planning and community involvement, restorative justice programs can easily perpetuate injustice by limiting programs to minor or first-time offenders; restricting programs to only some areas or to dominant languages; excluding people who are not "easy" to serve, such as women with children who need babysitting services, people without money for transportation to sessions, etc.; using language, vocabulary, and practices that are familiar or comfortable only to some participants; drawing program staff or participants from privileged groups only; focusing on the law-breaking act and ignoring the injustices and circumstances that may have contributed to it (Sharpe, 1998:94–98).

Still, others are not so trusting and optimistic about the potential benefits of programs based on healing and restorative justice principles. Some Aboriginal women insist that Aboriginal men, including Chiefs and Elders, must be held accountable in the Canadian justice system for the harms they have perpetrated on women and children. Leaders of the Native Women's Association of Canada have also expressed reservations about First Nations self-government, fearing that women and children in First Nations communities would not be protected if local chiefs and national leaders do not address violence in their communities (Faith, 1993:200–201; Hamilton & Sinclair, 1991:485). In Nova Scotia, women's groups successfully lobbied to have sexual offences excluded from the restorative justice process. These cases are all processed through the courts.

Law Reform

In spite of the series of "get tough" revisions to the YOA, and the belief by many that the YOA was a very good piece of legislation, albeit an underutilized one (Canadian Criminal Justice Association, n.d.), some interest groups (particularly law-and-order groups) continued to lobby for change. A major concern was the minimum and maxim age of jurisdiction for the youth justice system. The law and order lobby wanted the minimum age lowered to 10 and the maximum age lowered to 16. The federal

BOX 12.2

Genesee Justice: Victim, Offender, and Community Reconciliation

Traditional Adversary Approach	Restorative Approach
1. Community/Victim hurt by offender	1. Same
2. Government charges offender	2. Same
3. Government vs. offender	3. Community/Victim healing begins
4. Pretrial and trial proceedings take place	4. Victim/People assess Diversion/Affirmative Agreement
5. Time factor—6–15 months on average	5. Victim/Offender/People pursue restorative approach
6. Defendant guilty	6. Active community participation in Diversion/Affirmative Agreement
7. Defendant sentenced to prison or jail or community supervision	7. Time factor—time used as a positive means for offender to earn opportunity
	8. Victim and offender healing continues
	9. If successful, community-based sentence; reconciliation already achieved; community reintegration established

Problems

- Expensive
- Fosters overcrowding
- Divides rather than brings together
- Burdens heavy court calendar

Solutions

- Less costly
- Reduces overcrowding tendencies
- Focus on reintegration and restoration
- Frees up court calendar for more serious cases

Source: Adapted from Genesee Justice (1995:12).

government responded in the YCJA by maintaining the same minimum and maximum ages, but lowering the age of liability for adult sentences for presumptive and "serious" offences to 14. While some groups see "adult sentences for adult crimes" as a significant erosion of the fundamental principle of youth justice and a significant step away from the International Covenant on the Rights of Children (see Appendix, Chapter 2) (Canadian Criminal Justice Association, n.d.), the lobbying continues for legislators to lower the age yet again.

Another area of concern for the law and order lobby is the guarantee of privacy for young offenders. Through the short lifespan of the YOA, lobby efforts continued to demand publication of the names of young offenders. The YCJA has maintained the privacy of youth except for youth liable to adult sentences. This too is a regressive change. There is no reason to believe that there are any positive outcomes from such a practice. It is not likely to deter youth from crime, particularly if they are already marginalized, nor is it likely to make parents more accountable. As the Canadian Criminal Justice Association sees it, "parents who care for their children are [already] devastated when [their children] engage in crime, and those who have given up on their children, could not care less" (n.d.:8).

Other proposals have centred on this issue of parental responsibility. The federal Reform Party (and Alliance) pressed for federal legislation to make parents responsible for their children's crimes; Manitoba has already introduced parental-responsibility legislation, and Ontario Attorney General Charles Harnick asked the federal government to consider enacting national legislation that would address the issue. Other groups in favour of such legislation include Victims of Violence and the Canadian Police Association (Groundswell Against Youth Crime, 1996; Manitoba Parents, 1997:A26). The YCJA addresses these concerns by encouraging greater parental involvement in the justice process and holding parents responsible for their children's legal fees.

There are two major problems with proposed parental-responsibility laws. First, there is no guarantee that they will solve the problems of youth crime. There are limits to the ability of law to solve problems (Bala et al., 1994). Indeed, as we know from the short history of the YOA, the introduction of new laws is as likely to create new problems as it is to solve old ones. More important, these proposed laws ignore the reality that many youth in trouble with the law are oppressed, neglected, or victimized by their families. Fining or otherwise penalizing parents for their children's behaviours will very likely intensify these negative conditions for youth or further penalize those already dispossessed. Further, it places additional hardships on families already struggling with limited financial resources, particularly single parent families headed by women.

Parental-responsibility law is not new. The JDA contained such provisions, but they were seldom used. There is no reason to expect that justice personnel today would be any more inclined to apply parental-responsibility laws than their counterparts were in the past. As for lowering the minimum and maximum ages, all this is likely to accomplish is to lower the average age of offenders in both the youth and adult justice systems. Such a result will almost certainly lead to concerns about the wisdom of having very young people subject to the full force of law and begin the cycle of juvenile justice again. Past experience demonstrates that neither the lowering of ages nor parental-responsibility provisions offer solutions to youth crime.

More positive, creative law reforms would entrench healing and restorative justice as the primary principles underlying the juvenile justice system. Such reforms would also encourage or require a cooperative/collaborative approach involving the justice system and the social, health, and educational branches of government. Interestingly, in the federal government's law reform process (discussed in Chapter 2) the task force recommended a coordination of youth services (1996:630–31), but the standing committee failed to do so. Nonetheless, some provinces are already coordinating services. Ontario and British Columbia combine education and social services, while the Yukon combines health and human resources. Quebec had never abandoned a coordinated approach to youth issues. A more specific positive reform would be to remove administrative offenders from custody. A more appropriate response to youth who breach probation, fail to appear in court, escape, or run from detention is intensive supervision combined with appropriate programming. Such an approach would be cheaper than prison, would remove a considerable number of girls from custody, and would offer a better chance of yielding productive results for young people (Schwartz, 1994:179–80). Unfortunately, while the YCJA has entrenched restorative justice principles, it has subordinated these to crime control principles and has failed to advocate a coordinated and integrated approach to the administration of youth justice.

Policy

Victims' rights proposals for more prisons and longer prison terms are clearly regressive in that we know prisons neither deter nor produce desired rehabilitative effects. In introducing her reform package in May 1998, then-Minister of Justice Anne McLellan stated, "we must get past this uni-dimensional, myopic focus on the [idea] that somehow protection of society is achieved if we put more young offenders in jail for longer—that is simply not true, and it is a simplistic uninformed view" (cited in McIlroy, 1998b).

This view notwithstanding, the YCJA will send more youth to prison and more into the adult system. Recognizing that some youth will go to prison for "the protection of society," positive policy reforms would provide a mechanism for separating youth by age and offence such that older, "hard core" youth would be separated from younger, more impressionable youth. In addition, some youth require protection from victimization in prison from staff and offenders.

Victims' rights proposals can be problematic if they are tied to get-tough, law-and-order philosophies. With respect to increasing victim involvement in the justice process, the Aboriginal and restorative justice models whereby victims become part of a healing process would be a step in the right direction. In thinking about victim's rights, it is also important to remember that youth (including young offenders) are more likely than adults to be victims of crime. This fact underscores the need to have youth more actively involved in planning responses to youth issues, and for the justice system to acknowledge that young offenders are not just victimizers.

One policy that is being implemented for adults and young offenders in some U.S. jurisdictions is the **sentencing grid** (Castellano, 1986). A sentencing grid serves to reduce variability in sentencing by determining sentences on the basis of offence and prior record. While this type of sentencing does reduce variability, given the current political climate it would also likely result in substantial increases in the use of custody without increasing social protection (Bala, 1994:262).

More positive policies would be those seeking to establish cooperation, healing, and restoration as essential components of their mission statements. What is needed in policy is a commitment on the part of government to short-term crisis intervention and long-term support for youth and their families. An example of this type of policy initiative comes from the U.S. Department of Justice's SafeFutures project. Under the program, funding has been committed (for a five-year period) to six communities for the purpose of reducing youth violence and delinquency. These communities—which include neighbourhoods in Boston, Seattle, and St. Louis, two counties in California, and the Gros Ventre and Assiniboine Tribal Reservation community in Montana—were selected because of their demonstrated commitment to collaborative partnerships between local public and private community agencies. The funds from SafeFutures are intended to provide for services and needs in the areas of "family strengthening, after-school activities, mentoring, treatment alternatives for juvenile female offenders, mental health services, day treatment, and graduated sanctions for serious, violent, and chronic offenders" (Kracke, 1996). Intensive Intervention, the Newfoundland-based program described in Chapter 10, is another example of this type of program. It, however, focuses more on youth already in the justice system, largely because it lacks the funding required for more intensive preventative programming. Part of the federal government proposals for implementing the Youth Criminal Justice Act include funding for community-based crime prevention initiatives (McIlroy, 1998a). The extent to which government will institutionalize these funds rather than leave community agencies to raise their own funds after a few years remains to be seen.

Structural Change

There are those who would like to see the juvenile justice system abolished altogether. Indeed, as mentioned earlier, some of the YOA reforms moved in this direction and aspects of the YCJA continue this trend. Knowing what we do about the history of youth crime in Canada, this is clearly a regressive step. It was precisely the processing of youth in the adult system that led to reforms and proposals for a separate justice system for juveniles 100 years ago.

More positive structural changes would permit cooperative arrangements between coordinated welfare, health, education, and justice agencies and young people, crime victims, and communities. Youth Justice Committees are a step in this direction and, they could be enhanced with more financial support from government to allow an expansion toward a larger role in diversion and intervention. Youth justice committees could offer a positive alternative to punitive court judgments if they operated on the principles of healing, restoration, and community peacemaking circles (Sharpe, 1998:38).

A number of communities in the United States have effected change by having youth play active roles in the administration of juvenile justice. In Clovis, New Mexico, teens hear young offender cases as members of a jury and make recommendations regarding disposition and sentence. In Danville, California, teens serve as lawyers, clerks, and jurors on young offender cases. In Odessa, Texas, a teen court was developed to process alcohol offences, shoplifting, vandalism, and other minor offences. Teens here act as jurors and make recommendations for sentencing. If the young offender successfully completes his or her sentence, charges are dismissed and there is no criminal record. In all of these cases, youth recidivism has been reduced (Bynum and Thompson, 1992:466).

James Hackler (1991) recommends the adoption of a "social service judge." Like the judges found in the French youth justice system, this judge would play a less adversarial role. He or she would also be empowered to investigate alternatives (e.g., social services) to a legal or correctional response.

In 1993, a House of Commons committee stated, "our collective response to crime must shift to crime prevention efforts that reduce opportunities and focus increasingly on at risk young people and on the underlying social and economic factors associated with crime and criminality" (Standing Committee, 1993:2). Positive structural change will have to reflect a recognition that much crime occurs because young people are marginalized within, if not alienated from, their communities. New programs must focus on involving youth in both the community and the justice system so that they develop a sense of being genuine stakeholders. Of course, the definition of "community involvement" is open to debate. Does it mean bringing professional social workers into community activities? Or does it mean empowering community members to take responsibility for, and control of, their own problems? Empowerment of community members is required if such initiatives as Youth Justice Committees and community sentencing circles are to offer alternatives to punishment.

Programming for Change

Martinson's (1974) "nothing works" critique paved the way for a philosophy of radical nonintervention (Schur, 1973) in the 1970s. Diversion policies and programs were largely the result of this philosophy. It is a philosophy more recently reflected in Lundman's (1993) evaluation and analysis of delinquency, crime prevention, and treatment programs. With regard to minor property offenders, Lundman concludes that treatment is ineffective. He further argues that community restoration projects such as the Cambridge-Summerville Youth Study and the Chicago Area Project in the 1950s were a wasted effort and that "leaving these juveniles alone most certainly would have been just as effective and far less expensive" (Lundman, 1993:244). Nonintervention is certainly a good idea if it means keeping most young people out of prisons or institutions. However, a nonintervention policy that means leaving people to their own resources will essentially penalize those who lack personal, family, or financial resources.

Judge Maurice Cohill, Jr., a Chief Judge of the U.S. District Court in Pennsylvania, suggests that successful programming for young offenders requires first that we "look in their eyes"; upon doing this, we will discover that "these kids and their families (such as they are) are people" who need and deserve more than to be ignored (nonintervention) or to be locked up (crime control) (Cohill, 1991:129).

Correctional Programming

The most productive approach to programming is to think in terms of preventing crime before it happens. With respect to young people who break the law in serious ways, we need to think about what type of correctional programming will be most effective in reducing their chances of further involvement in crime. The most positive trend in programming has to do with intervention. This does not mean intervention designed to "rehabilitate" by means of intrusive therapy and counselling, but rather intervention that provides advocacy, support, skills training, and resources appropriate to a young offender's needs. In most cases, this will likely mean food, clothing, shelter, and meaningful employment. Successful programming must begin by providing what youth require for independent living. Beyond this, programming should include academic education, vocational training, community support for independent living, substance abuse programs, physical and sexual abuse survivor programs, family conflict resolution, and other support services (Schwartz, 1991:136).

In order for correctional programming to be positive, it must take us beyond "more of the same." Positive programming will

1. move away from punishing antisocial behaviour and toward rewarding prosocial behaviour (Gendreau et al., 1993);
2. provide what young people need, not what suits administrative or professional agendas (Doob and Brodeur, 1989);
3. listen to and learn from what youth have to say about their daily lives, needs, and experiences with the justice system and correctional programming (Barron, 2000:94–100);
4. recognize the socioeconomic and political basis of youth issues and not target individuals as failures or "criminals";

5. bring youth into the community by fostering their active involvement;
6. involve the community in programming and develop cooperative/collaborative models that treat the whole child (Krisberg and Austin, 1993); and, above all,
7. have a positive goal. The purpose of programs should be to benefit youth and the community. If the only goal is to deter individuals from crime, reduce recidivism, or lower crime rates, programs are bound to appear as failures (Cohen, 1985).

Prevention Programs

Community Intervention Recent theorizing about the causes of delinquency and evaluation research on what does and does not work in preventing delinquency suggests the need for holistic, long-term community-based intervention programs. Programs such as SafeFutures and Intensive Intervention, discussed earlier, are examples. While cautioning that what works for boys may not work for girls, Yoshikawa (1994) identifies some of the common elements of successful intervention programs:

1. Delinquency is not viewed as a single problem but rather as one with multiple causes and risks.
2. Interventions deal with a broad range of issues associated with a young offender's family, school, and friends.
3. Delinquency prevention is not a primary goal. Rather service and assistance for disadvantaged groups—urban low-income families—is a priority. The major objective is to improve children's life chances in the long term.
4. Intervention is long term—two to five years. A long-term commitment to improving life chances is required rather than efforts to prevent crime or delinquency.
5. The most effective intervention begins within the first five years of a child's life (Yoshikawa, 1994:44).

In the 1980s, two smaller-scale intervention programs were implemented in Montreal. These programs focused on school and family intervention and involved boys in kindergarten who were "disruptive" (Tremblay et al., 1991a) or "violent" (Tremblay et al., 1991b). In the case of the disruptive boys, intervention involved working with parents, social skills training, and teaching the boys to be critical of television. The intervention program lasted two years. The program for the violent boys also ran two years and was similar in that it involved social skills training for the boys and parenting training for parents. Both studies involved comparisons with matched control groups. Two years after treatment, the disruptive boys were less involved in fighting and theft than the control group. The violent boys were followed up at ages 9 through 12, considerably beyond the time of the intervention. Researchers report that the boys involved in the intervention program were less likely than the control group to be involved in fights either at home or away from home. They were also less likely to be involved in stealing from the home. In addition, rates of school failure and institutionalization were lower for the treated violent boys and they were less likely to have behavioural and academic performance problems.

Family Conferencing   Some programs accomplish prevention goals by shifting from an adversarial approach to a focus on restoration and healing. One such program is the Family Youth Conference, which has been adopted in New Zealand and some juris-dictions in Australia. Although the emphasis on restoration and healing recalls the community peacemaking circle, conferencing is more structured in format and has a slightly different philosophical orientation. Family conferences seek to "shame" the act and reintegrate the young offender into the community through a process called rein-tegrative shaming (Braithwaite and Mugford, 1994). In New Zealand, the family group conference has almost entirely replaced the youth court system. The only youth now going through youth court are those charged with murder or manslaughter; all other youth participate in a family conference. In these conferences, the accused and the victim, together with their relatives, meet with police and government officials to work out and agree on a suitable punishment or response to the offence. The conference is held in a place that is agreeable to all parties. Both the victim and the accused have a veto right over decisions, which ensures that outcomes will ultimately be acceptable to all parties. Young people also have the right to maintain their innocence or insist on a trial in court; if they do so, a family group conference is required beforehand so that efforts can still be made to divert the case from court.

The New Zealand system has succeeded in reducing the court caseloads. Only 20 percent of young offenders now go to court, while the crime rate for young offenders has declined by 29 percent over the past six years (Tyler, 1995:A21). The system also seems to have been effective in addressing aspects of crime and justice that are either hidden or absent in the formal justice system, such as feelings of aggrievement on the part of victims or offenders (Braithwaite and Mugford, 1994). The RCMP began adopting family conferencing in some jurisdictions by the mid-1990s as a means of diverting minor youth offences from its caseload and other similar "community justice forums" have followed (Smandych, 2001:193). The YCJA recommends family confer-encing as an appropriate extrajudicial measure so we should expect its use to increase across the country. A cautionary lesson to be learned from past experience, however, is that good intentions and benevolent ideas do not always translate into positive results (Rothman, 1980). There is a danger that community justice forums or family confer-ences may be viewed as a "quick fix" to youth justice reforms (Jackson, 1999). In iso-lation from other legal, structural, policy, and philosophical changes, conferencing alone is not likely to have a noticeable effect on youth crime.

Community Initiatives Some communities have taken the initiative to develop their own programs. One community-developed program is the Youth Empowerment Success Program in Whitehorse. Early on in the program's development, community youth were asked what help they needed. It was their idea to have a resource centre rather than a drop-in centre. They wanted a place where they could participate in literacy programs and programs designed to prepare them for jobs. At the centre, youth are also involved in social activities and have organized a "talking circle" and their own youth magazine (Bula, 1996:B2).

Some very creative initiatives have been undertaken to address specific crime problems. A school in Calgary, for example, addresses vandalism problems through a creative use of music. The idea was to make spaces that were most at risk of being vandalized less attractive to potential vandals. The school board decided to make these spaces less attractive by piping in "obscure operas, operettas and classical music." As the school board director explains, "We're making an atmosphere less conducive to people who wouldn't normally enjoy this type of music" (Different Note, 1996:C1). The school board reports that this technique has been highly successful in reducing vandalism and that it is an inexpensive solution to a costly problem.

Schissel (1997) envisions more fundamental school changes and argues that schools need to develop alternative models of teaching, learning, and curriculum to better serve youth who are marginal and "relatively disadvantaged." He cites the Princess Alexandria School and the Joe Duquette High School in Saskatoon and the St. Peter's College Alternative High School in Muenster, Saskatchewan, as examples of schools that are committed to "egalitarian and nonauthoritarian" teaching. All of these schools reject standardized inflexible curricula, offer a nonjudgmental and nonpunitive learning environment, reject discipline and punishment, and focus on empowering students in an atmosphere of mutual respect (Schissel, 1997:120–26). School boards also need to adapt to the needs of street youth by providing educational programs that address their remedial needs and acknowledge the realities of street life in physical spaces that are accessible (Schissel and Fedec, 1999:52).

Safe Homes for Kids No matter what other programs are implemented, residential facilities must be provided for abused and neglected children and for young people who, for whatever reason, are not able to live with their families. These alternate living arrangements must not follow a corrections model, as they have in the past. Children should not be locked in solitary confinement for misbehaving or acting out. Rather, homes for children and youth must provide a more caring, supportive environment. Runaway and homeless youth are the most victimized, the most vulnerable, and the most in need of protection, not only from the street, but also from uncaring, insensitive adult authority figures (Whitbeck et al., 2001:1200–202). Young people (and their

BOX 12.3

Family Conferences

A conference follows a basic sequence. The offender gives his/her version of events, followed by the version of events as perceived by the offender's supporters. Then it is the turn of the victim to provide what usually proves a startlingly different version. The victim's supporters also make a contribution here and these too often include surprising revelations. In a number of cases, for instance, evidence of feuds between individuals, families or larger groups have been revealed. An apparently straightforward assault may, in fact, be only one small part of a much larger picture. Differences stretching to over a decade have been revealed and addressed in the conferences. A long process of reconciliation has then been initiated.

More generally, conferences address problems that the old system ignored, problems such as the anger and resentment of victims and the possibility of compensation. The issue of compensation has proved less problematic than anticipated. In many cases, return of goods and monetary compensation for damage has been readily undertaken. In the event of damage to buildings, supervised repair work as agreed to by both parties has normally been arranged. Interestingly, nearly all young offenders offer to impose tougher demands on themselves than the victims consider appropriate. Offenders, wishing to emphasize their willingness to earn respect, argue the case for a tougher penalty. The group's collective compromise is rarely considered unfair.

Conferences also offer better solutions to those problems which the old system did address, problems such as need to disapprove of the offense and to discourage further offending.

Source: Moore and O'Connell (1994).

families, where appropriate) need to be protected from the life-threatening dangers of the streets through the provision of shelter, independent-living arrangements, street workers, and outreach agencies (Webber, 1991:239–48; Schissel and Fedec, 1999:51–52). We also need to implement in all provinces child advocacy programs such as Ontario's Office of Child and Family Services Advocacy Program that have the resources and mandate to investigate youth complaints of institutional abuse.

CONCLUSIONS

I have tried throughout this book to present young offenders as people just like "us"—people with hopes and dreams, wants and needs. What distinguishes many young offenders from youth who are not in conflict with the law is that they have been denied the skills and resources that would allow them to realize their hopes and dreams. Today, child poverty is a public issue, but its consequences are not fully appreciated in public discourse. Child poverty means more than not enough food on the table. It often means the denial of a rewarding and fulfilling childhood. It means children growing into adolescence and young adulthood without crucial skills and resources. It means, for many, not having their basic needs met, whether by their families or schools and other social institutions, including government.

In addition, many young offenders have been abused or neglected by the people who are supposed to love and cherish them, and this has nothing to do with class background. In the words of Supreme Court Justice Joseph Kennedy, most young people get into trouble because "nobody gave a damn about them after the novelty [of having children] wore off" (Smith, 1997). For all these young people, injustice is perpetuated when we, as a society, fail to create responses that recognize the reality of their abuse and neglect.

The fact that not all young people who have lived in poverty, or who have suffered abuse or neglect, resort to crime is not a justification for perpetuating injustice. A productive response to this fact is to acknowledge that there are indeed many more young people who are marginalized, impoverished, and victimized than we see in the youth justice system. Many of these youth are coping alone. Far too many are living on the streets; some are on the caseloads of child welfare agencies, in foster homes and institutions. Many are likely to be found in psychiatric hospitals and drug treatment facilities (Schwartz, 1989; Faith, 1993). According to Schwartz (1989), "hospitals are rapidly becoming the new jails for middle class and upper middle class kids" (135–36).

This "hidden dimension" merely underscores the need for a holistic, community-based approach to youth issues. Such an approach would focus on the real needs of youth and reduce their marginalization by making them active and productive stakeholders within their communities. In thinking about how to respond positively to youth crime, we might begin by considering the words of the National Council of Juvenile Family Court Judges:

> The way in which a society treats its children—its young people—says something about the future of a society, its beliefs, and the viability of its beliefs. The way in which a society treats children who deviate from the beliefs of that society, when those beliefs are expressed in laws, says something about its humanity, its morality, its resilience, its ability to be self-correcting. (cited in Cohill, 1991:125)

SUMMARY

An important lesson to be learned from the history of juvenile justice in Canada is that supervision and control by means of probation and institutionalization have not solved youth crime problems. In order to achieve genuine reform in the juvenile justice system, we need to stop recycling programs that have failed in the past and start thinking about holistic solutions. Holistic solutions to youth crime focus on all aspects of youth issues, not just criminal activity; they also involve a coordinated approach that addresses the "whole child" and require us to think in terms of prevention as well as appropriate justice system responses.

Positive and effective juvenile justice reform requires changes in philosophy, law, structure, institutional and social policy, and correctional programming. New philosophical approaches to justice involve healing and restorative justice rather than punishment and retribution. Positive policy and programming reforms focus on prevention and community-based intervention.

Recent negative reform proposals include parental-responsibility legislation, sentencing grids, house arrest, electronic monitoring, lowering the minimum age of youth criminal responsibility, "presumptive" transfers to the adult justice system, publication of young offenders' names, and establishing "protection of society" as the main goal of the youth justice system.

Positive structural changes would combine the efforts of welfare, health, education, and justice agencies in responding to youth issues. A holistic, community-based approach to youth issues would serve to reduce youth alienation and marginalization by providing young people with opportunities to be active and productive stakeholders within their communities.

Glossary

(Numbers in parentheses refer to the chapter(s) containing the main discussion of the term.)

Administrative offences - YOA, Youth Criminal Justice Act, and Criminal Code offences that are not behaviours generally considered criminal in the same manner as are property crimes or crimes against the person. They are charges that result from people failing to comply with justice system directives. Examples are failure to comply with probation orders, failure to appear in court, escape from custody. (3)

Aftercare - any range of programming and services provided after a young person has completed his or her court-imposed sentence or extrajudicial-measures contract. (10)

Aggregated - statistics on crime and other social behaviour are deemed aggregated when they are grouped into categories that make it impossible to match individuals on other characteristics. For example, UCR statistics for types of index crime, as they are published for public consumption, could not be rearranged to find out the age of individuals responsible for particular types of crimes or who their victims were. (3)

Alternative measures - defined under the Young Offenders Act as "taking no measures or taking measures other than judicial proceedings" with young persons in conflict with the law. In practice it involves a variety of programs such as mediation designed to prevent future crime and divert youth from the courts. The concept has been broadened under the Youth Criminal Justice Act to that of "extrajudicial measures." (8)

Androcentric - refers to male centered ideas, concepts or theories. Often terms are presented as neutral (**androgynous** [Ch. 6]), not referring to any particular sex, such as "gangs," when in fact, the research being discussed has been based on all male samples. Hence, the knowledge is about male gangs but is presented in a so-called generic manner—gangs. (7)

Anomie - a term coined by Emile Durkheim referring to a state of "normlessness" or no rules, and used by Robert Merton to develop a general theory of deviance. It is sometimes used by criminologists to classify "strain" theories of crime and delinquency. (5)

Antisocial personality - a term used by psychologists to classify people with traits of impulsivity, insensitivity to their own pain or the pain of others, and a lack of guilt or remorse. It is similar to the personality type referred to as "sociopath" or "psychopath." (5)

Behaviourism - a branch of psychology based on a set of behavioural principles first developed by B.F. Skinner. (5)

Bifurcated - divided into two parts. The youth justice system, for example, is bifurcated by the YCJA's formalization of diversion for more youth while at the same time requiring prison terms and adult sentences for more youth. In other words, the system will be a very different experience for youth depending on which "half" she or he falls into. (2)

Birth cohorts - a group of people born in the same time period. For example, all children born in 1974 would constitute a birth cohort and could be used as a basis for longitudinal research. (4)

Boot camps - a term borrowed from military training programs for recruits and used in criminology and corrections to refer to a place of confinement where programming follows a militaristic regime with emphasis on physical conditioning, discipline, and punishment and sometimes it also involves educational and life-skills programming. (10)

Care ethic - a term created by Merry Morash and Meda Chesney-Lind to refer to an ethic or moral standard that is based on nurturing attitudes of caring for the welfare and well-being of others. Hence, moral judgments based on this ethic will produce very different outcomes than those based on a legal ethic. The classic dilemma of a man stealing medicine for his dying wife is a case in point. Is he guilty of the crime of theft or not guilty of anything because he acted out of a desire to care for his dying wife? (6)

Child savers - a term used by Anthony Platt to refer to 19th-century North American middle-class reformers who believed that delinquency was the product of bad environments and that the state should act like a parent to "save" children from these environments, even if that meant removing them from their parents' homes and placing them in an institution. This group was instrumental in the creation of a separate system of justice for juveniles to protect children and youth from the full force of criminal law and the negative influences of adult criminal offenders. (2)

Chivalry hypothesis - a belief that crime rates are lower for women and girls because people, including the police, are less likely to view their behaviour as criminal. Hence, it is the belief that victims are less likely to complain to police when the assailant is a female person and/or police are less likely to charge women and girls even when there is a complainant. (6)

Classical school - in criminology this refers to the school of thought that assumes people are rational, intelligent beings who exercise free will in choosing criminal behaviour. The works of Cesare Beccaria are an 18th-century example. (5)

Clearance rates - refers to statistics that indicate the rate at which police process criminal incidents as charged offences. This rate is often ascertained by comparing persons charged to persons not charged or by comparing victimization survey results on crimes reported to police to police charges for similar offences during the same time. (3)

Cognitive - having to do with mental processes and how we develop knowledge about and understandings of ourselves and the world around us. (5)

Cognitive skills - in the field of corrections this refers to the ability of people to develop cognitive solutions to their problems rather than react emotionally. Many correctional programs, for example, are designed to get youth to think about why they got into trouble with the law and how they might have avoided such an outcome in the past and how they will avoid problems in the future. These programs focus on self-analysis, self-control, reasoning, critical thinking, and problem-solving. (10)

Community-based intervention - stepping into a person's life at the level of the community, with programs designed to prevent criminal activity either through supervision or providing supportive, rehabilitative or educational services, rather than having the person become involved in the justice system. (12)

Concept - a general or abstract term that refers to a class or group of more specific terms. Disaster, for example, is a concept that refers to any number of specific terms such as tornado, flood, hurricane, etc. Similarly, crime, as a concept, refers to any number of specific behaviours. (3, 5)

Conditional supervision - an order for supervision, usually directed by the court, which requires a person to abide by particular conditions set by the court. A common such condition is to attend drug or alcohol rehabilitation programs. (10)

Conditioned - in behaviourist theory this refers to behaviours that have been patterned to repeat or stop by a regime of rewards or punishments. (5)

Consensus theory - in criminology this refers to that group of theories that are based on a fundamental assumption that people are essentially law-abiding. As such, the central theoretical task of this group of theories is to explain why some people break the law. (5)

Control theory - in contrast to consensus theory, this group of theories is premised on an assumption that people will operate on the basis of self-interest unless constrained. The theoretical task for these theories is to explain why some people's behaviour is constrained and others are not. (5)

Correctional programming - refers to a range of structured activities within a correctional system that are designed to rehabilitate, educate, train, and otherwise facilitate a person's reintegration into society. This can include programs within the prison system or programs that are part of a system of community based programming. (10)

Corrections - in criminology, refers to that part of the justice system that is responsible for carrying out the sentence of the court and/or alternative and extrajudicial measures. (10)

Crime control - a theoretical model representing a particular set of beliefs and philosophies about crime and justice. A central premise in this set of beliefs is that criminal behaviour is motivated by free will and, as such, needs to be punished in order to deter further crime. The fundamental purpose of the justice system is to protect the public through laws and practices that are considered "tough enough" to deter crime. (2)

Crime index - refers to a Statistics Canada categorization scheme for classifying police crime statistics. All crimes reported by the police are classified into three index crimes: property, violent, and other. (3)

Criminal event - is a concept from routine activities theory suggesting that crime is more than a behaviour that violates the law, that it is an event involving a motivated offender, a suitable target or targets, and the absence of controls. (6)

Criminalization - the process whereby a person comes to be officially and/or publicly known as a "criminal"—a person with a police record, or prison record, or criminal conviction. Sometimes, groups of people such as black youth or street youth become criminalized through media coverage of crime issues and all individuals from these groups are perceived to be "criminal suspects." (6)

Criminalize - when a person has gone through a criminalization process, she or he is said to have been "criminalized." It is a term that differentiates between referring to a person as a "criminal" and acknowledging that criminal activity is but one aspect of a person's behaviour. (7)

Critical - in criminology, refers to the group of theories that begins with the assumption that structures of power and oppression are the source of crime—more specifically, race, class, gender and to some extent age structures in society. (6)

Cycle of juvenile justice - a phrase used by T. Bernard to refer to the tendency of North American juvenile justice systems to engage in a never ending cycle of reform from a system based on lenient (or harsh) punishments to harsh (or lenient) punishment and then the cycle begins again. (2)

Decarceration - the practice, begun in the 1970s, of removing individuals from institutional settings in favour of community facilities and programs. (6)

Decontextualize - to remove something from its context. Of concern in criminology is the misinformation promoted about crime by media stories, which, by their nature, decontextualize crime. (1)

Delinquent subculture - a concept in early criminology theory used to explain youth crime. It is generally viewed as a subculture with values, norms ,and behavioural expectations that deviate from the dominant culture. (5)

Demographic - the basic or vital statistics of a group, usually factors such as age, sex, ethnicity, marital status. (1)

Denied adulthood - refers to the notion that youth, because of their legal dependency in Western society, are prevented from attaining the things that many adults take for granted such as the right to a job, the right to make decisions about their own lives, the right to express their views, etc. (1)

Determinate sentences - sentences with a stated minimum and maximum term. (10)

Deterrence - a contemporary theory from the Classical school which holds that certain and speedy punishment will discourage or prevent future criminal behaviour both in a general and specific manner. (9)

Development theoryv as applied to an understanding of youth crime, it is theory that focuses on states of development and posits inadequate development or failure to progress to higher states in explaining criminal and delinquent behaviour. Piaget's theory of moral development is an example. (5)

Discourse - how things are talked about and understood both orally and in written form, including formal talk such as theory, professional talk such as reports, books, and media as well as conversation. (1)

Discretion - The decision making power that police and other criminal justice personnel such as judges and crown prosecutors have to make decisions without legal requirements. Under the YCJA, for example, discretional power was extended to police to keep youth out of the justice system but restricted regarding "presumptive" offences. (8)

Diversion - a practice based on a philosophy that justice, rehabilitation, and reintegration are better served by keeping most people out of the formal justice system. This practice has been formalized under the Youth Criminal Justice Act, for example, in that police are urged to use more discretion with the minor offences of young offenders to not charge and/or to use alternatives to formal justice processing for youth offences. (8)

Empirical - knowledge that is based on observation, experience, or experiment rather than theory or philosophy. For example, to say "that is an empirical question" is to suggest the question can only be answered by putting it to the test of systematic investigation. It cannot be answered through theoretical or logical reasoning. (3, 5)

Equality - a liberal based philosophy or belief that all is or should be the same. (11)

Ethnicity - a concept that refers to a person's group of origin, where origin is usually thought of in terms of geographical place and/or elements of culture such as language, style of dress, behavioural patterns, and social customs. It is a socially constructed category that is often imposed upon people or groups and a subjective concept in that individuals may or may not identify with a particular ethnic group. (4)

Ethnographic method - a particular method of research involving richly detailed descriptions and classifications of a group of people or behaviours. (4)

Etiological - having to do with cause or origins. A theory of causation or origin. (7)

Eugenics - a branch of science based on a belief in genetic differences between groups that result in superior and inferior strains of people. These beliefs are usually based on sex and class distinctions or socially constructed racial categories. (5)

Eurocentric - beliefs, attitudes, theories, philosophies, and practices that are specific to European experience, thinking, and world views. (11)

Extrajudicial measures - created and defined by Part II of the Youth Criminal Justice Act. The concept reinforces and expands to Young Offenders Act concept "alternative measures" and refers to processing accused young offenders by means other than through the youth or adult justice system. (8)

Extralegal - refers to factors affecting criminal or youth justice processing that are outside the jurisdiction of law. There are no legal requirements, for example, that a youth must have two parents living at home to avoid a prison sentence. Yet, there is research evidence suggesting that youth from broken homes tend to get different sentences for the same offences than other youth. (8)

Facts - in everyday terms it is usually meant as something that is true. In a scientific sense, a fact is something that has been established through the research process. (5)

Family conferences - in youth justice this refers to an alternative to processing youth through the justice system. Used extensively in New Zealand it involves a meeting of an accused youth, her or his family and supporters, with the victim, her or his family and supporters to work out a resolution to the reality of an offence having taken place. (12)

Family structure - refers to how families are structured in terms of living arrangements. The traditional western way of thinking about families is as "nuclear," two parents living with their own juvenile children. In reality families have many different structures. There are, for example, single parents with children, elderly parents with married children, blended families with two married adults living with their own juvenile children as well as children from previous marriages, to name a few. (7)

Field research - a research method where research is conducted outside of a laboratory in the setting where the behaviour of interest is occurring. (3)

First Nations - a term used and preferred by many Aboriginal tribal groups in North America to refer to themselves. Compared to the term Aboriginal, First Nations has clear political connotations because it defines a group in historically specific terms. It means the first people who were a nation, that is, a people with legal and political standing. (4)

Gender - refers to the socially constructed aspects of a person's biological sex. (4)

Gendered expectations - what is expected of a person because of their biological sex characteristics. (9)

Guardian - in legal terms this refers to a person who has been given legal authority over and responsibility for another person. With children and youth, parents automatically have this authority but the state can designate another person as a legal guardian. In either case, a principle of Western law is that guardians will act in the best interest of those in their care. (9)

Healing - a new principle of justice based on Aboriginal philosophy that posits crime as an injury that requires healing, not only of severed relations between an offender and victim but also for their families and the larger community. (11)

High-risk youth - a concept generally used in a crime prevention context to refer to youth with characteristics and/or living circumstances that are known to be criminogenic or crime producing. (8)

Holistic solutions - a theory and philosophy that posits there are no simple solutions to issues or problems. When applied to children and youth, it suggests that we cannot solve a behavioural problem by looking at only the "criminal child," rather, effective solutions require looking at and addressing the needs of the whole child. (12)

Human ecology - a branch of behavioural science that examines the relationship between people and their physical environment. (5)

Incapacitation - basically means to deprive a person. Hence, to put someone in prison is to incapacitate her or him in an absolute and fundamental manner. (9)

Indeterminate sentences - refers to sentences that are not absolute or definite. It is not clear with an indefinite sentence how long the person will be under control of the state. Parole, for example, turns a prison sentence for a definite time period into something indefinite. It is not clear how long a person will spend in prison because he or she might get out on parole. (10)

Indictable - in the Canadian Criminal Code this refers to offences that are of a serious nature and the maximum sentence is never less than two years. (2)

Intensive rehabilitative custody and supervision - a term created by the Youth Criminal Justice Act which refers to a sentence of the court whereby a youth must serve a custody term in a facility designated as a rehabilitation institution. (10)

Interactional theory - a theory proposed by Thornberry et al. (1991), which posits that relationships between delinquent behaviour and other variables are not unidirectional but rather bidirectional. So, for example, weak bonds with parents can impact on delinquent behaviour but engaging in delinquent behaviour can also impact on a young persons relationship with her or his parents. (6)

Interim release - Criminal Code provisions that allow an arrested person to be released, under specific conditions, into the community while waiting for their court appearance dates. Commonly referred to as "bail." (9)

Justice - a concept having a variety of meanings depending on a person's philosophy and world view. In this text, it refers to a philosophy and orientation to criminal justice that posits the rule of law as the primary means of achieving a "just" justice system. (2)

Juvenile delinquent - a concept popularized in the Victorian era referring to children and youth who were considered problematic for a variety of reasons. The term was legally defined by the Juvenile

Delinquents Act in 1908. It ceased to be a legal category with the passage of the Young Offenders Act in 1984. (1)

Juvenile justice system - a system of laws, policies, and practices designed under the guiding philosophy that children and youth, because of their age and maturity, should not be subject to the law in the same manner as adults. The first such system was created in Canada in 1908 with the passage of the Juvenile Delinquents Act. All legislative reforms since that time have maintained this principle. (1)

Law reform - the processes by which laws are changed. (12)

Legal advocate - generally considered to be the appropriate role for a defence lawyer to assume in relation to their client. That is, one where the lawyer is expected to make decisions and act in the best interests of his or her client particularly with regard to ensuring the client has every legal advantage possible. (9)

Liberation hypothesis - A belief that women and girls behaviour is becoming more like that of men and boys because of the women's liberation movement. This idea is sometimes used to explain women and girls' assumed increased involvement in violent behaviour. (6)

Lifecourse developmental theory - a theory positing that children undergo a succession of role and status changes as they grow older. (7)

Life skills - the behavioural, emotional, and philosophical skill set that one acquires that enables functioning in the social world. For example, communication, interpersonal relationships, sexual relationships, personal maintenance, etc. (10)

Limited accountability - a fundamental principle of any juvenile justice system because it posits that because of their age and level of maturity children and youth should not be held responsible or be considered or made accountable for their behaviour in the same manner as are adults. Children and youth are held accountable by the justice system, but in a limited manner compared to adults. (2)

Longitudinal studies - a type of research method that collects data on a group of people over a number of time periods rather than at only one point in their lives. (4)

Marginalized - in criminology this refers to a condition where people are excluded from mainstream society. This exclusion can be economic, social, cultural, political, or all four. An accused person in the justice system who does not speak either of the two official languages in Canada, French or English, will be marginalized because he or she will be unable to participate actively in her or his processing through the system. (1)

Mediation - a form of conflict resolution that involves a third party, usually a person with professional skills, to assist two parties with a grievance or unresolved matter to reach a mutually agreeable solution to the conflict. (8)

Meta-analysis - a type of analysis where the unit of analysis is the research results from other research reports. (7)

Microscopic - in sociology and criminology this is a theoretical approach that focuses on individuals and behaviour rather than social structures. (7)

Minorities - those groups of people who do not form the political, social, and/or cultural majority. These are social positions not determined by numerical minority or majority but rather an exclusion based on social, political, cultural and/or economic marginality. (11)

Misogyny - generally refers to a hatred of women. Hence, beliefs, behaviours, practices, attitudes, among many other things, are said to be misogynous when they support, promote, reinforce, or promulgate a hatred of women.

Modified justice - refers to a particular model of criminal or juvenile justice that is not in strict adherence to a pure justice philosophy but is modified somewhat by other justice principles such as crime control or welfare. (2)

Monolithic - a single uniform undifferentiated idea or structure. (11)

Moral panic - a term coined by Stanley Cohen that refers to situations where people, groups, circumstances, or events are defined and perceived to be a threat to security and public order. (1)

Near group - a concept used by Lewis Yablonsky to refer to criminal groups whose structure and activities are not as organized and stable as other groups more commonly referred to as "gangs." (7)

Net widening - a tendency for policies seemingly designed to reduce the number of people in the justice system to inadvertently result in more people under state control. (8)

Official crime - offender and offence data based on information collected by justice agencies such as police, courts and correctional institutions for their administrative purposes. Official crime statistics are usually based on aggregate records. (1)

Open custody - a form of youth custody designated by the Young Offenders Act as requiring less restrictions on movement both within and outside the institution than is required for secure custody. (10)

Oppression - occurs when a person or entire group of people are unable to exercise the rights and freedoms that others have because of sheer physical force from the oppressor or structural arrangements such as laws and political policies that prevent them from doing so. (6)

Parens patriae - a doctrine based on English common law which gives the state the power to take on a guardian or parenting role for children. It was a fundamental principle of youth justice in Canada under the Juvenile Delinquents Act. (2)

Patriarchy - a set of structural relations that creates, reinforces, and perpetuates male dominance and control over women. (6)

Peacemaking circle - in criminology this concept refers to an alternative method of resolving criminal conflicts. It comes from the healing philosophy of aboriginal peoples and can involve the healing circle, the sentencing circle, or the community peacemaking circle. (12)

Penitentiary - a 19th-century term for prisons based on a philosophy of penitence, punishment to atone for wrongs. (1)

Positivist - an 18th-century philosophical, theoretical, and methodological perspective positing that only that which is observable through the scientific method is knowable. (5)

Postmodernists - those who reject or challenge all that has been considered modern—Western theory, art, philosophy, and knowledge that developed from the 19th and 20th centuries. (5)

Power - from a Weberian point of view this refers to the ability of a person or group to force others to do what they wish. (6)

Power-control theory - a theory formulated by John Hagan et al. that attempts to explain class and gender differences in delinquency by the structure of family relations, whether egalitarian or patriarchal. (6)

Presumptive offence - defined by the Youth Criminal Justice Act as a serious violent offence, or any other violent offence for which an adult would be liable to a prison sentence of more than two years. (9)

Pretrial detention - holding an accused person in a prison or detention facility prior to their court appearance, trial, or while awaiting sentence. Sometimes also referred to as "remand." (9)

Prevention - in criminology this generally refers to policies and programs designed to curtail certain behaviours such as crime prevention programs. (12)

Primary data - information gathered through research directly from the source of interest, the original source. (1)

Principle of least possible interference - an important principle of juvenile justice first introduced in Canada through the Young Offenders Act. It is the idea that whatever action is taken should have the least impact on a youth's freedom. (8)

Probation - a sentence of the court that involves supervision in the community and set conditions that must be adhered to if the person is to remain in the community. First introduced in Canada through the Juvenile Delinquents Act in 1908. (2)

Proportionality principle - a principle of justice from the classical school, which maintains that sentences should be proportional to the offence that a person is guilty of committing. (9)

Public issues - a sociological concept from C. Wright Mills that refers to matters of public concern that become debated in a variety of forums and that usually involve demands for action or change.

Race - a socially constructed category based on beliefs about biological differences between groups of people that have no basis in scientific evidence. (4)

Reconciliation - an important component of healing philosophy and a cornerstone of restorative justice policy and practice. It is based on the notion that a more productive response to crime is to encourage all affected parties to participate in conflict resolution. Reconciliation is the desired outcome often of a mediation process. (8, 11)

Reformatories - a 19th-century term for juvenile prisons that were based on a belief in the ability of prisons to reform or change an individual. (1)

Rehabilitation - a correctional philosophy entrenched in the juvenile justice system by the Juvenile Delinquents Act. It is based on the belief that the appropriate treatment programs can reform or change an individual. (9, 10)

Reintegration - a correctional concept referring to policies and programs designed to introduce offenders back into their communities as productive, participating, law abiding members. (2, 11)

Reintegrative shaming - John Braithwaite's concept refers to shaming that has a productive, reintegrative effect on individuals as opposed to disintegrative shaming which is nothing more than public humiliation. (12)

Reliability - in behavioural science this concept refers to the extent to which variable measurement and research findings can be or have been repeated. (3)

Remand - holding an accused person in a prison or detention facility prior to their court appearance, trial, or while awaiting sentence. Sometimes also referred to as pretrial detention. (10)

Remedial - programs designed to help overcome a weakness as opposed to correct a problem. (4)

Reparation - in restorative justice models this involves offenders making amends in any variety of ways to their victims for the harm done by the offence. (2)

Research - a systematic process of information gathering, analysis, and reporting of findings. (5)

Restitution - is more specific than reparation in that it refers to payment in money or kind to compensate victims for their loss. Sometimes referred to as compensation. (8)

Restorative justice - a justice model that focuses on the harm caused by crime and seeks through responses to repair the damage done to offenders, victims, and communities. (2, 12)

Retribution - punishment for an offence committed. (9)

Reverse discrimination - occurs when policies designed to end discrimination against one group inadvertently create discrimination for another group. (11)

Role theory - theories attempting to explain criminal behaviour by understanding the processes whereby individuals acquire and become committed to deviant roles. (6)

Secondary data - in contrast to primary data this refers to information or data used for research that has been collected by a different researcher or person for another purpose. (1)

Secure custody - a form of youth custody designated by the Young Offenders Act as requiring more restrictions on movement both within and outside the institution than is required for open security. (10)

Self-fulfilling prophecy - a concept coined by Robert Merton to refer to instances where a situation or person is defined in a particular way and responded to as if these definitions were real. These responses in turn are likely to make the situation or person actually become as they were initially defined. (3)

Self-report survey - in criminology these are questionnaire surveys where individuals are asked to report on their actual involvement in criminal or delinquent activities. (3)

Sentencing circles - often used in Aboriginal communities where judges sit with community members to decide on an appropriate sentence for an individual case. (11)

Sentencing conference - introduced to the juvenile justice system by the Youth Criminal Justice Act, it involves a meeting of a group of professionals for the purpose of making recommendations to the court about appropriate sentences for individual cases. (9)

Sentencing grid - a computer software program used in some jurisdictions in the United States that allows judges to input case particulars and the program recommends a sentence. (12)

Social bond - from Travis Hirschi, the concept refers to the social ties that hold people together, that cause people to care about each other. (5)

Social capital theory - the theory that people possess varying degrees of useful and valuable social goods such as supportive family and neighbours and an education or good grades in school. (7)

Social class - a sociological concept with a variety of definitions depending on which theoretical perspective is used. It generally refers to one's economic position or standing in a particular social structure or society. (7)

Social control agencies - usually government agencies mandated to fulfill varying parts of the justice system such as police courts and correctional institutions. (3)

Social injustice - a situation or state of affairs where groups of people are disadvantaged relative to others because of societal laws, policies, or practices. (11)

Social learning theory - a set of theories explaining crime and delinquency through notions of imitation and modeling. (6)

Social order - a term referring to an assumed state of being for a society, one that is free of disorder. (6)

Socioeconomic status - similar to social class but it specifically refers to a person's social standing or position in terms of their education, occupation, and income. (4)

Status offences - behaviours only considered illegal because of the age status of the individual such as, in Canada under the Juvenile Delinquents Act, sexual behaviour, truancy, disobeying parents, incorrigibility. In other words, behaviours not legally sanctioned if engaged in by an adult. (2, 4)

Stigmatization - the negative consequences for an individual of having a particular negative label or definition attached to his or her behaviour. Having a criminal record, for example, is said to stigmatize a person in that he or she finds it more difficult to get a job. (8)

Strain theory - a group of theories that argue in a variety of ways that blocked opportunities are a cause of problem behaviours, one of which is crime and delinquency. (5)

Structural - refers to how something is ordered and organized, how its parts relate and connect to each other and to the whole. (1)

Structural change - refers to changes in how something is ordered and organized, or in how its parts relate and connect to each other or to the whole. (12)

Surveillance - the mechanisms and processes by which the state monitors and keeps track of people and their behaviour. In criminal justice this refers to the police, probation, and parole roles. (8)

Telescoping - a problem faced by researchers conducting self-report or victimization surveys where people tend to lump offences that may have occurred two or three years ago into something that occurred "last year." (3)

Theory - integrated sets of propositions that offer explanations for some phenomenon. (5)

Tracking - school policies that group and stream students into different programs based on their performance on standardized tests. (7)

Training schools - a common term for juvenile correctional institutions in the decades leading up to the introduction of the Young Offenders Act. (10)

Treatment - rehabilitative programs based on assumptions of correcting individual pathologies. (10)

Unfounded - events investigated by police as potentially criminal that are found not to be. (3)

Validity - refers to the extent to which research variables have been measured in a way that is consistent with the theoretical concept or what was intended. (3)

Victimization survey - a survey questionnaire where individuals are asked to report if they have ever been victimized over a particular time period and in what ways. (3)

Welfare - a model of juvenile justice based on a rehabilitative philosophy. (2)

Zero-tolerance policies - policies that curtail the use of discretion. Most commonly, zero-tolerance policies have been developed as a means of controlling violence. Many schools have implemented these policies with regard to bullying and other forms of aggressive behaviour. Zero-tolerance means every accused person is sanctioned in the same manner, no exceptions. Many police departments also have these policies for domestic violence complaints and police are required to lay charges. (3)

References

Abramovitch, M., M. Peterson-Badali, and M. Rohan. (1995). Young People's Understanding and Assertion of Their Rights to Silence and Legal Counsel. *Canadian Journal of Criminology* 37, 1–19.

Adelberg, E., and C. Currie. (1988). *Too Few to Count*. Vancouver: Press Gang Publishers.

Adler, F. (1981). *The Incidence of Female Criminality in the Contemporary World*. New York: New York University Press.

Adler, F. (1975). *Sisters in Crime*. New York: McGraw-Hill.

Agnew, R. (2001). Building on the Foundation of General Strain Theory: Specifying the Types of Strain Most Likely to Lead to Crime and Delinquency. *Journal of Research in Crime and Delinquency* 38(4), 319–361.

Agnew, R. (1993). Why Do They Do It? An Examination of the Intervening Mechanisms Between "Social Control" Variables and Delinquency. *Journal of Research in Crime and Delinquency* 28, 126–56.

Agnew, R. (1992). Foundation for a General Strain Theory of Crime and Delinquency. *Criminology* 30, 47–88.

Agnew, R. (1990). Adolescent Resources and Delinquency. *Criminology* 28, 535–66.

Agnew, R. (1985a). Social Control Theory and Delinquency. *Criminology* 23, 47–61.

Agnew, R. (1985b). A Revised Strain Theory of Delinquency. *Social Forces* 64, 151–67.

Akers, R. (1994). *Criminological Theories: Introduction and Evaluation*. Los Angeles: Roxbury Publishing.

Akers, R. (1985). *Deviant Behavior: A Social Learning Approach*. 3rd ed. Belmont, CA: Wadsworth. Reprinted 1992. Fairfax, VA: Techbooks.

Akers, R. (1977). *Deviant Behavior: A Social Learning Approach*. 2nd ed. Belmont, CA: Wadsworth.

Akers, R. (1973). *Deviant Behavior: A Social Learning Approach*. Belmont, CA: Wadsworth.

Albonetti, C. (1991). An Integration of Theories to Explain Judicial Discretion. *Social Problems* 38, 247–66.

Allen, R. (1991). Preliminary Crime Statistics—1990. *Juristat* 11(9). Ottawa: Canadian Centre for Justice Statistics.

Alvi, S. (1986). Realistic Crime Prevention Strategies through Alternative Measures for Youth. In D. Currie and B. Maclean, (Eds.), *The Administration of Justice*. Saskatoon: University of Saskatchewan, Department of Sociology.

Anderson, K. (1996). *Sociology: A Critical Introduction*. Scarborough, ON: ITP Nelson.

Andrews, D.A., and J. Bonta. (1994). *The Psychology of Criminal Conduct*. Cincinnati, OH: Anderson.

Annual Report of the Several Departments of the City Government of Halifax, Nova Scotia, for the Municipal Year 1898–99. Report of Chief of Police, 76.

Archambault, R.O. (1986). Young Offenders Act: Philosophy and Principles. In R.A. Silverman, J.J. Teevan, and V. F. Sacco, (Eds.), *Crime in Canadian Society*, 3rd ed. Toronto: Butterworths.

Armstrong, F. (1997, September 30). Cabbie's Killer Chooses Prison. *The Chronicle-Herald*, A6.

Armstrong, G. (1977). Females Under the Law—Protected but Unequal. *Crime and Delinquency* 23, 109–20.

Artz, S. (1997). *Sex, Power, and the Violent School Girl*. Toronto: Trifolium Books.

Austin, G., P. Jaffe, G. Peter, A. Leschied, and L. Sas. (1985). A Model for the Provision of Clinical Assessment and Service Brokerage for Young Offenders. *Canadian Psychology* 25, 54–62.

Awad, G. (1991). Assessing the Needs of Young Offenders. In A. Leschied, P. Jaffe, and W. Willis, (Eds.), *The Young Offenders Act: A Revolution in Canadian Juvenile Justice.* Toronto: University of Toronto Press.

Bailey, I. (1995, July 27). "Violence Panic" Hitting Nation. *The Chronicle-Herald*, A11.

Bala, N. (1994). What's Wrong with the YOA Bashing? What's Wrong with the YOA? Recognizing the Limits of the Law. *Canadian Journal of Criminology* 36, 247–70.

Bala, N. (1992). The Young Offenders Act: The Legal Structure. In R. Corrado, N. Bala, R. Linden, and M. Le Blanc, (Eds.), *Juvenile Justice in Canada: A Theoretical and Analytical Assessment.* Toronto: Butterworths.

Bala, N. (1989). Transfer to Adult Court: Two Views as to Parliament's Best Response. *Criminal Reports* 69(3), 172–77.

Bala, N. (1988). Young Offenders Act: A Legal Framework. In J. Hudson, J.B. Hornick, and B. Burrows, (Eds.), *Justice and the Young Offender in Canada.* Toronto: Wall and Thompson.

Bala, N., and K.L. Clarke. (1981). *The Child and the Law.* Toronto: McGraw-Hill Ryerson.

Bala, N., J. Hornick, M.L. McCall, and M.E. Clarke. (1994). *State Responses to Youth Crime: A Consideration of Principles.* Ottawa: Department of Justice.

Bala, N., and D. Mahoney. (1994). *Responding to Criminal Behaviour of Children Under 12: An Analysis of Canadian Law and Practice.* Ottawa: Department of Justice Canada.

Bala, N., and M. Kirvan. (1991). The Statute: Its Principles and Provisions and Their Interpretation by the Courts. In A. Leschied, P. Jaffe, and W. Willis, (Eds.), *The Young Offenders Act: A Revolution in Canadian Juvenile Justice.* Toronto: University of Toronto Press.

Bandura, A. (1977). *Social Learning Theory.* Englewood Cliffs, NJ: Prentice-Hall.

Baron, S.W., D.R. Forde, and L.W. Kennedy (2001). Rough Justice: Street Youth and Violence. *Journal of Interpersonal Violence* 16(7), 662–78

Baron, S.W. (2001). Street Youth Labour Market Experiences and Crime. *Canadian Review of Sociology and Anthropology/Andropology* 38(2), 189–216.

Baron, S. (1995). Serious Offenders. In J.H. Creechan and R.A. Silverman, (Eds.), *Canadian Delinquency.* Scarborough, ON: Prentice Hall Canada.

Barron, C.L. (2000). *Giving Youth a Voice: A Basis for Rethinking Adolescent Violence.* Halifax: Fernwood.

Baumrind, D. (1991). Parenting Styles and Adolescent Development. In R. Lerner, A. Peterson, and J. Brooks-Gunn, (Eds.), *Encyclopedia of Adolescence.* New York: Garland Publishing Company.

Baumrind, D. (1978). Parental Disciplinary Patterns and Social Competence in Children. *Youth and Society* 9, 239–76.

B.C. Anticipates Tougher Young Offenders Act. (1997, December 8). *The Chronicle-Herald*, A15.

Beaulieu, L. (1994). Youth Offenses—Adult Consequences. *Canadian Journal of Criminology* 36, 329–41.

Beccaria, C. (1819). *On Crimes and Punishments.* 2nd ed. Translated by Edward Ingraham. Philadelphia: Philip H. Nicklin.

Becker, H. (1963). *Outsiders: Studies in the Sociology of Deviance.* New York: Free Press.

Bell, S.J. (1995). *Young Offenders and Juvenile Justice in Nova Scotia: An Overview of the Young Offender Symposium.* Halifax: Atlantic Institute of Criminology.

Bell, S.J. (1994a). An Empirical Approach to Theoretical Perspectives on Sentencing in Young Offender Court. *Canadian Review of Sociology and Anthropology* 31(1), 35–64.

Bell, S.J. (1994b). Young Offenders and Family Violence: Implications for Justice Reform. Paper presented at the 29th annual meeting of the Atlantic Association of Sociology and Anthropology, Halifax.

Bell, S.J. (1993). Family Court under the Young Offenders Act: The Site of a Power Struggle. Paper presented at meetings of the American Society of *Criminology*, Phoenix, AZ.

Bell, S.J., and P. Smith. (1994). Youth and Adult Custody in the Province of Nova Scotia: A Test of the Assumptions Underlying "Get Tough" Proposals. Paper presented at meetings of the Canadian Sociology and Anthropology Association, Calgary.

Bernard, T. (1992). *The Cycle of Juvenile Justice*. Toronto: Oxford University Press.

Bernard, T.J. (1987). Testing Structural Strain Theories. *Journal of Research in Crime and Delinquency* 24, 262–90.

Besserer, S. and C. Trainor (2000). Criminal Victimization in Canada, 1999. *Juristat* 20(10). Ottawa: Canadian Centre for Justice Statistics.

Bibby, R. (1995). *The Bibby Report: Social Trends Canadian Style*. Toronto: Stoddart Publishing.

Biron, L. (1980). An Overview of Self-Reported Delinquency in a Sample of Girls in the Montreal Area. In A. Morris and L. Gelsthorpe, (Eds.), *Women and Crime*. Cambridge: Institute of Criminology.

Black, D., and A. Reiss. (1970). Police Control of Juveniles. *American Sociological Review* 35, 63–77.

Bodine, G. (1964). Factors Related to Police Dispositions of Juvenile Offenders. Paper presented at annual meeting of the American Sociological Association.

Bohm, R.M. (1997). *A Primer on Crime and Delinquency*. Belmont, CA: Wadsworth Publishing.

Bonger, W. (1916). *Criminality and Economic Conditions*. Reprinted Bloomington, IN: Indiana University Press, 1969.

Borden, S. (1998, May 14). YOA Changes "Right Approach." *The Chronicle-Herald*, A8.

Boritch, H. (1997). *Fallen Women: Female Crime and Criminal Justice in Canada*. Toronto: ITP Nelson.

Bortner, M. (1988). *Delinquency and Justice: An Age of Crisis*. Toronto: McGraw-Hill Ryerson.

Bourne, P. L., McCoy, and D. Smith (1998). Girls and Schooling: Their Own Critique. *Resources for Feminist Research* 26 (1 and 2): 55–68.

Bourque, B.B., R.C. Cronin, D.B. Felker, F.R. Pearson, M. Han, and S.M. Hill. (1996). *Boot Camps for Juvenile Offenders: An Implementation Evaluation of Three Demonstration Programs*. Washington, DC: National Institute of Justice, Research in Brief, May 1996.

Bowker, M.M. (1986). Juvenile Court in Retrospective: Seven Decades of History in Alberta (1913–1984). *Alberta Law Review* 24(2), 234–74.

Braga, A.A., D.M. Kennedy, E.J. Waring, and A.M. Piehl (2001). Problem-Oriented Policing, Deterrence, and Youth Violence: An Evaluation of Boston's Operation Ceasefire. *Journal of Research in Crime and Delinquency* 38(3), 195–225.

Braithwaite, J. (1989). *Crime, Shame, and Reintegration*. Cambridge: Cambridge University Press.

Braithwaite, J., and S. Mugford, (1994). Conditions of Successful Reintegration Ceremonies: Dealing with Juvenile Offenders. *British Journal of Criminology* 34, 138–71.

Brannigan, A. (2000). The Adolescent Prostitute: Policing Delinquency of Preventing Victimization. In J.A. Winterdyk ed. *Issues and Perspectives on Young Offenders in Canada*, 2nd. (ed.), Toronto: Harcourt.

Brayton, G. (1996). Adolescent Sexual Offenders. In John Winterdyk, (Ed.), *Issues and Perspectives on Young Offenders in Canada*. Toronto: Harcourt Brace & Company.

Brezina, T., A.R. Piquero, and P. Mazerolle (2001). Student Anger and Aggressive Behaviour in School: An Initial Test of Agnew's Macro-Level Strain Theory. *Journal of Research in Crime and Delinquency* 38(4), 362–86.

British Columbia Ministry of the Attorney General, Corrections Branch. (1996). *Annual Reports*, 1995–96.

British Columbia Ministry of the Attorney General, Corrections Branch. (1995, February). *Inventory of Alternative Measures and Diversion Programs*.

Brodeur, J. (1989). Some Comments on Sentencing Guidelines. In L. Beaulieu, (Ed.), *Young Offender Dispositions*. Toronto: Wall and Emerson.

Bromberg, W. (1953). American Achievements in Criminology. *Journal of Criminal Law, Criminology and Police Science* 47, 166–76.

Brownfield, D., and K. Thompson. (1991). Attachment to Peers and Delinquent Behaviour. *Canadian Journal of Criminology* 33, 46–60.

Bula, F. (1996, April 2). Teenagers Are Victims of Crime More Often Than Cause of Them. *Sun* (Vancouver), B2.

Burgess, R.L., and R. Akers. (1966). A Differential Association-Reinforcement Theory of Criminal Behaviour. *Social Problems* 14, 128–47.

Byles, J.A. (1969). *Alienation, Deviance and Social Control: A Study of Adolescents in Metro Toronto*. Toronto: Interim Research Project on Unreached Children.

Bynum, J., and W. Thompson. (1992). *Juvenile Delinquency: A Sociological Approach*. Toronto: Allyn and Bacon.

Campbell, A. (1990). Female Participation in Gangs. In C. Ronald Huff, (Ed.), *Gangs in America*. Newbury Park, CA: Sage, 163–82.

Campbell, A. (1984). *The Girls in the Gang*. Oxford: Basil Blackwell.

Campbell, M. (1998, October 30). A Perfect Carnival of Juvenile Horrors. *The Globe and Mail*, A6.

Canada, Department of Justice. (1991). *Aboriginal People and Justice Administration—A Discussion Paper*. Ottawa: Department of Justice.

Canadian Association of Elizabeth Fry Societies and Correctional Services of Canada (1990). *Creating Choices: The Report of the Task Force on Federally Sentenced Women*. Ottawa: Correctional Services Canada.

Canadian Criminal Justice Association (n.d.) *Comments on "Strategy for the Renewal of Youth Justice*. At http://home.istar.ca/~ccja/angl/youth.htm (November 11, 2001).

Caputo, T.C. (1987). The Young Offenders Act: Children's Rights, Children's Wrongs. *Canadian Public Policy* 13(2), 125–43.

Caputo, T., and D. Bracken. (1988). Custodial Dispositions and the Young Offenders Act. In J. Hudson, J. Hornick, and B. Burrows, (Eds.), *Justice and the Young Offender in Canada*. Toronto: Wall and Thompson.

Caputo, T., and S. Goldenberg. (1986). Young People and the Law: A Consideration of Luddite and Utopian Responses. *The Administration of Justice*. Saskatoon: University of Saskatchewan, Department of Sociology.

Caron, R. (1978). *Go-Boy!* Toronto: McGraw-Hill Ryerson.

Carrigan, O.D. (1991). *Crime and Punishment in Canada: A History*. Oxford University Press.

Carrington, P. (1998). Changes in Police Charging of Young Offenders in Ontario and Saskatchewan after 1984. *Canadian Journal of Criminology* 36(1), 1–28.

Carrington, P. (1995). Has Violent Youth Crime Increased? Comment on Corrado and Markwart. *Canadian Journal of Criminology* 37, 61–74.

Carrington, P. J. (1999). Trends in Youth Crime in Canada. *Canadian Journal of Criminology* 41(1), 1–32.

Carrington, P., and S. Moyer (1998). *A Statistic Profile of Female Young Offenders*. Ottawa: Department of Justice, Research and Statistics Division/Policy Sector.

Carrington, P., and S. Moyer. (1994a). Trends in Youth Crime and Police Response, Pre- and Post-YOA. *Canadian Journal of Criminology* 36, 1–28.

Carrington, P., and S. Moyer. (1994b). Interprovincial Variations in the Use of Custody for Young Offenders: A Funnel Analysis. *Canadian Journal of Criminology* 36, 271–90.

Carrington, P., and S. Moyer. (1990). The Effects of Defence Counsel on Plea and Outcome in Juvenile Court. *Canadian Journal of Criminology* 32, 621–37.

Castellano, T.C. (1986). Justice Model in the Juvenile Justice System: Washington State's Experience. *Law and Policy* 8, 479–506.

Cernkovich, S., and P. Giordano. (1987). Family Relationships and Delinquency. *Criminology* 25, 295–321.

Chambliss, W. (1973). The Saints and the Roughnecks. *Society* 11, 24–31.

Chesler, P. (1972). *Women and Madness*. New York: Doubleday.

Chesney-Lind, M. (1988). Girls in Jail. *Crime and Delinquency* 34, 151–68.

Chesney-Lind, M. (1970). Judicial Paternalism and the Female Status Offender. *Crime and Delinquency* 23, 121–30.

Chesney-Lind, M. and R. Sheldon (1998). *Girls, Delinquency and Juvenile Justice*, 2nd (Ed.), Belmont, CA: West/Wadsworth.

Chesney-Lind, M., A. Rockhill, N. Marker, and A. Reyes. (1994). Gangs and Exploring Police Estimates of Gang Membership Delinquency. *Crime, Law, and Social Change* 21, 201–28.

Chesney-Lind, M., and R. Shelden. (1992). *Girls, Delinquency and Juvenile Justice*. Pacific Grove, CA: Brooks/Cole.

Chisholm, P. (1997, December 8). Bad Girls: A Brutal B.C. Murder Sounds an Alarm about Teenage Violence. *Maclean's*.

Chunn, D. (1998). *Whiter than White: Sexual Offences, Law and Social Purity in Canada, 1885–1940* Paper presented at the Western Association of Sociology and Anthropology, Vancouver, May 15.

Cicourel, A. (1968). *The Social Organization of Juvenile Justice*. New York: John Wiley.

City Marshal. (1909–10). *Annual Reports*. City of Halifax: Nova Scotia Provincial Archives.

Clark, B., and T. O'Reilly-Fleming. (1994). Out of the Carceral Straightjacket: Under Twelve and the Law. *Canadian Journal of Criminology* 36, 305–27.

Clark, B., and T. O'Reilly-Fleming. (1993). Implementing the Young Offenders Act in Ontario: Issues of Principles, Programmes, and Power. *Howard Journal of Criminal Justice* 32, 114–26.

Clark R. and D. Cornish (1985). Modeling Offenders Decisions. In N. Morris and M. Tonry (Eds.), *Crime and Justice 6*. Chicago: University of Chicago Press 147–185.

Clark, R. and M. Felson (1993). *Routine Activity and Rational Choice*. New Bunswick, NJ: Transaction Books.

Cloninger, C., and I. Gottesman. (1987). Genetic and Environmental Factors in Anti-Social Behavior Disorders. In J. Mednick, T. Moffitt, and S. Stack, (Eds.), *The Causes of Crime: New Biological Approaches*. Cambridge: Cambridge University Press.

Cloward, R., and L. Ohlin. (1960). *Delinquency and Opportunity*. New York: Free Press.

Coflin, J. (1988). The Federal Government's Role in Implementing the Young Offenders Act. In J. Hudson, J. Hornick, and B. Burrows, (Eds.), *Justice and the Young Offender in Canada*. Toronto: Wall and Thompson.

Cohen, A.K. (1955). *Delinquent Boys*. New York: Free Press.

Cohen, L. and M. Felson (1979). Social Change and Crime Rate Trends: A Routine Activity Approach. *American Sociological Review* 44, 588–608.

Cohen, S. (1985). *Visions of Social Control: Crime, Punishment and Classification*. Cambridge: Polity Press.

Cohen, S. (1972). *Folk Devils and Moral Panics*. London: Granada Publishing.

Cohen, S. (M.P.) (1997). *Renewing Youth Justice*. Thirteenth Report of the Standing Committee on Justice and Legal Affairs. Canada: Queen's Printer.

Cohill, M., Jr. (1991). Why Do I Like Broccoli? (De Gustibus non est Disputandum). *Journal of Criminal Law and Criminology* 82, 125–30.

Coleman, J.S. (1990). *Foundation of Social Theory*. Cambridge, MA: Harvard University Press.

Coleman, J.S. (1988). Social Capital in the Creation of Human Capital. *American Journal of Sociology* 94, 95–120.

Colvin, M., and J. Pauly. (1987). A Critique of Criminology. *American Journal of Sociology* 89, 513–51.

Conly, C. (1993). *Street Gangs, Current Knowledge and Strategies*. Washington, DC: National Institute of Justice.

Conly, D. (1978). *Patterns of Delinquency and Police Action in the Major Metropolitan Areas of Canada during the Month of December, 1976*. Ottawa: Solicitor General, Canada.

Connell, R.W. (1987). *Gender and Power*. Stanford, CA: Stanford University Press.

Conway, J. (1992). Female Young Offenders, 1990–91. *Juristat* 12(11). Ottawa: Canadian Centre for Justice Statistics.

Cook, P. (1980). Research in Criminal Deterrence. In N. Morris and M. Tonry (Eds.), *Crime and Justice 2*. Chicago: University of Chicago Press.

Copperman, P. (1980). *The Literacy Hoax*. New York: Morrow.

Corrado, R. (1992). Introduction. In R. Corrado, N. Bala, R. Linden, and M. Le Blanc, (Eds.), *Juvenile Justice in Canada: A Theoretical and Analytical Assessment*. Toronto: Butterworths.

Corrado, R., and A. Markwart. (1995). Processing Serious Cases in British Columbia. In J. Creechan and R. Silverman, (Eds.), *Canadian Delinquency*. Scarborough: Prentice Hall Canada.

Corrado, R., and A. Markwart. (1994). The Need to Reform the YOA in Response to Violent Young Offenders: Confusion, Reality or Myth? *Canadian Journal of Criminology* 36, 343–78.

Corrado, R., and A. Markwart. (1992). The Evolution and Implementation of a New Era of Juvenile Justice in Canada. In R. Corrado, N. Bala, R. Linden, and M. Le Blanc, (Eds.), *Juvenile Justice in Canada: A Theoretical and Analytical Assessment*. Toronto: Butterworths.

Corrado, R., and A. Markwart. (1988). The Prices of Rights and Responsibilities: The Impacts of the Young Offenders Act in British Columbia. *Canadian Review of Family Law* 7(1), 93–115.

Corrado, R.R., C. Odgers, and I.M. Cohen (2000). The Incarceration of Female Young Offenders: Protection for Whom? *Canadian Journal of Criminology* 42(2), 189–207.

Costly Problem: Expensive to Lock Kids Up for Long. (1995, April 18). *Daily News*.

Cowie, J., V. Cowie, and E. Slater. (1968). *Delinquency in Girls*. London: Heinemann.

Cox, W. (1995, August 3). Law Breaking by Young Continues to Decrease. *The Chronicle-Herald*, A2.

Creechan, J. (1995). How Much Delinquency Is There? In J. Creechan and R. Silverman, (Eds.), *Canadian Delinquency*. Scarborough, ON: Prentice Hall Canada.

Cross, B. (1998, February 12). A Killing Lights a Prairie Fire, *The Globe and Mail*, A2.

Crow, C. (1994). Patterns of Discrimination: Aboriginal Justice in Canada. In N. Larsen, (Ed.), *The Canadian Criminal Justice System: An Issues Approach to the Administration of Justice*. Toronto: Canadian Scholars Press.

Dabbs, J., R. Frady, T. Carr., and N. Besch. (1987). Testosterone and Criminal Violence in Young Prison Inmates. *Psychosomatic Medicine* 49, 174–82.

Dabbs, J., R. Ruback, R. Frady, C. Hooper, and D. Sgoutas. (1988). Saliva Testosterone and Criminal Violence Among Women. *Personality and Individual Differences* 9, 269–75.

Daly, K., and M. Chesney-Lind. (1988). Feminism and Criminology. *Justice Quarterly* 5, 497–538.

Danger of the Street: Where Lieth Responsibility? (1908, January 11). *Evening Mail*, 16.

Dannifer, D., and R. Schutt. (1982). Race and Juvenile Justice Processing in Court and Police Agencies. *American Journal of Sociology* 87, 1113–32.

Dauvergne, M. and H. Johnson. (2001). Children Witnessing Family Violence. *Juristat* 21(6). Ottawa: Canadian Centre for Justice Statistics.

Davidson, W., and R. Redner. (1988). The Prevention of Juvenile Delinquency: Diversion from the Juvenile Justice System. In R. Price, E. Cowen, R. Orion, and J. Ramos-McKay, (Eds.), *Fourteen Ounces of Prevention*. Washington, DC: American Psychological Association.

Davies, L. (1994a). In Search of Resistance and Rebellion Among High School Drop-Outs. *Canadian Journal of Sociology* 19(3), 331–50.

Davies, L. (1994b). Class Dismissed? Student Opposition in Ontario High Schools. *Canadian Review of Sociology and Anthropology* 31(4), 422–45.

Defective Children Discussed at Annual Conference in Buffalo. (1909, June 8). *Morning Chronicle.*

DeFleur, L. (1975). Biasing Influences on Drug Arrest Records, *American Sociological Review* 40, 88–101.

Dell'Olio, J.M., and P.H. Jacobs. (1991). The CHILD Inc. of Delaware Experience. In I. Schwartz and S. Orlando, (Eds.), *Programming for Young Women in the Juvenile Justice System*. Ann Arbor, MI: Center for the Study of Youth Policy.

de Souza, P. (1995). Youth Court Statistics, 1993–94 Highlights. *Juristat* 15(3). Ottawa: Statistics Canada, Canadian Crime Statistics.

Dickson-Gilmore, J. (1992). Finding the Ways of the Ancestors: Cultural Change and the Invention of Separate Legal Systems. *Canadian Journal of Criminology* 34(3–4), 479–502.

Different Note, A. (1996, September 30). *The Chronicle-Herald*, C1.

Doherty, G., and P. de Souza. (1996). Youth Court Statistics, 1994–95 Highlights. *Juristat* 16(4). Ottawa: Statistics Canada, Canadian Crime Statistics.

Donzelot, J. (1979). *The Policing of Families*. Translated by Robert Hurley. New York: Pantheon Books.

Doob, A. (1992). Trends in the Use of Custodial Dispositions for Young Offenders. *Canadian Journal of Criminology* 34, 75–84.

Doob, A. (1991). Workshop on Collecting Race and Ethnicity Statistics in the Criminal Justice System. Toronto: University of Toronto, Centre of Criminology.

Doob, A. (1989). Dispositions under the Young Offenders Act: Issues without Answers. In L. Beaulieu, (Ed.), *Young Offender Dispositions*. Toronto: Wall and Emerson.

Doob, A., and L. Beaulieu. (1995). The Exercise of Judicial Discretion. In J. Creechan and R. Silverman, (Eds.), *Canadian Delinquency*. Scarborough, ON: Prentice Hall Canada.

Doob, A., and Beaulieu, L. (1992). Variation in the Exercise of Judicial Discretion with Young Offenders. *Canadian Journal of Criminology* 34, 35–50.

Doob, A., and J. Brodeur. (1989). Rehabilitating the Debate on Rehabilitation. *Canadian Journal of Criminology* 31, 179–92.

Doob, A., and J.B.L. Chan. (1995). Factors Affecting Police Decisions to Take Juveniles to Court. In J. Creechan, and R. Silverman, (Eds.), *Canadian Delinquency*. Scarborough, ON: Prentice Hall Canada.

Doob, A., V. Marinos, and K. Varma. (1995). *Youth Crime and the Youth Justice System in Canada: A Research Perspective*. Toronto: University of Toronto, Centre of Criminology.

Doob, A., and J.B. Sprott. (1996). Interprovincial Variation in the Use of the Youth Court. *Canadian Journal of Criminology* (October), 401–12.

Dorey, B. (1997, November 22). Justice for Kids. *The Chronicle-Herald*, B2.

Dorey, B. (1996, April 20). On the Inside, Looking Out. *The Chronicle-Herald*, C1.

Drucker, S., and M. Hexter. (1923). *Children Astray*. Cambridge, MA: Harvard University Press.

Duffy, A. (1996). Bad Girls in Hard Times: Canadian Female Juvenile Offenders. In G. O'Bireck, (Ed.), *Not a Kid Anymore*. Scarborough, ON: ITP Nelson.

Dugdale, R. (1888). *The Jukes: A Study in Crime, Pauperism, Disease and Heredity*. 4th ed. New York: Putnam.

Durkheim, E. ([1897] 1951). *Suicide*. Translated by John A. Spaulding and George Simpson. New York: Free Press.

Durkheim, E. ([1893] 1933). *The Division of Labour in Society*. Translated by George Simpson. London: Free Press of Glenceo.

DuWors, R. (1992). *Report on the Involvement of Children Under 12 in Criminal Behaviour.* Ottawa: Canadian Centre for Justice Statistics, Statistics Canada.

Edwards, P. (1992, February 17). Reform School Was a Nightmare: Woman Recalls Brutal Girlhood Behind Bars. *Toronto Star,* A8.

Ekstedt, J., and C. Griffiths. (1988). *Corrections in Canada: Policy and Practice.* Toronto: Butterworths.

Elder, G.H. Jr. (2000). Symposium on John Hagan and Bill McCarthy, *MeanStreets: Youth Crime and Homelessness.* Cambridge: Cambridge University Press, 1997. Extreme Situations in Young Lives. *Theoretical Criminology.* 4(20), 208–15.

Elder, G.H. Jr. (1985). Perspectives on the Life Course. In G.H. Elder Jr., (Ed). *Life Course Dynamics.* Ithaca: Cornell University Press: 23–49.

Elliott, D. (1966). Delinquency, School Attendance and Dropout. *Social Problems* 13, 307–14.

Elliott, D.S., D. Huizinga, and S. Ageton. (1985). *Explaining Delinquency and Drug Use.* Beverly Hills, CA: Sage.

Elliott, D., and H. Voss. (1974a). School Alienation and Delinquency. *Crime and Delinquency* 24, 355–70.

Elliott, D., and H. Voss. (1974b). *Delinquency and Dropout.* Lexington, MA: Lexington Books.

Ellis, D., and P. Austin. (1971). Menstruation and Aggressive Behaviour in a Correctional Center for Women. *Journal of Criminal Law, Criminology, and Police Science* 62, 388–95.

Enriquez, V. (1990). *Hellside in Paradise: The Honolulu Youth Gang.* Honolulu, HI: University of Hawaii at Manoa, Center for Philippine Studies.

Ericson, R. (1982). *Reproducing Order: A Study of Police Patrol Work.* Toronto: University of Toronto Press.

Ericson, R.V., and K.D. Haggerty. (1997). *Policing the Risk Society.* Toronto: University of Toronto Press.

Erikson, E. (1968). *Identity: Youth and Crisis.* New York: Norton.

Erikson, E. (1950). *Childhood and Society.* New York: Norton.

Eysenck, H. (1977). *Crime and Personality.* 2nd ed. London: Routledge & Kegan Paul.

Fagan, J. (1991). Social Processes of Delinquency and Drug Use Among Urban Gangs. In C.R. Huff, (Ed.), *Gangs in America.* Newbury Park, CA: Sage.

Fagan, J., E. Slaughter, and E. Hartstone. (1987). Blind Justice? The Impact of Race on the Juvenile Justice Process, *Crime and Delinquency* 33, 224–58.

Faith, K. (1993). *Unruly Women.* Vancouver: Press Gang Publishers.

Fasiolo, R., and S. Leckie. (1993). *Canadian Media Coverage of Gangs: A Content Analysis.* Ottawa: Solicitor General, Canada.

Featherston, D. (2000). The Law and Young Offenders in J.A. Winterdyk (Ed.), *Issues and Perspectives on Young Offenders in Canada.* 2nd ed. Toronto: Harbour Canada, 93–118.

Fedorowycz, O. (2000). Homicide in Canada—1999. *Juristat* 20(9). Ottawa: Canadian Centre for Justice Statistics.

Fedorowycz, O. (1999). Homicide in Canada—1998. *Juristat* 19(10). Ottawa: Canadian Centre for Justice Statistics.

Fedorowycz, O. (1997). Homicide in Canada—1996. *Juristat* 17(9). Ottawa: Canadian Centre for Justice Statistics.

Ferdinand, T.N., and E.G. Luchterhand. (1970). Inner-City Youth, the Police, the Juvenile Court, and Justice. *Social Problems* 17(Spring), 510–27.

Finckenauer, J.O. (1982). *Scared Straight! and the Panacea Phenomenon.* Englewood Cliffs, NJ: Prentice Hall.

Fingard, J. (1989). *The Dark Side of Life in Victorian Halifax.* Nova Scotia: Pottersfield Press.

Finkelhor, D., and J. Dziuba-Leatherman. (1994). Victimization of Children. *American Psychologist* 49, 173–83.

Finkelhor, D., and J. Dziuba-Leatherman. (1993). *Children as Victims of Violence: A National Survey.* Durham, NH: University of New Hampshire, Family Research Laboratory.

Fisher, J. (1989). *Missing Children's Research Project: Findings of the Study Executive Summary.* Ottawa: Solicitor General of Canada.

Fisher, L., and H. Janetti. (1996). Aboriginal Youth in the Criminal Justice System. In John Winterdyk, (Ed.), *Issues and Perspectives on Young Offenders in Canada.* Toronto: Harcourt Brace & Company.

Fisherman Murdered. (1995, July 16). *Sunday Daily News.*

Fishman, L. (1988). *The Vice Queens: An Ethnographic Study of Black Female Gang Behaviour.* Paper presented at the annual meetings of the American Society of Criminology.

Fishman, M. (1978). Crime Waves as Ideology. *Social Problems* 25, 531–43.

Flynn, A. (1995, July). Youth to Face Adult Court in Drive-By Slaying Case. *The Chronicle-Herald.*

Fogel, D. (1988). *On Doing Less Harm.* Chicago: University of Illinois at Chicago.

Foran, T. (1995). Youth Custody and Probation in Canada, 1993–94. *Juristat* 15(7). Ottawa: Statistics Canada.

Fowler, K. (1993). Youth Gangs: Criminals, Thrillseekers or the New Voice of Anarchy? In T. Fleming and B. Clark, (Eds.), *Youth Injustice: Canadian Perspectives.* Toronto: Canadian Scholars Press.

Frank, J. (1992). Violent Youth Crime. *Canadian Social Trends.* Ottawa: Statistics Canada.

Frank, J. (1991). Violent Offence Cases Heard in Youth Courts, 1990–91. *Juristat* 11(16). Ottawa: Statistics Canada, Canadian Centre for Justice Statistics.

Freire, R. (1990). *Pedagogy of the Oppressed.* New York: Continuum.

Freud, S. (1953). *A General Introduction to Psychoanalysis.* New York: Permabooks.

Freud, S. (1924). *A General Introduction to Psychoanalysis.* New York: Boni and Livelight.

Friedlander, K. (1947). *The Psychoanalytic Approach to Juvenile Delinquency.* London: Kegan Paul.

Frith, S. (1985). Sociology of Youth. In Michael Haralabos, (Ed.), *Sociology: New Directions.* Ormskiek: Causeway Press.

Gabor, P., I. Greene, and P. McCormick. (1986). The Young Offenders Act: The Alberta Youth Court Experience in the First Year. *Canadian Journal of Family Law* 5, 301–19.

Gabor, T. (1999). Trends in Youth Crime: Some Evidence Pointing to Increases in the Severity and Volume of Violence on the Part of Young People. *Canadian Journal of Criminology* 41(3), 385–92.

Gaffield, C. (1991). Labouring and Learning in Nineteenth-Century Canada: Children in the Changing Process of Family Reproduction. In R. Smandych, G. Dodds, and A. Esau, (Eds.), *Dimensions of Childhood: Essays on the History of Children and Youth in Canada.* Winnipeg: University of Manitoba Legal Research Institute.

Gagnon, M., and G. Doherty. (1993). *Offences Against the Administration of Youth Justice in Canada.* Ottawa: Statistics Canada, Canadian Centre for Justice Statistics.

Gamoran, A, and R. Mare. (1989). Secondary School Tracking and Educational Inequality. *American Journal of Sociology* 94, 1146–83.

Gandy, J. (1992). *Judicial Interim Release (Bail) Hearing That Resulted in Detention Prior to Trial of Youths Charged Under the Young Offenders Act in Three Ontario Cities.* Toronto: Policy Research Centre on Children, Youth, and Families.

Gartner, R., and A. Doob. (1994). Trends in Criminal Victimization, 1988–93. *Juristat* 14(13). Ottawa: Canadian Centre for Justice Statistics.

Gendreau, P., M. Paparozzi, T. Little, and M. Goddard. (1993). Does "Punishing Smarter" Work? An Assessment of the New Generation of Alternative Sanctions in Probation. *Forum on Corrections Research* 5, 31–34.

Gendreau, P., and R. Ross. (1987). Revivication of Rehabilitation: Evidence from the 1980's. *Justice Quarterly* 4(3), 349–407.

Genesee Justice. (1995). *Instruments of Law, Order, and Peace.* Batavia, NY: Genesee County Sheriff's Office.

Gilligan, C. (1982). *In a Different Voice.* Cambridge, MA: Harvard University Press.

Giordano, P. (1978). Girls, Guys, and Gangs: The Changing Social Context of Female Delinquency. *Journal of Criminal Law and Criminology* 69, 126–32.

Glassner, B.N., B. Ksander, B. Berg, and B. D. Johnson. (1983). A Note on the Deterrent Effect of Juvenile versus Adult Jurisdiction. *Social Problems* 31(2), 219–21.

Glueck, S., and E. Glueck. (1959). *Predicting Delinquency and Crime.* Cambridge, MA: Harvard University Press.

Glueck, S., and E. Glueck. (1956). *Physique and Delinquency.* New York: Harper.

Glueck, S., and E. Glueck. (1950). *Unravelling Juvenile Delinquency.* Cambridge, MA: Harvard University Press.

Goddard, H. (1912). *The Kallikak Family.* New York: Macmillan.

Godin, R. (1993, January 16). Crime Puts Squeeze on Businesses. *Mail Star,* A4.

Goff, C. (1997). *Criminal Justice in Canada.* Scarborough, ON: ITP Nelson.

Goldman, N. (1963). *The Differential Selection of Juvenile Offenders for Court Appearance.* New York: National Council on Crime and Delinquency.

Gomme, I. (1995). Theories of Delinquency. In J. Creechan and R. Silverman, (Eds.), *Canadian Delinquency.* Scarborough ON: Prentice Hall Canada.

Gomme, I. (1985). Predictors of Status and Criminal Offences Among Male and Female Adolescents in an Ontario Community. *Canadian Journal of Criminology* 27(2), 147–60.

Gomme, I., M. Morton, and G. West. (1984). Rates, Types and Patterns of Male and Female Delinquency in an Ontario Community. *Canadian Journal of Criminology* 26(3), 313–24.

Gordon, R.A. (1987). SES versus IQ in the Race-IQ Delinquency Model, *International Journal of Sociology and Social Policy* 7, 29–96.

Gordon, R.M. (1995). Street Gangs in Vancouver. In J. Creechan and R. Silverman, (Eds.), *Canadian Delinquency.* Scarborough, ON: Prentice Hall Canada.

Gordon, R.M. (1993). *Incarcerated Gang Members in British Columbia: A Preliminary Study.* Victoria: Ministry of the Attorney General.

Gorham, B. (1993, February 7). Island of Despair. *Province* (Vancouver), A34.

Gottfredson, M., and T. Hirschi. (1990). *A General Theory of Crime.* Palo Alto, CA: Stanford University Press.

Gottlieb, B. (1993). *The Family in the Western World: From the Black Death to the Industrial Age.* New York: Oxford University Press.

Greenberg, D. (1977). Delinquency and the Age Structure of Society. *Contemporary Crises: Crime, Law, and Social Policy* 1, 189–223.

Greenberg, P. (1992). Youth Property Crime in Canada. *Juristat* 12(14). Ottawa: Canadian Centre for Justice Statistics.

Griffiths, C.T., and R. Hamilton. (1996). Sanctioning and Healing: Restorative Justice in Canadian Aboriginal Communities. In B. Galaway and J. Hudson, (Eds.), *Restorative Justice: International Perspectives.* New York: Criminal Justice Press.

Groundswell Against Youth Crime Seeks to Make Bad Parenting Illegal. (1996, May 14). *Sun* (Vancouver), A7.

Hackler, J. (1991). Good People, Dirty System: The Young Offenders Act and Organizational Failure. In A. Leschied, P. Jaffe, and W. Willis, (Eds.), *The Young Offenders Act: A Revolution in Canadian Juvenile Justice.* Toronto: University of Toronto Press.

Hackler, J. (1978). *The Prevention of Youthful Crime: The Great Stumble Forward*. Toronto: Methuen.

Hagan, J., A.R. Gillis, and J. Chan. (1978). Explaining Official Delinquency: A Spatial Study of Class, Conflict and Control. *Sociological Quarterly* 19, 386–98.

Hagan, J., A. Gillis, and J. Simpson. (1985). The Class Structure of Gender and Delinquency: Toward a Power-Control Theory of Common Delinquent Behavior. *American Journal of Sociology* 90, 1151–78.

Hagan, J., and J. Leon. (1977). Rediscovering Delinquency: Social History, Political Ideology and the Sociology of Law. *American Sociological Review* 42, 587–98.

Hagan, J. and B. McCarthy (2000). Symposium on John Hagan and Bill McCarthy, *Mean Streets: Youth Crime and Homelessness*. Cambridge: Cambridge University Press, 1997. The Meaning of Criminology. *Theoretical Criminology*. 4(2), 232–42.

Hagan, J. and B. McCarthy (1997). *Mean Streets: Youth Crime and Homelessness*. Cambridge: Cambridge University Press.

Hagan J., J. Simpson, and A. Gillis. (1988). Feminist Scholarship, Relational and Instrumental Control and a Power Control Theory of Gender and Delinquency. *British Journal of Sociology* 39(3), 301–36.

Hagan, J., J. Simpson, and A. Gillis. (1987). Class in the Household: A Power-Control Theory of Delinquency. *American Journal of Sociology* 92, 788–816.

Hagedorn, J. (1988). *People and Folks: Gangs, Crime and the Underclass in Rustbelt City*. Chicago: Lakeview Press.

Hak, J. (1996). The Young Offenders Act. In John Winterdyk, (Ed.), *Issues and Perspectives on Young Offenders in Canada*. Toronto: Harcourt Brace & Company.

Hamilton, A.C., and C.M. Sinclair. (1991). *Report of the Aboriginal Justice Inquiry of Manitoba. Volume 1: The System and Aboriginal People*. Winnipeg: Queen's Printer.

Hare-Mustin, R.T. (1983). An Appraisal of the Relationship Between Women and Psychotherapy. *American Psychologist* 38, 593–601.

Harris, Mary. (1988). *Cholas: Latino Girls and Gangs*. New York: AMS Press.

Hartnagel, T.F., and S.W. Baron. (1995). It's Time to Get Serious: Public Attitudes Toward Juvenile Justice in Canada. In J.H. Creechan and R.A. Silverman, (Eds.), *Canadian Delinquency*. Scarborough, ON: Prentice Hall Canada.

Harvey, L., R. Burnham, K. Kendall, and K. Pease. (1992). Gender Differences in Criminal Justice. *British Journal of Criminology* 32, 208–17.

Hatch, A., and K. Faith. (1991). Female Offenders in Canada: A Statistical Profile. In R. Silverman, J. Teevan, and V. Sacco, (Eds.), *Crime in Canadian Society*. 4th ed. Toronto: Butterworths.

Hathaway, S., and E. Monachesi. (1953). *Analyzing and Predicting Juvenile Delinquency with the MMPI*. Minneapolis: University of Minnesota Press.

Havemann, P. (1992). Crisis Justice for Youth: Making the Young Offenders Act and the Discourse of Penalty. In D. Currie and B. MacLean, (Eds.), *Rethinking the Administration of Justice*. Halifax: Fernwood.

Healy, W., and A. Bronner. (1936). *New Light on Delinquency and Its Treatment*. New Haven, CT: Yale University Press.

Heimer, K. (2000). Symposium on John Hagan and Bill McCarthy. *Mean Streets: Youth Crime and Homelessness*. Cambridge: Cambridge University Press, 1997. A Model for Criminology in the Next Century. *Theoretical Criminology*. 4(2), 215–21.

Heitgerd, J.L., and R.J. Bursik, Jr. (1987). Extra-Community Dynamics and the Ecology of Delinquency. *American Journal of Sociology* 92, 775–87.

Hendrick, D. (1991). Youth Court Statistics Preliminary Data, 1990–91 Highlights. *Juristat* 11(14). Ottawa: Canadian Centre for Justice Statistics.

Henley, T. (1989). Rediscovery, Ancient Pathways: New Directions. *A Guide to Outdoor Education*. Vancouver: Vancouver Canada Wilderness Committee.

Herman, J.L. (1981). *Father–Daughter Incest*. Cambridge: Harvard University Press.

Hetherington, M. (1977). *Review of Child Development Research*. New York: Russell Sage Foundation.

Hindelang., M. (1979). Sex Differences in Criminal Activity. *Social Problems* 27, 143–56.

Hindelang, M., and J. McDermott. (1981). *Analysis of National Crime Victimization Survey Data on Study Serious Delinquent Behavior*. Monograph 2. Washington, DC: U.S. Department of Justice, Office of Juvenile Justice and Delinquency Prevention.

Hindelang, M., T. Hirschi, and J. Weis. (1981). *Measuring Delinquency*. Beverly Hills, CA: Sage.

Hirschi, T. (1989). Exploring Alternatives to Integrated Theory. In S. Messner, M. Krohn, and A. Liska, (Eds.), *Theoretical Integration in the Study of Deviance and Crime*. Albany, NY: State University of New York Press.

Hirschi, T. (1983). Crime and the Family. In James Q. Wilson, (Ed.), *Crime and Public Policy*. San Francisco: Institute for Contemporary Studies Press.

Hirschi, T. (1969). *Causes of Delinquency*. Berkeley, CA: University of California Press.

Hoare, E. (1995, September 21). Copycat Assault Worries Parents. *The Chronicle-Herald*, A6.

Hogeveen, B, and R. C. Smandych (2001). Origins of the Newly Proposed Canadian Youth Criminal Justice Act: Political Discourse and the Perceived Crisis in Youth Crime in the 1990's: In Smandych, (Ed.), *Youth Justice: History, Legislation and Reform*. Toronto: Harcourt Canada 144–68.

Hogeveen, B. (2001). Winning Deviant Youth Over by Friendly Helpfulness, Transformations in the Legal Governance of Deviant Children in Canada, 1857–1908 in R. C. Smandych (as above) 43–63.

Hohenstein, W. (1969). Factors Influencing the Police Disposition of Juvenile Offenders. In T. Sellin and M. Wolfgang, (Eds.), *Delinquency: Selected Studies*. New York: John Wiley & Sons.

Homeless Youth in Perspective. (1994). Halifax: Dalhousie University, Nova Scotia Public Interest Research Group.

Hood-Williams, J. (2001). Gender, Masculinities and Crime: From Structures to Psyches. *Theoretical Criminology*. 5(1), 37–60

Horowitz, R. (1990). Sociological Perspectives on Gangs: Conflicting Definitions and Concepts. In C. Ronald Huff, (Ed.), *Gangs in America*. Newbury Park, CA: Sage.

Horowitz, R. (1987). Community Tolerance of Gang Violence. *Social Problems* 34(5), 437–50.

Horowitz, R., and A. Pottieger. (1991). Gender Bias in Juvenile Justice Handling of Seriously Crime-Involved Youth. *Journal of Research in Crime and Delinquency* 28(1), 75–100.

Houston, S. (1982). The "Waifs and Strays" of a Late Victorian City: Juvenile Delinquents in Toronto. In J. Parr, (Ed.), *Childhood and Family in Canadian History*. Toronto: McClelland and Stewart.

Houston, S. (1972). Victorian Origins of Juvenile Delinquency: A Canadian Experience. *History of Education Quarterly* 12, 254.

Huizinga, D., and D.S. Elliott. (1987). Juvenile Offenders: Prevalence, Offender Incidence, and Arrest Rates by Race. *Crime and Delinquency* 33(April), 206–23.

Hylton, J. (1994). Get Tough or Get Smart? Options for Canada's Youth Justice System in the Twenty-First Century. *Canadian Journal of Criminology* 36, 229–46.

Hylton, J. (1981). Some Attitudes Towards Natives in a Prairie City. *Canadian Journal of Criminology* 23, 357–63.

Jackson, M. (1988). Locking Up Natives in Canada: A Report of the Committee of the Canadian Bar Association on Imprisonment and Release. Ottawa: Canadian Bar Association.

Jackson, S. (1999). Family Group Conferences and Youth Justice: The New Panacea? In B. Goldson, (Ed.), *Youth Justice: Contemporary Policy and Practice*. Aldershot, UK: Ashgate, 127–47.

Jankowski, M. (1991). *Islands in the Street: Gangs and American Urban Society*. Berkeley, CA: University of California Press.

Jensen, E.L., and L.K. Metsger. (1994). A Test of the Deterrent Effect of Legislative Waiver on Violent Juvenile Crime. *Crime and Delinquency* 40, 96–104.

Jensen, G., and K. Thompson. (1990). What's Class Got to Do with It? A Further Examination of Power-Control Theory. *American Journal of Sociology* 95, 1009–23.

Joe, D., and N. Robinson. (1980). Chinatown's Immigrant Gangs. *Criminology* 18, 337–45.

Joe, K., and M. Chesney-Lind. (1993). Just Every Mother's Angel. Paper presented at meetings of the American Society of Criminology, Phoenix, AZ, October 1993.

Johnson, H. (1995). Children and Youths as Victims of Violent Crimes. *Juristat* 15(15). Ottawa: Statistics Canada, Canadian Crime Statistics.

Johnson, H. (1986). *Women and Crime in Canada*. TRS NO9. Ottawa: Solicitor General of Canada, Communications Group.

Johnson, H., and G. Lazarus. (1989). The Impact of Age on Crime Victimization Rates. *Canadian Journal of Criminology* 31, 309–18.

Jolly, S. (1983). *Our Children Are Hurting: Fact Sheet on the Disproportionate Involvement of Indian Young People in the Juvenile Justice and Child Welfare Systems of Ontario*. Ontario Native Council on Justice.

Jones, A. (1988). Closing Penetanguishene Reformatory: An Attempt to Deinstitutionalize Treatment of Young Offenders in Early Twentieth Century Ontario. In R.C. MacLeod, (Ed.), *Lawful Authority: Readings in the History of Criminal Justice in Canada*. Toronto: Copp Clark Pitman.

Joyce, G. (2000, March 11). Friend of Accused Tells of Attack on Virk, *The Chronicle-Herald*, D32.

Kaihla, P. (1994). Kids Who Kill. *Maclean's* 107(33), 32–39.

Kaminski, L. (1994). *Children, Delinquency and the Community*. Unpublished Paper. Manitoba: University of Manitoba, School of Social Work.

Kaminski, L. (1993). *The Welfare Supervision Board, the Eugenic Argument and the Report on Juvenile Delinquency in Manitoba, 1934–35: Welfare vs. Justice*. Child and Family Services Research Group. University of Manitoba, Child and Family Research Group.

Kandel, E., and S. Mednick. (1991). Prenatal Complications Predict Violent Offending. *Criminology* 29, 519–20.

Kaplan, H.B. (1975). *Self-Attitudes and Deviant Behavior*. Pacific Palisades, CA: Goodyear.

Kappeler, V.E., Blumberg, M. and G. W. Potter (1996). The Mythology of Crime and Criminal Justice, 2nd ed. Prospect Heights, IL: Waveland

Katz, J. (1988). *Seductions of Crime*. New York: Basic Books.

Keane, C., A.R. Gillis, and J. Hagan. (1989). Deterrence and Amplification of Juvenile Delinquency by Police Contact: The Importance of Gender and Risk-Orientation. *British Journal of Criminology* 29(4), 336–52.

Keiser, L.R. (1969). *The Vice Lords*. New York: Holt, Rinehart and Winston.

Kelly, D. (1975). Status Origins, Track Position, and Delinquent Involvement. *Sociological Quarterly* 16, 264–71.

Kelso, J.J. (1907a). Delinquent Children. *Canadian Law Review* 6, 106–10.

Kelso, J.J. (1907b). Children's Courts. *Canadian Law Times and Review* 26, 163–66.

Kenewell, J., N. Bala, and P. Colfer. (1991). Young Offenders. In R. Barnhorst and L.C. Johnson, (Eds.), *The State of the Child in Ontario*. Toronto: Oxford University Press.

Klein, M. (1971). *Street Gangs and Street Workers*. Englewood Cliffs, NJ: Prentice-Hall.

Kohlberg, L. (1969). Stage and Sequence. In D. Goslin, (Ed.), *Handbook of Socialization and Theory*. Chicago: Rand McNally.

Kohlberg, L. (1964). Development of Moral Character and Moral Ideology. In M. Hoffman and L. Hoffman, (Eds.), *Review of Childhood Development Research*, (Vol 1). New York: Russell Sage Foundation.

Kong, R. (1998). Canadian Crime Statistics 1997. *Juristat* 18(11). Ottawa: Statistics Canada, Canadian Crime Statistics.

Kong, R. (1994). Urban/Rural Criminal Victimization in Canada. *Juristat* 14(17). Ottawa: Statistics Canada, Canadian Crime Statistics.

Konopka, G. (1966). *The Adolescent Girl in Conflict*. Englewood Cliffs, NJ: Prentice-Hall.

Kostash, M. (1987). *No Kidding: Inside the World of Teenage Girls*. Toronto: McClelland and Stewart.

Kracke, K. (1996, June). *SafeFutures: Partnerships to Reduce Youth Violence and Delinquency*. Fact Sheet 38. Washington, DC: U.S. Department of Justice, Office of Juvenile Justice and Delinquency Prevention.

Krisberg, B. (1975). *The Gang and the Community*. San Francisco: R&E Research Associates.

Krisberg, B., and J.F. Austin. (1993). *Reinventing Juvenile Justice*. Newbury Park, CA: Sage.

Krisberg, B., and J.F. Austin. (1978). The Children of Ishmael: Critical Perspectives on Juvenile Justice. Palo Alto, CA: Mayfield.

Kueneman, R., R. Linden, and R. Kosmick. (1992). Juvenile Justice in Rural and Northern Manitoba. *Canadian Journal of Criminology* 34, 435–60.

Kufeldt, K., and M. Nimmo (1987). Youth on the Street: Abuse and Neglect in the Eighties. *Child Abuse and Neglect* 11, 531–43.

LaPrairie, C.P. (1994). *Seen But Not Heard: Native People in the Inner City*. Reports 1–3. Ottawa: Department of Justice.

LaPrairie, C.P. (1988). The Young Offenders Act and Aboriginal Youth. In J. Hudson, J. Hornick, and B. Burrows, (Eds.), *Justice and the Young Offender in Canada*. Toronto: Wall and Thompson.

LaPrairie, C.P. (1983). Native Juveniles in Court: Some Preliminary Observations. In T. Fleming and L.A. Visano, (Eds.), *Deviant Designations: Crime, Law, and Deviants*. Toronto: Butterworths.

LaPrairie, C. (1995). Seen but Not Heard: Native People in Four Canadian Inner Cities. *The Journal of Human Justice* 6(2), 30–45.

LaPrairie, C.P. and C.T. Griffiths. (1982). Native Indian Delinquency: A Review of Recent Findings. Native People and Justice in Canada, Special Issue, Part 1. *Canadian Legal Aid Bulletin* 5(1), 39–45.

Laub, L., and R. Sampson. (1988). Unraveling Families and Delinquency. *Criminology* 26, 355–80.

Lauderback, D., J. Hansen, and D. Waldorf. (1992). Sisters Are Doin' It for Themselves: A Black Female Gang in San Francisco. *The Gang Journal* 1, 57–72.

Law Reform Commission of Canada. (1991). *Report on Aboriginal Peoples and Criminal Justice*. Ottawa: Minister of Justice.

Leah, R. (1995). Aboriginal Women and Everyday Racism in Alberta. *The Journal of Human Justice* 6(2), 10–29.

Le Blanc, M. (1993). The Prediction of Male Adolescent and Adult Offending from School Offence. In E. Vallieres and P. McDuff, (Eds.), *Canadian Journal of Criminology* 33(4), 459–78.

Le Blanc, M. (1992). Family Dynamics, Adolescent Delinquency and Adult Criminality. *Psychiatry* 55, 336–53.

Le Blanc, M. (1983). Delinquency as an Epiphenomenon of Adolescents. In N. Corrado, M. Le Blanc, and J. Trepanier, (Eds.), *Current Issues in Juvenile Justice*. Toronto: Butterworths.

Le Blanc, M., and R.E. Tremblay. (1988). Homeostasis: Social Changes Plus Modifications in the Basic Personality of Adolescents Equal Stability of Hidden Delinquency. *International Journal of Adolescence and Youth* 1(3), 269–91.

Legge, L. (1996, April 20). Last Hope for the Lost Boys. *The Chronicle-Herald*, C1.

Lemert, E. (1967). *Human Deviance, Social Problems and Social Control*. Englewood Cliffs, NJ: Prentice-Hall.

Lemert, E. (1951). *Social Pathology*. New York: McGraw-Hill.

Leon, J.S. (1977). The Development of Canadian Juvenile Justice: A Background for Reform. *Osgoode Hall Law Journal* 15, 71–106.

Leonard, E.B. (1982). *Women, Crime and Society: A Critique of Theoretical Criminology*. New York: Longmans.

Leonard, T. (1993). Youth Court Statistics. *Juristat* 13(5). Ottawa: Canadian Centre for Justice Statistics.

Leonard, T., R. Smandych, and S. Brickey. (1996). Changes in the Youth Justice System. In John Winterdyk, (Ed.), *Issues and Perspectives on Young Offenders in Canada*. Toronto: Harcourt Brace & Company.

Lerner, R. (1986). *Concepts and Theories of Human Development*. 2nd ed. New York: Random House.

Leschied, A., and P. Jaffe. (1991). Dispositions as Indicators of Conflicting Social Purposes Under the JDA and YOA. In A. Leschied, P. Jaffe, and W. Willis, (Eds.), *The Young Offenders Act: A Revolution in Canadian Juvenile Justice*. Toronto: University of Toronto Press.

Leschied, A., and P. Jaffe. (1988). Implementing the Young Offenders Act in Ontario: Critical Issues and Challenges for the Future. In J.P. Hudson, J. Hornick, and B. Burrows, (Eds.), *Justice and the Young Offender in Canada*. Toronto: Wall and Thompson.

Leschied, A., and P. Jaffe. (1987). Impact of the Young Offenders Act on Court Dispositions: A Comparative Analysis. *Canadian Journal of Criminology* 29, 421–30.

Leschied, A., P. Jaffe, D. Andrews, and P. Gendreau. (1992). Treatment Issues and Young Offenders: An Empirically Derived Vision of Juvenile Justice Policy. In R. Corrado, N. Bala, R. Linden, and M. Le Blanc, (Eds.), *Juvenile Justice in Canada: A Theoretical and Analytical Assessment*. Toronto: Butterworths.

Leschied, A., P. Jaffe, and G. Stone. (1985). Differential Response of Juvenile Offenders to Two Detention Home Environments as a Function of Conceptual Level. *Canadian Journal of Criminology* 27, 467–76.

Leschied, A., P. Jaffe, and W. Willis, (Eds.). (1991). *The Young Offenders Act: A Revolution in Canadian Juvenile Justice*. Toronto: University of Toronto Press.

Leschied, A., and K. Thomas. (1985). Effective Residential Programming for "Hard-to-Serve" Delinquent Youth. *Canadian Journal of Criminology* 27, 161–77.

Leyton, E. (1979). *The Myth of Delinquency: An Anatomy of Juvenile Nihilism*. Toronto: McClelland & Stewart.

Li, Peter S. (1990). *Race and Ethnic Relations in Canada*. Toronto: Oxford University Press.

Life's Too Short. (1997, January/February). *Society News*. Youth Alternative Society of Halifax, Nova Scotia.

Linden, R., and C. Fillmore. (1981). A Comparative Study of Delinquency Involvement. *Canadian Review of Sociology and Anthropology* 18, 343–61.

Lipsey, M.W. (1990). *Juvenile Delinquency Treatment: A Meta-Analytic Inquiry into the Variability of Effects*. New York: Russell Sage Foundation.

Liska, A., M.D. Krohn, and S.F. Messner. (1989). Strategies and Requisites for Theoretical Integration in the Study of Crime and Deviance. In Steven F. Messner, Marvin D. Krohn, and Allen E. Liska, (Eds.), *Theoretical Integration in the Study of Deviance and Crime*. Albany, NY: State University of New York Press.

Liska, A., and M. Reid. (1985). Ties to Conventional Institutions and Delinquency. *American Sociological Review* 50, 547–60.

Liska, A. and M. Tausig. (1979). Theoretical Interpretations of Social Class and Racial Differentials in Legal Decision-Making for Juveniles. *The Sociological Quarterly* 20, 197–207.

Loader, I. (1996). *Youth, Policing and Democracy*. London: Macmillan.

Loeber, R. (1988). *Families and Crime*. Washington, DC: U.S. Department of Justice.

Lombroso, C., and W. Ferrero. ([1895] 1959). *The Female Offender*. New York: Peter Owen.

Lundman, R. (1993). *Prevention and Control of Juvenile Delinquency*. 2nd ed. New York: Oxford University Press.

Lundman, R., R.E. Sykes, and J.P. Clark. (1978). Police Control of Juveniles: A Replication. *Journal of Research in Crime and Delinquency* 15(January), 74–91.

MacDonald, Jo-Anne. (1994a, September 4). 15 Years Old and Flush with Cash. *Sunday Daily News*, 6.

MacDonald, Jo-Anne. (1994b, September 5). Judging the Children. *Daily News*, 6.

MacDonald, Jo-Anne. (1994c, September 6). Locked Down. We're Treating Them as Human Beings. *Daily News*, 4.

MacKenzie, D.L., D.B. Wilson, G.S. Armstrong, and A.R. Gover (2001). The Impact of Boot Camps and Traditional Institutions on Juvenile Residents: Perceptions, Adjustment, and Change. *Journal of Research in Crime and Delinquency* 30(3), 279–313.

MacKinlay, S. (1995, July 26). Teens Charged in "Brutal Attack." *Daily News*, 3.

Manitoba Parents Can Be Responsible for Youth Crime. (1997, September 23). *The Chronicle-Herald*, A26.

Margolin, G. (1998). Effects of Domestic Violence on Children. In P.K. Trickett and C.J. Schellenbach (Eds.), *Violence against Children in the Family and the Community*. Washington, DC: American Psychological Association, 57–101.

Markwart, A. (1992). Custodial Sanctions Under the Young Offenders Act. In R. Corrado, N. Bala, R. Linden, and M. Le Blanc, (Eds.), *Juvenile Justice in Canada: A Theoretical and Analytical Assessment*. Toronto: Butterworths.

Markwart, A., and R. Corrado. (1989). Is the Young Offenders Act More Punitive? In L. Beaulieu, (Ed.), *Young Offender Dispositions: Perspectives on Principles and Practice*. Toronto: Wall and Thompson.

Marron, K. (1993). *Apprenticed in Crime: Young Offenders, the Law, and Crime in Canada*. Toronto: Seal Books.

Martinson, R. (1979). New Findings, New Views: A Note of Caution Regarding Sentencing Reform. *Hofstra Law Review* 7, 243–58.

Martinson, R. (1974). What Works? Questions and Answers About Prison Reform. *The Public Interest* 35(Spring), 22–54.

Matsueda, R.L. and K. Heimer (1997). A Symbolic Interactionist Theory of Role-Transitions, Role-Commitments, and Delinquency. In T. Thornberry, (Ed.), *Developmental Theories of Crime and Delinquency*. New Brunswick, NJ: Transaction Books: 163–213.

Matthews, F. (1993). *Youth Gangs on Youth Gangs*. Ottawa: Department of Justice.

Matza, D. (1964). *Delinquency and Drift*. New York: Free Press.

Maxon, C., M.A. Gordon, and M. Klein. (1985). Differences Between Gang and Non-Gang Homicides. *Criminology* 23, 209–22.

Maxon, C., and M. Klein. (1990). Street Gang Violence: Twice as Great or Half as Great? In C. Ronald Huff, (Ed.), *Gangs in America*. Newbury Park, CA: Sage.

Mayor's Report. (1862). *Annual Reports*. City of Halifax: Nova Scotia Provincial Archives.

McCarthy, B., and J. Hagan. (1992). Mean Streets: The Theoretical Significance of Situational Delinquency Among Homeless Youths. *American Journal of Sociology* 98(3), 597–627.

McCarthy, W. (1990). *Life on the Street: Serious Theft, Drug Selling and Prostitution among Homeless Youth*. Ph.D Dissertation, University of Toronto.

McCormack, A., M.D. Janus, and W.A. Burgess. (1986). Runaway Youths and Sexual Victimization: Gender Differences in an Adolescent Runaway Population. *Child Abuse and Neglect* 10, 887–95.

McCrossin, S. (1994). *Juvenile Justice and Youth Crime in Nova Scotia*. A Research and Discussion Paper. Nova Scotia Youth Secretariat, Halifax.

McCully, S. (1994). Detention Reform from a Judge's Viewpoint. In I.M. Schwartz and W.H. Barton, (Eds.), *Reforming Juvenile Detention: No More Hidden Closets*. Columbia: Ohio State University Press.

McDougall, D. (1992, August 27). No More Slap on the Wrist. *The Chronicle-Herald*, A1.

McEachern, R,. and R. Bauzer. (1967). Factors Related to Dispositions in Juvenile Police Contacts. In M. Klein, (Ed.), *Juvenile Gangs in Context*. Englewood Cliffs, NJ: Prentice-Hall.

McFarlane, J., and T. Williams. (1990). The Enigma of Premenstrual Syndrome. *Canadian Psychology* 31, 95–108.

McGuire, M. (1997). C.19 An Act to Amend the Young Offenders Act and the Criminal Code Getting Tougher. *Canadian Journal of Criminology* (April), 185–214.

McIlroy, A. (1998a, March 16). Ottawa Poised to Revamp Young Offenders Act. *The Globe and Mail*, A3.

McIlroy, A. (1998b, May 13). McLellan Proposes Youth Justice Changes. *The Globe and Mail*, A3.

Mednick, S., W. Gabrielli, and B. Hutchings. (1987). Genetic Factors in the Etiology of Criminal Behaviour. In S. Mednick, Terrie E. Moffitt, and Susan A. Stack, (Eds.), *The Causes of Crime*. Cambridge: Cambridge University Press.

Meehan, A.J. (1993). Internal Police Records and the Control of Juveniles: Politics and Policing in a Suburban Town. *British Journal of Criminology* 33(4), 504–24.

Meloff, W., and R. Silverman. (1992). Canadian Kids Who Kill. *Canadian Journal of Criminology* 34, 15–34.

Melville, K. (1988). *Marriage and the Family Today*. 4th ed. New York: Random House.

Merton, R.K. (1968). *Social Theory and Social Structure*. New York: Free Press/Macmillan.

Merton, R.K. (1938). Social Structure and Anomie. *American Sociological Review* 3, 672–82.

Messerschmidt, J. (1993). *Masculinities and Crime*. Lanham, MD: Rowman & Littlefield.

Messerschmidt, J. (1986). *Capitalism, Patriarchy, and Crime: Toward a Socialist Feminist Criminology*. Totowa, NJ: Rowman & Littlefield.

Mitchell, K.J. and D. Finkelhor (2001). Risk of Crime Victimization among Youth Exposed to Domestic Violence. *Journal of Interpersonal Violence* 16(9), 944–64.

Miller, W. (1980). American Youth Gangs. In Abraham Blumberg, (Ed.), *Current Perspectives on Criminal Behavior*. New York: Knopf.

Miller, W. (1958). Lower-Class Culture as a Generating Milieu of Gang Delinquency. *Journal of Social Issues* 14, 5–19.

Milne, H., R. Linden, and R. Kueneman. (1992). Advocate or Guardian: The Role of Defence Counsel in Youth Justice. In R. Corrado, N. Bala, R. Linden, and M. Le Blanc, (Eds.), *Juvenile Justice in Canada: A Theoretical and Analytical Assessment*. Toronto: Butterworths.

Milner, T. (1995). Juveniles' Understanding of Legal Language. In J. Creechan and R. Silverman, (Eds.), *Canadian Delinquency*. Scarborough, ON: Prentice Hall Canada.

Minister of Justice. (1994, June 2). *Department of Justice News Release*. Ottawa: Government of Canada.

Mitterauer, M. (1992). *A History of Youth*. Translated by G. Dunphy. Blackwell Publishers.

Moffitt, T., R. McGee, and P. Silva. (1987). Self-Reported Delinquency, Neuropsychological Deficit, and History of Attention Deficit Disorder. Paper presented at annual meeting of the American Society of Criminology, Montreal.

Montgomery, A. (1997). *Alternative Measures in Nova Scotia: A Comprehensive Review*. Nova Scotia Department of Justice.

Monture-OKanee, P.A. (1993). Reclaiming Justice: Aboriginal Women and Justice Initiatives in the 1990's. In *Aboriginal Peoples and the Justice System: Report of the National Round Table on Aboriginal Justice Issues*. Ottawa: Royal Commission on Aboriginal Peoples. 105–132.

Moogk, P.N. (1982). Les Petits Sauvages: The Children of 18th Century New France. In J. Parr, (Ed.), *Childhood and Family in Canadian History*. Toronto: McClelland and Stewart.

Moore, D.B., and P.A. O'Connell. (1994). Family Conferencing in Wagga Wagga: A Communitarian Model of Justice. In C. Alder and J. Wundersitz, (Eds.), *Family Conferencing and Juvenile Justice: The Way Forward or Misplaced Optimism?* Canberra: Australian Institute of Criminology.

Moore, J. (1991). *Going Down to the Barrio: Homeboys and Homegirls in Change.* Philadelphia: Temple University Press.

Morash, M. (1986). Gender, Peer Group Experiences and Seriousness of Delinquency. *Journal of Research in Crime and Delinquency* 23(1), 43–67.

Morash, M. (1984). Establishment of a Juvenile Police Record: The Influence of Individual and Peer Group Characteristics. *Criminology* 22 (February): 97–111.

Morash, M. (1983). Gangs, Groups and Delinquency. *British Journal of Criminology* 23, 309–35.

Morash, M., and M. Chesney-Lind. (1991). A Reformulation and Partial Test of the Power Control Theory of Delinquency. *Justice Quarterly* 8, 347–77.

Morash, M., and M. Chesney-Lind. (1989). Girls' Crime and Women's Place: Toward a Feminist Model of Female Delinquency. *Crime and Delinquency* 35, 5–29.

More Dressing Than Meat. (1998, May 14). *The Chronicle-Herald*, C1.

Morin, B. (1990). Native Youth and the Young Offenders Act. *Legal Perspectives* 14(4), 13–15.

Morris, A. (1987). *Women, Crime and Criminal Justice.* New York: Basil Blackwell.

Morris, R. (1964). Female Delinquencies and Relational Problems. *Social Problems* 43, 82–88.

Motiuk, M. (1995). Secure Detention and Short-Term Custody Youth Centres: A Social Service Perspective. In *Forum of Corrections Research* 7(1), 28–30.

Moyer, S. (1992). Race, Gender, and Homicide: Comparisons Between Aboriginal and Other Canadians. *Canadian Journal of Criminology* 34, 387–402.

Moyer, S., and P. Carrington. (1985). *The Attitudes of Canadian Juvenile Justice Professionals Towards the Young Offenders Act.* Ottawa: Ministry of the Solicitor General.

Muehlbauer, G., and L. Dodder. (1983). *The Losers: Gang Delinquency in an American Suburb.* New York: Praeger.

Myers, M. (2000). Symposium on John Hagan and Bill McCarthy, Mean Streets: Youth Crime and Homelessness. Cambridge: Cambridge University Press, 1997. Toward Theoretical Integration. *Theoretical Criminology.* 4(2), 221–25.

Myrskog, F. (1995, August 3). Canada Becoming a Safer Place. *Daily News*, 8.

Nelson, J. (1994). *Kids Who Kill Kids.* Los Angeles: Storm Publishing Company.

Neugebauer, R. (1992). Misogyny, Law and the Police: Policing Violence Against Women. In K. McCormick and L. Visano, (Eds.), *Understanding Policing.* Toronto: Canadian Scholars Press.

Neugebauer-Visano, R. (1996). Kids, Cops, and Colour: The Social Organization of Police–Minority Youth Relations. In G. O'Bireck, (Ed.), *Not a Kid Anymore.* Scarborough, ON: ITP Nelson.

Newfoundland and Labrador. (1996). *Annual Report*, 1994–95. Division of Youth Corrections.

Newfoundland and Labrador. (1994, January). *An Overview of the Alternative Measures Process for Young Offenders in Newfoundland and Labrador.* Division of Youth Corrections, Department of Social Services.

Newfoundland and Labrador. (1994, October). *Intensive Intervention Program.* Division of Youth Corrections, Department of Social Services.

NiCarthy, G. (1983). Addictive Love and Abuse: A Course for Teenage Women. In S. Davidson, (Ed.), *The Second Mile: Contemporary Approaches in Counselling Young Women.* Tucson, AZ: New Directions for Young Women.

Nova Scotia Department of Community Services. (1993). *Report of the Female Young Offender Review Committee.*

Nova Scotia Department of Corrections. (1994, October). *Nova Scotia Department of Justice, Department of Corrections, Policy and Procedures Young Offender Institutions.*

Nova Scotia Youth Secretariat. (1993). *Juvenile Justice and Youth Crime in Nova Scotia.*

Nye, F., and J. Short. (1957). Scaling Delinquent Behavior. *American Sociological Review* 22, 326–32.

O'Brien, D. (1984). Juvenile Diversion: An Issues Perspective from the Atlantic Provinces. *Canadian Journal of Criminology* 26, 217–31.

O'Brien, M.J., and W.H. Bera. (1986). Adolescent Sexual Offenders: A Descriptive Typology. *Preventing Sexual Abuse* 1, 1–4.

Ogrodnik, L. (1994). Canadian Crime Statistics, 1993. *Juristat* 14. Ottawa: Canadian Centre for Justice Statistics.

O'Hanlon. (1998, October 30). Justice Ministers Split on YOA. *The Chronicle-Herald*, D14.

Ontario Ministry of the Solicitor General and Correctional Services. (1995a, June 22). *Government of Ontario, Ministry of the Solicitor General and Correctional Services Information Paper.* Correctional Services Division.

Ontario Ministry of the Solicitor General and Correctional Services. *Women's Issues Task Force Report.* (1995b, June 22). Ministry of the Solicitor General and Correctional Services Information Paper, Correctional Services Division.

Oosterom, N. (1995, July 25). Drive-By Shooter Kills Boy, 13. *The Chronicle-Herald*, 3.

Palmer, T. (1974). The Youth Authority's Community Treatment Project. *Federal Probation* 38, 3–14.

Pate, K., and D. Peachey. (1988). Face-to-Face: Victim–Offender Mediation Under the Young Offenders Act. In J. Hudson, J. Hornick, and B. Burrows, (Eds.), *Justice and the Young Offender in Canada.* Toronto: Wall and Thompson.

Patterson, G. (1980). Children Who Steal. In T. Hirschi and M. Gottfredson, (Eds.), *Understanding Crime.* Beverly Hills, CA: Sage.

Pearson, G. (1983). *Hooligan.* London: Macmillan.

Pearson, J. (1991). Legal Representation Under the Young Offenders Act. In A. Leschied, P. Jaffe, and W. Willis, (Eds.), *The Young Offenders Act: A Revolution in Canadian Juvenile Justice.* Toronto: University of Toronto Press.

Peterson, E. (1996, June). *Juvenile Boot Camps: Lessons Learned.* Fact Sheet 36. Washington, DC: U.S. Department of Justice, Office of Juvenile Justice and Delinquency Prevention.

Peterson, M. (1988). Children's Understanding of the Juvenile Justice System: A Cognitive Developmental Perspective. *Canadian Journal of Criminology* 30, 381–96.

Phelps, R.J. (1982). *Wisconsin Juvenile Female Offender Project.* Madison: Youth Policy and Law Center, Wisconsin Council on Juvenile Justice.

Philip, M. (1998, October 29). Parenting Style Matters More Than Family Income, Study Says. *The Globe and Mail*, A9.

Piaget, J. (1932). *The Moral Judgement of the Child.* London: Kegan Paul.

Piliavin, I., and S. Briar. (1964). Police Encounters with Juveniles. *American Journal of Sociology* 70, 206–14.

Platt, A. (1969a). *The Child Savers.* Chicago: University of Chicago Press.

Platt, A.M. (1969b). The Rise of the Child Saving Movement: A Study in Social Policy and Correctional Reform. *The Annals of the American Academy of Political and Social Science* 381, 21–38.

Polk, K. (1983). Curriculum Tracking and Delinquency. *American Sociological Review* 48, 282–84.

Pollak, O. (1950). *The Criminality of Women.* New York: Barnes.

Pollock, L. (1983). *Forgotten Children: Parent–Child Relations from 1500 to 1900.* Cambridge: Cambridge University Press.

Porterfield, A. (1946). *Youth in Trouble*. Fort Worth, TX: Leopotishman Foundation.

Price, R.T. and C. Dunnigan (1995). *Toward an Understanding of Aboriginal Peacemaking*. Victoria: University of Victoria Institute of Dispute Resolution.

Prison Report. (1881, 1889–99). *Annual Reports*. City of Halifax: Nova Scotia Provincial Archives.

Pugliesi, K. (1992). Pre-Menstrual Syndrome: The Medicalization of Emotion Related to Conflict and Chronic Role Strain. *Humbolt Journal of Social Relations* 18, 131–65.

Purvis, A. (1997, December 8). Fury of Her Peers: A Teenagers Brutal Assault and Drowning Raise Questions in a Quiet Canadian Town. *Time* 1–3.

Quicker, J. (1983). *Homegirls: Characterizing Chicana Gangs*. Los Angeles: International University Press.

Rains, P., and E. Teram. (1992). *Normal Bad Boys: Public Policies, Institutions, and the Politics of Client Recruitment*. Montreal and Kingston: McGill-Queen's University Press.

Rankin, J., and E. Wells. (1990). The Effect of Parental Attachments and Direct Controls on Delinquency. *Journal of Research in Crime and Delinquency* 27(2), 140–65.

Ratner, R.S. (1996). In Cultural Limbo: Adolescent Aboriginals in the Urban Life-World. In G. O'Bireck, (Ed.), *Not a Kid Anymore*. Scarborough, ON: ITP Nelson.

Reckless, W. (1961). *The Crime Problem*. 3rd ed. New York: Appleton-Century-Crofts.

Reckless, W. (1953). The Etiology of Delinquent and Criminal Behavior. *Social Science Research Council Bulletin No. 50*. New York: Social Science Research Council.

Redl, F., and D. Wingman. (1956). *Children Who Hate*. New York: Free Press.

Reduced Sentences Sought for Boys Who Killed Toddler. (1996, April 18). *The Chronicle-Herald*, D8.

Regan, G. (1995). *A Report on Youth Issues from the Town Hall Meeting Held in Bedford, Nova Scotia*. Submission to the Standing Committee on Justice and Legal Affairs.

Regoeczi, W. C. (2000). Adolescent Violent Victimization and Offending: Assessing the Extent of the Link. *Canadian Journal of Criminology* 42(4), 493–505.

Regoli, R., and J. Hewitt. (1994). *Delinquency in Society: A Child-Centered Approach*. New York: McGraw-Hill.

Reid, S.A., and M. Reitsma-Street. (1984). Assumptions and Implications of New Canadian Legislation for Young Offenders. *Canadian Criminology Forum* 7, 1–19.

Reid-MacNevin, S. (1991). A Theoretical Understanding of Current Canadian Juvenile-Justice Policy. In A. Leschied, P. Jaffe, and W. Willis, (Eds.), *The Young Offenders Act: A Revolution in Canadian Juvenile Justice*. Toronto: University of Toronto Press.

Reitsma-Street, M. (1999). Justice for Canadian Girls: A 1990's Update. *Criminal Journal of Criminology* 41(3), 335–63

Reitsma-Street, M. (1993a). *Fifteen Years in the Lives of Canadian Girls in Conflict with the Law*. Ottawa: Canadian Association of Elizabeth Fry Societies.

Reitsma-Street, M. (1993b). Canadian Youth Court Charges and Dispositions for Females Before and After Implementation of the YOA. *Canadian Journal of Criminology* 35, 437–58.

Reitsma-Street, M. (1991a). A Review of Female Delinquency. In A. Leschied, P. Jaffe, and W. Willis, (Eds.), *The Young Offenders Act: A Revolution in Canadian Juvenile Justice*. Toronto: University of Toronto Press.

Reitsma-Street, M. (1991b). Girls Learn to Care, Girls Policed to Care. In C. Baines, P. Evans, and S. Neysmith, (Eds.), *Women's Caring*. Toronto: McClelland and Stewart.

Reitsma-Street, M. (1989–90). More Control Than Care: A Critique of Historical and Contemporary Laws for Delinquency and Neglect of Children in Ontario. *Canadian Journal of Women and the Law* 3(2), 510–30.

Reitsma-Street, M. (1984). Differential Treatment of Young Offenders. *Canadian Journal of Criminology* 26, 199–217.

Report of the Federal-Provincial-Territorial Task Force on Youth Justice. (1996). *A Review of the Young Offenders Act and the Youth Justice System in Canada.*

Riley, B. (1995, July 15). Boy, 7, Called Accomplice in Brutal Death of Youngster. *Daily News*, 13.

Roach, K. and J. Rudin (2001). Gladue: The Judicial and Political Reception of a Promising Decision. *Canadian Journal of Criminology* 42(3), 355–388.

Rogers, K. (1945). *Street Gangs in Toronto: A Study of the Forgotten Boy.* Toronto: Ryerson Press.

Rosenblum, K. (1980). Female Deviance and the Female Sex Role: A Preliminary Investigation. In S. Datesman and F. Scarpitti, (Eds.), *Women, Crime and Justice.* New York: Oxford University Press.

Ross, R. (1994). Duelling Paradigms, Western Criminal Justice versus Aboriginal Community Healing. In R. Gosse, Y. Youngblood Henderson, and R. Carter (Eds.), *Continuing Poundmaker and Riel's Quest.* Saskatoon: Purich.

Ross, R. (1992). *Dancing with the Ghost: Exploring Indian Reality.* Markham, ON: Octopus Publishing Group.

Rothman, D. (1980). *Conscience and Convenience.* Toronto: Little, Brown.

Royal Commission on Aboriginal Peoples (1996). *Bridging the Cultural Divide: A Report on Aboriginal People and Criminal Justice in Canada.* Ottawa: Minister of Supply and Services, Canada.

Rubington, E., and M. Weinberg. (1981). *The Study of Social Problems: Five Perspectives.* 3rd ed. New York: Oxford University Press.

Ryan, G., and S. Lane, (Eds.), (1991). *Juvenile Sexual Offending: Causes, Consequences, and Corrections.* Lexington, MA: Lexington Books.

Ryant, J., and C. Heinrich. (1988). Youth Court Committees in Manitoba. In J. Hudson, J. Hornick, and B. Burrows, *Justice and the Young Offender in Canada.* Toronto: Wall and Thompson.

St. Amand, C., and P. Greenberg. (1996). Youth Custody and Probation in Canada. *Juristat* 16(5). Ottawa: Canadian Crime Statistics.

Sampson, R.J., (1986). Effects of Socioeconomic Context on Official Reaction to Juvenile Delinquency. *American Sociological Review* 51(December), 876–85.

Sampson, R.J., and J.H. Laub (1993). *Crime in the Making: Pathways and Turning Points through Life.* Cambridge University Press.

Sandberg, D. (1989). *The Child Abuse–Delinquency Connection.* Lexington, MA: Lexington Books.

Sapers, H., and C. Leonard. (1996). Young Offenders Act Amendments—Principled Reform? In John Winterdyk, (Ed.), *Issues and Perspectives on Young Offenders in Canada.* Toronto: Harcourt Brace & Company.

Savelsberg, J.J. (2000). Symposium on John Hagan and Bill McCarthy, *Mean Streets: Youth Crime and Homelessness.* Cambridge: Cambridge University Press, 1997. Linking *Mean Streets* with Adverse Culture. *Theoretical Criminology.* 4(2), 225–32.

Savoie, J. (1999). Youth Violent Crime. *Juristat* 19(13). Ottawa: Canadian Centre for Justice Statistics.

Schissel, B. (1997). *Blaming Children: Youth Crime, Moral Panics and the Politics of Hate.* Halifax: Fernwood.

Schissel, B. (1995). Trends in Official Juvenile Crime Rates. In J. Creechan and R. Silverman, (Eds.), *Canadian Delinquency.* Scarborough, ON: Prentice Hall Canada.

Schissel, B. (1993). *Social Dimensions of Canadian Youth Justice.* Toronto: Oxford University Press.

Schrader, K. (1994). *Community Alternatives and Youth Justice: Needs, Interests, and Obstacles.* Master's thesis, Carleton University.

Schur, E. (1973). *Radical Non-Intervention: Rethinking the Delinquency Problem.* Englewood Cliffs, NJ: Prentice–Hall.

Schwartz, I. (1994). What Policy Makers Need to Know about Juvenile Detention Reform. In I. Schwartz and W.H. Barton, (Eds.), *Reforming Juvenile Detention: No More Hidden Closets.* Columbus: Ohio State University Press.

Schwartz, I.M. (1992). *Juvenile Justice and Public Policy: Toward a National Agenda.* Lexington, MA: Lexington Books.

Schwartz, I.M. (1991). Delinquency Prevention: Where's the Beef? *Journal of Criminal Law and Criminology* 82(1), 132–40.

Schwartz, I.M. (1989). *Justice for Juveniles.* Lexington, MA: Lexington Books.

Schwartz, I.M., and W.H. Barton. (1994). *Reforming Juvenile Detention: No More Hidden Closets.* Columbus: Ohio State University Press.

Schwartz, I., and S. Orlando. (1991). *Programming for Young Women in the Juvenile Justice System.* Ann Arbor: Center for the Study of Youth Policy.

Schwendinger, H., and J. Schwendinger. (1979). Delinquency and Social Reform. In E. Lamar, (Ed.), *Juvenile Justice.* Charlotteville, VA: University of Virginia Press.

Scott, W.L. (1908). The Juvenile Delinquent Act. *Canadian Law Times and Review* 28, 892–904.

Sellin, T. (1938). *Culture and Conflict in Crime.* New York: Social Science Research Council.

Sellin, T., and M. Wolfgang. (1964). *The Measurement of Delinquency.* New York: John Wiley & Sons.

Shahar, S. (1990). *Childhood in the Middle Ages.* London: Routledge.

Shannon, L. (1963). Types and Patterns of Delinquency Referral in a Middle-Sized City. *British Journal of Criminology* 4, 24–36.

Sharpe, S. (1998). *Restorative Justice: A Vision for Healing and Change.* Edmonton: Edmonton Victim–Offender Mediation Society.

Shaw, C., and H. McKay. (1942). *Juvenile Delinquency and Urban Areas.* Chicago: University of Chicago Press.

Shaw, C.R., and H.D. McKay. (1931). *Social Factors in Juvenile Delinquency.* Chicago: University of Chicago Press.

Sheldon, W.H. (1949). *Varieties of Delinquent Youth.* New York: Harper.

Sherr, S.A. (1996). *Our Children, Our Enemies: Media Framing of Children-at-Risk.* Paper presented at the Images of Youth in the Nineties Conference, Ryerson Polytechnic University, Toronto.

Shkilnyk, A.M. (1985). *A Poison Stronger Than Love: The Destruction of an Ojibway Community.* New Haven, CT: Yale University Press.

Shoemaker, D. (1990). *Theories of Delinquency: An Examination of Explanations of Delinquent Behavior.* 2nd ed. New York: Oxford University Press.

Silverman, R. (1990). Trends in Canadian Youth Homicide: Some Unanticipated Consequences of a Change in Law. *Canadian Journal of Criminology* 32(4), 651–56.

Silverman, R., and L.W. Kennedy. (1993). *Deadly Deeds: Murder in Canada.* Scarborough, ON: ITP Nelson.

Simon, R. (1975). *Women and Crime.* Lexington, MA: Lexington Books.

Simon, R., and J. Landis. (1991). *The Crimes Women Commit, the Punishments They Receive.* Lexington, MA: Lexington Books.

Simone, M.V. (1985). Group Home Failures in Juvenile Justice: The Next Step. *Child Welfare* 64, 4.

Simourd, L., and D. Andrews. (1996). Correlates of Delinquency: A Look at Gender. In R. Silverman, J. Teevan, and V. Sacco, (Eds.), *Crime in Canadian Society.* Toronto: Harcourt Brace and Company.

Singer, S.I., and D. McDowall. (1988). Criminalizing Delinquency: The Deterrent Effects of the New York Juvenile Offender Law. *Law and Society Review* 22, 521–35.

Skinner, B.F. (1953). *Science and Human Behavior.* New York: Macmillan.

Skinner, B.F. (1938). *The Behavior of Organisms.* New York: Appleton.

Smandych, R.C. (2001) Accounting for Changes in Canadian Youth Justice: From the Invention to the Disappearance of Childhood: in R.C. Smandych (as above) 4–23.

Smandych, R. (2001). Rethinking System-Based Responses to Young Offenders: International Trends and Perspectives. In R. Smandych (Ed.), *Youth Justice: History, Legislation and Reform*. Toronto: Harcourt, 191–95.

Smandych, R. (1995). Changing Images of Childhood and Delinquency. In J. Creechan and R. Silverman, (Eds.), *Canadian Delinquency*. Scarborough, ON: Prentice Hall Canada.

Smith, A. (1997, May 3). Locking Up Youth Not the Answer, Judge Says. *The Chronicle-Herald*, B8.

Smith, D.A., and C.A. Visher. (1981). Street-Level Justice: Situational Determinants of Police Arrest Decisions. *Social Problems* 29 (December), 167–77.

Smith, R., Bertrand, B. Arnold and J. Hornick (1995). *A Study of the Level and Nature of Youth Crime and Violence in Calgary*. Calgary: Calgary Police Service.

Snyder, H., and M. Sickmund. (1995). *Juvenile Offenders and Victims: A Focus on Violence*. Pittsburgh, PA: National Center for Juvenile Justice.

Solomon, P. (1992). *Black Resistance in High School: Forging a Separatist Culture*. Albany, NY: State University of New York Press.

Spergel, I. (1992). Youth Gangs. *Social Service Review* 66, 121–40.

Spergel, I., and D. Curry. (1991). The National Youth Gang Survey: A Research and Development Process. In A. Goldstein and C.R. Huff, (Eds.), *Gang Intervention Handbook*. Champaign-Urbana, IL: Academic Press.

Sprott, J.B., A.N. Doob, and J.M. Jenkins (2001). Problem Behaviour and Delinquency in Children and Youth. *Juristat 21(4)*. Ottawa: Canadian Centre for Justice Statistics.

Sprott, J. R. (1996). Understanding Public Views of Youth Crime and the Youth Justice System. *Canadian Journal of Criminology* 38(3), 271–90.

Standing Committee on Justice and the Solicitor General. (1993). *Crime Prevention in Canada: Toward a National Strategy*. Ottawa: Queen's Printer.

Stansell, C. (1986). *City of Women: Sex and Class in New York, 1789–1860*. New York: Alfred A. Knopf.

Statistics Canada (2000). *Youth Custody and Community Services Data Tables*, 1998–99. Ottawa: Canadian Centre for Justice Statistics.

Statistics Canada. (1999). *Canadian Crime Statistics, 1998* Ottawa: Canadian Centre for Justice Statistics.

Statistics Canada. (1999). Sex Offenders. *Juristat* 19(3). Ottawa: Canadian Centre for Justice Statistics.

Statistics Canada. (1998). *Youth Court Statistics, 1996–1997*. Ottawa: Canadian Centre for Justice Statistics.

Statistics Canada. (1997). Canadian Crime Statistics, 1996. *Juristat* 17(8).

Statistics Canada. (1997b). Youth Court Statistics, 1995–96 Highlights. *Juristat* 17(10). Ottawa: Canadian Centre for Justice Statistics.

Statistics Canada. (1996). *Youth Court Statistics*, 1994–1995. Ottawa: Canadian Centre for Justice Statistics.

Statistics Canada. (1995). Canadian Crime Statistics. *Juristat* 15(12). Ottawa: Canadian Crime Statistics.

Statistics Canada. (1993). *Youth Court Statistics*, 1992–93 Ottawa: Canadian Crime Statistics.

Statistics Canada. (1992). Crime Trends in Canada, 1962–1990. *Juristat* 12(7). Ottawa: Canadian Crime Statistics.

Statistics Canada. (1992b). Teenage Victims of Violent Crime. *Juristat* 12(6). Ottawa: Canadian Centre for Justice Statistics.

Statistics Canada. (1990a). Violent Offences by Young Offenders, 1986–87 to 1988–89. *Juristat* 10(5). Ottawa: Canadian Crime Statistics.

Statistics Canada. (1990b). Youth Crime in Canada, 1986–1988. *Juristat* 10(12). Ottawa: Canadian Crime Statistics.

Statistics Canada. (1990c). Youth Court Statistics Preliminary Data, 1989–90 Highlights. *Juristat* 10(13). Ottawa: Canadian Centre for Justice Statistics.

Statistics Canada. (1984). Data from the Juvenile Courts–1982. *Juristat* 4(3). Ottawa: Canadian Crime Statistics.

Statistics Canada. (1981). Juvenile Delinquents, 1980. *Juristat* 1(2). Ottawa: Canadian Crime Statistics.

Statistics Canada. (1947). *Canada Year Book*. Ottawa: Canadian Centre of Statistics.

Stevens, S. (1990). An Aboriginal View of the Canadian Justice System. *Legal Perspectives* (May), 10–12.

Stinchcombe, A. (1964). *Rebellion in a High School*. Chicago: Quadrangle Books.

Strauss, M.A., and R.J. Gelles. (1990). *Physical Violence in American Families: Risk Factors and Adaptations to Violence* in 8,145 Families. New Brunswick, NJ: Transaction.

Stuart, B. (1997). *Building Community Justice Partnerships: Community Peacemaking Circles*. Ottawa: Department of Justice, Aboriginal Justice Directorate.

Sudworth, M. and deSouza, P. (2001). Youth Court Statistics, 1999–2000. *Juristat* 21(3). Ottawa: Canadian Centre for Justice Statistics.

Sullivan, C., M. Grant, and J.D. Grant. (1957). The Development of Interpersonal Maturity: Applications to Delinquency. *Psychiatry* 20, 373–85.

Sundeen, R. (1972). A Study of Factors Related to Police Diversion of Departmental Policies and Structures, Community Attachment and Professionalization of the Police. Ph.D. Dissertation, University of Southern California.

"Suspended Sentences" and Dishonesty Among Minors in the City of Halifax. (1908, January 15). Evening Mail, 5.

Sutherland, E. (1939). *Principles of Criminology*. 3rd ed. Philadelphia, PA: Lippincott.

Sutherland, E.H., and D.R. Cressey. (1974). *Criminology*. 9th ed. Philadelphia: Lippincott.

Sutherland, N. (1976). *Children in English-Canadian Society: Framing the Twentieth Century Consensus*. Toronto: University of Toronto Press.

Suttles, G. (1972). *The Social Construction of Communities* Chicago: University of Chicago Press.

Sykes, G., and D. Matza. (1957). Techniques of Neutralization: A Theory of Delinquency. *American Journal of Sociology* 22, 664–70.

Sylvester, S. (1972). *The Heritage of Modern Criminology*. Cambridge, MA: Schenkman Publishing Company.

Tannenbaum, F. (1938). *Crime and the Community*. Boston: Ginn.

Tanner, J. (1996). *Teenage Troubles: Youth and Deviance in Canada*. Scarborough, ON: ITP Nelson.

Taylor, C. (1993). *Girls, Gangs, Women and Drugs*. East Lansing, MI: Michigan State University Press.

Taylor, L. (1984). *Born to Crime: The Genetic Causes of Criminal Behavior*. Westport, CT: Greenwood.

Teens Who Killed Woman Sent to Penitentiary. (1997, July 10). *The Chronicle-Herald*, A18.

Teen Charged with Assaulting Officer. (2000, August 3). *The Chronicle-Herald*. A6

Teilmann, K., and P. Landry. (1981). Gender Bias in Juvenile Justice. *Journal of Research in Crime and Delinquency* 18, 47–80.

Terry, R. (1967). Discrimination in the Handling of Juvnile Offenders by Social-Control Agencies. *Journal of Research in Crime and Delinquency* 4, 218–30.

Thomas, W. (1923). *The Unadjusted Girl*. New York: Harper & Row.

Thompson, A.H. (1988). Young Offender, Child Welfare, and Mental Health Caseload Communalities. *Canadian Journal of Criminology*, 135–44.

Thornberry, T. (1987). Towards an Interactional Theory of Delinquency. *Criminology* 25, 863–91.

Thornberry, T. (1973). Race, Socioecononic Status, and Sentencing in the Juvenile Justice System. *Journal of Criminal Law and Criminology* 64(March), 90–98.

Thornberry, T., A. Lizotte, M. Krohm, M. Farnworth, and S. Jang. (1991). Testing Interactional Theory: An Examination of Reciprocal Causal Relationships Among Family, School, and Delinquency. *Journal of Criminal Law and Criminology* 82(1), 3–33.

Thrasher, F. (1927). *The Gang: A Study of 1,313 Gangs in Chicago*. Chicago: University of Chicago Press.

Tobin, A. (1987). Creating and Operating Community-Based Mediation Programs. In C. Griffiths, (Ed.), *Northern Youth in Crisis: A Challenge for Justice*. Joint publication of the Northern Conference and Simon Fraser University.

Totten, M. (2000). *The Special Needs of Females in Canada's Youth Justice System: An Account of Some Young Women's Experiences and Views. Draft Report*, March. Canada: Department of Justice.

Tremblay, R.E., J. McCord, H. Boileau, P. Charlebois, C. Gagnon, M. Leblanc, and S. Larivee. (1991a). Can Disruptive Boys Be Helped to Become Competent? *Psychiatry* 54, 148–61.

Tremblay, R.E., R.M. Zhou, C. Gagnon, F. Vitaro, and H. Boileau. (1991b). Violent Boys: Development and Prevention. *Forum on Corrections Research* 3(3), 29–53.

Tribble, S. (1972). Socioeconomic Status and Self-Reported Juvenile Delinquency. *Canadian Journal of Criminology* and Corrections 14, 409–15.

Turk, A.T. (1969). *Criminality and Legal Order*. Chicago: Rand McNally.

Tyler, T. (1995, December 24). Justice for Youths Can Begin with a Hug. *Toronto Star*, A21.

Umbreit, M.S. (1995). *Mediation of Criminal Conflict: An Assessment of Programs in Four Canadian Cities*. Ottawa: Department of Justice.

Van Ness, D. W. and K. Heetderks Strong. (2002). Restoring Justice. 2nd ed. Cincinnati, OH: Anderson.

Vedder, C., and D. Somerville. (1975). *The Delinquent Girl*. 2nd ed. Springfield, IL: Charles C. Thomas.

Vincent, I. (1998, January 22). Police Arrest Members of Girl Gang. *The Globe and Mail*, A3.

Vincent, I. (1995, September 23). Ruthless Violence Part of Girl Gang Reality. *The Chronicle-Herald*, C2.

Visher, C. (1983). Gender, Police Arrest Decisions, and Notions of Chivalry. *Criminology* 21, 5–28.

Vold, G., and T. Bernard. (1986). *Theoretical Criminology*. 3rd (Ed.), New York: Oxford University Press.

Voter's Guide to the Issues, A. (1993, October 1). *The Globe and Mail*, A5.

Wallerstein, J., and S. Blakeslee. (1989). *Second Chances*. New York: Ticknor and Fields.

Wallerstein, J., and B.J. Kelly. (1980). *Surviving the Breakup*. New York: Basic Books.

Warr, M. (1993). Parents, Peers, and Delinquency. *Social Forces* 72, 247–64.

Warren, M.Q. (1970). The Case for Differential Treatment of Delinquents. In H.L. Voss, (Ed.), *Society, Delinquency and Delinquent Behavior*. Boston: Little, Brown.

Wattie, C. (1996, August 30). 11-Year-Old Taunted Cops. *The Chronicle-Herald*, A22.

Weagant, B., and C. Milne. (1992). Using the Criminal Code to Punish Group Home Residents: What Are We Teaching Them? Discussion paper presented at the National Youth in Care Conference, Victoria, British Columbia.

Webber, M. (1991). *Street Kids: The Tragedy of Canada's Runaways*. Toronto: University of Toronto Press.

Weinberg, M., E. Rubington, and S. Hammersmith. (1981). *The Solution of Social Problems*. New York: Oxford University Press.

Wells, E., and J. Rankin. (1991). Families and Delinquency: A Meta-Analysis of the Impact of Broken Homes. *Social Problems* 38, 71–93.

Werthman, C., and I. Piliavin. (1967). Gang Members and the Police. In D.J. Bordua, (Ed.), *The Police*. New York: John Wiley.

West, D., and D. Farrington. (1977). *The Delinquent Way of Life*. London: Heinemann.

West, G. (1991). Towards a More Socially Informed Understanding of Canadian Delinquency Legislation. In A. Leschied, P. Jaffe, and W. Willis, (Eds.), *The Young Offenders Act*. Toronto. University of Toronto Press.

West, G. (1984). *Young Offenders and the State: A Canadian Perspective on Delinquency*. Toronto: Butterworths.

Whitbeck, L.B., D.R. Hoyt, K.A. Yoder, A.M. Cauce, and M. Paradise (2001). Deviant Behaviour and Homeless and Runaway Adolescents. *Journal of Interpersonal Violence* 16(11), 1175–204.

Wiatrowski, M., S. Hansell, C. Massey, and D. Wilson. (1982). Curriculum Tracking and Delinquency. *American Sociological Review* 47, 151–60.

Wilbanks, W. (1975). *The Insertion/Diversion Decision at the Juvenile Police Level*. Ph.D. Dissertation, State University of New York at Albany.

Wilson, J., and R. Herrnstein. (1985). *Crime and Human Nature*. New York: Simon & Schuster.

Wilson, J.Q. (1968). *Varieties of Police Behavior*. Cambridge: Harvard University Press.

Wilson, L. (1982). *Juvenile Courts in Canada*. Toronto: Carswell.

Winslow, R.W. (1973). *Juvenile Delinquency in a Free Society*. 2nd ed. Encino, CA: Wadsworth.

Winterdyk, J.A. (1996). Trends and Patterns in Youth Crime. In Winterdyk, (Ed.), *Issues and Perspectives on Young Offenders in Canada*. Toronto: Harcourt Brace and Company.

Yablonsky, L. (1959). The Delinquent Gang as a Near-Group. *Social Problems* 7, 108–17.

Y.M.C.A. Making a Feature of the "Boy Problem." (1909, May 11). *Morning Chronicle*, 5.

York, G. (1990). *The Dispossessed: Life and Death in Native Canada*. London: Vintage.

Yoshikawa, H. (1994). Prevention as Cumulative Protection: Effects of Early Family Support and Education on Chronic Delinquency and Its Risks. *Psychological Bulletin* 115, 28–54.

Young, M. (1993). *The History of Vancouver Youth Gangs*, 1900–1985. Master's thesis, Simon Fraser University, School of Criminology.

Youth Alternative Society. (1997). Information Pamphlet on the Ally Project. Youth Alternative Society of Halifax, Nova Scotia.

Yumori, W.C., and G.B. Loos. (1985). The Perceived Service Needs of Pregnant and Parenting Teens and Adults on the Waianae Coast. Working Paper. Kamehameha Schools/ Bishop Estate.

Zatz, M. (1987). Chicago Youth Gangs and Crime: The Creation of a Moral Panic. *Contemporary Crisis* 11, 129–58.

Zatz, M. (1985). Los Cholos: Legal Processing of Chicano Gang Members. *Social Problems* 33(1), 13–30.

Zhang, S. X. (1998). In Search of Hopeful Glimpses: A Critique of Research Strategies in Current Boot Camp Evaluations. *Crime and Delinquency* 44(2), 314–34

CASES CITED

Gault, 387 United States 1 (1967)

R. v. G. K. [1985], 21 C.C.C. (3D) 558 (Alta. C.A.)

R. v. Gladue (1999) 133 C.C.C. (3D) 385 (S.C.C.)

R. v. James Albert C. (T) [1991] O. J. Number 936 (Provincial Division) (QL)

R. v. J. J. M. [1993], C. S. J. 14

R. v. Jones [1979] 4 C.R. (3D)

R. v. M. (J.J) [1993] 2 SCR 421

R. v. M. T. April 15, [1993] Yukon Territorial Court

R. v. O. [1986], 27 C.C.C. (3D) 376 (Ont. C.A.)

R. v. Richard I. [1985], 17 C.C.C. (3D) 523, 44 C.R. (3D) 168 (Ont. C.A.)

R. v. Shelson, S. [1990] 2 SCR 254

Index

Credits

Data Tables, Cat. No. 85-226-XIE, p. 48-49; **p. 296**, *Box 10.5*: The Ottawa-Carleton Young Offenders Unit: A Facility for Secure Detention and Short-Term Custody, adapted from Motiuk, Michelle, Secure Detention and Short-Term Custody Youth Centres: A Social Perspective, in *Forum of Corrections Research* 7(1): 28–30. Copyright © 1995. Reprinted with permission; **p. 299–300**, *Box 10.7*: Differing Views of a High Level Custodial Facility for Young Offenders, adapted from Dorey, B., On the inside looking out, *Chronicle-Herald* (4/20/1996:C1-5), and Legge, L., Last hope for the lost boys, *Chronicle-Herald* (4/20/1996:C1). Reprinted with permission from the Halifax Herald Limited; **p. 318**, *Box 11.1*: Different Views on Therapeutic Intervention, excerpted from Ross, R., *Dancing with the Ghost: Exploring Indian Reality.* Copyright © 1992, Octopus Publishing Group, p. 32–34; **p. 319**, *Box 11.2*: Different Views on Correctional Philosophy, excerpted from Ross, R., *Dancing with the Ghost: Exploring Indian Reality.* Copyright © 1992, Octopus Publishing Group, p. 168–169. Reprinted with permission; **p. 325**, *Box 11.4*: A Judge's Point of View on Girls in Detention, excerpted from McCully, S., Detention Reform from a Judge's Viewpoint, In I.M. Schwartz and W.H. Barton, eds., *Reforming Juvenile Detention: No More Hidden Closets.* Copyright © 1994, Ohio State University Press. Reprinted with permission; **p. 334–335**, *Box 12.1*: Youth Reflections on the Consequences of Their Criminal Actions, excerpted from youth letters, Youth Alternative Society files, Halifax/Darmouth, Nova Scotia. Reprinted with permission of Youth Alternative Society; **p. 339**, *Box 12.2*: Genesee Justice: Victim, Offender, and Community Reconciliation, adapted from Genesee Justice, *Instruments of Law, Order, and Peace* (1995:12). Reprinted with permission of the Genesee County Sheriff's Office; **p. 348**, *Box 12.3*: Family Conferences, adapted from Moore, D.B., and T.A. O'Connell, Family Conferencing in Wagga Wagga: A Communitarian Model of Justice, In C. Alder and J. Wundersitz eds., *Family Conferencing and Juvenile Justice: The Way Forward or Misplaced Optimism?* Copyright © 1994 Australian Institute of Criminology. Reprinted by permission of Dr. David Brian Moore.